PENGUIN BOOKS

THE PENGUIN CAREERS GU

Philip Gray began his career in teaching, later specializing in careers education and guidance. He held a variety of teaching, advisory and management posts, and was involved in many of the early vocational education initiatives. After writing a series of books on aspects of career choice and contributing to various publications, he worked as a magazine editor. He was founder editor of *Ucan* magazine for UCAS, then became the editor of *Insight, Lifeforce, Finance Futures* and *Careerscope*. He has also developed and produced a number of ISCO careers and higher education directory titles. He is now an independent publisher.

The Penguin Careers Guide is one of the longest established careers directories published in the UK. This edition takes forward the work of the four previous editors: Ruth Miller, one of the pioneers of careers writing, on whose original concept the *Guide* is based, Anna Alston, Anne Daniel and Jan Widmer.

The Penguin Careers Guide

FOURTEENTH EDITION

Philip Gray

Assistant Editor Carol Coe

PENGUIN BOOKS

Published by the Penguin Group

Penguin Books Ltd, 80 Strand, London WC2R ORL, England

Penguin Group (USA) Inc., 375 Hudson Street, New York, New York 10014, USA Penguin Group (Canada), 90 Eglinton Avenue East, Suite 700, Toronto, Ontario, Canada M4P 2Y3 (a division of Pearson Penguin Canada Inc.)

Penguin Ireland, 25 St Stephen's Green, Dublin 2, Ireland (a division of Penguin Books Ltd)

Penguin Group (Australia), 250 Camberwell Road, Camberwell, Victoria 3124, Australia (a division of Pearson Australia Group Pty Ltd)

Penguin Books India Pvt Ltd, 11 Community Centre, Panchsheel Park, New Delhi – 110 017, India

Penguin Group (NZ), 67 Apollo Drive, Rosedale, North Shore 0632,

New Zealand (a division of Pearson New Zealand Ltd)

Penguin Books (South Africa) (Pty) Ltd, 24 Sturdee Avenue, Rosebank, Johannesburg 2196, South Africa

Penguin Books Ltd, Registered Offices: 80 Strand, London WC2R ORL, England

www.penguin.com

First published as *The Peacock Book of Careers for Girls* 1966
Second edition published as *Careers for Girls* 1970
Third edition 1973
Fourth edition 1975
Fifth edition published as *Equal Opportunities:*
A Careers Guide for Women and Men 1978
Sixth edition 1981
Reprinted with revisions 1982
Seventh edition 1984
Reprinted with revisions 1985
Eighth edition 1987
Ninth edition published as *The Penguin Careers Guide* 1992
Reprinted with updating material 1993
Tenth edition 1996
Eleventh edition 2002
Twelfth edition 2004
Thirteenth edition 2006
Fourteenth edition 2008
This edition published exclusively for ISCO 2008
1

www.greenpenguin.co.uk

Penguin Books is committed to a sustainable future for our business, our readers and our planet. The book in your hands is made from paper certified by the Forest Stewardship Council.

Contents

Contents

Contents

Acknowledgements

I would like to thank the many organizations who have provided the information which has made this fourteenth edition of the *Guide* possible. I would also like to acknowledge the help of others who gave advice or direction in my research. I am greatly indebted for the support and encouragement I have been given by the previous editor, Jan Widmer. I am also extremely grateful to Carol Coe for her work as Assistant Editor on this edition.

Foreword

It is more than forty years since the first edition of the forerunner to this *Guide*. During that period there have been significant changes in education and employment patterns. When it comes to making future plans, most people today are influenced only by their own preferences and abilities. Educational and career opportunities are broader than ever. Given the ability and application, young people should be able to aspire to anything – and if expectations aren't met for any reason, a career change is entirely possible at a later stage.

But an increased level of opportunity brings the need for an awareness of the full range of career options available, supported by a realistic understanding of what the work involves, and what qualifications, education or training will be required.

Fortunately careers information is now instantly accessible. There are numerous websites offering information at the click of a mouse. But for those wanting ideas to follow up, a book is still easier to browse than the Web. This book aims to be a starting point for career decisions. This edition has been completely updated, offering structured and in-depth detail on many different occupations and sign-posting the reader to websites where the most recent information should be available.

Background to the *Guide*

The Penguin Careers Guide was first published in 1966 as *Careers for Girls*. At that time, when nursing, teaching and secretarial work were considered the main 'good' jobs for girls, it was a trailblazer, its purpose unambiguously to encourage girls to widen their career choices. When in 1978, following the passing of the Sex Discrimination Act, the book was renamed *Equal Opportunities: A Careers Guide for Women and Men*, there remained many hurdles to equality in employment. In 1992, by which time jobs and careers, with one or two statutory exceptions such as certain roles in the Armed Forces, were open to applicants regardless of their gender, the book was given its present title.

Looking ahead

Gender inequality has been an issue throughout the history of the *Guide*: a very recent University of Cambridge report shows that the gender gap in terms of pay and opportunities continues in Britain to this day. And there are other issues that may influence future work patterns, from population change to the growth of global-scale organizations.

Estimates of future population change, with current birth rates in Britain lower than the 'population replacement rate', suggest future skills shortages in key areas such as technological fields. Young people entering the workforce today can look forward to increasing life expectancy: many of them can now anticipate a working career spanning fifty years, with continuing education and professional development.

Economists and planners are now describing the development of a 'knowledge economy', with future success based on knowledge and skills rather than on more tangible natural resources. Knowledge-based companies, specializing in research and development projects, are increasingly developing the new products that are manufactured in China and then imported as finished goods.

As many large organizations continue to grow on a world scale, these global corporations offer increasingly international career opportunities. Opportunities for more flexible working patterns and career breaks, whether for family responsibilities or for personal development, are also developing in many professions and areas of employment. Employers that understand the need for an improved work–life balance, a notable example being the NHS, promote both flexible working and help with return to practice as a major recruitment inducement.

Looking ahead in the longer term, perhaps future editions of the *Guide* may be describing the decline of global corporations and the rise of a completely new type of small-scale ethical company in which carbon trading and low environmental impact are key concerns.

I hope that this book will help readers to take the longer view when considering their career or career change. I wish you all future success.

Philip Gray

Introduction to the *Guide*

Access to careers information, like access to all other information, has been revolutionized by the Internet. Universities, professional bodies and providers of qualifications all now have websites where up-to-date details can be found instantly.

So why publish a printed careers directory? The answer is, in the main, for the same reasons that it has ever been useful. This publication aims to provide unbiased information, and to bring it together so that different careers can be compared and contrasted. In addition it provides the sort of information not readily available on the Web, such as insights into the work and the sort of person likely to be good at/happy in it, based on experience and observation. This is what differentiates the information in this book from that provided by the sources mentioned above, in whatever media the information may be provided.

That said, the Internet is a most valuable tool for those researching careers information. Qualifications and education and training structures are constantly being changed and once a particular career has been identified, the Web can be used to seek out the latest information. Website addresses are provided within the text where appropriate or at the end of each chapter, although neither the editor nor the publisher has any responsibility for the content of external websites listed in the *Guide*.

WHO IS IT FOR?

The *Guide* is likely to be used mainly by young people as they research their education, training and career plans. However, it is also valuable for the increasing number of people in their twenties, thirties or forties who want to, or have to, change their occupation. Some people still make a traditional 'career for life' decision at 16, or occasionally even earlier, but for so many others a career has become something that evolves and adapts throughout life as personal preferences, circumstances, work patterns and opportunities all change. For many occupations maturity is seen as an asset; education and training facilities may well be available; and standard entry requirements may be relaxed for older people (see individual entries, Higher Education, p. 13, and Late Start and Return to Work, p. 23).

More than ever before, individuals are expected to take charge of their own careers. This applies to everyone, from those working for large organizations to unemployed people on government training schemes. From time to time we all need to assess where we are in job terms, decide what we are aiming at and what we need to achieve our aims. 'Buzz' phrases today are 'personal portfolio' – the individual's package of knowledge, skills and experience – and 'transferable skills' – those which can be put to good use in any work situation. The individual who is prepared to be flexible, to take advantage of (increasingly compulsory) continuing professional development (CPD), and who doesn't assume that any job is immune to change, is the one most likely to weather times of high unemployment.

HOW TO USE THIS *GUIDE*

Careers in this *Guide* are listed alphabetically. However, many if not most careers are really 'areas of work'. Look at the index and you see how many more jobs than careers sections there are. Usually one kind of training leads to jobs in a variety of settings and you can normally mould training plus experience to the kind of job you will want to do when you know more about the whole spectrum and about your own likes, dislikes, strengths and weaknesses.

We could not hope to include all occupational areas in one book, so we have had to make arbitrary choices. Since the future demand is expected to be for more highly skilled, highly trained people, we have left out jobs requiring few, if any, educational qualifications, concentrating instead on those which need formal training or which lead to the widest range of options. School-leavers needing information on other jobs and training opportunities should contact their Connexions service. Adults should consult the Jobcentre or local guidance centre. Use this *Guide* in conjunction with sources of help in Part One, combined with discussions with personal/careers advisers, family, friends who know you well and, if possible, with people doing the jobs you'd like to do.

Look at job advertisements. If you are a mature job-seeker you may be baffled by some of the newer or rarer job titles. Often it is only by reading the job specification that you discover it is something you know under a different name. Some are genuinely new occupations and you may need to dig more deeply to find out if your background and possible future training would make you a good candidate. Be adventurous, look at as wide a range as possible, using the 'Related careers' sections as signposts.

Part One

The Qualifications System

THE NATIONAL QUALIFICATIONS FRAMEWORK

Successive governments have tried to bring the academic and vocational qualifications which have grown up piecemeal over the years into some kind of logical structure, to aid equivalence and progression. The aim is to bring all qualifications – general, vocational and occupational – within the national qualifications framework. The framework has nine levels, ranging from entry level for students not ready for level 1 qualifications to level 8 which encompasses doctorates.

The Qualifications and Curriculum Authority is currently carrying out tests and trials on a new proposed unit-based qualifications framework (the Qualifications and Credit Framework). The QCF awards credit for units (parts of qualifications) and qualifications at different levels and provides a flexible system of credit accumulation and transfer.

Further information Qualifications and Curriculum Authority (QCA) website: *www.qca.org.uk*

GCSE

The General Certificate of Secondary Education is the main qualification awarded at 16+ to pupils in England and Wales. Grades are on a scale from A* to G; GCSEs at grades C and above are level 2 qualifications and at grades D to G level 1. Short course GCSEs,

2

which cover half the content and take roughly half the time of a full award, are available in a number of subjects. Four or five GCSEs at grades A–C is a common starting point for most of the careers and courses in this book.

GNVQs and Applied GCSEs

General National Vocational Qualifications have now been phased out; replacements for the Foundation and Intermediate level GNVQ include applied GCSEs, BTEC Introductory and First qualifications and OCR Level 1 and 2 National qualifications (see below). The applied GCSEs (previously known as GCSEs in Vocational Subjects) are currently available in eight subjects: Applied Art and Design; Applied Business; Engineering; Health and Social Care; Applied Information and Communication Technology; Leisure and Tourism; Manufacturing; and Applied Science. An applied GCSE is the equivalent of two traditional GCSEs and is graded A*–G in the same way.

ADVANCED LEVEL QUALIFICATIONS

The structure of advanced level qualifications changed in 2000 with the introduction of a modular unit-based curriculum designed to increase breadth of study and make it easier to mix academic and vocational programmes. All advanced level qualifications are now made up of a number of units assessed in stages or at the end of the course and awarded at grades A–E. Some changes will be made to A levels from 2008 as follows: the number of units will be reduced from six to four in most subjects; an A* grade is to be introduced for A level (not AS level); more challenging papers will be introduced at A2 and an extended project will be introduced as a separate qualification.

AS Level

The GCE AS (Advanced Subsidiary) is currently a three-unit qualification designed both to provide a bridge between GCSE and A level and to give students the opportunity to broaden their range of subjects. In practice the AS usually acts as the first half of an A level but it is a qualification in its own right.

A Level

GCE A levels are currently six-unit qualifications, and are made up of an AS plus a further three units called the A2, taken in a second year. Assessment is through varying combinations of course work and exams.

A Levels in Applied Subjects

A levels in applied subjects are designed to offer an introduction to a broad vocational area and encourage learning in work-based contexts. They follow the same AS/A2 structure as A levels with the difference that some subjects offer six units at AS and six units at A2 level, and equal two AS/A levels. These qualifications were introduced in 2005 and replace Vocational A levels, also known as VCE, which in turn replaced Advanced GNVQs.

14–19 Diplomas

New specialized Diplomas for 14–19-year-olds will be available from September 2008 in five 'Lines of Learning': Construction and the Built Environment, Creative and Media, Engineering, Information Technology and Society, Health and Development. Further Diplomas will be launched in 2009 and a total of seventeen subjects will be available by 2011. There are three levels of Diploma: Foundation, Higher and Advanced. As well as core subjects and skills relating to the specific occupational sector, other components of the Diplomas will include additional complementary learning, functional skills in English, ICT and maths (see p. 5) and work experience. The Diplomas can lead to further study or to employment with training.

Further information
http://yp.direct.gov.uk/diplomas

The International Baccalaureate

The International Baccalaureate (IB) Diploma is widely recognized by universities as an alternative to A levels and Highers. The qualification is achieved through a two-year programme, and is assessed through course work and examinations. It has three core elements: an extended essay, a cross-discipline theory of knowledge course, and a programme of art, sport and community work. Students then choose six subjects to study, one from each of six areas.

Key Skills Qualification

There are six key skills qualifications: communication, application of number, ICT, working with others, improving own learning and performance, and problem-solving. Introduced as part of the curriculum changes in 2000, they are available at different levels and are assessed on the basis of course work and a test. New functional skills qualifications in English, maths and ICT are to be introduced in 2010: Government policy states that achievement of a level 2 functional skills qualification will then be needed for the award of grade C+ in the related GCSE subject.

ENTRY TO HIGHER EDUCATION

The standard entry to higher education is two or three qualifications at advanced level and many higher education institutions now accept a range of qualifications at that level. However, degree level courses differ greatly in their requirements and universities and higher education colleges are not uniform in their response to the new curriculum. Prospective students should seek advice before choosing their advanced level programme and check carefully with individual institutions.

UCAS Tariff

The Universities and Colleges Admissions Service (UCAS) has developed a tariff which calculates advanced level qualifications on a points score system to evaluate achievement for entry to higher education. Additional qualifications are being added into the tariff year by year. Many institutions now use the tariff system to express their entry requirements but some still ask for specific A level grades.

Further information
www.ucas.com

SCOTTISH QUALIFICATIONS

The system in Scotland differs from the rest of the UK. The following is a basic guide to its structure.

Standard Grade

Standard Grade (formerly SCE Ordinary grade) is the equivalent of GCSE and is normally taken in Scottish fourth year. It is awarded on a scale of seven grades at three levels of study: foundation, general and credit. A credit pass in a certain subject may be a prerequisite for certain degree courses.

National Qualifications

This is a programme of units and courses offered in fourth, fifth and sixth year of secondary education and some schools offer these in fourth year instead of Standard Grade. In some areas, the lower levels of National Qualifications may be offered in the third year of secondary school.

The programme has five levels: Access, Intermediate 1, Intermediate 2, Higher and Advanced Higher. Students usually complete a course in one year but can take longer if desired. Students can progress from one level to the next or move sideways to other subjects at the same level.

The courses taken by students in fifth year are determined by the levels achieved at Standard Grade and/or previous National Qualifications. Students normally take five subjects in fifth year but may take a variety of subjects at different levels depending on how they have performed at earlier levels. Each course at each level is divided into three separate units and each unit has its own internal assessment. In order to get the course award a student must pass all three units.

At the end of the whole course – i.e. at the end of all three units – there is an external assessment. Its form is appropriate to the subject so it may be a traditional examination or it could be, for example, a performance. The final course grade is given on the basis of how well the student does in this external assessment/exam.

Vocational subjects such as care, hospitality and mechanics are offered in the same five-level course pattern as more traditional subjects like English and maths. Courses taught at further education colleges – as well as those taught at school – are within the same NQ programme.

Group Awards

Pupils can do five separate subjects of their choice or, if they choose a group of subjects that go together, they can get a Scottish Group Award (SGA). For example, they might get an SGA in technology or in languages. The SGA includes full courses, extra units and evidence of appropriate competence in five key core skills – communication, numeracy, using IT, problem-solving and working with others. There are no extra exams for the SGA – the award is made simply on the basis of having completed the necessary courses and units.

University Entrance

Universities use passes at Higher level as the basis of their offer, with some giving credit for Advanced Highers. For example, they may accept a grade at Advanced Higher as equivalent to one grade above that in the same subject at Higher level. Scottish universities may allow students with Advanced Highers direct entry on to the second year of a closely related four-year degree course (in the same way that they may allow A level students from elsewhere in the UK to do so). (See also UCAS Tariff, p. 6.)

Scottish Qualifications Certificate

Students are awarded the Scottish Qualifications Certificate, which lists all educational and training achievements to date. This includes a Core Skills profile showing the level achieved in communication, working with others, numeracy, problem-solving and IT. Those gaining Group Awards are given an additional certificate.

All Group Awards have compulsory Core Skills units. Core skills are also being developed through Highers.

Further information
Scottish Qualifications Authority (SQA), The Optima Building, 58 Robertson Street, Glasgow G2 8DQ.
www.sqa.org.uk

AWARDING BODIES

There are well over a hundred recognized awarding bodies in the UK offering over 4,000 qualifications. These range from the Assessment and Qualifications Alliance (AQA) and the Oxford, Cambridge and RSA Examination Board (OCR), which offer many of the school-age qualifications, to professional institutes to amateur sports associations. The three awarding bodies offering vocational qualifications most listed in this *Guide* are Edexcel (BTEC), the City & Guilds of

London Institute and the Scottish Qualifications Authority (SQA). OCR also offers work-related qualifications (see below).

Edexcel (BTEC)

Edexcel offers nationally recognized BTEC qualifications in a wide range of subjects. These include: business; health and care; art and design; media, music and performing arts; engineering; hospitality; IT and computing; travel and tourism; sport; public services; and science.

BTEC courses may be taken in schools, colleges of further and higher education, approved training centres and companies. Courses are modular, with a range of compulsory 'core' and optional subjects so students can tailor-make programmes to suit their needs and interests.

There are several levels of course and qualification.

- *BTEC Introductory Certificate and Diploma* Introduced in 2003, these are the first step to skills in a chosen vocational sector.
- *BTEC First Diploma* General education standard to four GCSEs grade D–G usually required. Programmes are usually one year and may be full-time or part-time. Equivalent to four GCSEs grade A*–C, the First Diploma is available in many schools.
- *BTEC Nationals* A minimum of four GCSEs (A*–C) or equivalent, or acceptable pass in First Diploma required, or at the discretion of the college. BTEC National qualifications (Award, Certificate and Diploma) are accredited to the National Qualifications Framework at advanced level and they are included in the UCAS Tariff. The Diploma is an eighteen-unit qualification, equivalent to three A levels.
- *BTEC Higher Nationals – HND and HNC* A minimum of one A level plus supporting GCSEs (A*–C) or equivalent or BTEC National required. The Higher National Certificate (HNC) usually takes two years part-time; the Higher National Diploma (HND) takes two years full-time or three years part-time or sandwich. They are generally accepted as equivalent to an ordinary degree.

- *Continuing Education* Edexcel also offers a range of individual units and programmes for adults wishing to update and acquire new skills.

Further information

Edexcel, 190 High Holborn, London WC1V 7BH.
www.edexcel.org.uk

OCR Nationals

OCR National qualifications (Awards, Certificates and Diplomas) are work-related qualifications offered at levels 1, 2 and 3 in different vocational areas, with level 3 included in the UCAS Tariff.

City & Guilds

City & Guilds awards its own qualifications in over 500 different subjects in a wide range of vocational areas, including catering and hospitality, construction, engineering, printing, travel and tourism, agriculture and horticulture, media, retail and distribution, and health and social care. City & Guilds does not run courses itself; these are held in centres such as colleges of further education, adult education institutes and training centres. Courses may be part-time, full-time or a mixture. Some are available by distance learning or through flexible-learning programmes.

In the main, no specific time limits or entry requirements are laid down for qualifications. Many certificates are awarded jointly with partners in industry. All City & Guilds awards are normally available at several levels and individuals often progress from one to the next. In addition, there are senior awards that people can work for and which depend solely on experience and demonstrated ability, not on conventional academic study: Licentiateship (higher technician or master craftsman level); Graduateship (equivalent to first degree); Membership (equivalent to a Masters degree or full corporate membership of a professional body); Fellowship (outstanding professional achievement at the highest level).

Further information
City & Guilds, 1 Giltspur Street, London EC1A 9DD.
www.cityandguilds.com

Scottish Qualifications Authority

SQA is the national body responsible for the development, accreditation, assessment and certification of qualifications in Scotland other than degrees. SQA qualifications are offered at approximately 1,750 approved centres. They include: National Qualifications including Standard Grade and National Units and Courses at Access, Intermediate, Higher and Advanced Higher levels (see 'Scottish Qualifications', p. 6); Higher National Certificates and Diplomas (HNC/ HND) and Scottish Vocational Qualifications (SVQ).

Further information
Scottish Qualifications Authority, The Optima Building, 58 Robertson Street, Glasgow G2 8DQ.
www.sqa.org.uk

NATIONAL VOCATIONAL QUALIFICATIONS/ SCOTTISH VOCATIONAL QUALIFICATIONS

National Vocational Qualifications (NVQ) and Scottish Vocational Qualifications (SVQ) are work-based qualifications which record the 'skills, knowledge and understanding' of an individual in relation to their work. They are based on national occupational standards developed by Sector Skills Councils. These identify the level of competence expected of people in their work.

Competence means the ability to perform tasks and this is assessed 'on the job'. This may be as an employee, through an Apprenticeship, or as a school or college student through a work placement. NVQs are unit-based and a unit is achieved when the candidate is assessed as competent in the skills and knowledge specified.

NVQs are awarded at the five levels of the qualifications framework. Level 1 is the most basic, level 3 broadly equates to two A levels, while level 5 represents higher professional qualifications. Levels 1–4 are in place in most sectors. Because each NVQ fits into a framework it should now be possible to relate one vocational qualification to another, regardless of what organization has awarded it, making it easier to move up the qualifications ladder.

NVQs are awarded by established organizations, such as City & Guilds and Edexcel (BTEC) (see pp. 9–10) and a host of organizations representing different industry sectors. In England the qualifications are approved by the Qualifications and Curriculum Authority; in Wales by the Qualifications, Assessment and Curriculum Authority for Wales; and in Scotland by the Scottish Qualifications Authority (the SQA differs in that it awards as well as accredits qualifications). These qualifications are not graded, since candidates are either competent or not yet competent.

APPRENTICESHIPS

Apprenticeships are designed to equip young people with the range of flexible skills needed in today's changing employment market and in England they are available in 80 different sectors within industry and commerce. The aim is to ensure that more young people obtain higher level vocational skills. They differ from old-style apprenticeships in three main ways:

- they are not 'time-serving'
- any young person aged between 16 and 24 can apply
- they are available not only in traditional industries but in occupational areas that formerly did not offer Apprenticeships.

An Apprenticeship is based on a training agreement between the apprentice and employer. Employers must follow strict guidelines. Time taken is flexible, depending on the apprentice's educational qualifications and experience at the start, but Apprenticeships usually take three years. Apprentices are normally paid a wage.

There are two levels of Apprenticeships in England: for apprentices and for advanced apprentices. Apprenticeships for apprentices last about a year and focus on achieving a level 2 NVQ and a technical certificate; those for advanced apprentices take at least two years and lead to an NVQ at level 3 and a technical certificate. There are no set requirements except that applicants should be aged 16–24. Both levels aim to equip young people with the key skills such as working with others and problem-solving.

Adult Apprenticeships (age 25+) were introduced in August 2007.

In Scotland Apprenticeships, usually leading to a level 3 qualification, are part of Scottish Enterprise's Skillseekers initiative.

A similar Apprenticeship scheme is also available in Wales.

Further information
England: *www.apprenticeships.org.uk*
Scotland: *www.scottish-enterprise.com*
Wales: *http://new.wales.gov.uk*

HIGHER EDUCATION

Degrees

Courses and qualifications in higher education are constantly evolving. The traditional route to a degree is still through a three-year or four-year full-time or four-year sandwich course, but part-time and even distance-learning modes of study are becoming more widespread. Students may specialize in a single subject or in two major subjects in a joint degree or take various combinations of subjects in a 'combined' degree. The great majority of degrees are now structured on a modular basis, with modules carrying a number of credits depending on their length. Modules are available at levels (normally 1, 2 and 3) and whereas some courses require students to take a level 1 before they take a level 2, others allow students to pick up modules at different levels in a different order. This way there is maximum choice and flexibility.

There is a nationally recognized credit rating of courses (under what is generally called CATS – the Credit Accumulation and Transfer

Scheme). For example, for an honours degree students need to accumulate 360 credits, with 120 credits being awarded after each of three years of full-time study. Credits may also be given by institutions to students for in-company training, professional studies and experiential learning, so long as these relate to the proposed course of study. The European Credit Transfer Scheme (ECTS) also provides for Europe-wide credit transfer. This is operated by Erasmus (now part of the Lifelong Learning Programme) which also offers HE students the opportunity to study at universities in other European countries.

Higher National Diplomas

These are full-time or sandwich courses in vocational subjects such as science, engineering and business. They may be taken as a qualification in their own right or, in some cases, as a stepping stone to a degree. Higher National Diplomas (HND) may be linked to a degree in the same subject at one or more universities and allow successful diplomates entry to the final year of the degree course. Others allow students on to the second year of a degree. In some cases students who start degree courses and find them too challenging can transfer to an HND programme. Higher National Certificates (HNC) are available in similar subjects, mainly followed by people in work who wish to study part-time. Some full-time HNCs are also available. Although of a similar standard to HNDs they do not generally cover such a full syllabus.

Foundation Degrees

Foundation degrees are flexible employment-related higher education qualifications introduced in 2001, designed by universities in partnership with employers. Courses develop work-specific skills relevant to a particular employment sector, and are the equivalent of two years' academic learning. Students who are already in employment can combine study at a higher education institution or further education college with distance or Internet-supported learning and work-based learning in programmes to suit their circumstances. A Foundation degree is a stand-alone qualification (usually carrying 240 credits) with guaranteed articulation with at least one related honours degree and with professional qualifications.

Diploma of Higher Education – England and Wales Only

Most Diploma of Higher Education (DipHE) courses take two years full-time or three years part-time at higher education institutions. Nursing DipHEs take three years (except for graduates). Entry requirements for school-leavers vary – some, but not all, require a minimum number of UCAS points (i.e. A levels or equivalents).

Courses are comparable in standards and sometimes similar or identical in content to the first two years of an honours degree. As free-standing courses they are available only in a small number of subject areas. Most are vocationally related, for example in health care or management studies. They may form an integral part of vocational training. Many diplomates go on to degree courses towards which their DipHE may count; some universities award a DipHE after successful completion of two years of a degree course.

Entry Requirements – Widening Access

Traditionally to enter a degree course one normally needed two or three passes at A level (or four or five Scottish Highers). For an HND normally one pass at A level is required. In recent years, however, many universities have accepted applicants with alternative qualifications such as International or European Baccalaureate or Vocational A levels. Recent changes in post-16 examinations in England, Wales and Scotland mean that some universities are making offers based on the UCAS Tariff, which allocates points to qualifications included in the Tariff (see p. 6). Many universities have welcomed applications from 'mature' candidates without these kinds of school or college leaving qualifications. In 2005 nearly 90,000 accepted student applications for full-time courses were from people aged 21 or over. Over 8,000 of these were aged over 40. Mature applicants are required to show evidence of recent academic study to demonstrate that they will be able to cope with the course. Those with a suitable background (of education, work or training) may be admitted straight on to a course. For those without such a background there are various ways to prepare (see below). The proposed Qualifications and Credit Framework aims to provide a flexible system of credit accumulation and transfer which recognizes smaller units of achievement (see p. 2).

Foundation years

These are also known as year 0 and are taught in universities (occasionally colleges) and lead straight on to the first year of the degree, making a four-year course in total. These are mostly in disciplines such as science or engineering where students without a strong background in specific subjects can catch up.

Access to higher education courses

These courses have been around even longer and are run at adult and further education institutions. They may be directly linked to degree courses at a nearby university or may be free standing. They are in subjects ranging from teaching to social work, science to law or humanities. All include an element of numeracy, information technology and English.

Other preparatory programmes range from courses which help students to improve A level grades to those which update special areas of knowledge, to those which deal with study skills. They may have titles such as Return to Learn, Wider Opportunities, or Make Your Experience Count. Some universities run summer schools as a 'taster' for potential students. Residential colleges are intended for those over 21. They run a variety of courses, some intended as preparation for higher education or professional training, others designed to stretch students' minds and open up their horizons.

For a list of access courses see the website: *www.ucas.com*, click 'students', then 'before you apply' and 'access programmes'.

Associate student schemes

Students are not formally enrolled on degree programmes, but sample some units of degree courses. Assessment is optional. Some students decide to progress to degree study.

The Open University

The Open University is the UK's largest institution of higher education. No academic qualifications are required for admission for undergraduate degrees, but places are limited and students are admitted on a first-come basis. Students study at home in their own time using specially prepared materials, such as books, videos, radio and TV programmes, and, increasingly, online. There are also weekend and residential summer schools. Students build up credits towards ordinary and honours degrees. It is possible to complete a degree in three years but most people take four to six years, combining study with work or family responsibilities. There is also an associate student programme and many shorter courses for professional people, scientific and technical updating, community and personal interest. There are various postgraduate programmes and a range of management courses taught through the OU Business School.

Further information

The Open University, Walton Hall, Milton Keynes MK7 6AA.
www.open.ac.uk (includes addresses of regional centres)

University of London External System

The External System has a long history. It differs from the much newer Open University in offering in-depth study of single subjects rather than interdisciplinary courses. London University acts only as an examining body, with students studying either independently or, more commonly, at a college or by correspondence course. The basic entry requirement is two A levels and three GCSEs, or equivalent, but mature applicants are assessed on an individual basis. Successful students gain a London University degree (or a more recently introduced Diploma which, as in other universities, may allow progress to a degree).

Further information
The External System, Senate House, University of London, Malet Street, London WC1E 7HU.
www.londonexternal.ac.uk

Financing Your Studies

The system of funding students through further and higher education has changed radically in recent years and continues to change. At the time of writing the position is as follows.

NON-ADVANCED COURSES

These are courses run mainly in further, tertiary or adult education colleges.

Students aged 16–18 studying in their local (non-private) colleges do not have to pay fees. Students aged 19 and over are normally expected to make a contribution, based on income, although tuition may be free for some courses. Education Maintenance Allowances, which offer some young people between the ages of 16 and 18, who are staying on in full-time education after year 11, a weekly income dependent on their household income, are available (details at *http://ema.direct.gov.uk/ema.html*). Students with financial difficulty may also apply for help from Learner Support funds, administered and distributed by the colleges. Contact the college's Student Support or Welfare Officer. Help may also be available for certain kinds of specialist residential course (e.g. agriculture or horticulture) outside the area.

Students aged over 18 are eligible for Career Development Loans for vocational courses (see p. 22).

Further information

For students aged 16–19, see 'Money to Learn' section on the Direct Gov website at *www.direct.gov.uk* (click 'Education and Learning', then '14–19').

For information on funding and financial support for adults, telephone the learndirect helpline: 0800 100 900, or visit the Direct Gov website at *www.direct.gov.uk* (click 'Education and Learning', then 'Adult Learning' and 'Extra Financial Help'). A booklet *Financial Help for Adults* is also downloadable here.

ADVANCED COURSES

From 2006 the maximum that universities can charge in tuition fees will differ within the UK. Student finance now has many variables and prospective applicants should consult the information sources at the end of this section. In essence there are two elements to the cost of studying: tuition fees and living costs.

Tuition Fees

From 2006 until 2009 tuition fees charged by English and Northern Ireland universities have been set at a maximum of £3,000, variable by the rate of inflation. Eligible Scottish students have free tuition at Scottish universities (they may pay a graduate endowment on completion of their course, although the Scottish Government is currently planning to abolish this) but English, Welsh and Northern Irish students attending Scottish universities in 2007/08 pay up to £1,735 (except for courses in medicine for which the fees are £2,760). In Wales students will pay up to £3,145 for 2008/09, but for students who normally live in Wales and who are studying in Wales a fee grant of up to £1,890 is available.

Full-time undergraduate students not wishing to pay tuition fees before or during their time at university can apply for a student loan for fees, and the money will be paid directly to the university on their behalf. This loan is repaid after they have graduated and are earning over £15,000.

Part-time students on low incomes can apply for a means-tested non-repayable fee grant; the maximum amount will depend on how intensive their course is (see below).

Living Costs

From 2008 non-repayable maintenance grants of up to £2,835 are available for low-income full-time students. Low-interest loans for maintenance, of which a proportion is means-tested, are also available, repayable when students have finished their studies and are earning over £15,000.

Again, part-time students can apply for means-tested support; for the most intensive courses a maximum of £1,435 (for 2008/09) is available, through the fee and course grants combined.

Bursaries

Universities and colleges charging maximum tuition fees award non-repayable bursaries to students receiving the full maintenance grant to make up the shortfall.

Students studying certain vocational degree courses, for example health-related or social work, may be eligible for subject-specific bursaries which cover all their fees.

Other Sources of Help

Universities and colleges administer Access to Learning Funds. Some universities offer other scholarship and bursary schemes – ask individual institutions or check the websites. Some charities also have funds available for students in particular categories.

Reference libraries will have directories of grant-making trusts.

CAREER DEVELOPMENT LOANS

These are deferred-repayment bank loans available by an arrangement between the Learning and Skills Council (LSC) and three banks (Barclays, Co-operative and Royal Bank of Scotland). Borrowers do not need to have an existing account with these banks to qualify. The loans are intended only to help with vocational courses and training, which can be at any level from NVQs to postgraduate awards. Study can be full-time, part-time or by distance learning. Students can borrow between £300 and £8,000 to help fund training costs over two years or less, plus one year of practical work experience if it is part of the course. The LSC pays the interest until a month after the course finishes, when the student starts to repay the loan.

Further information

Details from the above banks or the CDL Information Line: 0800 585 505.

> *www.direct.gov.uk* (click 'Education and Learning', then 'Career Development Loans')

SOURCES OF INFORMATION

England: For a copy of *A Guide to Financial Support for Higher Education Students* call the Student Finance information line: 0800 731 9133, or for information and a downloadable copy of the *Guide* visit the Direct Gov website at *www.direct.gov.uk* (click 'Education and Learning', then 'University and Higher Education' and 'Student Finance')

Wales: *www.studentfinancewales.co.uk*

Scotland: Student Awards Agency for Scotland, telephone: 0845 111 1711, or look at the website: *www.student-support-saas-gov.uk*

The Student Loans Company Ltd, 100 Bothwell Street, Glasgow G2 7JD. Helpline: 0800 40 50 10, or look at the website: *www.slc.co.uk*

The Lifelong Learning Guide (UCAS).

Late Start and Return to Work

A VARIETY OF ROUTES FOR RETURNERS, CAREER CHANGERS AND MATURE ENTRANTS

There have never been as many or as flexible opportunities for lifelong learning as there are now. Adults who need educational or vocational qualifications – or simply more knowledge – for courses or careers they want to start or return to after a gap of some years can choose from an ever-increasing variety of courses and methods of study. For details of what is available nationally and locally see guides listed under 'Especially for career changers and mature entrants' on p. 40.

PREPARATORY COURSES

Most re-entry courses were started by women, for women wishing to return to work, but men are rarely excluded. These preparatory courses have various titles, such as Women into Work, Women Returners and New Opportunities for Women.

Courses vary in content, organization, level and quantity of work expected. Some are mainly confidence-restoring and 'diagnostic': they help students to sort out their aims, motivation, level of confidence and circumstances, and then balance these with the available job opportunities and obstacles which may arise. Others include work experience or work-related skills training, introduction to new technology and job-hunting techniques.

OPEN LEARNING

(The terms *open learning* and *distance learning* are often interchangeable.)

What is open learning? Essentially it is a system which enables more people to make use of educational and training facilities. Flexibility and accessibility are the key words. All colleges are trying to attract more adults to their courses, whatever their chosen method of study. Open learning aims to remove traditional barriers to education and training, such as rigid entry requirements, the need for full-time attendance, fixed-length courses, and the need to live or work within daily travelling distance of the college or training centre.

Flexibility is provided in two ways: by making entry requirements less rigid and by giving students a choice of study methods to fit in with their work or domestic commitments. For example, distance-learning courses have been steadily increasing in recent years. These can be a kind of 'enhanced' correspondence course with printed material being supplemented by other course materials, e.g. video, CD, DVD, or Web-based, plus personal, telephone or email contact with a tutor. One of the best-known distance learning providers is the National Extension College (NEC, Michael Young Centre, Purbeck Road, Cambridge CB2 2HN: *www.nec.ac.uk*). Many distance learning courses have websites, with online course material and online conferencing available. For information about the Open University, which offers 'supported open learning', see p. 17.

Accessibility partly depends on where courses are held – some areas are much better provided for than others. Students can generally enrol on open-learning courses at any time and work at their own pace. Many courses require attendance on one or two days a week or even less, making it possible for many more people to participate than in the past. The growth of multimedia provision and the potential offered by the Internet have given a boost to open learning and are opening it up to many more people.

Open learning is increasingly used to train people who are in work (see 'learndirect', p. 26). The definition of the term 'open learning' is complicated by the fact that it refers both to a concept and to specific institutions and initiatives.

OPEN COLLEGE NETWORKS

These should not be confused with the Open University. Open College Networks do not themselves run courses, but consist of groups of colleges which collaborate to provide accreditation for adult learning in their geographical area. This is carried out through a system of credits and levels (see 'CATS', pp. 13–14). These can help individual learners plan their pathways through their local further and higher education system and, in many cases, enable them to have their achievements recognized by other Open College Networks. Although the eleven Networks differ in the way they work, they all adhere to a framework giving four levels of award, ranging from entry to A level/ NVQ level 3.

Further information
National Open College Network, 9 St James Court, Friar Gate, Derby
  DE1 1BT.
  www.nocn.org.uk

THE OPEN COLLEGE OF THE ARTS

This was set up in 1987 to provide training in the arts by open-learning methods to people wishing to develop their artistic and creative abilities at home. It is affiliated to the Open University (see p. 17). Courses currently available are in painting, drawing, sculpture, textiles, art and design, interior design, garden design, calligraphy, photography, creative writing, music, singing, understanding art, dance. The two main elements of a course are: books, tapes and videos; and tutorial support. Students can choose to study either by correspondence via post or email, with help and guidance from a personal tutor, or by face-to-face study at locations throughout England, Wales,

Scotland and Ireland. Many tutors are based in colleges and art centres, while others are practitioners with an interest in teaching. Optional summer schools, life classes, visits, etc., are arranged by many tutors.

Some courses carry the option of assessment for academic credit points awarded by the University of Glamorgan, and OCA has a credit transfer agreement with the Open University. The college now offers a full BA (Hons) degree. The OCA can be particularly useful for people who think they might want to work in the arts, but need to test their abilities and build up a portfolio, including those who have to study at home because of domestic circumstances.

Further information
Open College of the Arts, Unit 1B, Redbrook Business Park, Wilthorpe Road, Barnsley S75 1JN
www.oca-uk.com

LEARNDIRECT

learndirect is a government-supported online course provider. The aim is to enable people to acquire specific knowledge, mostly work-related, without enrolling for a traditional course which may involve many months of study before they come to the particular area of learning they need. Courses may be as short as fifteen minutes or take several hours. They can be assessed through a personal computer at home, at work, or at one of the learndirect centres set up in easily accessible locations including shopping malls, sports centres and railway stations. Courses do not lead to national qualifications but some can help in preparing to work towards a formal qualification.

Further information
www.learndirect.co.uk (click 'Skills & Qualifications')

Employment Legislation

This is a very brief outline of the main legislation and regulations affecting employment. Many of these acts and regulations extend beyond employment provision.

EQUALITY AND DISCRIMINATION

Sex Discrimination Act 1975

This Act makes discrimination against men or women unlawful in employment, vocational training and education. It is also makes discrimination in employment or training unlawful on the grounds of marriage or civil partnership.

Equal Pay Act 1970

The Equal Pay Act 1970 stipulates that women must be paid the same as men when they are doing equal work, and vice versa.

Disability Discrimination Acts 1995 and 2005

These Acts make it unlawful to discriminate against anyone in education, training, recruitment or employment on the grounds of disability.

Race Relations Act 1976

This Act makes it unlawful to treat a person less favourably than others on racial grounds. It covers grounds of race, colour, nationality (including citizenship) and national or ethnic origin.

Employment Equality Sexual Orientation Regulations 2003

These regulations make discrimination and harassment in employment and vocational training, on the grounds of sexual orientation, unlawful.

Employment Equality (Religion or Belief) Regulations 2003

These regulations make discrimination and harassment in employment and vocational training, on the grounds of religion or certain beliefs, unlawful.

The Employment Equality (Age) Regulations 2006

These regulations make discrimination in recruitment, promotion and training on the grounds of age unlawful.

Further information
www.equalityhumanrights.com

WORKING TIME AND PAY

Working Time Regulations 1998 (plus later amendments)

This European Union law defines the maximum number of hours a person should work without regular genuine breaks. Certain sectors, including transport, offshore work and doctors in training, were excluded when the directive was originally introduced. Further directives specific to these sectors have been implemented. Basic rights for the majority of workers include a maximum 48-hour working week, and four weeks' paid holiday a year. At present, employees can opt out of the working time requirement and agree to work longer hours if they wish.

The National Minimum Wage Act 1999

This resulted from a directive from the European Union. The Minimum Wage is increased each year in line with the rise in the cost of living. The level is set by the government each year, based on the recommendations of the independent Low Pay Commission. The rates from 1 October 2008 will be:

- adults (which means people aged 22 and over), £5.73 an hour
- workers aged 18–21, £4.77 an hour – the 'development rate'
- young people (those older than school leaving age and younger than 18 (you're under school leaving age until the end of summer term of the school year in which you turn 16)), £3.53 an hour.

Further information
www.berr.gov.uk

OTHER ENTITLEMENTS
Maternity Leave

Women employees are entitled to a minimum of 26 weeks of Ordinary Maternity Leave, normally paid, regardless of how long they have worked for their employer. Employees are also entitled to a period of Additional Maternity Leave. This starts at the end of the Ordinary Maternity Leave period and can last for up to a further 26 weeks.

Paternity Leave

To be eligible for paternity leave an employee must be the biological father of the child or expect to have responsibility for the upbringing of the child and fifteen weeks before the child is due he must have worked continuously for his employer for 26 weeks. Most employees are also entitled to Statutory Paternity Pay and can choose to take one or two weeks' consecutive leave. The leave can start following the child's birth but should be completed within 56 days of the first day of the expected week of birth. The government has indicated an intention to extend the period of paternity to 26 weeks; a possible implementation date is currently under discussion.

Parental Leave

Parents who have completed one year's qualifying employment are entitled to take up to thirteen weeks of unpaid leave for each child, or up to eighteen weeks of unpaid leave for a child entitled to a disability living allowance. Parents' rights to return to the same or similar job are also protected. Parental leave can be taken at any time up until the child's fifth birthday or until five years after adoption or, in the case of children with a disability, up until their eighteenth birthday.

Adoption Leave

To qualify for adoption leave an employee must be newly matched with a child (i.e. not a step-parent adopting a partner's children) by an adoption agency and have worked continuously for an employer for 26 weeks before the date of notification of matching. Adoption leave is available to an individual or to one of a couple adopting jointly and equates with maternity leave, starting from the date of placement or from a fixed date which can be up to fourteen days before the expected date of placement. Partners of adopters are entitled to paternity leave.

Flexible Working

Parents of children under 6, or of a disabled child under 18, can apply to work flexibly, and employers have a statutory duty to consider their application seriously – although employers do not have to agree. Flexible working can include flexitime, job-sharing, term-time working, voluntary reduced working time. To qualify an employee must have worked continuously for an employer for 26 weeks before applying. A carer who cares for a spouse, partner or relative living at the same address can also apply.

Time off for Dependants

Employees have a legal right to take time off for family emergencies such as unexpected illness or accident, or childcare breaking down. Employers are not obliged to pay for the time taken but are not able to penalize employees for their absence as long as the reason is genuine.

Part-time Working

The Part-time Workers (Prevention of Less Favourable Treatment) Regulation 2000 ensures that part-time workers are not treated less favourably than their full-time colleagues doing comparable work. This means they must receive comparable treatment regarding rates of pay (including overtime when they have worked more than the normal full-time hours), access to career-break schemes, maternity, paternity and parental leave, holiday entitlement, training and development, company pension schemes, promotion and transfer and redundancy. Protection is also provided for employees wishing to return to part-time work where formerly they were employed full-time.

Further information
www.direct.gov.uk

Working in Europe

An increasing number of people spend part of their working lives abroad. Many professionals set themselves up in practice by applying for comparable posts and others are employed by multinational companies. In many countries the process of obtaining permission to work is complex, but every EU citizen has a right to work or set up a business in any European Union (EU) or European Economic Area (EEA) member state.

The situation is complicated by the differing nature of qualification systems throughout Europe, and the need to obtain recognition of qualifications obtained in another member state. The European Commission has introduced a number of directives in an attempt to address these issues.

SECTORAL DIRECTIVES

Initially the Commission aimed to harmonize qualifications profession by profession. Sectoral Directives were issued for the professions of doctor, dentist, midwife, general care nurse, pharmacist, veterinary surgeon and architect. This means that those qualified in these jobs in one EU member state can work in another member state, although they do need to register with the appropriate professional body.

GENERAL DIRECTIVES

The sectoral approach proved to be lengthy and difficult and so the Commission decided to tackle the remaining professions by means of General Directives based on the principle of mutual recognition of qualifications. General Directive 89/48/EEC covers professionally regulated qualifications at degree level and above, and General Directive 92/51/EEC covers professionally regulated qualifications at below degree level.

Further information

More information about the directives and who to contact to have qualifications recognized in other member states is available on the Europe Open for Professions website at *www.dfes.gov.uk/europe-open*

THE CERTIFICATE OF EXPERIENCE

EC Directive 99/42/EC enables crafts- and tradespeople within the EU who wish to work in another member state to do so without having to attain the relevant national qualification for that trade or craft in the host member state. A Certificate of Experience provides proof of qualifications and previous work experience in a particular profession in the UK, but it is only required if a profession is regulated in a particular member state.

The Certificate of Experience service is run by the National Recognition Information Centre for the United Kingdom (UK NARIC) in association with the Department for Innovation, Universities and Skills (DIUS).

Further information

More information about eligibility and an online application form are available at *www.certex.org.uk*

The majority of professional and trade associations will also advise members.

NATIONAL REFERENCE POINTS FOR VOCATIONAL QUALIFICATIONS

The National Reference Point network is an organization of centres across Europe that can help and advise on the recognition of qualifications. The UK National Reference Point for Vocational Qualifications operates an assessment service, which can produce an evaluation report detailing the comparable UK level and closest award, modular equivalence, background information and grading system conversion.

The main focus of this service initially is to provide information to individuals, employers, professional associations and other interested organizations in the UK about European vocational qualifications. However, the UK NRP will also act as a signpost to the other NRPs across Europe for those wanting information about the validity of their UK qualifications in Europe.

Further information
More information is available from the UK National Reference Point
   for Vocational Qualifications website at *www.uknrp.org.uk*

EUROPASS

This initiative is designed to help people wanting to work or enter education and training in member countries of the EU, other than their own, by helping them to present their competencies, skills and qualifications in a way understood by education and training providers and employers in all European countries. The five Europass documents are:

- *CV template*, containing personal information in addition to details of any work experience, education and training, personal skills and competences
- *Language Passport*, a self-assessed record of language proficiency to standard European level

- *Mobility document*, a record of periods of learning attended in another country
- *Certificate Supplement*, recording competences and qualifications gained through vocational training
- *Diploma Supplement*, recording educational achievements at higher education level.

Further information
www.uknec.org.uk

THE LIFELONG LEARNING PROGRAMME

The Lifelong Learning Programme (LLP) 2007–2013 supports education and training across Europe by funding activities at school, at college, at university, in the workplace and in the community. LLP programmes include:

- *Comenius* – school and further education projects
- *Erasmus* – higher education study and work placement mobility
- *Leonardo* – skills and training development
- *Grundtvig* – adult education partnerships
- *Transversal study visits* – exchange programmes for teachers.

In the UK the LLP programmes are managed by the British Council and ECOTEC.

Further information
www.lifelonglearningprogramme.org.uk
Further information on all aspects of careers and working in Europe and further afield is available from Careers Europe, 72–74 Godwin Street, Bradford, West Yorkshire BD1 3PT.
www.careerseurope.co.uk

Sources of Help

CAREERS ADVISORY SERVICES

As a result of devolution the different countries of the UK now all have their own careers advisory services.

England

In England the main source of information and guidance for young people is the Connexions Service (see NOTE below). Connexions is a support service for young people aged between 13 and 19, offering help in a range of areas including careers. Local Connexions Partnerships are the best point of contact for information on initiatives such as Apprenticeships as well as advice on further and higher education and career choice. The address of local Connexions Services can be found on *www.connexions-direct.com*.

Some Connexions Partnerships also offer a service to adults but adult guidance is more normally provided through a network of Information Advice and Guidance Partnerships. Details on local services can be obtained from Connexions Partnerships or Jobcentres. Adults can also contact the free learndirect helpline – 0800 100 900 – to talk to an adviser or to be referred to a local IAG Partnership adviser, or find online information on the website: *www.learndirect-advice.co.uk*.

NOTE: The Connexions Service is in transition: for further information visit *www.everychildmatters.gov.uk/youthmatters/connexions*. This website states that the funding that currently (at the time of writing) goes directly to the 47 Connexions Partnerships will by April

2008 go to the 150 local authorities. The latter, working under Children's Trust arrangements, will commission and manage Information, Advice and Guidance services. Connexions Direct at *www.connexions-direct.com* continues to offer online information and advice to 13–19-year-olds in England, complementing local services.

Scotland

Careers information, advice and guidance in Scotland is provided by Careers Scotland, an all-age service with centres throughout the country. It operates a helpline – 0845 8 502 502 – or information on careers and learning or details of local centres can be accessed through the Careers Scotland website: *www.careers-scotland.org.uk*.

Wales

In Wales careers information, advice and guidance can be obtained from Careers Wales, an all-age service bringing together the seven careers companies which cover all areas of Wales. Information on careers and learning can also be found on the Careers Wales website: *www.careerswales.com* which also gives details of the local careers companies. Adults can also ring the learndirect helpline – 0800 100 900.

Northern Ireland

The Northern Ireland Department for Employment and Learning provides an information, advice and guidance service for young people and adults. Careers officers are based in 35 JobCentres and Jobs and Benefits Offices throughout Northern Ireland. Careers and learning information can be accessed on *www.careersserviceni.com*.

Higher Education Careers Services

Universities and colleges/institutes of higher education have their own guidance services tailored to the needs of their students and graduates. As well as information on local courses and career opportunities they provide a vast amount of national information produced by AGCAS (Association of Graduate Careers Advisory Services). Students of all ages are advised to make early contact with their service.

The addresses of HE Careers Services can be found on *www.prospects.ac.uk.*

GENERAL HELPLINES AND WEBSITES

- learndirect national helpline: 0800 100 900 – help and information on finding courses.
  www.learndirect-advice.co.uk
- The Direct Gov website offers information on a wide range of topics. The Education and Learning sections offer information for parents, young people and adult learners. The Employment sections provide information and advice for young people and adults on jobs and careers. A dedicated jobs and skills section at *http://jobseekers.direct.gov.uk* facilitates searching for jobs, training, career information, childcare providers and voluntary work across the UK.
  www.direct.gov.uk
- The Connexions website is designed specifically for young people, with information to help in making decisions about careers and education, and addresses of local Connexions services. Also includes jobs4u, a careers database.
  www.connexions-direct.com
- The UCAS website provides information on applying to higher education, and a course search facility leading to a developing database of entry profiles, which give in-depth information on course content and requirements and direct links to university and college sites.
  www.ucas.com
- Prospects is the UK's official graduate careers website offering careers advice and information for graduates. The website covers

how to choose a career, information and advice on jobs and employers, the graduate job market, work experience and working abroad along with job vacancies and resources for further study, and provides a range of information in downloadable formats. *www.prospects.ac.uk*

PUBLICATIONS

Many of the sources listed below are available in careers libraries and reference libraries. There are growing number of computer programs providing help with career decisions, occupational information and course choice, and many Connexions services, schools, colleges and universities will have these available for use by clients.

Higher and further education information
The Big Guide, published annually by the Universities and Colleges Admissions Service (UCAS).

The Scottish Guide, published annually by UCAS.

Directory of University & College Entry, Trotman (Crimson Publishing).

CRAC Degree Course Guides, Trotman (Crimson Publishing). Compare individual courses within disciplines.

The Student Book, Trotman (Crimson Publishing). Contains facts as well as opinions on subjects of study and institutions.

The Sixthformer's Guide: The Annual Guide to Visiting Universities and Colleges. Lists open days and gives advice on what to ask and look out for on a visit. From The Inspiring Futures Foundation (see *www.inspiringfutures.org.uk*).

Directory of Vocational and Further Education, Trotman (Crimson Publishing). Lists full-time and part-time vocational courses at all levels outside universities.

The Disabled Students' Guide to University, published by Trotman.

Sources of Help

Careers information

AGCAS (Association of Graduate Careers Advisory Services) publishes a series of regularly updated booklets covering most graduate career areas, some of which can be downloaded from the Prospects website: *www.prospects.ac.uk*

Working Abroad: The Complete Guide to Overseas Employment by Jonathan Reuvid, published by Kogan Page.

Especially for career changers and mature entrants

Second Chances – A National Guide to Education and Training for Adults, published by Lifetime Careers Wiltshire. A comprehensive guide to education and training at all levels.

The Mature Students' Directory: Lifelong Learning Opportunities for the 21 Plus, published by Trotman.

The Which? Guide to Changing Careers, published by Which? Books.

Major careers publishers include Kogan Page, Trotman (Crimson Publishing), How To Books and Lifetime. Check catalogues for current publications.

Part Two

Main Careers in Alphabetical Order

Accountancy

PROFESSIONAL ACCOUNTANT

Entry qualifications Majority graduate entrance. Still substantial non-graduate recruitment opportunities for which National Qualifications Framework Level 3 (A levels, BTEC National awards) or Scottish Credit and Qualifications Framework equivalent generally required. (See also Accounting Technician, p. 51.)

In Scotland, for training with the Institute of Chartered Accountants of Scotland, either a degree or membership of the Association of Accounting Technicians.

The work The image of accountants as deskbound number-crunchers is quite wrong. An accountancy qualification leads to a vast variety of jobs, in virtually any environment: manufacturing industry or television; retail or merchant banking; professional consultancy; public service. There is scope for accountants interested in the intricacies of accounting procedures and their technological development, or in high finance, or as a way into general management, or self-employment. (See Working for Oneself, p. 625.)

There is a vast variety of jobs in all types and sizes of business and in the public sector. An accountancy qualification is also an excellent preparation for jobs in merchant and other banking, insurance and the City.

There are some opportunities for employment (but not in private practice) in the EU, and in most other countries.

Work falls broadly into three categories:

- *Private practice*
- *Industrial and commercial accountancy*
- *Public sector accountancy.*

Private Practice

Private practice firms (i.e. accountancy firms) vary in size and type from high-powered global organizations which deal mainly with large companies and are at the very centre of the country's commercial activities, to small suburban practices which deal mainly with private clients and local businesses.

As the financial scene becomes ever more complex, many accountants now specialize in one particular accountancy aspect: for example, taxation, computer systems, mergers, corporate finance. However, the bulk of private practice work is taxation and accounting-service auditing. Auditing means analysing and verifying clients' books and ensuring that the annual balance sheet presents a 'true and fair' picture of the client's financial affairs. Auditing is done on clients' premises so it involves meeting people and possibly travelling. Audits take anything from a few hours to several months, depending on the client's size and type of business. Audits may be done in streamlined offices using the latest technologies, or it may mean having to create order out of chaos when, for example, a sole trader's accounting system consists of a file full of receipts. Auditing is largely desk-work, but it also involves discussions with clients – anyone from clerk to managing director – if specific items in the books are not clear. Some accountancy firms provide management consultancy services (see p. 355).

Industrial and Commercial Accountants

These can be divided into financial accountants, concerned largely with internal audits, taxation, wage and salary structure, financial record-keeping; and management accountants. This is a major accountancy specialization (and it overlaps with management consultancy). Management accountants assess the relative importance, value and cost of all aspects of a business (or public service): labour, raw materials, transport, sites, administration, marketing, etc. Every person's, machine's, department's, vehicle's, etc., contribution to the effectiveness of an organization, and their interdependence, can, with the help of computer systems and mathematical models, be assessed separately and as part of the whole operation. Management accountants might, for example, compare the relative cost of using a cheap new raw material, which would necessitate more expensive machine maintenance and require a marketing campaign to launch the changed product, against the cost of going on using the more expensive traditional raw material – taking into account, among other factors, what the competition abroad might do, and how staff would feel about the change. Or they might assess the cost of moving a factory to a cheaper site, considering increased transport costs, recruiting and training new staff. Like management consultants, their work requires interviewing all the people whose work affects the efficiency of the organization concerned. Having compared the financial results of alternative courses of action, management accountants present the information to the decision-makers at the top of the organization and may be involved in future strategic planning and forecasting.

Because management accountants take part in decision-making and business control they need a broader understanding of business organization in general and of the type of business with which they are concerned than do financial accountants. They often move into consultancy sections of auditing firms, or into management consultancy (see p. 355).

Public Sector Accountants

Accountants and auditors working in local and central government, the health service, national audit and other public service bodies are, like industrial and commercial accountants, concerned with all aspects of financial management. The emphasis of their work is on the efficient and effective use of funds and the need for public accountability.

In the 1990s public service organizations became more commercially orientated. Involvement in the management of change, e.g. contracting out of services and advising on alternative options for the use of limited funds, are important aspects of the finance manager's job. Work in the national audit bodies involves auditing public income and expenditure, certifying accounts and carrying out value-for-money studies.

Companies providing services to the public sector increasingly seek to recruit public service accountants and auditors. Significant numbers of finance managers become top-level general managers.

Training

There are six main professional qualifications, awarded by the following organizations:

- The Institute of Chartered Accountants in England and Wales (ICAEW)
- Institute of Chartered Accountants of Scotland (ICAS)
- Institute of Chartered Accountants in Ireland (ICAI)
- Association of Chartered Certified Accountants (ACCA)
- Chartered Institute of Management Accountants (CIMA)
- Chartered Institute of Public Finance and Accountancy (CIPFA).

There are differences between the syllabuses and the training programmes that each body offers. There is a core element of accountancy knowledge which all accountants must master – but emphasis varies.

Accountancy courses cover: economics; statistics; computer applications and systems; corporate finance; financial management; taxation; trustee work; share organization; management accounting; relevant law; EU accountancy implications; auditing. The emphasis on different aspects of accountancy differs in the various professional bodies' examinations; some syllabuses overlap more than others.

The various qualifications are equally marketable. Choice of one qualification over another only partly depends on the ultimate career aim: it also depends on what training is available locally; and on the type of training method preferred. The chartered accountancy bodies except CIMA can approve their members to be registered auditors.

Chartered management accountants' training concentrates more on running a business and planning its future than do the others. So people who definitely want to go into industry/commerce might choose this qualification. They too can choose to work in the public sector.

The *Chartered Institute of Public Finance and Accountancy* qualification differs from the others in that it is specifically tailored to the very large amount of work in the public sector: public utilities; National Health Service; local and central government.

Training methods vary among the various bodies, and they are complicated. (Candidates should read carefully all the accountancy bodies' training literature.) The essential differences in the various bodies' training methods are:

The Institute of Chartered Accountants in England and Wales (ICAEW)

To train as an ACA (Associate of the Institute of Chartered Accountants in England and Wales) chartered accountant students must complete a training contract with an organization authorized to train by the ICAEW (the employer). This ensures that they receive the correct work experience, which is a vital part of the qualification. Training contracts can last between three and five years depending on the route to entering training, although a graduate will normally receive a three-year contract. Authorized training organizations can vary from small accountancy firms to large international firms (more commonly known as the 'big four') to commercial organizations and public sector and not-for-profit organizations such as the NHS or National Audit Office. The work experience will be varied and every client will be different.

As well as a minimum of three years on a training contract, students must also pass the Institute's exams. There are two stages: the Professional Stage comprising the knowledge and application modules, totalling twelve exams; and the Advanced Stage which consists of two technical papers and a case study. These are linked into work experience and personal skills development. ACA training develops a blend of technical knowledge, communication skills and commercial awareness with structured training in ethics.

Institute of Chartered Accountants of Scotland

The majority of students who train with ICAS enter through the graduate entry route. Depending on degree studied, ICAS awards exemptions from the first level of exams. They also provide a route into chartered accountancy training for those students who decide to go straight into employment, rather than going to university. This new route involves up to three years' study towards membership of the Association of Accounting Technicians (AAT). Students who qualify for AAT membership can continue their professional development and progress on to chartered accountancy training. To qualify as a chartered accountant, students must secure a training contract with an approved employer authorized by ICAS. The three-year training programme combines classroom-based study and exams with supervised work-based training in employer training offices. Students can train with ICAS anywhere in the UK.

Association of Chartered Certified Accountants

This body's training is the most flexible although it must total three years. Students do not have to enter into training contracts but can train while in part-time or full-time salaried employment by various part-time methods. Alternatively they can study for the exams full-time and get practical experience afterwards. They may change employers, and type of employer, during their training and thus can get varied experience. They need not make up their mind at the outset whether they wish to go into industry/commerce or into private practice. Three years' training in an Approved Training Practice is obligatory for those who ultimately want to become Registered Auditors in private practice. This experience can be gained before, during or after passing the professional exams. Exams leading to Associate Membership (ACCA) are at two levels. Those with a relevant HND/HNC or foundation course may be exempt from all or part of level 1. Study can be full-time, by day or block release, evening classes or correspondence courses, or online. Certified accountancy students are not automatically entitled to study leave, but companies registered on the Employer Accreditation Scheme offer it.

Chartered Institute of Management Accountants

To gain Associate membership, CIMA students need a minimum of three years' relevant practical experience and to pass three stages of examinations. They can gain the practical experience (which could include a sandwich year taken in industry) before or after passing the examinations and they can be working in a variety of business areas, including public and private sectors, industry and commerce. They may change employers during this period. Students qualified above the minimum entry level may be given exemptions from parts of the syllabus. The method of study chosen will depend on the employer and the student: options include full-time, part-time, evening, week-end and correspondence courses.

Chartered Institute of Public Finance and Accountancy

CIPFA's professional accountancy qualification is at three levels: certificate, diploma and the Final Test of Professional Competence. Entry requirements are two A levels and three GCSEs including maths and English at either level or equivalent. Exemptions are given for those with the AAT Accounting Qualification (see accounting technician 'Training', p. 52) or other related qualifications. CIPFA students are normally employed in a public service finance post. They follow a structured practical experience scheme integrated with theory studied through open-learning packages which can be supplemented with taught college courses. The whole scheme takes around three years to complete. Both the syllabus and work experience reflect the increasingly commercial focus of public service and the need for financial management skills.

Personal attributes (generally) Academic ability; numeracy; ability to speak and write concisely; business sense; logical mind; ability to negotiate without self-consciousness with people at all levels within an organization; tact in dealing with employers and clients; a liking for desk-work. Training demands determination, motivation and staying power.

Mature entry and career change All applicants are considered on an individual basis.

Work–life balance A career break should be no problem although it will probably be necessary to update before returning to practice. There are lectures and journals which help to keep accountants up to date with developments. It is possible to work in most parts of the country and also to run a small practice or consultancy from home.

Part-time opportunities are increasing, especially in private practice. Job-sharing should be possible.

Further information

The Institute of Chartered Accountants in England and Wales (ICAEW), Learning and Professional Development, Level 1, Metropolitan House, 321 Avebury Boulevard, Milton Keynes MK9 2GA.
www.icaew.com/careers

Institute of Chartered Accountants of Scotland, CA House, 21 Haymarket Yards, Edinburgh EH12 5BH.
www.icas.org.uk

Institute of Chartered Accountants in Ireland, CA House, 83 Pembroke Road, Dublin 4 & The Linenhall, 32–38 Linenhall Street, Belfast BT2 8BG.
www.icai.ie

The Association of Chartered Certified Accountants, 2 Central Quay, 89 Hydepark Street, Glasgow GB3 8BW.
www.accaglobal.com

The Chartered Institute of Management Accountants, 26 Chapter Street, London SW1P 4NP.
www.cimaglobal.com

The Chartered Institute of Public Finance and Accountancy, 3 Robert Street, London WC2N 6RL.
www.cipfa.org.uk

Related careers *actuary – banking – chartered secretary – information technology – insurance – management – purchasing and supply – science: Statistics – tax inspector*

Accounting Technician

Entry qualifications There are no prescribed entry requirements for the Association of Accounting Technicians' Education and Training scheme or ACCA's Certified Accounting Technician (CAT) scheme, but students are advised that they need reasonable numeracy and literacy skills in order to cope with the qualifications.

The work There is no legal requirement for accountants to be professionally qualified; 'accountant' is not a 'protected title' in the way 'solicitor' or 'architect' is. This 'second tier' technician qualification was created because there is so much accountancy work which, while requiring responsibility, expertise and training, does not require the breadth of professional accountancy education (see p. 43).

Broadly, professional accountants conduct audits (which technicians are not empowered to do) and deal with complex financial management and advice, etc.; accounting technicians collate the information on which professional accountants base their decisions, and deal with routine accountancy. This involves more desk-work than professional accountancy, but it also involves contact with clients.

The vast majority of accounting technicians work in professional accountants' offices or under the direction of professional accountants in industry, commerce or the public sector. However, some are 'sole' or 'company' accountants in firms too small to warrant employing a professional accountant, and some accounting technicians set up on their own, dealing with private clients' (individuals, shopkeepers, etc.) VAT, income tax and similar matters. Some keep small firms' books and visit such clients at regular intervals on a contract basis.

AAT members who want to become professional accountants (see above) normally get exemption from at least the professional accountancy bodies' (see above) Foundation examinations.

Training Trainees can work towards AAT Accounting Qualifications either by a work-based NVQ route or by a college-based Diploma route. Both routes are 'competence-based' and are at three levels, each a qualification in its own right. Assessments are conducted through exams, skill tests and work-based projects.

The CAT scheme from ACCA is assessed by exams and requires a year's practical experience in the workplace. It can be achieved through distance learning, face-to-face tuition or self-study.

Personal attributes A methodical approach, willingness to take responsibility, ability to keep to deadlines.

Mature entry and career change There is very good scope for mature entrants such as unqualified but experienced accountancy staff, returners to office occupations and mid-career changers. Mature entrants with relevant experience or knowledge may be exempted from some examinations.

Work–life balance Career breaks are unlikely to present any problems as long as people keep up with changes in taxation and other accountancy matters. AAT offers reduced membership subscriptions for those on maternity break. There is very good scope for part-time work, both in employment and working on one's own. Job-sharing should be possible.

Further information

Association of Accounting Technicians, 140 Aldersgate Street, London EC1A 4HY.
www.aat.org.uk
The Association of Chartered Certified Accountants, 2 Central Quay, 89 Hydepark Street, Glasgow GB3 8BW.
www.accaglobal.com

Related careers *banking – insurance – logistics – purchasing and supply – stock exchange and securities industry*

Actuary

Entry qualifications Almost exclusively a graduate profession.

The work Actuaries use probability and finance theory together with statistical techniques to highlight and solve financial problems, to suggest appropriate courses of action and to model/assess the financial implications of such actions. In other words, they 'work out the odds' and their work has a strong mathematical bias. Over a third of actuaries work for insurance offices, concentrating on the technical side of life assurance and pension funds. They investigate such matters as relative life expectancies of various groups in the population, and assess the effects of lifestyles and characteristics on premiums and policies and investment. In other insurance branches – accident, fire, motor – actuaries assess risks and pinpoint variables in the light of changing conditions and lifestyles, and advise on reserves necessary to cover long-term liabilities. In the Government Actuary's Department actuaries advise on public service pensions and insurance schemes.

About 50 per cent of actuaries work in consultancy. Much of their work involves advising pension funds, insurance companies or the companies which finance the funds. Good communication skills are essential to this work, as is increasingly the case in other areas of the profession.

There are also openings in the Stock Exchange and other financial institutions, as well as some opportunities (usually to do with pensions) in industry and commerce.

Actuaries can go into middle and higher business management, especially in life assurance companies and pension funds.

Training On-the-job training and on average three to six years' (depending on degree subject) part-time study leading to membership of the Institute of Actuaries (England and Wales) or Faculty of Actuaries (Scotland). A good degree in maths, statistics or economics qualifies a student for exemption from some early parts of the professional examinations. A first or postgraduate degree in actuarial subjects can lead to further exemptions.

In 2008 an Associate-level qualification is being launched, which students can obtain having completed foundation exams. They will be able to call themselves 'actuary' and use the letters AFA (Associate of the Faculty of Actuaries (Scotland), or AIA (Associate of the Institute of Actuaries (England and Wales). This will allow students to complete an actuarial qualification within a shorter period, on average around three years.

Personal attributes An analytical brain; probing curiosity; ability to interpret mathematical and statistical information and express results clearly; good communication skills.

Mature entry and career change All applicants require strong mathematical skills and need to take into account the long training.

Work–life balance A career break may be possible for experienced actuaries who have kept up with developments, especially relevant legislation. Actuaries tend not to work the long hours that are common in the City. In theory the work could be done part-time and by job-sharers or freelancers although most actuaries work full-time for large financial companies. Opportunities exist in investing, banking or management consultancy worldwide.

Further information

Institute of Actuaries, Staple Inn Hall, High Holborn, London WC1V 7QJ.

The Faculty of Actuaries, Maclaurin House, 18 Dublin Street, Edinburgh EH1 3PP.

www.actuaries.org.uk

Related careers *accountancy – banking – civil service – insurance – stock exchange and securities industry*

Advertising

Entry qualifications No rigid requirements; in practice usually National Qualifications Framework Level 3 (A levels, BTEC National awards) or Scottish Credit and Qualifications Framework equivalent. Most entrants are now graduates.

Graphic design, typography, etc., require art-school training (see Art and Design, p. 104).

The work Advertising specialists work in:

- Agencies
- Company advertising departments
- The media and for suppliers of advertising services (e.g. studios, film production, market research).

AGENCIES

Agencies plan, create and place advertisements on behalf of advertisers who appoint them to handle their 'account'. This may be a detergent, a package holiday, government information or financial services. Not all advertising expenditure is concerned with persuading people to buy; advertisements are also used to attract money for charities, votes for political parties, support for legislation, to encourage energy saving or investment, to fill jobs.

Agencies vary in size, speciality and scope. A very few employ up to 500 people, most under 50. Some specialize: for example, in business-to-business or recruitment advertising. Some will be responsible for creating the communications (creative agencies) and others will be responsible for media planning and buying (media agencies). Online agencies specialize in new media opportunities, such as Internet and SMS advertising.

Some agencies offer a full service (i.e. they have creative and media under the same roof). The largest agencies are now usually part of a communications group which can offer clients a wide range of specialist services ranging from packaging design (see p. 107) to broadcast production (see p. 597), market research, marketing and/or brand consultancy, sponsorship, public relations (see p. 484) and promotional marketing, etc. Some agencies, especially regional agencies, will offer these services in-house and yet others will buy in services as and when needed from outside suppliers.

Account Executive/Account Planner

Agency staff work in groups on individual accounts. The *account executive*'s main responsibility is liaison with the client; the *account planner*'s with organizing and interpreting research into consumer attitudes and developing the strategy on which the advertising will be based. Account executives are usually in charge of several accounts, each dealing with a different product, and are the link between clients and agency. They acquaint themselves thoroughly with each client's product, investigate the competition's product and ensure the client's claims for the product can be substantiated. Account planners acquaint themselves with the potential consumers who form the target group (the people at whom the advertisement is to be aimed) and commission the necessary research. Once the group has decided upon a campaign proposition or theme, the account executive discusses it with the client. When the brief and the budget are agreed, work on creating the advertisement starts.

The account executives coordinate the work, control the budget and present progress reports to the client. Their work involves travelling if clients are scattered over the country or abroad.

The executive's job requires self-confidence and diplomacy, as clients often have to be persuaded that the type and tone of a campaign suggested by the agency will be more effective than the client's own idea. Planners' jobs tend to be more strategic and intellectual in approach.

Media Executive

Planning, research and buying are the three media functions; they may be carried out by different people within the department, or the whole media operation may be the responsibility of a group of individuals assigned to a particular campaign.

Media planners are crucial to the success of any campaign. In consultation with account handlers and creative staff they work out how best to spend the available budget in order to generate most sales/influence. They choose the channels of communication – newspapers, magazines, radio, television, websites, posters and so on – which are most appropriate for any particular campaign and reach the target group most economically. Media planning decisions are based on information and statistics provided by *media research* and an understanding of media consumers. Computers are widely used to compare effectiveness and costs, but creative requirements – for colour, movement or sound – require subjective judgement.

Media buyers are responsible for negotiating the purchase of advertisement space or air time and the selection of different options within a medium (e.g. different magazines).

Market Research

Before an advertising campaign is planned, facts are compiled about the product's uses, its advantages and limitations, competitors' products, distribution and so on. Facts and opinions are also gathered about its potential users – the target group: not just in terms of who they are, how much money they have and where they live, but in terms of their attitudes and behaviour. Some facts come from desk research, collecting information from a variety of published sources and the client's own records. Others may need specially commissioned research, ranging from statistics compiled by part-time interviewers questioning members of the public to sophisticated behavioural studies involving trained psychologists (see also Marketing, p. 362).

Creative Department

Once the account group has been briefed and a strategy agreed with the client, the creative team of *copywriter* and *art director* together develop the advertisement.

The advertising 'message' is translated into a 'communication' that makes an instant impact on the target group. Words and pictures must complement each other.

Copywriters must be literate and imaginative, but they must choose their words under considerable constraints – from the disciplines of the brief and the restrictions of the space or time available, to the obligations of the Code of Advertising Practice and legal requirements. An interest in commercial success and an understanding of people's ways of life and priorities are far more useful than literary leanings.

Copywriters and art directors work with television producers and directors to create television and cinema commercials. There is no hard-and-fast rule about who exactly does what, and whether the visual or verbal aspect is the more important.

The *art director* is responsible for the visual appearance of advertisements, deciding whether to use photography, illustration, computer graphics or typography, and commissioning and supervising their production. The typographer chooses type which is easily readable, fits the layout and reflects the character of the product. The artist (only the larger agencies employ their own) may produce anything from a 'rough' to a finished 'visual'.

The atmosphere in agencies is often relaxed and informal, but the pace and pressure are very demanding indeed. The decline in the number of people in agencies means fierce competition for any openings. Considerable talent, the right kind of personality and commitment are needed to survive and succeed.

Traffic and Production Manager

This role involves liaising between other departments within an agency and clients and keeping up with all projects, in order to ensure that they are completed in time and within budget. The production manager makes sure that creative departments have necessary approvals and scripts, organizes print buying and the purchase of services such as photography when needed, and keeps track of overall expenditure.

COMPANY ADVERTISING DEPARTMENTS

Many large companies incorporate advertising into marketing (see p. 362).

Brand managers are responsible for the marketing policy for a product, including its advertising. Relatively few have their own advertising departments. If a manufacturer creates and places all the advertising directly, the department may be much like a small agency. There is less scope for employees to work on different types of products simultaneously, but there may be a broader range of work covering different aspects of marketing.

Retailers' advertisement departments may deal with store and window displays, exhibitions, fashion shows, promotions, sponsorship, Internet activity, classified recruitment advertising and public relations, for example, using an advertising agency only for display advertisements.

Advertising departments are useful training grounds, giving experience in a range of work.

MEDIA

The advertising departments of media owners are responsible for selling space or air time to advertisers, directly or through agencies. The *research section* provides information about readers or viewers; it helps advertisers pinpoint target groups. The *promotions section* may have its own creative department, which works in three areas: projecting the medium to advertisers, to distributors and to retailers on behalf of advertisers. *Sales representatives* are responsible for selling advertisement space or air time; this may include telephone selling, trying to get classified advertisements (which may involve having to put up with being rebuffed, and trying again). *Media managers* are responsible for ensuring that advertisements comply with the Code of Advertising Practice, which may involve checking copy claims and possibly asking for changes to be made before accepting copy.

Training Considerable patience – as well as talent – is needed to get a job. Nearly three-quarters of jobs are in London. Once in, training is a combination of practice and theory. Agency policy varies concerning how far vocational qualifications listed below are looked for or encouraged and possession is no guarantee of a job.

Pre-entry training is not essential. The larger agencies tend to run in-service training schemes, sometimes supplemented by external courses. The Institute of Practitioners in Advertising runs a phased programme of courses designed to cater for the training needs of executives employed at IPA member agencies at each stage of their career development. Some agencies take several graduates (any discipline) each year; many advertisers have management training schemes which can lead to advertising jobs.

Administrative staff occasionally progress to executive or copywriting positions; their chances are better with a small specialist agency (for example, a recruitment agency) or in an advertising department, but they are never great. Other ways into the industry are through production departments (see Publishing, p. 488 and Printing, p. 462) and 'traffic control' (progress chasing – keeping the work flowing to schedule through all the different departments and processes).

Those wanting to take a pre-entry course can choose from the following.

- A growing number of university courses – degrees and higher national diplomas – with a substantial advertising component.

- Foundation degree in Business (Advertising & Marketing Communications), two years full-time, or postgraduate Advanced Professional Diploma in Advertising, 30 weeks full-time at West Herts College.
- Full-time, part-time or distance-learning courses leading to the CAM Foundation's Certificates (available at pre-entry stage or when in employment).

However, these vocational qualifications do not necessarily increase the chance of entry as the advertising industry recruits from a wide base of subjects in order to vary the range of knowledge and experience within a team.

Personal attributes Business acumen; interest in social and economic trends; flair for salesmanship; numeracy; communication skills; ability to work in a team; ability to stand criticism whether justified or not; ability to work under pressure; stamina; resilience; persistence; interest in popular culture.

For creative people: Discipline; originality; strong feeling for uncomplicated images and 'messages'; willingness to produce the kind of words/artwork that are best for the campaign, whether artistically first-rate or not.

For planning and research: Objectivity; a logical, analytical brain but ability to make lateral strategic leaps – often based on intuition – that then have to be backed by solid evidence and a creative appreciation.

Mature entry and career change Little opportunity without previous relevant commercial experience although some agencies do look at more varied working backgrounds when recruiting for the account planning department.

Work–life balance The advertising industry has produced a guide to best practice in work–life balance for both agencies and individuals. There is increasing recognition of the need to accommodate more flexible working to retain talented individuals – both male and female – particularly given the development of technological support. There is also increasing incidence of flexible working to accommodate outside pressures – such as further study, other creative endeavours, children and other dependants – on staff who have demonstrated their worth.

Prospects for career breaks are reasonable for experienced planners or for successful executives who have 'kept their hand in' with freelance work.

Further information

CAM Foundation, Moor Hall, Cookham, Berkshire SL6 9QH.
www.camfoundation.com

Advertising Association, 7th Floor North, Artillery House, 11–19 Artillery Row, London SW1P 1RT.
www.adassoc.org.uk

Institute of Practitioners in Advertising, 44 Belgrave Square, London SW1X 8QS.
www.ipa.co.uk

Related careers *management – marketing and selling – public relations – retail management*

Agriculture and Horticulture

Entry qualifications Entry at all levels, from no qualifications to degree and postgraduate awards.

The work Agriculture and horticulture cover a wide range of land-based industries, both traditional and, increasingly, non-traditional. Dairy and beef production, arable and industrial crops, pig and poultry rearing, fish and deer farming, fruit, vegetable and flower growing, shooting, nature trails, vineyards – these and many other activities make up an industry that in the last few years has been going through one of its biggest ever changes, more particularly on the agricultural side. This is due to a number of factors: most recently changes to EU agricultural policy 'decoupling' subsidies from production levels and linking payments to food safety, animal welfare and environmental standards. Government schemes to pay farmers to 'set aside' land from production and to subsidize the planting of woodlands were the start of an escalating movement which sees farmers not just as producers of food, but as custodians of the countryside.

Over recent decades farmers' incomes have dropped significantly, meaning fewer staff can be employed and more farmers and their families work part-time rather than full-time. Smaller units are disappearing, while larger ones survive by becoming even more efficient. Numbers employed in general farm work have dropped dramatically and anyone looking to a career in farming in future must be prepared to develop good management and/or specialist skills. Bad publicity about chemical pollution, intensive farming and recent food scares, plus pressures from a more health-conscious public, mean more farmers have been switching to less intensive, organic methods of production. Recent disease outbreaks hit farming in some areas especially badly but all farmers are having to find other ways to use their resources, for example by diversifying into the tourism or recreation industries (e.g. bed and breakfast, golf driving ranges). This may not mean a big increase in income, and many farms are not suitable for such developments, but somehow farmers have to find ways of 'adding value' to their products or activities – perhaps making their own sheep's or goat's cheese, or growing energy crops, such as willow or poplar.

Management posts in agriculture and horticulture are often held by people who started out in practical work and then became supervisors. Increasingly, though, qualifications such as HNDs and degrees are essential for such jobs as farm manager, unit manager, manager of a country park. As farms and horticultural units grow in size, the range but not the number of management jobs is increasing. A manager of, for example, an animal unit needs scientific, technological, veterinary, accounting and IT knowledge. Marketing skills are increasingly in demand.

Research is usually concerned with a particular aspect of crop production or of animal husbandry. This could be pest control, plant disease, soil chemistry, genetics, nutrition, taste preservation (researchers work closely with technologists in the food industry (see p. 520). Work may be wholly or largely theoretical, involving study of scientific journals and papers as well as collaboration with scientists from other disciplines. It often involves experimental work in the laboratory or in trial growing areas. Researchers work for research establishments, for botanical gardens, in industry, in the Civil Service (mainly the Department for Environment, Food and Rural Affairs – Defra).

Advisory work is carried out by government (through Defra) and by commercial firms which supply agricultural and horticultural goods and equipment. Advice may be given on pest control, selection of the best variety of crop, choice of feed, marketing, finance, and diversification.

AGRICULTURE

The main branches of 'traditional' practical farm work are:

Animal Husbandry

Beef cattle: work varies according to size and type of farm. Some farms only rear calves, others fatten cattle through to slaughter.

Dairy cattle: a 100-cow herd can be worth a large sum of money, so this is highly responsible work. Tasks involve feeding, milking and following strict hygiene maintenance routines.

Pigs: farms breed pigs for sale, or buy young pigs and fatten them for sale as bacon or pork, or they do both. Extent of automation varies.

Poultry: highly specialized holdings concentrate either entirely on egg production or on hatching chicks – often in fully automatic giant incubators – or on rearing table birds. Some poultry units resemble a cross between a laboratory and a modern factory with indoor, clean work. Increased demand for free-range eggs means more scope for alternative forms of egg production but there are still few farms where looking after poultry means feeding birds in the farmyard.

Sheep: hill farms usually concentrate on large flocks; on lowland farms sheep may form part of a unit and shepherds also do other work. Shepherds work with, and may train, dogs.

Arable Farming

The wide variety of crops grown on British farms includes cereals such as wheat, oats and barley, animal fodder crops and and increasing number of non-food or 'industrial' crops such as fibres, specialist oils and biofuel materials. Intensive arable farming tends to be concentrated in South East England, with crops varying according to soil type, weather and suitability of the land for appropriate machinery. Most arable work is highly mechanized, but requires considerable skill in operating and maintaining increasingly sophisticated machinery.

General Farm Work

People who do not want to specialize can carry out general duties, driving tractors, helping with livestock, repairing buildings, clearing ditches, etc. The range of jobs depends on the type and size of farm.

HORTICULTURE

There are two main divisions: commercial – growing plants for sale – and amenity – making and maintaining gardens as pleasant environments. Horticulturalists, therefore, may work in different settings – as sole employee or as one of a large team; in the depths of the country or in the middle of a town.

Commercial Horticulture

This includes the production of fruit, vegetables, flowers, plants of all kinds in market gardens, nurseries, garden centres, greenhouses and fruit farms. Some sell directly to the public, while others sell only to other horticultural concerns. Some specialize in, for example, bulb production, soft fruit, cut flowers or house plants. Others grow a wide variety of plants. Many tasks are now mechanized, but some are still done by hand – some pollination, disbudding, collecting seed, grafting, for example. Much effort now goes into producing strains that are disease-resistant and/or have a longer growing season (e.g. through genetic engineering). Computer systems are often used to control the environment in order to produce exactly the right conditions for different plants. Garden centres are a feature of most towns, offering pot-grown plants which customers can plant in their gardens at any time of year, plus a huge range of garden tools and accessories. Jobs in these offer the most contact with members of the public, who expect staff to be knowledgeable. Experienced horticultural workers can become plantation assistants on fruit stations or quality inspectors for commercial canning and quick-freezing stations, or manage 'pick your own' farms (weekend work).

Amenity Horticulture

Its purpose is to provide pleasant open-air environments in town and country. It includes town and country parks; picnic areas off motorways; National Trust and similar properties; nature trails; theme parks; bowling greens; golf courses. It frequently involves nursery work and arboriculture (see 'Forestry', p. 70). Staff have to cope with the sometimes conflicting demands of the gardening programme and events held in the park (e.g. open-air concerts). A park manager may spend a large proportion of time on such non-horticultural activities as paperwork and rubbish disposal. Current reductions in staffing levels often affect types of planting, e.g. bedding plants may give way to grass and shrubs. The work involves contact with the public and often helping with recreational activities, such as sitting at cash-desks for open-air concerts, usher and patrol duty, although in some parks these duties are carried out by keepers with no horticultural training (see also Leisure/Recreation Management, 'Training', p. 332). *There may be more of a career structure (and day release) in this type of horticulture than in commercial concerns.*

Landscape and Garden Contractors

This work overlaps with landscape architecture and amenity horticulture. It includes design and construction of new gardens and regular maintenance of existing gardens. Increasingly contractors are employed by local authorities (and even by the Royal Parks) to maintain public gardens and parks.

Training

Although it may still be possible to get a job in farming and horticulture without going to college, there is much more chance of a proper career for those with formal training. Expertise and management skills are of increasing importance. The main training routes are apprenticeships – available in both agriculture and commercial horticulture – and NVQs/SVQs – available in agriculture and horticulture at levels 1–4. Work-based training with part-time courses can lead to these; some full-time courses also lead to credits towards NVQs.

Edexcel BTEC/SQA route BTEC First Diploma and National Certificate and Diploma/SQA Scottish Group Award courses can be in general agriculture or horticulture, or specialized. Examples are livestock, crop husbandry, land-based business and farm diversification. Higher National Diplomas (three-year sandwich) offer an alternative to a degree course for those looking for a career in practical farming or horticulture. A range of additional courses are available, mainly in new technologies, management and farm organization; these are especially suitable for people who have spent some time working in the industry.

Degrees Three or four years. Entry requirements normally include one or two sciences at A level or equivalent. There is a wide variety of courses: examples of titles, apart from general agriculture or horticulture, are Crop Science, Crop Technology and Resource Management, Agriculture and Land Management, Agricultural Botany, Agricultural and Food Marketing, Agroforestry, Animal Production Science. Little actual farm work is included in degree courses, which are intended for future advisers, researchers, teachers or managers. Entrants to full-time courses are frequently required to have had one year's practical experience. This is a good idea even where it is not obligatory.

Full-time and part-time Foundation degree courses, sometimes including a year's work experience, are also available.

Kew Diploma in Horticulture Three-year, degree-level course in amenity and botanical horticulture. Entry requirements are minimum five GCSEs, including English, maths and a science, plus two A levels, preferably in science subjects, in addition to formal horticultural training to at least NVQ level 2. All applicants are required to have a minimum of two years' work experience in a recognized horticultural establishment before beginning the course.

Applicants without the required qualifications but with greater experience are considered on an individual basis.

SPECIALIZATIONS

Forestry

This is a small specialization, although until recent tax changes made it less attractive, commercial conifer planting had been increasing. Woodland grant schemes encourage farmers to plant trees instead of crops; and environmentalists would like to see the planting of more hardwoods (which take a long time to grow and attract a wide range of wildlife) and fewer conifers. In commercial forestry trees are grown as a renewable resource and harvested like any other crop. Other woodlands are maintained for sporting or recreational purposes. Urban forestry is growing in importance; known also as arboriculture, it covers the establishment, care and maintenance of trees for amenity purposes (see p. 68).

Employers include the Forestry Commission, local authorities, commercial companies that own forests all over the country, cooperatives and individual landowners. There are opportunities to work abroad. Managers – senior forest officers – plan afforestation programmes and may be in overall charge of a single plantation, a group of forests or a whole district. Though an administrative job, it involves driving and walking. It includes responsibility for fire protection, wildlife protection, disease identification and control, planning and control of recreational areas, possibly marketing. Forest workers carry out practical tasks, usually under the supervision of foresters or forest officers.

Training Forest workers do not need formal qualifications, but may be given in-service training and/or sent on block release for courses leading to NVQs levels 1 and 2, First Diploma or City & Guilds/SQA certificates.

Most foresters or forest officers train by taking either a National Diploma or SQA-based college diploma or a degree or Foundation degree in a forestry-related subject or a postgraduate course. Those seeking the highest level management posts may need to take the Professional Examination of the Institute of Chartered Foresters.

Traditionally diploma holders have been taken on as supervisors, responsible for overseeing day-to-day operations, and graduates as assistant or area managers. Graduates have more scientific knowledge than diplomates, but the distinction has become blurred and promotion is possible for both types of entrant.

Fish Farming and Fisheries Management

This is the breeding and rearing of various types of fish for food or sport. Most fish farms are small owner-run businesses, but there are larger ones employing several staff. Other employers of fisheries managers are water authorities, angling clubs, estate owners, fish processors. Like all animal husbandry this is usually a seven-day-a-week job and involves unsocial working hours.

Training There is no prescribed entry and training route: the usual ways into this growing industry are through a National Award in Fish Management (Fish Production), a sandwich Higher National Diploma, or the Institute of Fisheries Management correspondence course for its certificate and diploma (no entry requirements). Work-based training may lead to NVQs/SVQs at levels 2 and 3.

For research posts: degree in biological or agricultural science, usually followed by a postgraduate course. It is possible to progress to management from a technician post.

Engineering in the Land-based Sector

Engineers in the land-based sector apply engineering principles to all kinds of agriculture and horticulture as well as in amenity-related fields. As the world's non-renewable and slowly renewable resources are being rapidly used up, it is essential to make the most efficient use of natural resources. This involves recycling processes; exploring and using new sources of energy; and, above all, incorporating new and sustainable technologies in the design and manufacture of agricultural equipment. Engineers in this sector may be involved in the sales, marketing and servicing of equipment; in designing and constructing farm and horticultural installations; in product planning; mechanizing procedures; crop storage and processing, and the design and maintenance of outdoor sports surfaces.

Training For levels of engineering see p. 213. NVQs/SVQs are available at levels 1–3 and can be achieved individually or as part of an Apprenticeship or Advanced Apprenticeship. Courses are available leading to BTEC/SQA awards, as well as degrees in agricultural engineering. Holders of a Higher National Diploma or a degree in a related subject (geography, science, agriculture) can take a postgraduate course in agricultural engineering.

Farm/Garden Mechanic

All farmworkers must be able to cope with running repairs; many arable units which use machinery worth thousands of pounds employ their own farm mechanics who are in charge of maintenance, repairs and adaptation of all types of mechanical gadgets. On large units there may be several mechanics; usually there is only one. However, the majority of mechanics are employed by agricultural and garden machinery dealers, carrying out servicing and repairs in a workshop or in the field where the machinery is being used.

Training Training schemes are accredited by the British Agricultural and Garden Machinery Association.

Social and Therapeutic Horticulture

This covers the use of horticulture in a range of therapeutic activities. It may form part of a planned rehabilitation of a physically disabled patient or it may provide education, recreation or vocational training for people with learning difficulties. Most therapists (who may be called horticultural instructors/organizers or project workers) work in sheltered workshops, hospitals, residential homes, training centres or in special education.

Training There is as yet no career structure, although the majority of the work is carried out by professional care staff and horticulturalists. A few colleges are introducing diploma courses and Thrive (a registered charity) offers a Professional Development Diploma in Therapeutic Horticulture, a part-time one-year, flexible-learning course studied through a combination of workshop blocks and home study. Exemptions apply for those with related qualifications. A certificate course has also been developed for individuals new to this field to provide them with a basic understanding of the principles and practice of horticultural therapy.

Personal attributes (generally) For most jobs: attention to detail; physical robustness and ability to cope with irregular hours; reliability; good powers of observation; ability to work without supervision.

For managers: ability to recruit and cope with permanent and seasonal staff; ability to take decisions, knowing that these may be subject to the vagaries of nature; enjoyment of responsibility.

Mature entry and career change On the whole this is not advisable as trainee vacancies tend to go to young applicants (partly because the pay structure is age-related), although there are no age limits on training schemes or courses. Some farmers' children return to farming as a second career when their parents wish to retire.

Work–life balance A career break should be no problem for those in management jobs before the break, except that competition for jobs is fierce. The Forestry Commission has a career-break scheme for men and women who retire temporarily for domestic reasons. Many more people than in the past are working part-time, especially in agriculture.

Further information

Lantra, Lantra House, Stoneleigh Park, Nr Coventry, Warwickshire CV8 2LG.
www.lantra.co.uk

Royal Botanic Gardens, Kew, Richmond, Surrey TW9 3AB.
www.rbgkew.org.uk

Institute of Chartered Foresters, 59 George Street, Edinburgh EH2 2JG.
www.charteredforesters.org

Institute of Horticulture, 9 Red Lion Court, London EC4A 3EF.
www.horticulture.org.uk

Institute of Fisheries Management, 22 Rushworth Avenue, West Bridgford, Nottingham NG2 7LF.
www.ifm.org.uk

The Institution of Agricultural Engineers, West End Road, Silsoe, Bedford MK45 4DU.
www.iagre.org

British Agricultural and Garden Machinery Association, Entrance B, Level 1, Salamander Quay West, Park Lane, Harefield, Middlesex UB9 6NZ.
www.bagma.com

Thrive (Horticultural Therapy), The Geoffrey Udall Centre, Beech Hill, Reading RG7 2AT.
www.thrive.org.uk

Related careers *animals: Veterinary Nurse/Surgeon – landscape architecture – science: Scientist; Technician*

Animals

VETERINARY SURGEON

Entry qualifications All graduate profession. Normally at least National Qualifications Framework Level 3 (A levels, BTEC National awards) or Scottish Credit and Qualifications Framework equivalent, including chemistry and/or biology (some courses require three sciences). This is a highly competitive degree course; very high grades are required. Veterinary schools require applicants to have gained practical work experience, such as working in a veterinary surgery, on farms or in stables, kennels or catteries. Some universities require applicants to take the BioMedical Admissions Test (BMAT) before applying.

Registration with the Royal College of Veterinary Surgeons.

General Practice

Some veterinary practices deal mainly or exclusively (except in cases of emergency) with small or 'companion' animals; others deal with farm animals or horses; some are mixed practices, but even here veterinary surgeons are likely to develop particular areas of interest and expertise. Veterinary surgeons must provide a 24-hour service, but most practices are organized so as to provide reasonable time off and holidays.

Veterinary surgeons treat animals both in their surgeries and at their owners' premises. It is important for them to be able to communicate effectively with animals' owners. This means a different approach for pet-owners, who have an emotional attachment to their 'companion animals', and for farmers to whom their animals are an investment. While always committed to the welfare of an animal, the veterinary surgeon must allow a farmer to balance an expensive new treatment against an economic return. In farm animal practice, veterinary surgeons are concerned not just with treating individual animals but with advising on the well-being and productivity of the entire stock.

Veterinary surgeons in practice often take on additional part-time appointments. Farm practitioners may be Local Veterinary Inspectors for the Department for Environment, Food and Rural Affairs, testing cattle for tuberculosis or brucellosis or carrying out inspections at cattle markets. Some practices carry out supervision of meat hygiene in abattoirs or poultry slaughterhouses; others work at licensed greyhound tracks. District councils need veterinary surgeons to inspect the riding establishments, zoos, pet shops and dog-breeding and boarding kennels which they license.

Newly qualified veterinary surgeons normally start as assistants in established practices, moving on to a more senior assistantship and then to a partnership in an existing practice or setting up a new practice.

Government Service

Veterinary officers employed by the State Veterinary Service are not concerned with individual animals. Their responsibilities include: the control and eradication of notifiable disease; diagnostic and consultancy work on notifiable and non-notifiable disease; epidemiological studies; disease monitoring and surveillance; special investigations and surveys; public health liaison and human diseases related to animals; red meat and poultry hygiene; the operation of animal health schemes; improved farm animal health.

Other public service opportunities include the Veterinary Laboratories Agency, which provides veterinary scientific research, diagnostic services and animal disease surveillance to all sectors of the animal health industry, the Food Standards Agency and the Meat Hygiene Service. The Department for Environment, Food and Rural Affairs

(Defra) also employs vets to monitor animal health and to prevent the spread of diseases.

Other Opportunities

Veterinary surgeons are also employed in research institutes; animal welfare societies; the Royal Army Veterinary Corps; industry, mainly pharmaceutical companies and those making animal feeds and fertilizers; universities; and the Animal Health Trust, a voluntary organization for veterinary research and the promotion of postgraduate veterinary education. There are also opportunities in developing countries, and veterinary surgeons who qualify from one of the six UK veterinary schools may practise in EU member states. However, they have to satisfy that country's registration requirements.

Training Degree courses last five years (six at Cambridge) and are divided into pre-clinical (animal husbandry, anatomy, physiology, biochemistry), para-clinical (pathology, pharmacology) and clinical (medicine and surgery, veterinary public health). During the vacations students must spend six months gaining experience in aspects of veterinary work under the supervision of veterinary surgeons in practice, in veterinary laboratories and in other areas of veterinary work.

To practise as a veterinary surgeon in the UK you must be registered with the Royal College of Veterinary Surgeons.

Personal attributes Scientific interest in animals and their behaviour and development, rather than sentimental fondness for pets; powers of observation; a firm hand; the ability to inspire confidence in animals (i.e. total absence of nervousness) and in their owners; self-reliance and adaptability; indifference to occasional physically disagreeable conditions of work.

As veterinary surgeons deal with owners as well as animals, excellent communication skills are essential, as are time management, leadership and the ability to work well in a team.

Mature entry and career change As there is such stiff competition for degree-course places, it is unlikely that anyone over 30 would be accepted, though there is no official upper age limit.

Work–life balance In general practice, a career break would have to be negotiated with partners. A retraining course has been organized every other year for those wishing to return to practice. Veterinary surgeons in the State Veterinary Service are civil servants (see p. 153).

There are opportunities to work part-time or as a locum.

Further information

Royal College of Veterinary Surgeons, Belgravia House, 62–64 Horseferry Road, London SW1P 2AF.
www.rcvs.org.uk
British Veterinary Association, 7 Mansfield Street, London W1G 9NQ.
www.bva.co.uk

VETERINARY NURSE

Entry qualifications Work-based training route: Five GCSEs (A–C) or equivalent, including English language and either two physical or biological sciences or one science and maths. Alternative qualifications of a comparable or higher standard may be accepted in lieu of the usual requirements at the discretion of the RCVS. Higher education route: A levels or equivalent, usually in chemistry and biology, and five GCSEs (A–C)/S grades (1–3) including English language and maths and two sciences. Registration with the Royal College of Veterinary Surgeons.

The work Veterinary nurses assist veterinary surgeons in their practice and occasionally on visits, undertaking a wide variety of veterinary care and supporting work. In the practice they assist with consultations and look after hospitalized animals, monitoring their condition and providing necessary care and treatment. Veterinary nurses prepare the operating theatre, ensuring that it is clean and that equipment is maintained. They also assist veterinary surgeons during operations and help to monitor anaesthesia. Veterinary nurses also undertake a range of veterinary investigations and treatments, under the direction of their employing veterinary surgeon. These can include the collection and examination of specimens, dental hygiene work, administration of vaccines, dressing changes, 'well pet' clinics and puppy parties, etc. In addition to providing nursing care for animals, veterinary nurses are also responsible for ensuring the hygiene of clinical areas of the veterinary practice. They work mainly in 'small animal' practices, i.e. those dealing with domestic animals kept as pets, and for the RSPCA and other animal welfare and research organizations. Opportunities also exist for training in equine veterinary nursing, in specialized veterinary practices dealing with horses.

The hours are usually long and irregular. Animals become sick and have to be cared for at weekends and during the night, which will mean going to work on Saturday and Sunday, and sometimes overnight.

Some veterinary surgeons' practices employ only one veterinary nurse who may then have little companionship. Most of the working day will be spent with the employer.

While predominantly a young person's job, there are a growing number of opportunities for career development and progression. These include senior nursing posts in specialized veterinary hospitals, veterinary nurse teaching posts, commercial work with pharmaceutical companies, practice management and specialization into areas such as pet behaviour or nutrition.

Training Work-based route: minimum age for enrolment as trainee is 17; practical work may start earlier. Training for the Veterinary Nursing Certificate is work-based, incorporating NVQs at levels 2 and 3, plus study by day-release or block-release courses.

A potential trainee must first find a job with a veterinary practice or hospital approved by the Royal College of Veterinary Surgeons as a training centre and then enrol with the RCVS as a trainee. The syllabus covers anatomy and physiology, hygiene and feeding, first aid, side-room techniques (analysing specimens and preparing slides) and the theory and practice of breeding and nursing. Trainees are continuously assessed at work and external examinations are taken at the end of the first and second years of training.

The veterinary nursing section of the RCVS website includes detailed lists of those veterinary practices and centres that are approved as training practices. Some practices offer specialist training in equine veterinary nursing.

Higher education route Veterinary nurse training is also available alongside an RCVS-approved veterinary nursing degree or HND course, which includes work experience placements. This route will take longer than work-based training, but could give you more career opportunities. Advanced qualifications in veterinary nursing are available.

Veterinary nurses are required to register with the Royal College of Veterinary Nurses.

Personal attributes A love of animals and a scientific interest in their development, behaviour and welfare; lack of squeamishness; a willingness to respond to instructions, and yet to act independently when necessary; readiness to work well both alone and with others; a sure, firm, but gentle grip; patience. Ability to type and drive is helpful.

Mature entry and career change There is no upper age limit, but most trainees are under 25. This is to some extent dictated by the low wages received during training.

Work–life balance There are many opportunities for part-time and locum work for qualified veterinary nurses. Most trainees work full-time. Any career break would have to be negotiated with employer.

Further information
Royal College of Veterinary Surgeons, Veterinary Nursing Department, Belgravia House, 62–64 Horseferry Road, London SW1P 2AF.
www.rcvs.org.uk

WORK WITH HORSES

Entry qualifications Four GCSEs or equivalent, including an English subject, for riding instructors, but requirements waived for entrants over 18. None for grooms and stable managers. But see 'Training', below.

The work Looking after horses nearly always means hard physical work that has to be carried out daily in all weathers. Hours tend to be long, especially in summer, and most people work a six-day week. Most new entrants have had unpaid experience. Staff may live in or out, but grooms and stable managers usually live on the premises because of the early-morning start. Meals may be provided.

Riding Instructor

They teach children and adults, in both private lessons and classes, and accompany riders out on 'hacks'. Classes may be held early in the morning or late in the evening, to suit pupils coming before or after work. Some instructors work for one establishment full-time, others work freelance or part-time. Many combine teaching with general stable work. Setting up one's own riding school requires considerable capital, experience and business knowledge.

Groom/Stable Manager

They work in and may eventually manage a variety of establishments, e.g. hunt, racing, showjumping and eventing stables, livery yards (which look after other owners' horses), riding schools, studs. They clean stables, feed and water horses, watch out for and report any symptoms which indicate a horse may be sick, clean and maintain tack. They prepare horses for competition – eventing, showjumping, dressage, driving, polo, showing, etc. At a stud, grooms also look after the brood mares and care for their foals. They may also assist with breaking and training. This is highly skilled work. 'Plum' jobs like travelling with show horses are rare. However, British grooms are in great demand abroad.

Training *Instructor*: The two main examining bodies in the horse industry are the British Horse Society and the Association of British Riding Schools. The BHS Stage Exams consist of two parallel streams: riding, and horse knowledge and care. Intending instructors must take both, together with teaching tests. The route is:

Stage 1 (minimum age 14).

Stage 2. Candidates for Stage 2 must first have passed the separate BHS Riding and Road Safety Test. This, together with the Preliminary Teaching Test (minimum age $17\frac{1}{2}$), leads to the Preliminary Teaching Certificate. On completion of 500 hours of teaching experience, and completion of Stage 3 (minimum age 17), the full Assistant Instructor Certificate (AI) is awarded.

Stage 4 (minimum age 18 for riding, 19 for care). This, together with the Intermediate Teaching Examination and a full Health and Safety at Work first aid certificate, leads to the Intermediate Instructor (II) award.

Stable Manager's Certificate (minimum age 22). Those who pass this plus the Equitation/Teaching Examination gain the full Instructor's Certificate.

BHS instructional qualifications are currently recognized in 32 countries through the International Group for Equestrian Qualifications.

NVQ/SVQ qualifications are available at levels 1 and 2 in Horse Care and Level 3 in Horse Care and Management through work-based training. Accredited NVQ/SVQ include equestrian centres, colleges and other training agencies.

Groom: People who want to become grooms and stable managers, but have no particular riding ambitions, can take either the BHS horse knowledge and care tests, Groom's Certificate, Intermediate Stable Manager's Certificate and Stable Manager's Certificate (without the riding tests) or the ABRS exams. These consist of Preliminary Horse Care and Riding, the Groom's Certificate (minimum age 16) and

Groom's Diploma (minimum age 20). No educational qualifications are required for the ABRS exams.

Training for horse exams is normally at an equestrian college or riding school/training yard. Duration of training depends on a student's ability and standard when starting. It is also possible to work for these exams while working as a groom. There are also some fee-charging schools. It is important to check that any training establishment is approved by the BHS and/or is a member of the ABRS. Increasingly, equestrian studies courses are being offered at colleges of agriculture and further education colleges, leading to BTEC National and Higher National awards and incorporating BHS qualifications. Degree courses are now also available. It is anticipated that in future people with qualifications will have the most opportunities in managing equestrian establishments of all kinds.

An Apprenticeship in the Equine Industry is available, as are NVQs at levels 1–3.

Personal attributes Physical stamina and ability to work outside in all weathers; indifference to getting dirty; willingness to work 'unsocial' hours and sometimes by oneself.

For instructors: authority; ability to express oneself clearly; patience; a liking for children.

Work–life balance There may be some part-time work for riding instructors at local riding establishments. Part-time work is on the increase.

Further information
British Horse Society, Stoneleigh Deer Park, Kenilworth, Warwickshire CV8 2XZ.
www.bhs.org.uk
Association of British Riding Schools, Office No. 2, Queens Chambers, 38–40 Queen Street, Penzance TR18 4BH.
www.abrs-info.org
Lantra, The Sector Skills Council for the Environment and Land-

based Sector, Lantra House, Stoneleigh Park, Nr Coventry, Warwickshire CV8 2LG.
www.lantra.co.uk

Other Work with Animals

There is a wide range of other opportunities to work with animals. They range from guide dog trainer to gamekeeper, pet shop assistant to RSPCA inspector, zookeeper to dog beautician. Some of these fields offer a very limited number of openings. Often no specific academic qualifications are needed and training is in-house.

Archaeology

Entry qualifications Degree course entry is usually at National Qualifications Framework Level 3 (A levels, BTEC National awards) or Scottish Credit and Qualifications Framework equivalent (normally requiring maths or a science and modern language at GCSE or equivalent). For *classical archaeology*, classical civilization or ancient history at either GCSE or Λ level, or equivalent, may be required; for *conservation*, chemistry at A level or equivalent. Archaeology A level or equivalent is available, but is not required.

The work Archaeology is the science of gaining knowledge from the past through the study of material remains and environmental traces. Excavations tend to be the most publicized aspects of the work, but the actual digging up and recording work is becoming less centre stage as emphasis on preservation and limiting of damage to sites increases. Though archaeologists need a broad knowledge of the whole field, they normally specialize in one geographical area or period, for example landscape, regional, prehistoric, Anglo-Saxon or interpretative archaeology. Some archaeologists also specialize in particular artefacts, for example coins, weapons or inscriptions.

Among the many broad archaeological specializations are archaeological science, conservation, heritage management, underwater archaeology, environmental archaeology, geophysical survey, archaeological computing and landscape archaeology. These can be studied through a wide variety of postgraduate courses.

Some archaeologists work in museums (see p. 381). Most work for national agencies, local authorities or utility companies. National agencies employing archaeologists include English Heritage, Historic

Scotland, Cadw: Welsh Historic Monuments, the Environment & Heritage Service (Northern Ireland), the National Trust, the National Trust for Scotland, national parks, Forestry Commission. Other opportunities include museum work and university teaching. There are many more archaeologists than related jobs.

Training BA or BSc in archaeology as a single subject or in combination with a wide variety of other disciplines. These can be followed by a one-year Masters degree in various specializations.

The Institute of Field Archaeologists is the professional institute for archaeologists, with various membership levels.

Personal attributes Deep curiosity about the past; intellectual ability well above average; artistic sensibility; patience; manual dexterity (for handling delicate and valuable objects). For excavation, physical stamina.

Mature entry and career change Advisable only for people who already have a relevant degree or scientific skills and/or hobby experience. Archaeological degrees tend to attract mature students.

Work–life balance Prospects for returners depend on previous experience.

A report published by the Cultural Heritage NTO in 2003 found that under 15 per cent of those working as field archaeologists or in a museum/visitor services worked part-time although opportunities were better in educational and academic research.

Further information

The Council for British Archaeology, St Mary's House, 66 Bootham, York YO30 7BZ.
www.britarch.ac.uk

The Institute of Field Archaeologists, SHES, Whiteknights, University of Reading, PO Box 227, Reading RG6 6AB.
www.archaeologists.net

Related careers *archivist – museums and art galleries*

Architecture

ARCHITECT

Entry qualifications Entry to a school of architecture course is usually at National Qualifications Framework Level 3 (A levels, BTEC National awards) or Scottish Credit and Qualifications Framework equivalent – schools may require specific GCSE and A level passes or equivalent. The Royal Institute of British Architects (RIBA) recommends students should have a minimum of two academic subjects at A level or equivalent (which will ordinarily be a mix of arts and science subjects) and five GCSEs or equivalent (these to include English, maths and double award science).

Registration with Architects Registration Board.

The work Architecture is a multidisciplinary profession requiring a combination of artistic, technological and sociological expertise. The challenge of architecture is to produce, within a given budget, an aesthetically pleasing design which will stand up to wear and tear and is the kind of building in which people will want to live or work. Architects must fully understand traditional and new building methods and materials and appreciate their potential and limitations. They must also understand and be interested in contemporary society and changing lifestyles, the community's expectations and needs, and social problems which may lead to loneliness or vandalism. They need to create a design for a building that is 'user friendly' and which works. For example, the design and layout of a housing estate and its walkways can provide a haven for muggers; a redesign can mean a dramatic drop in antisocial behaviour. This, together with strict financial constraints, makes architecture today a more demanding discipline than it has ever been.

Architects receive instructions (the 'brief') from their clients or employers on the type, function, capacity and rough cost of the building required. Then they do their research – and at that stage they may question some assumptions on which the client based the brief.

When the type of the building has finally been decided upon, the design work begins. This starts with producing, perhaps jointly with colleagues, a sketch scheme of the floor plans and the elevations, and perspective drawings. Several designs may have to be produced before one is finally approved.

The next stage is to prepare contract documents, which will include detailed drawings and specifications, estimates of cost and applications for necessary planning consents from the local authority. At this stage, especially if the scheme is a big one, consulting engineers (see p. 225) and quantity surveyors (see p. 571) may be appointed. When the contract for the work has been awarded to a building contractor, the architect will usually coordinate the project team, with responsibility for certifying payment to contractors, and for inspecting the work in progress. This involves regular visits to the building site, issuing instructions to the contractor's agent or foreman and discussing any problems that might arise. Site visits may involve walking through mud and climbing scaffolding.

The architect is normally also responsible for the choice or design of fittings and the interior design of the buildings (see p. 104).

An architect can work in different settings: in private practice; in the architects' and planning departments of a local authority; in a cooperative; with a public body; with a ministry; or in the architect's department of a commercial firm large enough to have a continuous programme of building or maintenance work.

In *private practice* the client may be an individual, a commercial firm, a local authority or other public body. It is usual for private practices to specialize, but not exclusively, in houses, schools or offices, etc. In private practice architects normally work only on design and not, as in other categories, on design and maintenance.

In *local authorities* architects may work on a wide variety of buildings, such as one-family houses, blocks of flats, schools, sports centres and clinics. They also collaborate with private architects employed by the authority for specific schemes.

For other public bodies such as government departments, the architect's work is less varied and is largely confined to the organization's particular building concern: e.g. hospitals for the Department of Health.

The same applies to architects working for a *commercial concern*. Their work is confined to that organization's particular type of building: e.g. hotels and restaurants for a large catering organization; shops for a retail chain.

The majority of architects are salaried employees, but they may become junior partners and later principals in a firm, or set up on their own. But to start a firm requires a good deal of experience, capital and contacts. More than half of practices employ five or fewer full-time architects.

Architects' prospects can be badly affected by recessions and at these times they have to be prepared to take on any work they can find. There are reasonable opportunities to work abroad and UK qualified architects are often in demand overseas. Architects qualified in the UK can register in other EU member states subject to local regulations.

Training The normal pattern of training is a five-year full-time course, with one year of professional experience after the third year and a second year of professional experience at the end of the course, making a minimum of seven years. Besides full-time courses, some schools of architecture offer part-time courses, but this method of training is not suitable for everyone, as students need to be working in an architectural practice to be accepted and it takes even longer than the normal training; however, it does provide a route to qualification for self-funding students. Subjects studied include architectural history, design and construction, town planning, environmental science, materials science, building control, some sociology, economics, law. The development of design and CAD (computer-aided design) skills through projects is central to an architect's education.

For *interior designers*, architectural training need only be up to degree level. It must be followed by a specialized art-school course (part-time or full-time) and practical experience.

Courses should be chosen with care: practising architects, whether in private practice or public employment, must be registered with the Architects Registration Board (ARB) and only qualifications pre-scribed by ARB lead to admission to the Register. For further infor-mation and a list of schools of architecture offering prescribed qualifications see *www.arb.org.uk*. Course titles can be misleading, e.g. Architectural Studies may or may not be a recognized course.

NOTE: For candidates who are not quite certain whether to commit themselves to a seven-year training course, it is useful to know that the first three-year stage of training, on most courses, leads to an honours degree in its own right, and therefore to all the graduate jobs for which no particular discipline is specified. Architecture, planning and land-scape architecture are related disciplines and there are some courses which start with a combined-studies year so that students can delay specialization until they know more about the whole field.

Personal attributes A practical as well as creative mind; an interest in people and an ability to respond to changing lifestyles; self-confidence to put over and justify new ideas; mathematical ability; drawing skills; the ability to deal with legal and financial questions; a reasonably authoritative personality; an aptitude for giving clear instructions and explanations.

Mature entry and career change The RIBA has a well-established system of external examinations offering a route to qualification for mature students with relevant experience.

Work–life balance Career breaks are possible for those who keep up by reading journals and attending occasional lectures and seminars. Architects are strongly advised to 'keep their hand in' and do some work throughout the break, however sporadic – although current Professional Indemnity Insurance can now make this a somewhat expensive undertaking.

Updating courses are a feature of the profession under its CPD (continuing professional development) requirement for all architects, and some returners take one of the postgraduate courses available to develop a new specialization in, for example, urban design, planning or conservation of historic buildings.

A fair proportion of women architects work part-time, but combining domestic and professional responsibilities will take its toll on career development. While there is little opportunity for part-time work in the public sector, up to middle-level jobs it should be possible to organize job-sharing and other flexible working. However, with increasing numbers of women choosing to study architecture, government legislation to support family-friendly working, and the RIBA's stated commitment to supporting equality of opportunity in the profession, this may be set to change.

Further information

Royal Institute of British Architects, 66 Portland Place, London W1B 1AD.
   www.careersinarchitecture.net and *www.architecture.com*
Royal Incorporation of Architects in Scotland, 15 Rutland Square, Edinburgh EH1 2BE.
   www.rias.org.uk
The Royal Society of Architects in Wales, Bute Building, King Edward VII Avenue, Cathays Park, Cardiff CF10 3NB.
   www.architecture-wales.com
Royal Society of Ulster Architects, 2 Mount Charles, Belfast, N. Ireland BT7 1NZ.
   www.rsua.org.uk
Architects Registration Board, 7 Portland Place, London W1B 1PP.
   www.arb.org.uk

Related careers *Architectural Technologist/Technician (see below) – art and design – engineering – landscape architecture – surveying – town and country planning*

ARCHITECTURAL TECHNOLOGIST/TECHNICIAN

Entry qualifications For architectural technologist minimum usually two A levels or equivalent, but entry increasingly with relevant HND/C or degree. Minimum entry requirements vary for technician entry.

The work Architectural technologists are specialists in the science of architecture, building design and construction. They provide the essential link between the architect's concept and the completed construction. They work in partnership with other professionals such as architects and planners, both in private practice and in public employment as well as with large firms of building contractors. Responsibilities may include: collecting, analysing and preparing technical information required for a design; preparing technical drawings for the builder and presentation drawings for the client; administration of contracts; liaison with clients and with specialists such as quantity surveyors; site supervision; collecting information on performance of finished buildings (which means contact with satisfied and possibly dissatisfied clients); office management. Technologists do responsible work but on the technical rather than the creative side. Those with a few years' experience in employment can set up on their own and, working for private clients or building contractors, design conversions; or help out in architectural firms which need occasional extra staff.

Architectural technicians provide support to other architectural professionals by ensuring the necessary technical information is available, and use CAD or traditional methods to produce the specifications and plans needed throughout a building project. They cannot practise on their own account.

Training – *Technologists* – an accredited degree or HND/C in architectural technology; *Technicians* – a relevant HND/C, Foundation degree or NVQ/SVQ level 4 in Architectural Technology.

Having gained the necessary academic qualifications to gain professional status it is necessary to complete CIAT's Professional and Occupational Performance Record (or POP record). For Architectural Technologists, this takes two to three years followed by a professional assessment interview; for Architectural Technicians one to two years.

Personal attributes Accuracy and attention to detail; ability to visualize and draw (although much of this can be done with a PC); technical ability; communication skills; interest in architecture, materials, structures and the environment (natural and within buildings); liking for teamwork; some design flair.

Mature entry and career change Part-time study can be combined with part-time or agency work. CIAT offers a non-standard route for those aged 30-plus who have a minimum of ten years' experience.

Work–life balance Theoretically there is no reason why qualified technologists should not return, although professional membership may require a reassessment of skills, expertise and knowledge.

There is not much opportunity for part-time employment, although flexible working hours and practices are available, especially for those who are self-employed.

Further information

Chartered Institute of Architectural Technologists, 397 City Road, London EC1V 1NH.
www.ciat.org.uk

Related careers *surveying: Surveying Technicians – engineering: Engineering Technicians*

Archivist

Entry qualifications Good honours degree (subject not strictly relevant).

The work Archivists' work involves the selection, preservation, arrangement, description and making available of records, such as those of central and local government, the courts of law, businesses, charities, universities or other organizations as well as famous people and families. Archivists help members of the public with their research, whether they are professors of history, solicitors in search of evidence, students working on projects, or genealogists. They may also be involved in promotional activities including exhibitions, presentations or media work. At a more senior level, archivists will undertake traditional management tasks as they take control of budgets, staff and strategy. There is considerable scope for trained archivists who prefer to specialize in records management.

About half of all archivists in the UK work in central and local government. Other posts can be found in large businesses, the NHS, universities, ecclesiastical foundations, charities and other independent cultural institutions, like museums and libraries.

Training Nearly all posts now require formal training: one-year postgraduate course for an MA or Diploma in Archives and Record Management. Subjects include palaeography, record office management, research methods, conservation methods, editing, information technology, some history and law. It is recommended that applicants have at least some work experience in an archive or records management service before applying to one of the six courses in the UK.

Personal attributes Communication and people skills; a logical mind; an understanding of new technologies and research techniques; a commitment to continuing professional development.

Mature entry and career change In general the profession welcomes mature entrants, although there may be practical difficulties involved in undertaking pre-course work experience, as the majority of such opportunities are solely on a voluntary basis.

Work–life balance The attitudes of different employers will obviously vary, but part-time posts are available and job-sharing may also be possible. It is usually necessary to go wherever there is a vacancy, both for the first job and later for promotion. Vacancies can be very scarce in some parts of the country.

Further information

Society of Archivists, Prioryfield House, 20 Canon Street, Taunton, Somerset TA1 1SW.
www.archives.org.uk

Related careers *archaeology – information science – museums and art galleries*

Armed Forces (Officer Entry Only)

The Armed Forces are currently in action more than at any time in the last 40 years. But in addition to the conflict in Afghanistan, service personnel are taking part in numerous peacekeeping, peace enforcing and humanitarian aid operations. The Army is currently deployed in more than 80 countries around the world. The Armed Forces work at many levels and service personnel have to be flexible, ready to deal with many different situations and rapid deployment to anywhere in the world.

Entry qualifications Minimum level usually National Qualifications Framework Level 3 (A levels, BTEC National awards) or Scottish Credit and Qualifications Framework equivalent. See individual forces.

The work Front-line service personnel operate and maintain increasingly technically sophisticated equipment, but in a peacekeeping role their primary weapon is often their own communication skills and ability to respond coolly to a sensitive situation. All three services have to be self-sufficient, i.e. they have to house, feed, clothe, equip, transport, select, train and provide medical and welfare services to servicemen and servicewomen at home and overseas. Many jobs are unique to the services, but all now offer opportunities to gain qualifications relevant to civilian life. Recruiters look for a particular mix of abilities and personal qualities to try to select people who will fit in and enjoy the way of life. Although many will spend their time without experiencing combat, nevertheless they can never forget that at any time they might have to take part in action against an enemy.

Most officers have a dual responsibility: as a leader and manager of a group of men and women, and as a specialist. All three forces have been actively recruiting more women and most jobs are open to them with new ground being broken all the time.

As jobs are so diverse, and training for them is so specific, it is not possible to give more than an outline of the various entry routes in this book. A great deal of information and help is available to people considering joining any one of the services; they should contact their school or university liaison officer, or local recruiting office, or use the information sources given below.

THE ARMY

The Army is divided into the Combat Arms and Service Support Arms, which are then both divided further into Corps and Regiments. Combat Arms, which include the Royal Armoured Corps and the Infantry, comprise units who become actively involved in the fighting of any battle. Combat Support and Combat Service Support units provide support to the Combat Arms. Each has its own responsibilities, e.g. the Royal Electrical and Mechanical Engineers (REME) handle engineering and construction services for all three forces. Potential officers apply to a regiment or corps, though not all are open to all entrants. Age limits vary, as do entry requirements. Over 80 per cent of recently commissioned officers are graduates.

Entry requirements as a commissioned officer Minimum age 17 years 9 months and up to 28; 180 UCAS Tariff points and GCSEs at grade C or above, or equivalent, including English language, maths and either a science or a foreign language.

Main Entry Routes and Types of Commission

Short-Service Commission (SSC) – minimum three years but can be extended up to eight years.

Intermediate Regular Commission (IRC) – the IRC entitles officers to serve for a minimum of ten years but they may apply to convert to a full-career Regular Commission (Reg C) after a period of service, subject to being recommended.

Regular Commission (Reg C) – the Reg C offers a full career to age of 55 (in some cases to age 60) although officers may leave at any time subject to meeting minimum notice periods and specified return of service following career courses.

Various schemes offer financial support to sixth-formers and undergraduates.

The Army Sixth Form Scholarship scheme is designed to attract candidates of the highest ability into a career as an Army officer by giving financial assistance to parents or guardians towards the cost of the candidate's sixth-form education. Entry to Royal Military Academy Sandhurst is guaranteed after sixth form or university.

Welbeck – The Defence Sixth Form College – is a residential college which offers a two-year A2 level course to motivated young people who would like, in the future, to commission in technical branches of the three Services or the MOD Civil Service. Those going into the Army will be commissioned into one of the following corps: Royal Engineers, Royal Signals, Royal Logistic Corps, Royal Electrical and Mechanical Engineers. The Welbeck course is designed both to qualify students to take degrees in engineering and science and to develop their personalities and leadership qualities prior to their officer training at Sandhurst.

The Army Undergraduate Bursary scheme provides financial support and opportunities for paid training that supplement usual student finance. Bursaries can be awarded for any degree course including veterinary science, nursing and pharmacy. Those awarded bursaries have to commit themselves to the minimum of a three-year SSC after graduation and the 44-week officer training course at Sandhurst.

Medical and Dental Cadetships are available to suitable candidates who are applicants for the Royal Army Medical Corps and Royal Army Dental Corps and who are undergoing the final three years of medical and dental training.

Women in the Army

Over 10 per cent of Army officers are women. They are eligible for all branches except the Combat Arms – Household Cavalry, Infantry and Royal Armoured Corps.

ROYAL NAVY

The Navy has four fighting arms, the Surface Fleet, the Fleet Air Arm, the Submarine Service and the Royal Marines. Different branches provide specialist services:

Warfare officers are part of the team responsible for the safe and efficient handling of a ship while on watch and they may also operate weapons systems. They can go on to specialize, for example training to serve in the submarine service or in mine warfare and clearance diving, or as a hydrography, meteorology and oceanography officer, advising the command team on the environmental conditions and how they will affect aircraft or weapon performance. In eight to ten years they can qualify as a Principal Warfare officer, with the tactical expertise to direct fighting operations.

Aircrew officers develop the exacting skills necessary to fly the Navy's high-performance aircraft not only in defence situations but also in humanitarian roles such as search and rescue sorties. Pilots and observers work together as a team, carrying out equally demanding tasks. Job opportunities also exist within the Fleet Air Arm for air traffic control officers, who use some of the most sophisticated radar and communications equipment available to ensure the safety of both naval and civilian aircraft, and air engineer officers, who lead the teams of technicians who maintain and repair naval aircraft.

Engineer officers work with highly advanced technology and its complexity means that they specialize as one of the following: weapon engineer officers, marine engineer officers, engineering (training management) officers and engineering (information systems) officers. Weapon engineer officers are responsible for a ship's weapon and sensor system, and marine engineer officers are responsible for the ship's engines, power generation and water and waste systems. Training management officers are responsible for education and much of the training, from general academic studies to advanced technical training, both of ratings and officers. Information systems officers are responsible for the management of complex IS systems ashore and afloat.

Logistics officers work in ships and also at shore establishments. They are concerned with both the technical and the personnel aspects of a ship's organization. Their main duties are overseeing the work of their departments in: administration; correspondence; welfare and personnel matters; naval stores; catering; pay and cash. While at sea, Logistics officers also have extra operational duties in areas such as damage control.

Medical and Dental officers, Nursing officers in Queen Alexandra's Royal Naval Nursing Service, take care of the health and well-being of naval personnel.

The Royal Marines are the Navy's amphibious infantry and they have their own training course at the Commando Training Centre, Lympstone, in Devon. The training is the physically hardest of all in the forces and includes the very demanding Commando course.

All entrants join on an initial commission of twelve years for RN officers and eight years for RM officers. They are eligible for competitive selection to a career commission (sixteen years) or for selection to a full-term commission (to age 55).

Main Entry Routes

There are two main entry routes for Warfare, Logistics, Fleet Air Arm and Royal Marines officers:

- Non-graduate entry for those with 140 UCAS points (with the exception of Royal Marines officers, who require a minimum of five GCSE passes or equivalent). On completion of their initial professional training, non-graduate Warfare, Logistics and Fleet Air Arm officer entrants receive a Foundation degree in Naval Studies and subsequent accreditation towards an in-service honours degree with the Open University, at no financial cost to the individual. The exact degree title is dependent on the branch joined.
- Direct Graduate Entry on completion of a university degree. Entrants who have a degree join with more seniority and at a higher salary level.

Financial support through scholarships or sponsorship is available at both levels of entry. University sponsorship is offered as either a bursary or a university cadetship.

Engineering, Medical and Dental officers may apply for cadet entry (and be sponsored through university) or for Direct Graduate Entry on completion of their degree. Engineers can also apply for the Defence Technical Undergraduate Scheme.

Engineering (Training Management) and Engineering (Information Systems) officers enter by Direct Graduate Entry only. They must hold a degree or equivalent in a mathematical, computing, engineering or scientific discipline and be under 34.

Women in the Royal Navy

Entry and conditions of service are the same as for men. Currently women cannot serve in the Submarine Service, the Royal Marines Commandos or as mine clearance divers, although the All Arms Commando course is open to both men and women.

ROYAL AIR FORCE

The RAF is organized into a Strike Command and a Personnel and Training Command, comprising stations and squadrons. Each squadron is managed by commissioned officers undertaking a specialist role: air operations officers include pilots and navigation officers; operational support officers include air traffic controllers and RAF Regiment officers; engineering and logistics officers include aerosystems and communications electronic engineers; support service officers include security, training and physical education specialists. Officers are also recruited with specialized qualifications, such as medical and dental officers, nursing officers, chaplains and legal officers.

For most branches in the RAF there are two types of commission: *permanent* (up to age 40 or for eighteen years, whichever is the longer, with possible extension to age 55) and *short service* (three to six years, varying from branch to branch; twelve years for pilots and navigators, with the option to leave after six years' 'productive service').

Main Entry Routes

Minimum entry is at least five GCSEs (A–C)/S grades (1–3), including English language and maths, and two A levels/three H grades, or equivalent qualifications. Upper entry age varies with specialization: aircrew officers are recruited up to 23 years; officers in support services are usually recruited to 36 years. The minimum age for entry to some professional fields such as nursing is 23 years.

Various types of sponsorship are available, including sixth-form scholarships and university bursaries.

Women in the RAF

Women now serve in all branches except the RAF Regiment.

Personal attributes Depend very much on the branch or job, but all officers need certain qualities of leadership, initiative, ability to get on with people from all kinds of background, liking for teamwork, adaptability, physical fitness. Must enjoy and be willing to contribute to community life.

Further information
Your local Army, Royal Navy or RAF Careers Office or Jobcentre or
 Careers/Connexions Service.
Army: *www.army.mod.uk* or 0845 730 0111
Royal Navy: *www.royalnavy.mod.uk* or 0845 607 5555
Air Force: *www.raf.mod.uk* or 0845 605 5555

Art and Design

Entry qualifications See 'Training' below.

Continually changing concepts of what is meant by art and design, the development of new techniques and media, and the impact of digital technology together ensure that this is a very rapidly changing career field. The increasing requirements for multi-skilling have blurred the boundaries between areas of work, and any distinction between artist and designer has become far less certain. Art and design is usually referred to as two-dimensional, taking in areas from magazine and webpage design to photography and textiles, and three-dimensional, covering a huge range of creative activity from sculpture and fashion to theatrical set design and industrial design. Artists and designers may specialize in one material, such as oils or metals, but increasingly they choose or are required to bring a range of skills to their work.

Fine Art

Post-Turner prize this can mean performance art, installations and artistic video as much as painting and sculpture. Although commissions for murals and sculpture are more common since the influx of lottery money, it is still very hard to make a living through fine art although some do manage it. Artist-in-residence posts and Community Art work projects provide opportunities for some fine artists.

Many fine artists also teach and for that they need Qualified Teacher Status (see p. 586). Part-time teaching can be difficult to find. Others combine fine art with applied art, such as pottery, jewellery-making or illustration but success can depend on a certain amount of business acumen.

A fine art degree can lead to a career in related areas such as arts administration in galleries, museums or funding bodies.

Design
(see also *engineering – design*, p. 222)

The function of the designer, who is, broadly, a specialist combining artistic talent and training with sufficient technical and business knowledge to appreciate the requirements of an industry, is still evolving. Design careers tend not to be structured, although the last twenty years have shown that there are certain employment patterns that new entrants can aspire to. Most designers start as assistants and work first in the area of specialization in which they trained. Later, with experience and evolving interests, they can switch specializations, or at least sub-specializations. For example, a three-dimensional designer might switch from light engineering to furniture or interior design; a graphic designer from typography to photography; a fashion/textile designer from fashion (see p. 112) to floor-covering or wallpaper, etc. Sometimes three-dimensional-trained designers switch to visual communication – but the switch the other way round is less likely. A few later combine several design categories.

Titles in industry are arbitrary and mean little; an assistant designer may have more scope for creativity and decision-making than a designer or even design director. Not all industrial employers are used to working with designers; the contribution the designer is expected or indeed allowed to make varies from one job to another. For example, sometimes the bias is towards technical expertise: the designer is expected to state, through design, exactly how a product is to be manufactured or printed. Sometimes the bias is towards creativity, and the designer is expected to put forward ideas for totally new products. Usually, the visual appearance of the product is the most important aspect of the designer's brief.

Designers usually work with a team of experts from different disciplines, both technical (engineers, printing technologists, etc.) and business (buyers, marketing people, etc.). This teamwork is one of the important differences between artists and designers. Designers cannot just please themselves: their ideas on what is good design and what is not have to be adapted to fit in with commercial and technical requirements.

Though the designer's work varies from one field of design to another, the end-product always has to fulfil at least three demands: it must look up to date, perform its function adequately, and be economically produced so that it is profitable. For example, a poster must attract attention and be easily readable; a tin-opener or a fridge must work well, look good and last; a biscuit pack must attract attention, fit into shelf displays, keep its contents fresh, and open easily; a machine tool must serve the engineer's stated purpose, be easy and safe to handle and clean; and all these products must be manufacturable within given cost-limits. Designers must fully understand the purpose of the product they are designing and its marketing and manufacturing problems. They must know the limitations and potential of materials and machines available for production. Sometimes a change in technology allows the designer to develop revolutionary designs: e.g. in the commercial application of developments in nanotechnology.

Starting as design assistant, the trainee designer gains useful experience when carrying out simple 'design-technician' rather than design tasks. For example, the beginner may translate a designer's idea for a product into detailed working drawings: this requires technical knowhow rather than creativity. In furniture design, for example, the task might be specifying how to fix A satisfactorily to B in manufacturing terms without spoiling the appearance.

One designer is usually responsible for several design assistants (now sometimes called design technicians); the size of design teams varies greatly. Designers and design assistants work in various settings: in advertising agencies; manufacturing concerns' design departments; architects' offices; interior design studios; design consultancies, and many others. Organizing freelance work either on one's own or with colleagues on a design consultancy basis is complex and requires experience: newly trained designers should try to gain experience as staff designers first. They need to know a lot not only about production problems and organization, but also about how to deal with clients and finance.

The ratio of opportunities to qualified applicants is more favourable in the less glamorous and more technical field of product design than in interior, set or textiles and fashion design.

There will never be as many creative top-level jobs as there are aspiring designers, but there is scope for design assistants or 'technicians' whose work varies in creativity and responsibility; for example, making working drawings from designers' scribbled outlines; model-making; or, in communication design, trying to get as near the designer's intended effect as possible with a restricted number of colours and within printing constraints. There is a vast range of jobs in product design which require technical competence, an appreciation of what constitutes good design and some creativity rather than creative genius.

Prospects are reasonable for people who want to design for industry and appreciate that it is teamwork, but not for failed artists. Many of the best product and fashion designers go abroad where British training is greatly appreciated.

Graphics or Graphic Design or Visual Communication

This is concerned with lettering; page design; illustration, including photography; the design of symbols or 'logos'. It ranges from the design of books, magazines, websites, all kinds of advertisements (posters, packaging, etc.), to the visual corporate identity symbol of organizations, i.e. presenting the image of that organization in visual, instant-impact-making terms. Nearly all graphic design work is carried out on computers and experience with relevant software is usually essential.

Visual communication includes 'visual aids' for industrial and educational application. This is an expanding area: instructions and/or information are put over in non-verbal language, with symbols taking the place of words. Symbols are used as teaching aids in industrial training; as user-instructions in drug and textile labelling; as warning or information signs on machinery; on road signs. Symbols may be in wall-chart or film-strip form, or on tiny labels as on medicine and detergent packages, or on textile labels, or on huge posters. Symbol design, whether single or in series, requires great imagination, social awareness, logical thinking.

Visual communication also includes TV graphics: captions, programme titles, all non-verbal TV presentation of information, such as election results, trade-figure trends, etc.; packaging, publicity and advertising; stamp and letterhead design. Graphic designers work in advertising agencies, in design units, or in manufacturing firms and other organizations' design departments. Television absorbs only a tiny proportion. Web design is a growing specialization, employing freelancers as well as in-house designers (see p. 283).

There are few openings in general book and magazine illustration and design, but there is considerable scope in technical and medical graphics, which require meticulous accuracy rather than purely creative imagination. There is also some scope in the greeting-card trade and in catalogue illustration. Much of this is considered hackwork by creative artists.

Three-dimensional Design

This can be divided conveniently into product design and interior design. Almost all 3D design is produced on computers.

Product design This covers the design of all kinds of consumer goods (e.g. domestic appliances, or suitcases) and of machine tools, mechanical equipment, cars, as well as pottery, furniture, etc.

There is pressure on manufacturing industry to pay more attention to design than it has in the past. But there is no general agreement on how this is to be brought about. Many engineers and manufacturers still believe that with a bit more design training, engineers can cope with the aesthetics and ergonomics (ease of handling and cleaning, convenience in use, legibility of instructions). Many of the more progressive manufacturers now agree that engineers must work with design specialists who, for their part, must have a thorough understanding of engineering principles and production constraints. The engineer designs the components and says how they must be arranged to do the job; the industrial designer is primarily concerned with the appearance and ergonomics of the product.

Between the first sketch and the final product there may be many joint discussions, drawings, modifications, working models and prototypes. The designer negotiates with the engineer; design technicians develop the product through the various stages. Designers and engineers work in teams – whether the team leader is an engineer or a designer varies according to the type of product, the firm's policy and, last but by no means least, the engineer's and designer's personalities.

Product designers need such extensive knowledge of relevant engineering and manufacturing processes that they tend to stay within a particular manufacturing area. The greatest scope is in plastics, which cover a wide range of products, from toys to complex appliances and equipment.

Interior design Interior designers work in specialized or general design consultants' studios; large stores; for a group of hotels or supermarkets; in private practice or local authority architects' offices. A considerable knowledge of architecture is required in order to know how to divert drains, move walls safely, or enlarge a shop window satisfactorily. The job of the interior designer, besides being responsible for such things as the management of contracts, is to specify the nature of an interior – how it is made, built and finished – as well as selecting the finishes and fixtures and fittings.

Planning interiors for a hotel, shop, aircraft, etc., needs research before the design starts. Beginners often spend all their time on fact-finding: the different items of goods to be displayed; the number of assistants required in a new shop; the kind of materials suitable and safe for furnishing a plane. They also search for suitable light fittings, heating equipment, furnishing materials, and they may design fixtures and fittings.

The term 'interior design' is often interpreted rather loosely, and some jobs require less training and creativity. This applies particularly to work done by assistants in the design studios of stores or architects' offices; in showrooms of manufacturers of paint, furniture, furnishings, light fittings, wallpaper, etc.; in the furnishing departments of retail stores, and in specialist shops. In these settings, interior designers may advise customers or clients on the choice and assembly of the items needed. This may mean suggesting colour schemes, matching wallpaper and curtains, sketching plans for room decoration, or advising on the most suitable synthetic fabric for a particular furnishing purpose. As stores' estimators and home advisers, they may go to customers' houses to give advice or even only to measure up for loose covers and curtains. Some stores and specialist shops employ interior designers as buyers in furniture and furnishing departments, and paint, wallpaper and furnishing fabric manufacturers may employ them as sales representatives. In these jobs 'interior designer' is a courtesy title rather than a job description.

Set Design

The work requires knowledge of period styles, structures and lighting techniques, an understanding of drama and an ability to analyse a play, to help visualize the right kind of set for a theatre production or TV programme. Limited scope.

Exhibition and Display Design

Combines some of the work of interior and set design with model-making and graphic design. Exhibition design is usually done by specialist firms. Exhibitions are often rush jobs, and designers may help put up stands and work through the night before opening. Exhibition designers also work in museums. See also Television, Film and Radio, p. 597.

Display Design

Closely allied to exhibition design, but can be a specialization on its own. The essence of window and 'point-of-sale' design is communication: the display designer must present the store's or shop's image, attract attention and persuade the passer-by to buy. Window display can consist of merely putting a few goods in the window or a show case, or it can be a highly sophisticated exercise in marketing, using specially designed models (see 'Model-making', below) and specially chosen merchandise to convey a 'theme' and marketing policy. In stores there may be a display manager, a display designer and several display assistants or technicians who make/arrange the props and merchandise. Reasonable scope.

Studio-based Design (Glass, Jewellery, Silverware, Stained Glass, etc.)

Design and production by designer-craftspeople who run their own small-scale studios or workshops where each article is made individually. This is a fairly precarious way of making a living. However, some studios survive, especially in tourist areas, selling to local shops and individual customers. They have 'studied the market', and perhaps compromised, producing designs which sell rather than those which they would ideally like to produce.

Model-making

This includes the design and/or making up of models for window and exhibition display, and the making of scale models for architects, planners, and interior-design and product-design studios. Many designers, architects, etc., find that their clients are better able to judge a design if they see it in three-dimensional model form rather than as drawings.

Model-makers use the traditional materials – wood, plaster, fabric, etc. – and also the new synthetics. They usually work in specialist studios and firms, but some work in other types of design studio. There is more scope here for manual work requiring some creative ability than for pure artistic design. It is an expanding field.

Textiles and Fashion Design
(see also *Fashion and Clothing*, p. 244)

Textile design includes printed and woven textiles, carpets and other floor coverings, wallpapers, and plastic surface coverings and decoration. There are few openings in manufacturing firms. One of the difficulties is that thorough knowledge of manufacturing methods is essential, but it is difficult to get a job with suitable firms.

Textile designers work on their own more frequently than do other designers. They usually work through agents who show their designs to manufacturers. Fashion collections are held two or more times a year, furnishing collections usually twice.

Training (generally)

There are entry routes at all levels.

BTEC National awards, SQA Scottish Group Award or Applied Art and Design A level Nearly all of these are two-year full-time courses for people aged 16 or more. For those with no particular educational qualifications there is a BTEC First Diploma in Art and Design; the National Diplomas/Certificates in Design are for those who already know in which area they want to become involved.

The National Diploma has been replaced in many colleges by the double award Applied Art and Design A level. This is a broad-based course equivalent to A level standard and acceptable for degree entry. In Scotland there is a named Scottish Group Award in Art and Design.

Foundation courses One-year full-time (two-year part-time) Art Foundation (in Scotland incorporated into a four-year art and design degree course) for students aged 17 or more, most of whom have several GCSEs or equivalent and have studied in the sixth form. This course should be 'diagnostic' to help students decide on their eventual specialization. There are many aspects of design which school-leavers cannot know about, and by taking a Foundation course students may be drawn to one of the less well-known design fields. However,

Foundation courses are not all the same, so students need to look carefully at what is on offer.

Access courses These are designed for adults returning to education after a break. They usually last one year and may be full-time or part-time.

Higher education courses The number and variety of art and design courses can be confusing. Course titles are not always indicative of course content and prospectuses should be studied carefully before a choice is made. (A detailed listing of all higher education Art and Design courses can be found in *The Art & Design Directory*, published by Trotman-Crimson Publishing.) Entry requirements vary considerably and a student's portfolio of work may be a deciding factor.

HNDs/HNCs These vary considerably and some may be almost indistinguishable from degree courses while others are much more employment-focused. Some incorporate a work placement. Many lead on to the final year of an honours degree.

Foundation degrees In many higher education institutions Foundation degrees are replacing Art and Design HNDs. These are work-related courses, and usually take two years full-time and three to four years part-time.

Degrees Entry qualifications vary – a minimum one A level and three GCSEs (A–C) or equivalent plus – normally but not invariably – a one-year Foundation course; or BTEC National Certificate or Diploma or Scottish equivalent. Individual colleges vary in their precise requirements; some demand, for example, GCSE (A–C) maths or craft design and technology and English. Acceptance also very much depends on applicant's portfolio, i.e. on proof of creative ability.

Again, course content varies considerably. Art and Design subjects can be studied individually or in combination, either with a related subject or with another subject such as a language. Most courses are modular and offer a range of electives in addition to the compulsory modules. Some are academically focused while others put more emphasis on developing skills. Institutions are not uniformly equipped and it is worth checking that they are up to date with technology where appropriate. Prospective students who expect to work freelance should look out for modules on marketing and business start-up.

Art and Design teachers in schools need to achieve Qualified Teacher Status (see p. 586). Art and Design lecturers in further education and higher education usually need professional experience as well as a relevant degree and increasingly a teaching qualification.

Postgraduate training Although a degree or HND is the basic requirement for anyone wanting to get on in the design world, it is usually necessary these days for artists and designers to update their skills or acquire new ones at some stage, often between three and ten years after gaining their first degree or HND. There are postgraduate courses in most design specializations, for example in film, in TV graphics, computer-assisted art and animation, conservation, theatre design.

The Open College of the Arts Set up in 1987, the Open College of the Arts (OCA) provides home-based education in the arts using similar methods to those of the Open University (p. 17), to which it is affiliated. Courses that can be taken by distance learning, with or without tutorial support provided by one of a network of tutorial centres, include basic art and design, drawing, painting, sculpture, interior design, textiles and photography. It is possible to study for a full honours degree in creative arts with OCA.

ART THERAPY

The work This is a growing field. Its purpose is twofold: painting and other art forms help withdrawn patients to express themselves and relieve tension, and seeing patients' work helps psychiatrists pinpoint patients' thoughts and problems. The majority of art therapists work

– usually on a sessional basis – in hospitals and institutions for those with psychiatric problems and learning difficulties, with children and with adults, individually and in groups; some work with children with special needs. Art therapy is not so much a career in itself as a field in which practising artists with the necessary personal qualities can do useful work.

Training Postgraduate approved one-year full-time or two-year part-time courses are essential. In order to practise, art therapists must be registered with the Health Professions Council.

Personal attributes (generally) All careers in art and design require resilience, self-confidence and exceptional talent.

Especially for design: Ability to work as one of a team; creative sensibility and imagination coupled with a logical analytical mind; an interest in science and technology; curiosity and a desire to solve technical problems; perseverance; an interest in the social environment and in the community's needs, tastes and customs; the ability to take responsibility and criticism; willingness at times to lower one's artistic standards in the interests of economic necessity or technical efficiency.

For freelancers and senior staff jobs: Business sense; the ability to communicate with employers and clients who commission the work but are possibly not themselves interested in art.

For 'technician' jobs: Considerable manual dexterity, technical ability and some creativity.

Mature entry and career change It is not unusual for people to do a fine art degree in later life. On vocationally orientated courses qualifications may be waived for applicants with experience.

Work–life balance If experienced and established, designers can set up on their own; some return to outside employment after a career break, but competition from recent art-school leavers is likely to be stiff. Freelancers can work their own hours but these may be longer than if in employment.

Further information

National Society for Education in Art and Design (NSEAD), The Gatehouse, Corsham Court, Corsham, Wilts SN13 0ES.
www.nsead.org

Design Council, 34 Bow Street, London WC2E 7DL.
www.designcouncil.org.uk

Chartered Society of Designers, 1 Cedar Court, Royal Oak Yard, London SE1 3GA.
www.csd.org.uk

British Association of Art Therapists, 24–27 White Lion Street, London N1 9PD.
www.baat.org

British Display Society, 12 Cliff Avenue, Chalkwell, Leigh-on-Sea, Essex SS9 1HF.
www.britishdisplaysociety.co.uk

Open College of the Arts, The Michael Young Arts Centre, Unit 1B, Redbrook Business Park, Wilthorpe Road, Barnsley S75 1JN.
www.oca-uk.com

Related careers *advertising – architecture – cartography – engineering – fashion and clothing – landscape architecture – museums and art galleries – photography – teaching – television, film and radio*

Banking (and Building Society Work)

Takeovers and mergers, along with the introduction of Internet and telebanking, continue to bring about branch closures and a reduction in traditional face-to-face customer services. Institutions offering high street financial services have gone through a period of rapid and dramatic change. Competition has intensified, spurred on by new technology and legislation. Distinctions between different institutions have blurred, with activities and services formerly offered by one particular kind of institution now being offered by others. Banks offer mortgages and insurance, while building societies offer cheque accounts. The retail or 'high street' banks have investment banking divisions or subsidiaries, while the investment banks have bought stockbroking firms. The term 'financial services group' conveys the range of financial activity. The Financial Services Authority (FSA) regulates the financial services industry, setting standards of competence and financial soundness appropriate for undertaking regulated activities.

Banking can be broken down into services to personal and business customers. There is growing specialization in terms of both activity and career paths.

RETAIL/PERSONAL BANKING

Entry qualifications Entry requirements vary, but many banks usually ask for a minimum of four GCSEs (A–C), or equivalent. Those with higher level qualifications including A levels or degrees may be recruited to an accelerated training programme. Graduate entry is increasing.

The work Banks and building societies provide a wide range of financial services to personal customers, largely through their branch networks. They take deposits and make loans, transmit money from one account to another, exchange foreign currency and travellers' cheques, offer mortgages, insurance policies, pensions and investment schemes. They also offer financial advice on a range of matters.

The rapid take-up of telephone and Internet banking means that many financial services staff now work in call centres. UK-based call and contact centres still represent major employment opportunities within the sector despite an ongoing trend to relocate many such operations abroad.

From an early stage in training, considerable emphasis is placed on the ability to relate to customers, identify their needs and promote the bank's services.

Trainees normally start by learning basic procedures such as sorting and listing cheques so that they can be 'read' electronically and operating a terminal linked to the central computer on which customers' accounts are updated. Trainees usually commence duties as a cashier. Cashiers or customer services assistants are in the front line of the intensifying battle for customers so they must make a good impression. Courtesy, efficiency and helpfulness are important.

After a spell at the counter, trainees undertake other customer service duties, for example setting up standing orders/direct debits and opening accounts. Promotion to senior clerical duties involves the development of supervisory skills and the more specialized technical knowledge needed to deal with, for example, customers' investments; the approval of small personal loans and analysis, with the management team, of more detailed lending propositions; or executor and trust work, dealing with trusts and wills in which the bank may look after customers' or their dependants' interests, advise people who have been left money on investment, or explain complex money matters to bewildered heirs. As clerical officers are promoted to junior management grades they take on increased responsibility for customer service and the smooth running of the branch.

Managers may be responsible for one branch or several. Within policy laid down by the bank, they have considerable responsibility for approving loans, dealing with business customers, from the small to, sometimes, the very large. (Depending on the operational structure of the individual institution, very large loans may need the approval of the central risk unit of a bank.) Other managerial responsibilities include overseeing the smooth running of their branches, leading their team of staff and marketing the bank's growing range of services and 'products'.

Those on accelerated management training programmes might spend only very short periods in the clerical functions. They are not necessarily expected to master the tasks but need to appreciate their importance in the overall service the bank offers its customers. There are also opportunities in regional and head offices where, for example, specialist advice is available and new 'products' are developed. A career with a bank can also develop into non-banking functions, e.g. human resources.

New technology has led to large cuts in staff among the banks. The impact is more marked in lower-level jobs; in an intensely competitive climate, the banks continue to recruit and train those who have the potential to become senior managers. Many banks have well-developed graduate recruitment and training programmes, but in theory it is still possible to reach senior levels from a modest start. (Alternatively many graduates also opt to develop their careers on the corporate side of the business.)

Training Training is largely 'in-house', with residential courses at more senior levels. A range of professional qualifications at different levels is offered by the ifs School of Finance and the Chartered Institute of Bankers in Scotland. The Financial Services Skills Council (FSSC) in partnership with employers is responsible for training, education and development in the sector and maintains a list of appropriate qualifications to equip individuals to perform regulated activities competently. The FSSC has now had new frameworks for apprenticeships in retail banking approved: Level 2 Apprenticeship in Retail Financial Services (Retail Banking pathway) and Level 3 Advanced Apprenticeship in Retail Financial Services (Retail Banking).

Call/contact centre staff can obtain a range of qualifications which are offered either by external providers or internally through their employer. Qualifications are available for various levels of staff, from customer advisers to supervisory and management levels.

Personal attributes Meticulous accuracy; the interpersonal skills to deal with customers; a clear, logical mind; tact; courtesy; numerical and IT skills.

Mature entry and career change Experience, e.g.: in business and customer service, and the right personal qualities are important.

Work–life balance Most of the major banks operate a career-break/ return-to-work scheme. They vary in detail but, broadly speaking, are open to male and female staff, for a period of two to five years. Some guarantee a return to the organization at one's previous grade. Normally the member of staff is expected to undertake refresher training for two to four weeks a year and to keep abreast of developments. Developments such as telebanking have increased opportunities for flexible working.

CORPORATE BANKING

Entry qualifications Usually degree or National Qualifications Framework Level 3 (A levels, BTEC National awards) or Scottish Credit and Qualifications Framework equivalent: non-graduates may start in clerical positions. Opportunities for school-leavers at National Qualifications Framework Level 2 (GCSEs A*–C, BTEC Diplomas and Certificates), or Scottish Credit and Qualifications Framework equivalent, are now more limited. Most banks recruit mainly graduate trainees.

The work Companies, other financial institutions and governments require complex financial services. Among the services offered by the banks to their corporate customers are: banking, which is basically taking deposits, transferring funds and lending money; corporate finance, which includes advising on mergers and acquisitions, raising capital and other advisory services; and treasury, which involves buying and selling foreign currency to protect against disadvantageous currency movements, and many other services. The banks are also involved in investment management on behalf of institutional investors of large sums of money, such as pension funds and investment trusts, and the securities business (see p. 562) – making issues and buying and selling shares.

Corporate banking can start with the local branch manager, but the more complex work will be done in the corporate divisions of the retail banks, their investment banking subsidiaries and the investment banks. Not all banks offer the same range of services. Staff are required for a range of tasks from research and analysis to sales. Teamwork is a common feature of this area of banking.

An important related activity is dealing – in currencies and various financial 'products' designed to help firms finance their businesses or manage their risks. Banks may deal speculatively on their own account to make a profit, or on behalf of clients to help them manage financial risks.

Wider, global economic factors and influences all have an impact on opportunities in the sector. Though the level varies, the larger banks maintain regular recruitment and for those who are successful, the financial rewards are high. The high rewards, however, are often balanced by high risks, especially on the dealing side. It is not a business that carries 'passengers'.

Most 'bankers' and corporate financiers will be graduates and the same is increasingly true for new recruits as dealers. Specialist staff, e.g.: experts in a particular industry, have good opportunities to move between banks.

Training Largely in-house with the opportunity and encouragement to obtain relevant qualifications. The FSSC maintains a list of appropriate examinations.

Personal attributes High intelligence; ability to work as a member of a team and to relate to clients at a high level; flexibility; competitive drive; ability to think analytically and practically. *For dealers*: confidence, quick wits, entrepreneurial flair, independence.

Mature entry and career change Relevant industrial/professional experience, e.g.: accountancy, is important.

Work–life balance In corporate banking job-sharing and part-time work are not widespread and mainly confined to clerical/secretarial areas and possibly support functions like human resources. Employers claim resistance from clients who want continuity of service from their bankers. The work often involves meeting tight deadlines and long hours.

Further information
Financial Services Skills Council, 51 Gresham Street, London EC2V 7HQ.
www.fssc.org.uk
ifs School of Finance, 4–9 Burgate Lane, Canterbury, Kent CT1 2XJ.
www.ifslearning.ac.uk
Chartered Institute of Bankers in Scotland, Drumsheugh House, 38b Drumsheugh Gardens, Edinburgh EH3 7SW.
www.ciobs.org.uk
London Investment Banking Association, 6 Frederick's Place, London EC2R 8BT.
www.liba.org.uk
Building Societies Association, 6th Floor, York House, 23 Kingsway, London WC2B 6UJ.
www.bsa.org.uk

Related careers *accountancy – actuary – insurance*

Beauty Specialist

Entry qualifications For school-leavers, minimum two or more GCSEs or equivalent may be required for entry to some courses; higher education courses are also available; see 'Training', below.

The work Practitioners may use one of several job titles, but the two most common terms are *beauty therapist* and *beauty consultant*.

BEAUTY THERAPIST

Most beauty therapists use the full range of available treatments on the face and body. These extend from make-up, facials and wax or electric depilation (removal of superfluous hair) to massage, saunas, diet and exercise. They know when to deal with a skin complaint themselves or when to advise the client to see a doctor. It is possible to learn one or two techniques only, e.g. a beautician works on the face and neck only; a manicurist/pedicurist on the hands/feet; the electrologist (or epilationist) uses various means to remove unwanted hair; a masseur/masseuse performs face/body massage. (Aromatherapists massage with aromatic oils.)

Beauty therapists work in private high street salons (sometimes combined with hairdressers) in their own or clients' homes, in health spas or cosmetic firms' salons. Clients may be of all ages, male or female.

Some beauty specialists set up on their own; the initial financial outlay on equipment depends on the treatments offered. The town hall will advise on necessary licences (see p. 625). For those trained in hairdressing there are some opportunities in television (see p. 597) and with psychiatric and other patients for whom beauty care can be part of their rehabilitation.

BEAUTY CONSULTANTS (SALES CONSULTANTS, SALES REPRESENTATIVES)

Usually work in the perfumery department of large stores, occasionally in luxury hotels (at home or abroad), on liners or at airports. They are usually under contract to a cosmetics firm and travel round the country, working for a week or two each in a succession of stores or shops.

They sell and promote the firm's products and try to win regular customers. They answer questions on skin-care and make-up problems, and may give talks and demonstrations.

Top jobs are as cosmetic buyers for stores, at the head offices of cosmetics firms, and as training consultants.

Professional training For jobs in a reputable salon or health farm, it is important to take a course leading to one of the mainstream qualifications. NVQs are available at levels 1 to 4 and students should make sure that courses lead to these qualifications, as they are likely to become very important in the future (e.g. for getting insurance cover). Courses are available both in further education colleges and in private schools. The advantage of maintained college courses is that they are free for younger students, although they generally last longer than private ones. Most good private courses last from five to twelve months (some are longer). Fees for private colleges range from a few hundred pounds to several thousand, depending on the range of skills taught. Syllabus includes theory – anatomy, physiology, diets, salesmanship, salon organization – and practical work: giving facials, different types of massage, make-up, sometimes electrical treatments, etc. Main courses are:

- In-house training leading to N/SVQs levels 2 and 3, while working as a junior therapist. This may be as part of an apprenticeship programme.

- Full-time or part-time National Certificate/Diploma courses, usually combined with a work placement. Some distance learning courses are available.
- Courses leading to awards of one of the national or international beauty therapy examining bodies, for example, the Confederation of International Beauty Therapy and Cosmetology and ITEC (International Therapy Examination Council). Minimum age usually 18.
- A number of universities and colleges offer two-year BTEC HND courses in Beauty Therapy Sciences or related subjects; two-year Foundation degrees and related three-year or four-year honours degree courses are also available.

NOTE: It is important to check the usefulness of courses not included above with one of the organizations mentioned under 'Further information'.

Courses given by cosmetics houses for sales consultants Minimum age depends on age range at which product is aimed, e.g. teenagers or mature people. Majority need to be 24+ and must have several years' selling experience and must be good salespeople. Training is mainly in-store and lasts a few weeks. Subjects dealt with are facials, simple massage, eyebrow shaping and make-up, for both day and evening. These courses qualify students as sales consultants, but not as beauty therapists.

It is useful to take hairdressing training as well as beauty training. It widens the choice of jobs later.

Personal attributes A liking for people of all ages; a friendly, confident manner; tact; courtesy; an attractive, well-groomed appearance; good health; business sense; ability to express oneself easily; foreign language sometimes an asset.

Mature entry and career change Beauty specialists' work is very suitable for late entrants. Many salons prefer women who are nearer in age to the majority of clients than young school-leavers are. Nurses and physiotherapists sometimes choose this work as a second career.

Work–life balance Career breaks present no special problem, except for the need to find new clients. Part-time work is relatively easy to obtain for experienced people.

Further information

Hairdressing and Beauty Industry Authority, Oxford House, Sixth Avenue, Sky Business Park, Robin Hood Airport, Doncaster DN9 3GG.
www.habia.org.uk

ITEC, 2nd Floor, Chiswick Gate, 598–608 Chiswick High Road, London W4 5RT.
www.itecworld.co.uk

Confederation of International Beauty Therapy and Cosmetology (CIBTAC), Meteor Court, Barnett Way, Gloucester GL4 3GG.
www.cibtac.com

Related careers *television, film and radio: Make-up Artists/Designers*

Bookselling

Entry qualifications None laid down, but good general education essential. Many entrants are graduates.

The work All bookselling is a branch of retailing, but there is a difference between a specialist bookshop, where customers expect to find knowledgeable staff, and non-specialist bookshops with a limited range of titles and various non-book products on sale. The latter are more suitable for people interested more in a retailing career than in books. Specialist bookshop staff must be well read in order to be able to advise customers and answer queries. Reading should cover a wide field rather than only one's own interests, but in large bookshops staff usually specialize in one or two subjects. Customers are often left to browse undisturbed among the stock and are offered help and advice only when they want it. Specialist bookshops range from small, independent businesses to nationwide chains of large stores. There are further opportunities with book wholesalers, online booksellers and second-hand bookshops.

Assistants' duties include daily dusting and filling and tidying shelves and display tables. This also helps them to learn the stock and remember where titles are shelved. Assistants also write out orders, keep records and may do some bookkeeping. In many bookshops, ordering, stock control, etc. are now computerized. Assistants may pack and unpack parcels and carry them to the post; bookshop work is physically quite hard.

One of the most interesting and most skilled parts of the job is helping customers who have only a vague idea of what they want or cannot explain what they have in mind. It may involve tracing titles in bibliographies and catalogues.

Book-buying – selecting a small proportion of the vast number of new titles published each month – is a highly skilled and often tricky task. Several members of staff may be responsible for buying within one or more subject areas. They have to be able to judge what will interest their particular customers, whether to buy a new title at all and how many copies to order. New titles are ordered before reviews have appeared so staff must trust their own judgement. They must also judge how much reliance to place on the recommendation of publishers' representatives.

Managers may take part in or do all the buying – it depends on how experienced their staff are and how large the shop is. Above all, the manager tries to give the shop an 'image' to attract a nucleus of regular customers. This is done partly by the choice of books in stock and partly by the method and type of display and arrangement of the shop as a whole. The manager is also responsible for the stock-control system (as would be the case in any other kind of shop).

Far more people want to work in bookshops than there are vacancies. Bookselling is not a high margin business; nevertheless some owner-managers of small bookshops do reasonably well if they have researched the market thoroughly before setting up shop (see p. 625). The Booksellers' Association publish *The Complete Guide to Starting and Running a Bookshop*.

Training Mainly in-house, although some large shops and chains have formal training schemes. The Booksellers' Association sell a training package covering the retail and administrative know-how necessary to run a bookshop.

Personal attributes An excellent memory; commercial sense; wide interests and extensive general knowledge; pleasure in reading and handling books; a liking for meeting people with various interests; a helpful friendly manner and the knack of making diffident customers who are not well read feel they are welcome; the ability to work well in a large team or in a very small shop or department; a calm temperament.

Work–life balance A career break should not present any problems. There is good scope for part-time work especially in bookshops with extended working hours.

Further information
The Booksellers' Association, Minster House, 272 Vauxhall Bridge Road, London SW1V 1BA.
www.booksellers.org.uk

Related careers *information science/librarianship – retail management*

Career Guidance

Entry qualifications Usually, although not exclusively, at degree level. Previous experience of work with young people is usually required for work with that age group. Previous employment experience is usually required for work in higher education.

Working with Young People

In *England* most careers guidance is offered through Connexions Partnerships. These provide a service for young people aged 13–19 and involve a range of social, health and educational agencies. Advisers are employed with the generic title Personal Adviser but some may specialize in providing careers guidance. In some areas the Connexions Partnership subcontracts careers advisory work to companies specializing in providing careers services. From April 2008 Connexions services will be funded by individual local authorities through a local Children and Young People's Trust.

In *Scotland, Wales and Northern Ireland*, careers advisers working with young people are based in all-age guidance services – Careers Scotland, Careers Wales and Careers Service Northern Ireland – which also carry out careers work in schools and colleges.

Careers work covers a wide range of activities from encouraging an unemployed school-leaver back into education or training to helping a school to plan an ongoing careers education programme to suit various age and ability groups. Personal/careers advisers need to keep abreast of developments, trends and impending changes in education, training and the jobs market. Some may specialize in information work, publishing local careers information in print or on websites and overseeing careers/Connexions libraries in centres and schools. Others may work solely with young people with special needs.

Personal advisers currently work in Connexions centres, in youth and community centres, in outreach work – anywhere where young people may be found – and may work with students in groups or as individuals. Since the introduction of the Connexions Service, individual work with young people has tended to focus on young people at risk of dropping out of education and training.

Working in Higher Education

Career advisers in higher education carry out a range of activities similar to those in Connexions/careers services but at a level appropriate to the age, maturity, sophistication and educational level of their clients. A degree and employment experience are essential; beyond that, backgrounds vary enormously. There is no pre-entry training; in-service training may be arranged by the employer or by the Association of Graduate Careers Advisory Services.

Working with Adults

Educational guidance for adults in England is provided through local Information Advice and Guidance (IAG) networks which operate under different names or initiatives. Advisers working in these networks aim to help adults understand and take advantage of the full range of educational and training opportunities available. The work includes information, assessment, advice and counselling; so, again, a wide variety of backgrounds may be appropriate.

Other Careers Work

There are opportunities for careers work in a number of other organizations, but they are limited in number and the entry qualifications of practitioners are very varied. Employers of careers advisory staff include professional bodies, charities and vocational guidance organizations. Again, backgrounds differ widely. Some people have experience in careers work, in teaching, in personnel or in the relevant profession. Vocational guidance organizations often look for psychology graduates.

An increasing number of experienced careers advisers are working on a self-employed basis.

Training

- One-year full-time (two-year part-time) course leading to the Qualification in Career Guidance (QCG). Courses are offered by a number of universities. After completion, careers advisers wishing to work in the Connexions Service must also undertake an NVQ/SVQ in Advice and Guidance level 4 (see below).
- A combination of work-based and off-the-job training leading to NVQ/SVQ in Advice and Guidance level 4. This qualification is a requirement for career guidance specialists working within Connexions providers. Various awarding bodies currently offer this qualification – City & Guilds, Edexcel, OCR, SQA and the Open University.
- Some Scottish universities offer a two-year MSc programme in Career Guidance and Development in place of the QCG award.
- Personal Advisers are also required to undertake in-house Connexions Service training programmes.

A guidance qualification is not mandatory for work in higher education or with adults but 60 per cent of higher education careers advisers now have a qualification, as do an increasing number of adult guidance workers. The Association of Graduate Careers Advisory Services offers post-experience qualifications at three levels – Certificate, a postgraduate Diploma and an MA.

Psychometric testing is increasingly being used in careers work, and careers advisers using such tests are usually required to have a certificate of competence from the British Psychological Society.

Personal attributes Ability to get on with and understand people of all levels of intelligence and temperament; interest in industrial and other employment trends and problems; sympathy with rather than critical attitude towards other people's points of view; organizing ability; willingness to work in a team; ability to put facts across clearly and helpfully; ability to gain people's confidence and to put them at ease however shy and worried; insight and imagination to see how young people might develop and to understand adults' particular difficulties; ability to communicate with individuals, with groups and in writing.

Mature entry and career change Applicants are normally over 21 and maturity and variety of experience are assets in this work. Relevant jobs are those which involve dealing with a variety of people, preferably in a work situation.

Work–life balance There are opportunities for part-time work and job-sharing and other flexible work patterns are now common.

Further information

Institute of Career Guidance, Third Floor, Copthall House, 1 New Road, Stourbridge, West Midlands DY8 1PH.
www.icg-uk.org

Association of Graduate Careers Advisory Services, Administration Office, Millennium House, 30 Junction Road, Sheffield S11 8XB.
www.agcas.org.uk

National Association for Educational Guidance for Adults (NAEGA), Meeting Makers Ltd, Crawfurd Building, Jordanhill Campus, 76 Southbrae Drive, Glasgow G13 1PP.
www.naega.org.uk

Connexions
www.connexions.gov.uk/partnerships

Related careers *personnel/human resources management – psychology – teaching – youth and community work*

Cartography

Entry qualifications *For cartographer*: degree or Higher National award. A levels or equivalent in geography, maths or science often required. *For cartographic technician*: National Qualifications Framework Level 2 (GCSEs A*–C, BTEC Diplomas and Certificates) or Scottish Credit and Qualifications Framework equivalent, including maths and English or equivalent.

The work Cartographers are concerned with map-making. A map in this context covers any type of chart, plan, three-dimensional model or computer image representing the whole or sections of the earth, or of other parts of the universe. While their work in producing 'traditional' maps and wall charts with which everyone is familiar, such as those used in schools and universities, by walkers and motorists and for land and air surveying, is as important as ever, there is steady demand for more specialist maps and charts. Planning professionals may need maps showing traffic flow or the distribution of housing, employment or industry; forest officers need to see areas of planting, thinning and felling; highly accurate details of the seabed are needed by scientists looking for oil or minerals. There are increasing calls for charts showing the spread, or contraction, of animal and plant populations and human habitation. The penetration of space and of the earth's crust has extended cartographers' horizons and set new challenges in finding new ways of representing the results of such exploration.

Cartographers are concerned with every stage of preparation and interpretation. They have to determine what data are needed for any particular map, discuss how to collect it, evaluate the information that comes in and apply it to map production. This is the editorial function. The actual collection of data is done by other specialists such as surveyors (see p. 568), specialists in remote sensing and geographical information systems or by historical or archaeological researchers. Infra-red photography, often taken from satellites, remote sensing and seismic measurements are techniques widely used in data collection. Information technology is having enormous impact on the way cartographers work, as is shown by the importance of GIS – Geographical Information Systems. These enable the storage, processing and display of information on a computer screen. GIS consist of a database, a statistical/mathematical analysing capacity and a means of graphic display. One of the many benefits of GIS is that they enable data to be scanned from existing 'hard copy', manipulated and processed before being displayed in new and graphic ways on a screen or printed out. Cartographers are developing electronic map forms which are replacing at least some products previously printed on paper.

This is a fairly small profession and entry and training opportunities have changed very much in the last few years. While editing is done by cartographers, production is usually the responsibility of the cartographic technician, although there is often overlap. The cartographic technician's traditional skill with hand and pen is now supplemented or replaced by the manipulation of computer images. Traditionally the Ordnance Survey was the largest employer of cartographic staff; owing to reorganization and the introduction of GIS, staff numbers have been reduced. Other government departments, such as the Ministry of Defence, that used to use large numbers of staff are in a similar situation. The main civilian employers are BT, the Civil Aviation Authority, utility companies and, of course, map publishers. There are some openings in universities and with local authorities.

Training In-house training with part-time study is rare; a relevant degree is normally required, often to be followed by further study.

There are various first degree courses in mapping science, geographical information systems, geoinformatics or topographic science. Geographical information systems can also be studied in combination with subjects such as geography, maths, computer science or surveying. There are some postgraduate courses in subjects related to geographical information systems. For a list of recommended courses see the British Cartographic Society website: *www.cartography.org.uk.*

Personal attributes Patience; diligence; great accuracy; good colour vision; powers of observation and interpretation; willingness to experiment; sense of design useful.

Work–life balance In principle, a career break should be no problem for qualified cartographers who have kept up to date, though it is likely to prove difficult when jobs are decreasing. Part-time work is possible, but again affected by the job situation.

Further information

British Cartographic Society, Administration, 12 Elworthy Drive, Wellington, Somerset TA21 9AT.
www.cartography.org.uk

Related careers *architecture*: *Architectural Technologist – art and design – surveying*

Chartered Secretary and Administrator

Entry qualifications None laid down for entry to first level of Institute of Chartered Secretaries and Administrators qualifications. Entry to higher level qualifications with appropriate vocational awards, professional qualifications, NHD, Foundation degree or honours degree (see 'Training', below).

The work This has nothing to do with personal secretarial work (see p. 530). Instead, it is general administration and management in public, private and voluntary sectors.

The main element in professional administration, wherever it is carried out, is coordinating (and possibly also controlling) various individuals and/or departments within an organization. Administrators are generalists who coordinate the activities of specialists. They form a link between people and their separate activities; they make sure that different sections or departments dovetail, and fit into the whole. Increased use of information technology in all organizations means they need a good grasp of information systems – how they work and what they can do. At senior level, administrators have an 'overview' over whatever their organization does; at junior level, they may, for example, coordinate the work of the accounts department; at middle level they ensure that, for example, production, distribution and personnel departments are informed of each other's needs. Professional administrators often work for a time in the various departments, to find out how each works and where it fits into the whole.

Like other professional qualifications, professional administration can lead to the top in whatever the type of organization. The work is immensely varied, and so are the top jobs. Senior administrators may be involved in the choice and design of complicated computer systems aimed at improved decision-taking by top managers.

Qualified chartered secretaries can become company secretaries: public companies are by law required to have company secretaries, i.e. people who have either a legal, accountancy or the ICSA qualification. According to type and size of company, company secretaries can be chief executives – possibly called director, or secretary-general – responsible only to the Board or whoever are the policy-makers; or they can be the chief administrative officer responsible to the director or chief executive.

As it is an adaptable qualification, chartered secretaries have a wide choice of jobs. They can also set up in private practice, offering clients a range of services.

Training The Institute's qualifying scheme consists of three stages: Certificate in Business Practice, Diploma in Business Practice and a two-part Professional programme, all modular. The first two programmes give a broad business education, covering law, finance, administration, corporate governance, company secretaryship and management. The Certificate programme requires no entry qualifications, while the Professional Programme is at postgraduate level. Exemptions are given for relevant or non-relevant BTEC/SVQ Awards, Foundation degrees, specified NVQs or other professional qualifications.

Study can be full-time or part-time by distance learning. Typically students take four modules a year.

Personal attributes A flair for administration; common sense and good judgement; numeracy; interest in current affairs; tact; discretion.

Mature entry and career change Good opportunities, especially now that access to ICSA examinations is 'open'.

Work–life balance A career break should be no problem for people who had responsible jobs before the break. Because of the flexible examination structure it is possible for people to study while on a break. There are fair opportunities for part-time work, particularly in small firms.

Further information

The Institute of Chartered Secretaries and Administrators, 16 Park Crescent, London W1B 1AH.
www.icsa.org.uk

Related careers *accountancy – health services management – law*

Chiropractic

Entry qualifications Usually National Qualifications Framework Level 3 (A levels, BTEC National awards) or Scottish Credit and Qualifications Framework equivalent, including biology and chemistry. Mature students with suitable alternative qualifications are considered. Foundation years are available for those without the standard qualifications.

Registration with the General Chiropractic Council.

The work Chiropractors diagnose, treat and prevent mechanical disorders of the musculoskeletal system and the effects of these disorders on the function of the nervous system and general health. In practice this usually involves using their hands to 'adjust' or 'manipulate' the spine and joints where signs of restriction in movement are found, and can also involve working on muscles. Patients consult them for a wide range of disorders, arising from accidents, stress, lack of exercise, poor posture or illness. Chiropractors may use x-rays for diagnosis but largely rely on their own diagnostic skills. They do not use drugs or surgery and they support their treatment with advice about their patients' work, diet and exercise.

Chiropractic is a complementary medicine with statutory recognition and regulation. It is illegal to practise unless registered with the General Chiropractic Council following qualification at a recognized college (see 'Training' below).

Chiropractors work in private practice, either on their own or within a group practice. Many NHS GPs endorse chiropractic and will refer patients for treatment which may be funded through the NHS. However, most patients consult chiropractors privately.

Training Three institutions offer courses leading to qualifications recognized by the General Chiropractic Council: the Anglo-European College of Chiropractic (AECC), the University of Glamorgan and the McTimoney College of Chiropractic.

AECC and The Welsh Institute of Chiropractic at the University of Glamorgan offer four-year full-time honours degree courses, with an optional foundation year for those without the standard entry requirements. These courses are recognized by the Higher Education Funding Council, and entry is via the UCAS system.

The McTimoney College of Chiropractic offers a five-year, 'mixed-mode' course, combining home study with college contact time at weekends. Students can follow the course while employed but this is a demanding option. An access course is available for those who do not meet the normal entry requirements.

Specialist postgraduate qualifications are available.

The regulating body, the General Chiropractic Council, requires continuing professional training for annual re-registration.

Personal attributes Dexterity; interest in the working of the body; empathy; interest in wellness and health promotion; communication skills; ability to work alone; business acumen.

Mature entry and career change About 40 per cent of entrants to the Anglo-European College are mature students. An access course or Open University science foundation course may be suggested as good preparation for those without the necessary academic background.

Work–life balance Chiropractors are self-employed so once established can choose their own hours. Practitioners wishing to be restored to the register after a career break will have to meet the mandatory requirement for re-registration.

Further information
General Chiropractic Council, 44 Wicklow Street, London WC1X 9HL.
www.gcc-uk.org

Chiropractic

British Chiropractic Association, 59 Castle Street, Reading RG1 7SN.
www.chiropractic-uk.co.uk

Related careers *medicine – occupational therapy – osteopathy – physiotherapy*

Civil Aviation

AIR TRAFFIC CONTROL OFFICER

Entry qualifications Usually National Qualifications Framework Level 3 (A levels, BTEC National awards) or Scottish Credit and Qualifications Framework equivalent. Graduates or people with other qualifications welcomed. High standard of physical fitness, eyesight and hearing required.

The work Teams of ATCOs control and monitor the movements of aircraft taking off, landing and when en route in designated controlled airspace. An aircraft leaving a controller's area of responsibility is coordinated with the next ATC unit, which may be an airfield or an air traffic control centre in the UK or in Europe. Pilots of aircraft are, in fact, in two-way radio communication with controllers from the time they request permission to start engines until the engines stop at their destination.

The work is responsible and highly skilled: it may involve the safe 'stacking' of aircraft in an airfield's 'holding area' while awaiting approach; the 'sequencing' of aircraft using radar to maintain a safe distance between them, and ensuring that aircraft flying the same routes at varying speeds, heights and directions are always safely separated horizontally and vertically. ATCOs use computers in their calculations. After gaining operational experience, a small proportion of ATCOs specialize in ATC computer work.

Most air traffic controllers work in area control centres, controlling the en route stage of a flight, using radar and other technology to track aircraft. Others work in airport control towers, guiding pilots as they approach and land. The international language of ATC is English, so UK ATCOs talk and are talked to in their own language. Foreign pilots sometimes have problems expressing themselves clearly, especially when under pressure. Although ATCOs must make quick decisions, they can ask pilots to repeat anything which is not quite clear.

The great majority of operational ATCOs work shift duties and all ATCOs must be prepared to do so; as far as possible shifts are planned well in advance, but last-minute changes are sometimes necessary.

Training Aerodrome controllers start with upwards of six months' training at the College of Air Traffic Control near Bournemouth; area controllers start with approximately twelve months, followed by a two-year period of in-house training.

Personal attributes Good eyesight (including normal colour vision); medically fit; a calm cool temperament; ability to conceal and control excitement in emergencies; ability to concentrate both in busy and in quiet periods; a good quick brain, with quick reactions and the ability to be decisive; the ability to work as part of a team.

Mature entry and career change Normal maximum age 36 unless with substantial relevant experience.

Work–life balance Career breaks are available. Most ATCOs work on a shift basis. There is no initial part-time work but some flexible working can be considered during career to suit personal needs.

Air Traffic Service Assistants assist ATCOs in their tasks by undertaking certain routine functions, particularly with data preparation and display, at both airfields and airways control centres.

Further information
National Air Traffic Services (NATS), Fifth Floor, 4000 Parkway, Whiteley, Fareham PO15 7FL.
   www.nats.co.uk and *www.natscareers.co.uk*

CIVIL PILOT

Entry qualifications Airlines sponsoring pilot training courses require applicants to have at least five GCSE passes at grade C or higher or equivalent (including English language and maths) and two A level passes or equivalent, preferably in maths and physics. CAA Class 1 Medical.

The work The pilot has to fly the aircraft safely at all times, in accordance with the company's operating procedures, complying with instructions from Air Traffic Control. The pilot is required to have a very good knowledge of the aircraft and to be able to deal with any emergency situation arising while in flight or on the ground. In a multi-crew aeroplane, one of the pilots is captain of the crew of the aircraft.

In an airline, the first job is as First Officer. Promotion to Captain, which is not automatic, may come between three and fifteen years later (earlier in small airlines and later in the largest airlines). The captain has total responsibility for the aircraft, crew and passengers. He/she usually has a co-pilot and there may be up to four pilots on long-haul flights.

The captain begins to plan the flight at least an hour before start-up time. After meeting the other flight-crew members in the operations department, and checking on the serviceability of the aircraft and its systems for the flight, the pilot studies the procedures to be used for the take-off and climb, en route, and descent and landing, together with the availability of diversion aerodromes along the route and any Notices To Airman (NOTAMs) affecting the route. After study of the meteorological forecast, the pilot works out the amount of fuel to be carried, taking account of the weights of the passengers and cargo. The pilot then calculates the take-off and landing weights (vital data in case of emergency action) and the optimum cruising heights for the route. Finally, at the aircraft, having carried out external and internal checks, the pilot signs a technical log accepting the aircraft as being fit for the flight. In modern aircraft, a great deal of this planning work is computerized and the pilot can load the route data into a Flight Management System computer within the aircraft.

On most aircraft, apart from take-off and landing, the flight is flown using the autopilot, and one of the pilot's tasks is to set its controls and then monitor it to see that it flies the required route. On 'short hauls' (within Europe) the pilot and crew are busy all the time. On long hauls there can be long hours flying at cruising height over the ocean, with only routine monitoring checks to go through. This can be difficult in an unexpected way: pilots get bored, especially at night, yet the need for alertness is as great as ever.

UK pilots are increasingly working for companies within Europe. There is some small demand for pilots (aeroplane or helicopter): on air taxis; crop spraying; aerial photography; oil rig support operations; weather and traffic observation; flying privately or flying company aircraft; and especially for instructors in flying clubs.

Fixed Wing (i.e. Aeroplanes)

Training The majority of UK students at approved Flying Training organizations are sponsored by airlines. While the major sponsor of UK pilots is British Airways, larger airlines such as EasyJet also offer sponsorship schemes. Competition is intense and airlines are increasingly entering arrangements with Commercial Training Providers who supply suitable candidates when vacancies arise.

Basic training lasts about fifteen months on full-time courses. The syllabus includes aviation law, flight performance and planning, human performance and limitations, meteorology, navigation, operational procedures, principles of flight, communication and multi-crew cooperation training. Flight training is carried out both in aircraft and in simulators.

The first qualification is the Commercial Pilot's Licence (CPL), but to fly in an airliner as co-pilot the basic requirement is the CPL plus Instrument Rating (IR), and the pilot must also have passed the Airline Transport Pilot's Licence Aeroplanes (ATPL) ground examinations and have at least 1,500 flying hours. Ratings are qualifications in particular aspects of flying and in flying particular types of aircraft.

The type of aircraft a pilot may fly depends on the aircraft ratings included in the licence. To become qualified as captain of a large airliner a pilot must have the ATPL, and several thousands of flying hours.

Trainee pilots can qualify by attending a full-time, integrated course in flying and ground training. This course costs from £55,000 and this route is usually only followed by sponsored students. An alternative route is to first gain a Private Pilot's Licence (PPL) and then 150 hours' flying experience before undertaking modular courses for the ground examinations, for the CPL and then the IR. This route still costs about £55,000 but the courses may be taken when funds permit.

Some experienced armed services pilots transfer to civil aviation flying, with further training and testing.

Rotary Wing (i.e. Helicopters)

Demand for commercial helicopter pilots fluctuates but due to a decrease in the number of military-trained pilots leaving the forces, prospects for commercially qualified helicopter pilots are improving. A full-time integrated course leading to a commercial pilot's licence lasts around nine months and costs about £45,000. A flexible modular course is also available which can be completed on a part-time basis. Commercial operators run occasional sponsorship schemes.

Personal attributes At least average intelligence; commitment; dedication; enthusiasm for aviation; mental agility; high standard of fitness; justifiable self-confidence; leadership qualities; ability to take decisions; well-balanced personality; ability to get on with others.

Mature entry and career change Airline sponsorship schemes have upper age limits.

Work–life balance A career break should be possible as all pilots need retraining throughout their career. Work is often irregular.

Further information

British Helicopter Advisory Board, Graham Suite, West Entrance, Fairoaks Airport, Chobham, Woking, Surrey GU24 8HX.
www.bhab.org

British Airline Pilots Association, 5 Heathrow Boulevard, 278 Bath Road, West Drayton UB7 0DQ.
www.balpa.org.uk

Related careers *Air Traffic Control Officer* (see above) – *engineering – surveying*

CABIN CREW (STEWARDESS AND STEWARD)

Entry qualifications Minimum and upper age limits for trainees and minimum height requirements vary between airlines. No set educational qualifications, but good GCSE or equivalent standard, preferably including English and maths, and conversational ability in a foreign language. Some catering or nursing experience, or minimum one year in a responsible job which involved dealing with people, e.g. in a travel agency.

The work The cabin crew welcome passengers, supervise seating and safety-belt arrangements, and look after air-sick travellers, babies, and children travelling alone. Stewards and stewardesses serve meals, and sell drinks, cigarettes, etc. in a variety of currencies.

They 'dress the plane' to see that blankets, head-rests, magazines, cosmetics, etc. are available and in good order, and make necessary announcements over the public-address system. They deal with any emergencies and write reports after each flight, with comments, for instance, on the behaviour of unaccompanied children.

Most of the time cabin crews are airborne waiters and waitresses. From the moment the plane is airborne they are continuously busy, working at great speed in a confined space.

Duty hours vary from one airline to another and are likely to be changed at the last minute because of weather and other 'exigencies of the service'. Normally on European routes cabin crews are 'on' for four to six days with a good deal of night duty; they are then off-duty for two to four days. On long-distance trips they may be away from home for three weeks, but that would include several days' rest at a foreign airport.

The farther the destination, the more chance of sightseeing. On short routes cabin crews may fly backwards and forwards for a month without seeing more than the airport at their destination. On long-distance trips crews often change planes at 'slip-points' and stay for a few days' rest, living in luxury hotels at their airline's expense.

British-trained crews are in demand by American and other foreign airlines if they speak the appropriate language.

Training About four to six weeks at airline training school. Subjects include food service, first aid, documentation, airborne procedure, foreign currency exchange, security procedures, emergency drill with swimming-pool lesson in the use of the inflatable dinghy and life-jacket, practical fire drills, customer service, grooming and deportment. Recognized qualifications include the BTEC Certificate in Preparation for Air Cabin Crews and the EAL Certificate in Air Cabin Crewing.

Personal attributes A likeable personality; calmness in crises; common sense; efficiency; sensitivity to anxious passengers' needs; well-groomed appearance.

Further information Individual airlines.

GROUND STAFF – SOME EXAMPLES

Passenger Service Assistant/Agent (titles vary)

Entry qualifications Minimum usually at National Qualifications Framework Level 2 (GCSEs A*–C, BTEC Diplomas and Certificates) or Scottish Credit and Qualifications Framework equivalent. Previous customer service experience useful. Minimum age usually 18.

The work Passenger service assistants see that passengers and luggage get on to the right plane, with the minimum of fuss. They check-in luggage, which involves checking travel documents, and check-out passengers at boarding gates. They answer passengers' questions on travel connections and similar matters.

Other duties carried out by experienced PSAs include: load-control – preparing information for aircraft loaders on luggage weight; cargo documentation for customs clearance; checking that planes leave with the right meals, cargo, baggage.

PSAs work in uniform, and do shift work. They move about the airport all day, rarely sit down.

Training Several weeks' induction and on-the-job training.

Sales Staff (titles vary)

Entry qualifications Minimum usually at National Qualifications Framework Level 2 (GCSEs A*–C, BTEC Diplomas and Certificates) or Scottish Credit and Qualifications Framework equivalent.

The work Sales staff sit in airport and city offices and answer questions on international flight connections; make fare calculations (in various currencies); sell tickets over the counter and over the phone. Bookings are made to and from all over the world; each reservation must be related to reservations made elsewhere and reservation vacancies available for any particular flight at any given moment. This is called 'space control'. Reservations staff use computerized information systems: they can see on their computer terminal exactly what the present reservation situation is on any flight of their airline.

Senior sales staff may call on travel agents, business houses and other important customers to explain ancillary services such as car hire, hotel accommodation, package holidays, and 'sell' their own particular airline, both passenger and cargo services.

Sales staff may do shift work, though less so in senior positions.

Training Short on-the-job training with some lectures.

Personal attributes For all 'public contact' jobs: an orderly mind; communication skills; a liking for meeting many people very briefly; a calm, helpful manner; good speech and appearance.

Commercial Management, Flight Operations and Flight Planning

Entry qualifications Vary with different airlines and according to supply and demand. Some promotion from sales staff; most entrants have A levels or equivalent; many have degrees or higher awards.

The work The administration of flight programmes, which cover many thousands of flight-miles, millions of tons of freight and ever-growing 'passenger throughput', is a highly complex undertaking. Staff organize the airline's fleet of planes over its network, making the most efficient use of each aircraft, e.g. ensuring that as far as possible outgoing freight is replaced with return-flight freight, and that the 'turn-round' time in airports is as short as possible, while allowing time for maintenance, loading, etc. 'Aircrew management' involves arranging individual crew members' schedules, taking into consideration maximum flying hours allowed; rest-days ('stop-overs') abroad, etc.

Apart from this planning work, staff are also responsible for ensuring that at all times aircrew have all the information they need before each take-off, throughout the planned itinerary. This involves discussions with a variety of departments and individuals; keeping detailed records; being prepared for emergencies.

Training Through airlines' own training schemes, lasting two to three years, or BTEC/SQA Higher awards or degree, followed by shorter airline training. Schemes vary between companies and according to expansion or contraction of airline industry.

Personal attributes Drive; organizing ability; liking for working under pressure.

Mature entry and career change May be possible for cabin crew, passenger service assistants and sales staff (see 'Entry qualifications', above).

Work–life balance A career break may be possible, but depends on vacancy situation. Also, returners have to start again with basic training. Part-time opportunities in some jobs, for example cabin crew, passenger services, but this affects promotion. Also some short-term contracts with 'package tour' companies for cabin crews.

Further information Individual airlines.

Related careers *hospitality and catering – languages – travel agent/ tour operator*

Civil Service

The UK Civil Service supports the government of the day by helping them develop and carry out their policies and administer the public services for which they are responsible. Every department has different priorities, providing a wide range of services to the public across the United Kingdom. This means that within the Civil Service there is a uniquely diverse mix of jobs and opportunities; the Civil Service is one of the largest employers in the country with more than half a million members of staff.

Historically, people joined the Civil Service straight from university or school and remained in the Civil Service for their entire career, working in policy areas and delivering services to the public sector. Now, the Civil Service is much more dynamic and professional; civil servants are no longer faceless bureaucrats, they are professionals bringing their expertise to the organization, such as accountancy, law, IT, project management, economics, marketing and policy – this represents the sheer size of the Civil Service.

People join government at different stages in their career and move between the public and private sector. Opportunities exist at all educational levels. There is a strong tradition of continuous development and upskilling the workforce to enable members of staff to perform much more effectively and progress through to Senior Civil Service (SCS) level. Training may be work-based, or on courses as appropriate, and may cover anything from policy-related areas and operational delivery, to specialist areas like finance, procurement and human resources development. There are also courses on understanding government and parliament.

Over the last few years, the Civil Service has been undergoing major changes with far-reaching developments still taking place. The aim is to make sure that government works much more effectively and professionally to deliver better public services.

The work of government departments – and their staff members at all levels – is immensely varied. It affects virtually every aspect of modern life – health, education, the environment, transport, agriculture, defence, international relations and development, poverty, energy policy and taxation. These broad headings cover the breadth and complex range of activities and issues of which it is possible here to give only a few examples.

The Department for Environment, Food and Rural Affairs (Defra) offers opportunities for senior staff to participate in meetings in Brussels on the development, negotiation and implementation of EU agricultural policy, but it is also responsible for the management of sea fisheries and consumer protection. The Ministry of Defence (MoD) is one of the largest consumers of the products of British industry with vast annual expenditure to manage. In the Home Office, members of staff might be concerned with the administration of prison management and reform. The Scottish Executive and the National Assembly for Wales, with their regional responsibilities, embrace a range of activities handled by different departments elsewhere, e.g. education, agriculture and fisheries, transport and health.

Across all departments and levels there is a broad spectrum of roles and responsibilities, both strategic and operational. Some civil servants advise ministers; others deal direct with members of the public; some research the implications of policy options; others provide support services in, for example, computer operations, human resources and finance.

Civil servants face similar pressures to those in industry, and the work is no less stimulating. The Civil Service has begun to operate in a much more professional and businesslike manner, with all the demands and satisfactions for its members of staff which that implies. Management is increasingly decentralized, allowing more flexibility in decision-making and managing budgets and teams.

Many people in the Civil Service now work in 'executive agencies' which operate like businesses under a Chief Executive who sets the financial and quality of service targets and who is given the financial and management freedom to pursue them. The idea is to ensure that managers are more accountable and visible and for the new ethos to filter down through to members of staff, with financial rewards for outstanding performance.

With regard to recruitment for job opportunities across the Civil Service, individual government departments advertise through national or local press and e-media including the Civil Service Recruitment Gateway. People join the Civil Service at different stages/levels of their career, from the wider public and private sector; whether they join straight from school, as graduates, or as executives from the private sector, the Civil Service looks for able and committed people to be part of delivering better government. Please see below the different entry routes into the Civil Service.

Fast Stream Graduate Programme

The Civil Service Fast Stream, the Civil Service's accelerated training and development programme, is aimed at current and/or previous graduates with the potential to reach Senior Civil Service level. This is a highly competitive centralized recruitment competition and although the basic qualification asked for is a 2:2 degree, candidates need to be in the top 10 per cent of students in terms of intellect, interpersonal skills and personal qualities. Candidates can apply for the Graduate Fast Stream which has a number of options including: Central Departments covering all the major departments except the Diplomatic Service; Science and Engineering; the Diplomatic Service; the Department for International Development (DfID) Technical Development Option; and Clerkships in Parliament. There are also Fast Stream schemes for statisticians, economists, technology in business, the Government Communications HQ (GCHQ) and the Secret Intelligence Service (SIS).

People already working in the Civil Service can also apply to the Fast Stream, though there is usually a two-year service requirement.

Entry qualifications A 2:2 degree in any discipline but this minimum requirement does not reflect the intensive competition for places. Generally applicants need to be British nationals.

Application and assessment process The initial application process is online and Fast Stream candidates are required to take an online self-assessment test before applying. Practice qualifying tests are also available online.

The application process begins with online tests in verbal and numerical reasoning and a competency-based questionnaire. Successful candidates proceed to a supervised reasoning test and exercise which takes place at a regional centre and, if again successful, candidates are invited to London to a one-day assessment centre. Candidates for the Diplomatic Service, DFID Technical Development Option and Clerkships in Parliament have to attend a final selection board.

Fast Stream entrants begin with a series of intensive placements or 'postings' which last from one year to eighteen months. They are given real responsibility from the start and may be seconded to other government departments, business or industry, or to work abroad, and can expect to be appointed to senior manager within four to five years.

Key areas of work and responsibility Senior civil servants are responsible, under ministers, for formulating and implementing the policy of the government of the day. As indicated above, the subject matter of the work varies considerably, but the work of civil servants at this level falls into several broad categories. It includes researching and analysing policy options; developing the organization and procedures necessary to translate policy objectives into practice; dealing with parliamentary business, including briefing ministers and drafting replies to parliamentary questions; drafting legislation; dealing with operational matters affecting the day-to-day responsibilities of a department; working in a minister's Private Office. There is scope for liaison and negotiation at a senior level within and between departments, with outside organizations, and with foreign governments. The balance of responsibilities varies between different postings.

As mentioned above, the Civil Service is moving towards greater accountability and responsibility for individual managers. Ultimately, however, ministers make final decisions. These decisions are made on the advice and recommendations of their civil servants, so there is a real opportunity to contribute to matters of national and international importance from an early stage of a Fast Stream career. There is also considerable intellectual challenge in mastering complex issues and giving impartial advice, whatever one's own politics or those of the government of the day.

Personal attributes Skills of delivery, intellectual capacity and interpersonal skills are all core competencies that potential candidates for the Fast Stream programme must possess. It is important that people demonstrate high intellect, capacity to analyse and weigh up complex and weighty documents; can deal with conflicting opinions and advice and make a decision; have the ability to write balanced and concise reports; can hold and delegate authority; enjoy responsibility; possess the ability to manage various stakeholders and resources and the ability to communicate and work well with other people at all levels – junior members of staff, colleagues, external stakeholders and ministers.

Junior Manager

Entry qualifications Requirements vary according to individual government departments and specific roles but candidates are expected to have achieved at least National Qualifications Framework Level 3 (A levels, BTEC National awards) or Scottish Credit and Qualifications Framework equivalent. However, many applicants who apply to the Civil Service have obtained a degree. There may also be nationality requirements.

Method of entry and training Entry is by competitive tests and competency-based interview. As HR processes are devolved to individual government departments or agencies, they are responsible for running their own recruitment competitions. Most of the career opportunities are advertised on individual government departments' websites as well as the Civil Service Recruitment Gateway website.

Training is largely achieved in-house, with regular opportunities to review progress and further development. All junior members of staff are encouraged to seek a mentor and/or buddy to help them develop a personal training programme to meet their own career plans. There are opportunities for more specialized training leading to external qualifications as appropriate and many departments organize their own management development programmes. The National School of Government, a business school for government delivers various training programmes that cover the core areas such as policy, operational delivery and corporate services delivery (specialist areas).

Key areas of work and responsibility Junior managers, also called executive officers, are the first line of management in the Civil Service. Their role is more operational than strategic and generally involves applying policy to key deliverable outcomes. The subject matter obviously varies a great deal from one government department or agency to another, but they may be involved in several broad types of work. Junior managers manage staff and resources, allocating, monitoring and controlling the team's work, motivating staff members and helping them to develop their potential. Many handle casework, making decisions on the basis of often complex law, regulations and precedent. A major area of responsibility includes dealing with the public, which may include opportunities within the voluntary sector, the NHS and local government. General operational and administrative responsibilities are an essential part of the work and essential to the smooth running of a department or agency; they may include finance, human resources, estate management, purchasing and support for senior colleagues, including arranging high level meetings and drafting reports/briefs.

Some junior managers have more specialized responsibilities and are recruited and trained accordingly. Particular examples include the Immigration Service, HM Revenue and Customs and the Diplomatic

Service (see below). There are also opportunities to train in accountancy (see p. 43) or information technology (see p. 280).

Promotion is generally linked to regular formal appraisals and reviews, and junior managers can move into senior posts at a fairly rapid rate depending on their performance and motivation. They may also apply to join the Fast Stream.

Personal attributes Overall, candidates must demonstrate practical intelligence; the ability to prioritize and organize their workload; a sense of pride and passion in their approach to work; strong interpersonal skills and the ability to build relationships with teams; and the capability to manage people.

Administrative Assistant

Entry qualifications Requirements may vary, but in practice, most candidates must have achieved four or five good GCSEs or equivalent.

Key areas of work and responsibility Administrative assistants are employed by all government departments to support operational staff members and ensure that the administrative areas such as filing, data recording, sorting and keeping records are managed efficiently. They may also deal with inquiries from the public, and may operate computer systems or electronic mail equipment. They are actively encouraged to upskill themselves by taking appropriate training to help support their career development. There are good prospects for promotion across the Civil Service.

THE DIPLOMATIC SERVICE

Entry qualifications For Diplomatic Fast Stream (see p. 155) candidates have to pass a medical (special provision is made for people with disabilities) and security vetting. No particular language skills are normally required but they can be a definite advantage. A language aptitude test measures candidates' aptitude for 'hard' languages.

In addition to the entry levels already mentioned, which are found in other areas of the Civil Service, the Diplomatic Service employs additional grades of staff who are generally expected to go on overseas postings: *Operational Officers* – minimum qualifications five GCSEs (grades A*–C) including maths and English language, or equivalent, plus three years' office experience (applicants with A levels or a degree must still achieve GCSE maths); *Policy Officers* – minimum qualification is a degree in any discipline at a minimum 2:2 or above plus proven ability to learn languages.

There are also occasional openings for research officers, economists, legal advisers, architects, surveyors, engineers and other specialist areas.

Key areas of work and responsibility Members of staff spend about a third to a half of their career working at the Foreign and Commonwealth Office in London. For the remainder of their time, they are serving overseas in any of the more than 160 countries with which the UK maintains diplomatic relations or with UN or NATO postings. During a working lifetime, anything from six to ten 'tours' of two to four years each are spent working at British embassies, high commissions and other missions in a variety of countries. The willingness to serve anywhere in the world is therefore vital.

There is huge diversity in the work. In the course of their careers, staff members may work on trade promotion, political reporting and analysis (especially in the Fast Stream), consular services to British nationals living or travelling overseas, immigration work, aid administration, human resources and financial management or combating international crime or terrorism.

Promotion is generally on the basis of performance on the job and there is a continuous process of appraisals and reviews.

Training New entrants at all levels usually undertake a short induction course which acquaints them with the organization, the working of the service and its place in the machinery of government. Specialized job-related courses are arranged for staff members who are appointed to roles, in for example, commercial or consular work, and there are also courses designed to develop individual skills and potential, for example in management, effective speaking or international economics. Not surprisingly, the Diplomatic Service attaches great importance to language training. For some of the positions, full-time language training for up to two years is provided; all members of staff, even when it is not an essential part of their jobs, are encouraged to learn something of the local language and are entitled to at least 100 hours of free tuition. Language allowances are paid to members of staff who reach a certain level of proficiency. Diplomats usually have demonstrable experience of mastering several languages during their careers.

Personal attributes Members of the Diplomatic Service must demonstrate excellent influencing and persuasive skills, strong political acumen and sound stakeholder management. The ability to be adaptable and resourceful and cope with the constant upheaval of travelling from one place/country to another is important. The Diplomatic Service is not so much a job as a way of life. It demands balance, staying power, and curiosity about other nations' governance and way of life and the confidence to be ambassadorial in representing the UK and its policy priorities.

SPECIALISTS AND PROFESSIONALS IN THE CIVIL SERVICE

The Civil Service employs a wide range and substantial number of specialists and professionals. There are opportunities for those with considerable experience gained outside the Civil Service, particularly newly qualified specialists and those seeking opportunities to obtain professional qualifications.

The basic entry and training structures of these careers and their different functions and applications are discussed in detail in other sections of this book. This section looks at their roles within the Civil Service. Most departments and agencies do their own recruitment; although there is specialist central graduate recruitment, the Fast

Stream graduate programme also recruits specialists including engineers, economists and statisticians. Non-Fast Stream entrants are usually required to have a good degree in the appropriate subject. Information on specialist recruitment opportunities can be found on *www.careers.civil-service.gov.uk.*

Scientists
(see also *science*, p. 507)

Scientists in the Civil Service may be involved in research and development; they may also provide scientific services, statutory advisory and inspection duties and scientific contributions to the formulation of government policies. Within these broad areas of work is a vast range of activity and interest covering aspects of life as diverse as the 'food we eat, the air we breathe and the weapons that defend us'.

For example, scientists in Defra tackle and study problems caused by animals, from the causes of BSE to bird collisions with aircraft. Others are concerned with the compulsory EU beef labelling system, food additives, the evaluation of new food products and processes, including high profile issues such as the trialling of genetically modified crops. The Defence Science and Technology Laboratory (DSTL) is one of the largest employers of scientists and engineers and recruits graduates from a range of disciplines. The Home Office maintains the Forensic Science Service, which provides the scientific backing to the search for criminal evidence, using sophisticated techniques to analyse a wide range of materials such as blood, fibres, glass, paint and soil.

There are opportunities in most scientific disciplines, both major areas like chemistry, physics and computer science, and smaller, more specialized fields like animal nutrition, meteorology and plant pathology.

Engineers
(see also *engineering*, p. 213)

There are opportunities for every type of engineer in the Civil Service. The MoD is keen to have engineers who can design and test software for combat simulators and develop and improve helicopter rotor blades. At the Department for Transport (DfT), while civil engineers might design new roads and bridges and manage huge projects, electrical engineers are responsible for developing computer-based traffic control systems.

Surveyors
(see also *surveying*, p. 568)

There is a variety of opportunities for surveyors in the Civil Service. The Valuation Office Agency provides valuation services to HM Revenue and Customs (HMRC) and other government departments throughout the UK. Surveyors in the Defence Estates Agency are responsible for all the property owned by the MoD, one of the largest landowners in the UK; there are also overseas projects to be managed. Defra offers advice, often as a chargeable service, to farmers, growers and landowners on all aspects of land and estate management. There are also opportunities available in other departments including the Department of Health (DH), Ordnance Survey and national museums. All types of surveyors are needed, but individual government departments will have specific requirements.

Economists
(see also *economics*, p. 210)

Economists work in about 30 government departments such as HM Treasury and the Department for Children, Schools and Families (DCSF), analysing the economic implications of virtually every aspect of government policy. A key part of this work is the interpretation of economics and other statistics and the wider impact on national and international issues. In some departments, for example in HM

Treasury, economists would specialize in applying economic principles to a variety of different situations.

Statisticians
(see also *mathematics and statistics*, p. 368)

Across the range of government activities, statisticians collect, analyse and interpret data on a variety of subjects and for a variety of purposes. Statistics on subjects as diverse as transport, health, education, trade and household expenditure are used both to shape and reflect policy and to inform industry, the academic world and the general public on aspects of modern life.

Press and Publicity
(see also *public relations*, p. 484)

The Civil Service is one of the largest employers of press and public relations specialists. Overall, their role is to explain government policies and measures to the public. This might involve advising a minister on dealing with the news media; planning a publicity and information campaign on, for example, drink-driving; organizing an exhibition to promote British trade overseas; or working on a range of publications dealing with subjects as diverse as recruitment, overseas aid or detailed statistics on social trends. The Central Office of Information offers the greatest number of opportunities, but there are openings in most government departments both for new graduates and for experienced professionals.

Lawyers
(see also *law*, p. 316)

Lawyers in government service have a great number of roles, many of which mirror work done in private practice and industry, some of which are unique to government. Lawyers have a key role in drafting legislation and assisting ministers in steering it through Parliament. They are also advisers on the formulation and implementation of policy. Many are involved in prosecution and litigation over, for example, serious VAT fraud. Lawyers working on the administration of justice might be advising on the discipline, conduct and welfare of the judiciary or settling cases before the European Court. There are also opportunities to advise on a range of matters concerning the Civil Service as a large and diverse organization covering areas such as employment relations/legislation, performance management, conveyancing and pay agreements. There are opportunities for both qualified lawyers and for graduates who wish to qualify through government service.

Accountants
(see also *accountancy*, p. 43)

Accountants in the Civil Service are at the forefront of many developments designed to promote accountability and governance and introduce financial management disciplines. They are also involved with government's dealings with industry and commerce and tax matters. There are career opportunities for those with a professional accountancy qualification and opportunities for some administration trainees and junior managers to be trained and become qualified accountants.

Research Officers

Research officers study the impact of government policies and provide information on which policy is based. Most career opportunities are with the MoD, DfT and Department for Work and Pensions (DWP).

Information Systems and Technology
(see also *information technology/information systems*, p. 280)

The Civil Service is investing in improving information technology to ensure that information systems and infrastructure are robust. Computers are in widespread use throughout the Civil Service. Applications range from sophisticated weather forecasting and research into climatic change, through to a Home Office electronic photofit system to help catch offenders.

Mature entry and career change (general) There may be increasing opportunities for mature candidates, especially those with managerial, professional, technical or scientific qualifications and/or experience. In 2006/07, the average age of new entrants to the Civil Service at senior level was 44 years old (source: SCS database, Cabinet Office).

Work–life balance The Civil Service has been at the forefront of introducing flexible working practices, having introduced career breaks and job-sharing in the 1980s and, more recently, term-time working and work-sharing. The government White Paper *Changing Patterns in a Changing World* published in 2000 required Civil Service departments to offer work–life balance options to their staff members. Under the Modernising Government and Civil Service Reform Programmes, all government departments have been innovative with regard to opportunities for flexible working and in introducing initiatives such as a cross-department database and register, through which to introduce potential job-sharers to each other. Current action on work–life balance includes addressing the issue of individuals having to choose between a good work–life balance and progression in their career, and encouraging support for work–life balance practices at senior levels, where possible.

Further information
   www.cabinet-office.gov.uk
   www.civil-service.gov.uk
   www.careers.civil-service.gov.uk
   www.faststream.gov.uk

Related careers *local government*

Complementary and Alternative Medicine

Complementary and Alternative Medicine (CAM) is the generic name for a number of different healthcare techniques, which aim to treat the whole person. These may include acupuncture, osteopathy, chiropractic, herbal medicine, homoeopathy, naturopathy, psychotherapy, massage, reflexology and aromatherapy. This guide includes sections on osteopathy and chiropractic. Public uptake of and interest in these approaches to healthcare has increased rapidly in recent years and currently very few of these treatments are available via the NHS. A demand for more treatment is bound to lead to a demand for more practitioners.

Training Training opportunities are growing very rapidly: there are many courses at various levels. Courses range from those for qualified doctors only, through four-year degree courses, to those lasting only a few days, with, in many fields, little objective guidance as to the quality or otherwise of courses. However, following the completion of the regulatory process (see below) a review of the National Occupational Standards for major disciplines has been undertaken. This provides the basis for 'Safe Practice'. The stated ethos of the British Register of Complementary Practitioners (BRCP) is that of its members working towards 'Best Practice', which enables appropriate practice for the assessed clinical need of each individual. This Register includes different categories of recognition of levels of competence. To be admitted to the Register practitioners must meet standards agreed by the Registration Panel and specialist Advisors. In addition, the BRCP has created a Career Pathway from Therapist to Fellow, to enable members to continue to develop their specialist skills and to encourage personal growth and continuing professional development.

With the exception of osteopathy and chiropractic there is currently no statutory regulation for CAM. (The Government will consider in 2008 the statutory regulation of acupuncture, herbal medicine and traditional Chinese Medicine). Following the House of Lords Select Committee report, the CAM profession is moving towards voluntary regulation, with the aim of safeguarding the public who access treatment and of raising the profile of the profession.

The Department of Health has now asked the Prince of Wales Foundation for Integrated Health to set up the Natural Healthcare Council from April 2008. This new independent body will develop voluntary regulation for a range of currently unregulated professions. It will set minimum standards (in adherence to National Occupational Standards, see above). Practitioners can register with the Council if they have a recognized professional qualification, are insured and have signed a code of conduct. The Council can strike incompetent practitioners off the Register.

Further information

Institute for Complementary Medicine, PO Box 194, London SE16 7QZ.
www.i-c-m.org.uk

The Prince's Foundation for Integrated Health, 33–41 Dallington Street, London EC1V 0BB (Natural Healthcare Council information).
www.fih.org.uk

Construction

Entry qualifications *For degree* usually National Qualifications Framework Level 3 (A levels, BTEC National awards) or Scottish Credit and Qualifications Framework equivalent – to include maths/ science for some courses. For technician training usually National Qualifications Framework Level 2 (GCSEs A*–C, BTEC Diplomas and Certificates) or Scottish Credit and Qualifications Framework equivalent. *For craft training:* none specified.

The work The construction industry is one of Britain's largest, employing one in fourteen people. It is made up of companies ('contractors') of all sizes, from international giants employing thousands of skilled craft workers and professional staff, including architects, chartered builders, surveyors and chartered engineers, to small 'jobbing builders' employing one or two craftsmen/women and taking on additional people as required. Many small builders work partly on their own and partly as sub-contractors to larger firms, sometimes providing a specialist skill which the main contractor may not be able to offer. Large companies have their own design departments and execute large-scale projects such as housing estates, large office blocks, hospitals, etc. Smaller firms – and often large ones too – work to plans drawn up by the client's architect and may sub-contract work to specialist firms of plumbers, tilers, smaller general builders, etc. On large projects the client, or the client's representative, appoints a clerk of works.

The construction trade (particularly, but not only, firms concerned with large projects) is very dependent on the economic climate. Currently the industry is buoyant, boosted by the successful bid for the 2012 Olympics, and needs to recruit half a million people into all levels. There are still too few registering on construction degrees, so experienced managers are usually in demand.

Levels and organization of work are very much less well defined than, for example, in the engineering industry. In the construction industry it is possible to start at any level and work your way up the career ladder or to owning your own business. There is currently a drive to ensure that the construction workforce is 100 per cent qualified, whether at operative or management level. There is, therefore, increasing scope for people with specialist and management qualifications, but there will always be scope for craftsmen and craftswomen who are qualified, good at their job and also have organizing ability to build up their own business. Knowledge of basic crafts like bricklaying, carpentry and plumbing is useful even for managers; knowledge of new materials and technologies is essential in all parts of the industry.

Graduate Route – Design, Engineering, Finance, Management and Planning

Creative people, financial experts and legal professionals all play a part in getting the project off the ground. Once the construction work begins, construction managers, engineers and surveyors organize all the people working on site to ensure that what is built matches the original designs.

Some job titles in this area include: architect (see p. 87), architectural technologist (see p. 92), landscape architect (see p. 305), building services engineer (see p. 214), civil engineer (see p. 214), structural engineer (see p. 214), building surveyor (see p. 572), quantity surveyor (see p. 571), town planner (see p. 612) and construction manager.

Construction Manager

Unlike many of the other construction occupations, construction managers tend to manage people and work processes rather than having specialist knowledge of engineering or design. They must see that work is carried out in the right sequence with the right materials – which must be available at the right time – and at the right cost. They organize the labour force, so must understand the work of bricklayers, carpenters, etc. Depending on the size of the firm, work may include organizing the financial side (paying wages, paying for materials, etc.). Some construction management jobs are site-based (there may be a site office), some are office-based; nearly all jobs involve some site visits; and many jobs, at least for large firms, involve working away from home at times, occasionally overseas.

As well as the construction manager there are other jobs and specializations which may be needed on a construction site (which vary very much between firms):

Planner – at pre-tender stage is involved in the decision about how the tender can be adjusted. When tender is accepted, produces charts showing sequence of operations. Works closely with contract manager. In large companies will use a computer for this. Planners need experience of estimating, buying or contracts management.

Site engineer – in charge of technical side of an individual project. Sets out the positions and levels of the building to ensure it is placed in the correct position in accordance with the designs. Oversees all the work on site, including quality control (see also pp. 213–14).

Site manager/site agent (used to be called 'general foreman') – in charge of the contract. Ensures the designs and specifications are understood by the foremen/women; plans and coordinates materials and labour. Sees that building keeps to the plan and time schedule (see 'Technician' below and also p. 577).

Production controller – works on incentive schemes; measures work done by operatives as part of productivity control; takes part in construction planning at site level. Some specialize in work study and/or industrial relations.

Contract manager – oversees several projects. Moves from site to site ensuring that work is progressing according to plan. Plans movement of machines and labour to minimize delays and time-wasting. Has overall responsibility for completion of projects to correct standard at the right time.

Clerk of works – other construction management specialists work for the contractor; the clerk of works is employed by the client (or client's representative). May be employed full-time on a contract basis or on a self-employed private practice/consultant basis. Works from an office on site and is responsible for seeing that the work is carried out according to the specification. As the only person on site not working for the contractor the clerk of works can be rather isolated, so needs to be confident and self-sufficient. On large schemes duties may include supervising several other clerks of works specializing in, for example, heating and ventilating or electrical installation.

Building control officers – are responsible for checking sites to see that work complies with building regulations. In certain circumstances they may advise contractors on alternative methods of construction. Up until recently they worked only for local and other public authorities, but they can now work in the private sector.

Technician

Technicians support the work of engineers, architects, quantity surveyors, etc. The role of technicians overlaps with that of managers and, in fact, many managers start as technicians (see 'Training'). Technicians do many of the detailed costings, work out quantities and prepare drawings. On site they may be involved in surveying, measuring and detailed planning of the work. They are the people who make things happen. Some jobs that mainly exist at technician level are:

Buyers – select from the design drawings the materials and services needed; contact suppliers and sub-contractors to obtain the most competitive prices; ensure materials are available on time and within budget.

Estimators – calculate the likely cost of materials (from door handles to concrete), labour and plant equipment, and the time needed for the project when the firm is tendering for a contract. Also analyses costs of existing projects to provide a guide for future estimates.

Craft

There is a huge range of occupations that craftspeople work in, for example bricklaying, painting and decorating and roofing. Other more unusual or specialist trades are shopfitting, plant operating, demolition and steeplejacking (for a full range of information visit *www.bconstructive.co.uk*).

Training

- *Manager* – Either in-house by training first as a technician (see below) and then taking BTEC/SQA Higher National awards or other professional qualifications; or Foundation degree, three-year full-time or four-year sandwich degree in construction management, building studies, built environment. Most give full exemption from Chartered Institute of Building's Final examination. Entrants with degrees in non-related subjects can take the Chartered Institute of Building graduate diploma conversion course. Further professional training to higher level awards and chartered status is available.
- *Building control officer* – Qualify in building, surveying or relevant engineering subjects at BTEC/SQA or degree level.
- *Technician* – Either via a technician apprenticeship programme, including part-time study; or as a trainee with a company and day or block release (both may lead to BTEC/SQA National awards); or by studying full-time for BTEC National Diploma (or SQA equivalent). Courses can be in construction or building services engineering (see p. 213).
- *Craft* – Either via the CITB Construction Apprenticeship Scheme (in Scotland, the Scottish Building Apprenticeship and Training Council Scheme), leading to specialist N/SVQ awards; or full-time

college courses, usually two years, leading to N/SVQ or City & Guilds qualifications.

NOTE: The construction industry has introduced CSCS (Construction Skills Certificate Scheme) Cards at all levels, from craft or technical trainee to senior management. This proof of competency is an increasing requirement for employment across the whole industry and is mandatory on many construction sites. (For further information see *www.cscs.uk.com.*)

Personal attributes *For construction crafts* – some manual dexterity; an inquiring and logical mind; willingness to work both in a team or alone with minimal or no supervision; good attention to detail; a reasonably careful nature or at least awareness of dangers unless basic rules are observed. *For construction technicians and management* – ability to work with all kinds of people and help them work as a team; technical and practical aptitudes; good at organization; willing to work outdoors in all weathers; commercial sense.

Mature entry and career change Most apprenticeships have an age limit of 23. There may be training and retraining schemes for adults with or without related experience and/or qualifications, e.g. as surveying technician (see p. 577).

Work–life balance Depending on the length of absence, a career break may be difficult without retraining. So far nothing is known about returners (see p. 625). Part-time work may be possible if working for small contractor or for oneself.

Position of women There are almost 200,000 women employed across all occupations in the construction industry, making up 12 per cent of the workforce. Almost 50,000 of these women are in professional, technician or management roles. Women in the craft trades accounted for 1 per cent of the workforce in 2005. Women currently make up 3 per cent of sole traders in the construction industry.

Further information

CITB-Construction Skills, Bircham Newton, King's Lynn, Norfolk
PE31 6RH (for England and Wales); or 32 Inglis Green Road,
Edinburgh EH14 2ER (for Scotland).
www.citb.org.uk and *www.bconstructive.co.uk*

Scottish Building Apprenticeship & Training Council, Scottish Building, Carron Grange, Carrongrange Avenue, Stenhousemuir
FK5 3BQ.
www.sbatc.co.uk

Chartered Institute of Building, Englemere, King's Ride, Ascot, Berks
SL5 7TB.
www.ciob.org.uk

Institute of Clerks of Works, 28 Commerce Road, Lych Wood,
Peterborough PE2 6LR.
www.icwgb.org

Women and Manual Trades, 52–54 Featherstone Street, London
EC1Y 8RT.
www.wamt.org

Related careers *agriculture and horticulture – architecture – engineering: Civil Engineering – surveying*

Consumer Scientist

Entry qualifications None laid down; depends on 'Training' (see below).

The work Consumer scientists, formerly known as home economists, act as a link between producers of household goods and services and their consumers. This covers a wide range of jobs. Within industry they also act as a link between technologists who design and develop new products but may know little about consumer preferences and requirements, and marketing and general management staffs. So consumer science, at least at senior level, requires communication skills as well as an understanding of technological and of social trends.

Consumer scientists work in various settings: industry, social services, public relations, public utilities, consumer advice and protection, retailing, hotels and catering. Increasingly they are working in community care and in health and welfare fields. As food technology teachers they are involved in health and design and technology education. There is nothing clear-cut about the professional consumer scientist's work: people with related kinds of training may do the same, or similar, jobs; and once qualified may branch off into related fields such as catering, marketing, consumer and trade magazines, and books.

The majority work in manufacturing industry on development, quality control, promotion and marketing of products, appliances and equipment used, or services provided in the home. Before new or improved food and washing products, dishwashers, cookers, central heating systems, etc. are put into production, consumer scientists discuss details of design and performance with engineers, scientists, designers, marketing people. They put the customer's point of view; they test prototypes in the laboratory under 'ideal conditions', and they also use them in the same way as the customer might – being interrupted in their work and not always following the instructions as they should. For instance, they test whether a new type of butter-substitute creams easily, even if kept in the fridge too long and if clumsily handled; how a washing machine behaves if switches are turned on in the wrong order; or how easily a new cooker cleans when it is really dirty. As a result of laboratory and 'user' tests, alterations are often made before a product is put into production. In the retail industry, consumer scientists work in, or manage, laboratories testing food and textiles; some become management trainees and then go into retail management (see p. 500).

Some consumer scientists are involved with educating the public, for example in the need for, and methods of, energy conservation (e.g. home insulation and other fuel-saving devices). The work combines dealing with lay people who have much less technical knowledge, and with experts who have very much more.

Under the heading customer relations or marketing, work involves writing clear, concise user instructions for explanatory labels and leaflets which accompany fish-fingers, freezers, synthetic-fibre carpets, baby foods, etc., as well as dealing with inquiries and complaints correspondence.

Consumer scientists also identify demand for new products or changes in existing ones. This may involve fieldwork – interviewing potential customers in their homes (see p. 362) and thinking up innovations which could be marketed profitably.

In the media consumer scientists prepare features and programmes: they cook and cost elaborate as well as very cheap dishes, or arrange and cost domestic interiors which are then photographed and described, or demonstrated on TV. They also use their skills in assessing and reporting on equipment and on issues relevant to the consumer at home and at work.

In local authority social services departments consumer scientists advise low-income families on budgeting and general household management; and they may run the home-help service and advise on the efficient running of the authority's residential homes. Those who have studied a housing option may work in local authority or private housing management. There are also openings in health education.

In hospitals they become domestic administrators at top management level.

They may also work in the Trading Standards Department (see p. 616) in consumer services.

Experienced consumer scientists can work as freelance consultants: firms may wish to research and/or promote a new product and need a consumer scientist for a particular project rather than permanently. For example, they work as freelancers, writing explanatory leaflets, developing and checking recipes and equipment, etc. Some prepare food for magazine photography or TV commercials; some write books and articles for consumer magazines.

Job prospects are good, especially for graduates, although competition for top jobs (most are in cities) is keen. However, the combination of technical knowledge and understanding of family and consumer needs can be useful in a variety of jobs; consumer scientists willing to be adaptable can find work in a wide range of organizations. Greatest scope is in food and domestic appliance manufacturing, in retail, fuel and energy industries.

Training No particular qualification leads to any particular type of job. It is possible for anyone with basic approved training or related training (see p. 256) and the right experience and personality ultimately to do as well as a graduate. But the more thorough the training, the wider the scope of job.

Academic route: Degree course in food and consumer studies/science, food and consumer product management or combined subjects such as consumer science and marketing. Entry requirements are two A levels plus five GCSEs (grades A–C) or equivalent. Higher National Diploma courses are also offered; entry requirements are one A level and four GCSEs (grades A–C) or equivalent. There are a few two-year full-time or part-time Foundation degrees in related subjects. (See also p. 586.)

Work-based route: Apprenticeships in Food and Drink Manufacturing lead to a level 2 or 3 NVQ. There is also a range of NVQs/SVQs in related occupations.

Personal attributes Practicality and organizing ability; interest in consumer affairs, ability to understand both consumers' and manufacturers' points of view; ability to communicate easily both with more highly qualified professionals and with often poorly educated, possibly illiterate consumers; liking for people.

Mature entry and career change Mature entrants are welcome on all courses and may be given exemptions if they have relevant experience.

Work–life balance A career break should be no problem for people who keep up with developments. Good opportunities for part-time working; no reason why job-sharing should not be tried. Some part-time courses are being developed.

Further information
Improve Ltd – Food and Drink Sector Skills Council, Providence House, 2 Innovation Close, York YO10 5ZF.
www.improveltd.co.uk
Institute of Food Science and Technology, 5 Cambridge Court, 210 Shepherd's Bush Road, London W6 7NJ.
www.ifst.org

Related careers *dietetics – hospitality and catering – public relations – teaching – trading standards officer*

Dance

Teaching and performing are two separate careers. There are three kinds of performer in Western dance: *classical ballet; contemporary; musical theatre.*

PERFORMING

Entry qualifications No specific educational requirements, but because of the precarious nature of a career in dance, students are advised to take full advantage of their general education and obtain as high a standard of academic qualifications as possible. Many dance schools offer A levels and GCSEs, and A levels or equivalent are essential for students interested in the growing number of degree courses in dance performance or teaching.

Ballet Dancer

The work Ballet dancers lead dedicated lives. Their days are spent practising, rehearsing and performing, which may leave little spare time for activities outside dance.

They are usually attached to one particular company and may be on tour for much of the year.

Ballet companies have only a few vacancies each year so opportunities are limited. Once a member of the corps de ballet, a talented dancer has a chance of rising to solo parts and understudying bigger roles, but it is rare indeed to rise to principal dancer status. Even a successful dancer's professional life is short; only the very exceptional still get engagements in their middle thirties. There are some opportunities abroad – dance is a very international activity.

Training Serious training must have started by the age of 11 and certainly no later than 16 with a professional teacher who prepares pupils systematically for one of the officially recognized major dancing examinations: e.g. those of the Royal Academy of Dance, the Imperial Society of Teachers of Dancing, the British Ballet Organization or the British Theatre Dance Association (RAD, ISTD, BBO, BTDA).

The best training is given at professional schools which give general education for GCSE, or equivalent, and a thorough drama and dance training. It is advisable to apply only for courses accredited by the Council for Dance Education and Training.

There are part-time ballet schools all over the country but pupils from the few full-time vocational schools (some of which are attached to companies) probably stand a better chance of getting into a company when they finish.

Ballet training includes national and character dancing, mime, history, art and literature, and usually French (most technical terms are in that language).

Before accepting a pupil, good schools insist on a thorough orthopaedic examination, which is repeated at regular intervals throughout training.

NOTE: Since the ending of local authority discretionary grants, government-backed Dance and Drama awards have been introduced for vocational courses leading to recognized qualifications at leading private training providers. These provide funding towards tuition fees and means-tested help with other expenses. For further information see *www.direct.gov.uk/danceanddrama*. Dance and drama students at institutions affiliated to the Conservatoire for Dance and Drama are eligible for the same financial support as other HE students.

Personal attributes Suitable physique, including strong back and feet; intelligence; intuition; emotional depth; musical talent; the ability to take criticism without resentment; a strong constitution; complete dedication; a distinct personality.

Contemporary Dancer

The work The work and lifestyle of the contemporary dancer is very like that of the ballet dancer, requiring the same degree of dedication. As contemporary dance groups are structured differently from classical ballet companies and are often much smaller, there is not the same hierarchy and route to principal dancer.

Training This is quite different from that of classical ballet, although contemporary dancers may have started with classical training as children and may continue to take classical dance classes occasionally (as classical dancers may take contemporary classes). Their kind of dance makes different aesthetic and physical demands and requires specialized training. Students frequently take a foundation course before starting their vocational training, which should begin by age 18. Most contemporary dance courses are degrees (for example the degree in Contemporary Dance run by the London Contemporary Dance School).

Personal attributes Similar to those of a ballet dancer; however, physical requirements are more flexible as contemporary dance aims to be inclusive of all body shapes and sizes.

Musical Theatre Dancer

The work Modern stage dancers perform in musicals, pantomime, cabaret, on TV, and in light entertainment generally. They are not usually attached to a company, but appear in individual shows. As well as learning dances, they often have to learn scripts and songs. They are more likely to be on short-term contracts and to have longer periods out of work than other dancers. Even when not working, they have to keep up their practice, which means paying for private classes at a dance centre.

For the fully trained first-rate dancer prospects are fair. But like other entertainers, a dancer must be prepared for months of 'resting', meanwhile earning a living in some other way yet being available to attend auditions. If lucky, they may get a long run in the West End, a tour or a television series.

Training Three years full-time, preferably. Most start vocational training at 16. Over 80 per cent of dancers currently employed in the West End have been through accredited vocational dance courses. At auditions, dancers must show potential; and do not rely on examination passes (they may be expected to have reached Elementary). The modern stage dancer should also have some training in voice production, drama and singing.

Personal attributes A strong stage appearance and presence; resilience; versatility; enterprise in tracking down jobs; sense of rhythm.

TEACHING

Entry qualifications To teach dance in state primary and secondary schools (i.e. not dance schools) Qualified Teacher Status is required: either a degree leading to QTS or a degree in dance or in performing arts (titles and content vary) followed by a Postgraduate Certificate in Education (see p. 586). Entry requirements may be waived for mature entrants.

The work A dancing teacher may teach both children and adults, or may specialize in teaching one or the other. Adults are taught in private schools/classes or in local authority adult education centres. Children are taught in ordinary schools; dancing schools; specialized professional schools.

In ordinary schools full-time or visiting part-time teachers teach dance to GCSE, mainly to improve children's poise and deportment.

Dancing schools are intended for children who do not have dancing lessons at school. They may be run by a teacher who hires a hall for the purpose, or they may be in a dancing school which caters for both children and adults.

Children are usually prepared for recognized dancing examinations (see 'Ballet Dancer' 'Training', p. 181). This ensures that children are being properly taught even though they do not intend to become professionals.

In professional schools dancing is an essential part of the curriculum in what is generally an arts-orientated private school; the teacher deals with especially talented children who hope to become professional dancers.

Job prospects are good for teaching adults and children. Royal Academy of Dance and Imperial Society of Teachers of Dancing examiners often go abroad to organize, teach and examine.

Training Applicants to degrees in dance should check prospectuses very carefully before choosing a course, as the 'dance component' varies from a few hours to a substantial proportion.

The dance teaching societies (e.g. ISTD and RAD) have their own entrance requirements for student teachers and need to be contacted individually. Students can teach only the syllabus they have been trained in, and usually work in private schools and classes. Degree courses are available for the ISTD and RAD syllabuses. A fast-growing area, in which there are some specialized teaching courses, is that of community dance. The emphasis is frequently on contemporary or ethnic dance.

Other courses A number of vocational schools now offer three-year degree courses. Universities and colleges around the country also offer BA Honours courses which include dance but there is considerable variation in the balance between academic study and practical work.

Personal attributes The ability to explain and demonstrate steps and movements; a fine sense of rhythm and some proficiency at the piano;

a liking for people of all ages; imagination; endless tact and patience; good appearance; graceful movements. (See also p. 586)

Teaching Keep Fit and Exercise

This area has expanded rapidly in the last few years. Movement classes have mushroomed, changing their style frequently in order to follow the latest (often imported) fashion. Many people have cashed in on the dance/exercise craze without a proper knowledge of how the body works and what kind of movement is suitable for each type of student. The most suitable basic training for teachers in this area is: a proper dance course; or physical education teacher training; or a two-year part-time course organized by the Keep Fit Association and run in conjunction with local education authorities; or courses leading to the OCR Certificate in Exercise & Fitness (Exercise to Music).

CHOREOGRAPHY

The work The dancer who has exceptional imaginative powers and the ability to interpret music in terms of dancing may ultimately do choreography. This is dance composition: the grouping of dancers and sequence of dances which make up the entire ballet. In musical theatre, a choreographer may direct within a wide range from the production numbers on TV which involve scores of dancers, to the unexacting dances of a seaside concert party.

Choreography is not a career for which a novice can be trained unless there is a noticeable talent. Years of experience of classical or contemporary dance and a musical training are needed (see p. 387). However, some dance courses now include choreography or offer it as an option.

Work–life balance Many dancers take up teaching after a break from performing. There are good opportunities to teach part-time.

Further information

Council for Dance Education and Training, Old Brewer's Yard, 17–19 Neal Street, London WC2H 9UY.
www.cdet.org.uk

Imperial Society of Teachers of Dancing, 22–26 Paul Street, London EC2A 4QE.
www.istd.org

British Ballet Organization, Woolborough House, 39 Lonsdale Road, Barnes, London SW13 9JP.
www.bbo.org.uk

British Theatre Dance Association, The International Arts Centre, Garden Street, Leicester LE1 3UA.
www.btda.org.uk

Keep Fit Association, 1 Grove House, Foundry Lane, Horsham, West Sussex. RH13 5PL.
www.keepfit.org.uk

Royal Academy of Dance, 36 Battersea Square, London SW11 3RA.
www.rad.org.uk

Related careers *drama – music – teaching*

Dentistry

DENTAL SURGEON

Entry qualifications Entry to training at National Qualifications Framework Level 3 (A levels, BTEC National awards) or Scottish Credit and Qualifications Framework equivalent – usually including at least two sciences – biology and chemistry are preferred. (See 'Training' for arts A level candidates and graduates.)

Registration with the General Dental Council.

The work Dentists (or dental surgeons) look after oral health by offering both preventive and restorative treatment. In addition to fillings and repairing teeth, dentists also extract teeth and design and fit artificial dentures. Some also carry out surgical operations on the jaw, while others specialize in orthodontics, which is the improvement of irregular teeth, mainly in children. The preventive aspects of dentistry are very important, especially encouraging good oral health care at home. Prospects are good and qualifications are accepted in the EU.

General Practice

The majority of dentists work in general practice. Most general practitioners are self-employed, often offering a combination of NHS and private treatment.

Dentists in general practice have the best financial prospects and the greatest independence. They may be in a partnership, or in practice on their own, working in their own premises with their own equipment and employing their own dental nurses (see p. 192).

It is usual to begin as an assistant or associate in a practice, perhaps with a view to becoming a partner later. An associate takes on his or her own patients and rents practice space from the practice owner.

Salaried Primary Dental Care Service (formerly Community Dental Service)

The Salaried Primary Dental Care Service (SPDCS) works within the community, largely providing care to those who may find it difficult to get treatment in general practice, such as those with disabilities. Those working within the SPDCS are also responsible for things like school dental checks. Unlike general practitioners, they are employed by the local NHS primary care trust.

Hospital and University Dental Practice

Dentists working in a hospital environment are usually specialists in a particular field and will require further training following their dental undergraduate degree. For those who go on to practise surgery, their work will include reconstructive surgery, for example for those involved in car accidents or whose mouth has been affected by disease or illness such as cancer. A large part of their work involves extractions under general anaesthetic.

Another option for dental graduates is dental teaching or research. Teaching posts are generally based in dental schools (attached to universities) and hospitals. Those going into dental research can look forward to working on the development of new treatments as well as looking at the causes of dental disease.

Training Five-year course (approved by the General Dental Council) at dental schools attached to universities. Some dental courses may be preceded by a one-year preliminary science course for students without the appropriate A levels (students with A level physics, chemistry, biology, zoology or maths are exempt from it), although not all dental schools offer this option.

Courses include anatomy, physiology, biochemistry, pathology, behavioural sciences and dental materials science, as well as practical training in all aspects of dental work.

Four-year accelerated courses are available at a few dental schools for graduates who have a good degree with sufficient elements of biology and chemistry.

Most dental schools require applicants to take a pre-admission test such as the UK Clinical Aptitude Test (UKCAT).

Before they can practise, dentists are required to register with the General Dental Council.

A year's vocational training in a practice under the supervision of an experienced dentist is required for new graduates who want to work in the NHS. Hospital dentists will need several further years of training in their chosen specialty.

Personal attributes Manual dexterity; a methodical and scientific approach; good personal skills; good health. Left-handedness is not a disadvantage.

Dentist in general practice especially: The ability to establish easy relationships quickly with people, and give confidence to the nervous (the growth of the practice may depend almost entirely on the patients' personal recommendations); organizing ability.

Community dental surgeon especially: The ability to get on with children.

Hospital dentist especially: The ability to work well as a member of a team.

Further information

General Dental Council, 37 Wimpole Street, London W1G 8DQ.
www.gdc-uk.org
The British Dental Association, 64 Wimpole Street, London W1G 8YS.
www.bda.org
NHS Careers, PO Box 2311, Bristol BS2 2ZX.
www.nhscareers.nhs.uk

Related careers *medicine*

OTHER DENTAL CARE PROFESSIONALS

For people interested in dentistry but without the necessary qualifications for dental training, there are four careers: *dental therapist, dental hygienist, dental nurse* and *dental technician/technologist*. Following recent legislation all dental care professionals will in future have to be registered with the General Dental Council.

Dental Therapist

Entry qualifications Entry requirements for approved courses vary but are normally at National Qualifications Framework Level 3 (A levels, BTEC National awards) or Scottish Credit and Qualifications Framework equivalent. A recognized dental nursing qualification may be accepted. Experience of working as a dental nurse is helpful.

The work Dental therapists do 'operative work'; they work in hospitals and community dental services, but also, increasingly, in general dental practice. They work under the direction of a dentist who prescribes the treatment to be given; this includes simple fillings, extraction of deciduous teeth, cleaning, scaling and polishing teeth and giving guidance on general dental care. Dental therapists always work under the direction and prescription of a registered dentist. Many of the patients are very young – in welfare clinics under 5, in school clinics mostly under 11. In the past dental therapists worked in hospitals and community dental services but since July 2002 they have been able to work in all areas of dentistry including general practice. There are now more training schools delivering courses, therefore it has become easier to access training.

Training 27-month full-time diploma course approved by the General Dental Council. Most dental therapy and dental hygiene courses are combined, giving a dual qualification.

BSc in Oral Health Science – three-year full-time course.

The NHS provides financial support to eligible students on approved training courses in dental hygiene and dental therapy.

Personal attributes Considerable manual dexterity; conscientiousness; some interest in science; good teamwork and communication skills.

Further information
British Society of Dental Hygiene and Therapy (see p. 192).
www.bsdht.org.uk

Dental Hygienist

Entry qualifications Entry to training is usually at National Qualifications Framework Level 3 (A levels, BTEC National awards) or Scottish Credit and Qualifications Framework equivalent. A recognized dental nursing qualification may be accepted.

The work Dental hygienists also do 'operative work'. They do scaling and polishing under the direction of dentists, but do not do any fillings, etc. An important aspect of the work is preventive dentistry.

They work with adults as well as with children, in general practice as well as in community health clinics and hospitals.

Dental therapists and hygienists may, after gaining experience, become practice managers, take on teaching roles, or move on to work as orthodontic therapists.

Training Two-year full-time diploma course approved by the General Dental Council. Most training schools now offer integrated courses in dental therapy and dental hygiene giving a joint qualification.

A BSc in Oral Health Science is available.

The NHS provides financial support to eligible students on approved training courses in dental hygiene and dental therapy.

Personal attributes As for therapists, plus the ability to express oneself lucidly.

Further information

The British Society of Dental Hygiene and Therapy, 3 Kestrel Court, Waterwells Business Park, Waterwells Drive, Quedgley, Gloucester GL2 2AT.
www.bsdht.org.uk
NHS Careers, PO Box 2311, Bristol BS2 2ZX.
www.nhscareers.nhs.uk

Dental Nurse

Entry qualifications None laid down, but most hospital training schools demand some GCSE passes or equivalent, which should include English language and a science. None required for admission to the examination for the National Certificate of the Examining Board for Dental Nurses.

The work Dental nurses support the dentist during dental procedures, e.g.: passing instruments, mixing materials. Dental Nurses are responsible for the preparation of the environment and maintaining a sterilized working area and instruments. Some dental nurses carry out reception duties including making appointments.

Dental nurses work wherever dentists work, i.e. in general practice, in community dental clinics and in hospitals.

Training In-house, in addition to attending approved college courses, leading to an approved qualification. To qualify for access to the General Dental Council register, nurses should hold either the National Examining Board for Dental Nurses National Certificate plus two years' experience; or the N/SVQ level 3 in Oral Health Care. Registration is mandatory from 31 July 2008.

Personal attributes Good communication skills; some manual dexterity; a smart appearance.

Further information

British Association of Dental Nurses, PO Box 4, Room 200, Hillhouse
International Business Centre, Thornton-Cleveleys FY5 4QB.
www.badn.org.uk
NHS Careers, PO Box 2311, Bristol BS2 2ZX.
www.nhscareers.nhs.uk

Dental Technician/Technologist

Entry qualifications For BTEC National Diploma: four GCSEs (A–C)
or equivalent, including maths and a science. For SQA Higher
National Certificate in Dental Technology: completion of National
Certificate, Accreditation of Prior Learning, and interview.

The work Dental technologists construct and repair dentures, crowns
and other orthodontic appliances. They work either in commercial
dental laboratories where work for individual dentists is carried out,
or in hospital dental laboratories. It is highly skilled work. From July
2008, all dental technicians must be on the GDC register. Registration
from that time is on the basis of an approved qualification only.

Training Either a trainee post with day release for part-time study or
full-time study leading to the degree in Dental Technology.

Personal attributes Great manual dexterity; patience; accuracy.

Further information

General Dental Council, 37 Wimpole Street, London W1G 8DQ.
www.gdc-uk.org
The Dental Technologists Association, Waterwells Drive, Waterwells
Business Park, Gloucester GL2 2AT.
www.dta-uk.org
NHS Careers
www.nhscareers.nhs.uk

Mature entry and career change (general) *For dentists*: Dental schools judge each application on its merits. All applicants need to provide evidence that they have the ability to cope with the demands of the course as well as commitment to a career in dentistry. *For dental care professionals*: All applicants are considered on an individual basis.

Work–life balance There are good opportunities for part-time employment. Those working in the NHS have access to the flexible working practices – part-time, job-sharing, term-time working, etc. – being introduced under the Improving Working Lives standard. There are refresher courses for dentists, dental therapists and dental hygienists who have taken a career break. Continuing professional development is mandatory for dentists and dental care professionals.

Related careers *medicine – nursing – science*

Dietetics

Entry qualifications Entry to training is usually at National Qualifications Framework Level 3 (A levels, BTEC National awards) or Scottish Credit and Qualifications Framework equivalent. Working in the NHS requires registration with the Health Professions Council (HPC).

The work The dietitian's special skill is to translate the science of nutrition into understandable and practical information about food and health. Career opportunities have greatly diversified as healthy eating habits become increasingly recognized as a vital part of preventing disease and promoting good health.

Dietitians are concerned with food and health in its widest sense and their work is preventive and therapeutic. They have to know about food production and processing; social, economic and psychological factors that influence food choice; the digestion, absorption and metabolism of food, its effect on nutritional well-being; how to treat disease and prevent nutrition-related problems.

Dietitians work in many different settings. Currently about half of the profession are employed in the National Health Service, where they work in hospitals or in the community as 'hands-on' dietitians or as managers.

Hospital dietitians advise people who need special diets as part of their medical treatment, e.g. a carefully controlled diet for kidney disease or an appropriately formulated liquid feed which is passed through a tube. With other health professionals they work as part of a clinical team. They also help in developing food policies and liaise with the catering services to ensure that healthy food is available for both patients and staff, and special dietary needs are met. Many hospital dietitians eventually specialize, e.g. in the treatment of children, diabetes or eating disorders. Whatever the reason for referral, the dietitian works with the patient (or carer) to plan changes to their eating patterns. As well as treating the medical condition, diets must take into account usual food habits, cultural customs and social and financial position in a non-discriminatory way. The dietitian must provide support and encouragement through sometimes difficult times of adjustment.

Community dietitians' work is more about health education, although many run clinics in doctors' surgeries and health centres for people needing specialist dietary advice. As there are so few dietitians, an important part of their job is to work closely with primary health care teams. This includes keeping nurses, doctors, health visitors and other health professionals up to date on the latest food issues so that they in turn can communicate important health messages as widely as possible. Dietitians also work with the media and speak to groups and societies to ensure that accurate nutrition information is available to their local communities.

Another important aspect of community work is working in partnership with local people to tackle food issues that they are concerned about, e.g. cooking skills, access to affordable, healthy food. Community dietitians may also work with schools, social services, agencies involved with the under-5s, workplaces, services for elderly people and local authorities to help promote positive, enjoyable changes in food choice. This work may involve: helping to develop and implement food policies; developing educational resources; nutrition education for staff or carers; liaison with catering services; and individual advice for people with special dietary needs, e.g. people with chewing or swallowing difficulties.

Outside the NHS dietitians work in rapidly expanding areas such as:

- *education,* for example as educators in centres of higher and further education, for other health care workers such as doctors and community nurses and for the media.

- *research,* for example into evaluating and improving dietetic treatment and developing the science of nutrition and dietetics.
- *industry,* for example with trade associations, food retailers, food manufacturers, catering organizations, public relations and marketing companies – in a consultancy role, giving advice on nutrition to businesses and their customers.
- *freelance dietetics,* for example in private practice, sports nutrition and the media.

Experienced dietitians are in demand, but getting that first job may mean moving to another part of the country. There are some openings in the developing countries and in the EU (for dietitians who speak the relevant languages). British qualifications are not automatically recognized in the USA, Canada and Australia, but reciprocity of recognition may be obtained in the future.

Training Registration with the Health Professions Council is required for a dietitian wishing to work in the UK. Courses must be approved by the British Dietetic Association and recognized by the HPC:

- A recognized four-year degree course. The syllabus includes: physiology; biochemistry; microbiology; nutrition and food science; diet therapy; health education; catering; psychology and sociology.
- Graduates with degrees which include an acceptable level of human physiology and biochemistry may take a recognized two-year postgraduate diploma.

All courses include a period of approved practical clinical training in hospital and community settings.

Personal attributes An interest in science, people and food; enjoyment of communicating with people from all walks of life; an ability to explain complex things in a simple manner; a positive and motivating attitude and an understanding, non-discriminatory approach; confident spoken and written communication skills; patience and a sense of humour.

Dietetics

Mature entry and career change Mature students are welcome on degree courses.

Work–life balance A career break should present no problem. The British Dietetic Association offers an open/flexible-learning programme for returners to the profession. Individual NHS primary care trusts may offer return-to-practice opportunities.

Opportunities for part-time work and job-sharing at all levels of seniority. At present there are no part-time training opportunities.

Further information

The British Dietetic Association, 5th Floor, Charles House, 148/9 Great Charles Street, Queensway, Birmingham B3 3HT. *www.bda.uk.com*

NHS Careers, PO Box 2311, Bristol BS2 2ZX. *www.nhscareers.nhs.uk*

Related careers *hospittality and catering – consumer scientist – medicine – nutritionist – science: Biochemist; Chemist; food science and technology*

Drama

ACTING

Entry qualifications No rigid requirements (see 'Training', below).

The work Acting is an unpredictable and highly competitive career, and most people who join and remain in it are passionate about their vocation. The work is varied, and some actors specialize in a particular area, such as musical theatre or theatre in education. Others work across the board, experiencing diverse environments and conditions. Constant change, new artistic partners and challenges are some of the positive aspects of acting. It involves working physically as well as mentally, collaborating closely with others and mastering adrenalin. On the negative side, most actors go through regular periods of unemployment, have additional jobs and spend a lot of time travelling. It can be hard to stay disciplined and positive, and casting breaks can depend as much on chance as on ability.

Though no formal training is necessary to practise, most actors take full-time vocational courses. Drama school training hones acting talent, but perhaps more importantly, it is the best way to equip oneself physically and emotionally for the challenges of this career. The final showcase is an opportunity to be seen and potentially signed by agents, which is crucial for professional advancement. It is therefore important to pick a school that is well respected by the industry.

Television

Auditions for television are arranged through agents, and usually involve being filmed reading the script. Screen work requires specific skills, with an emphasis on stillness and subtle changes of expression. Each scene is split into camera shots, which are recorded repeatedly in 'takes'. Actors may have to film scenes out of story order, requiring some discipline. In general, each scene is rehearsed on set, and recorded immediately. It is important to maintain concentration as a great deal of time can be spent waiting. Days are often long and very full, particularly on programmes with a high production rate, such as soap operas. Actors have little control over the finished product as they can't predict what shots will be used. Television usually pays better than theatre work and exposes the actor to a wider audience.

Theatre

As with all acting, theatre is competitive. Parts are cast by auditions, and actors may hear about them through agents, adverts in publications like *The Stage* or online, or by word of mouth. Work in theatre varies according to the scale of the production. West End theatres often produce musicals, usually requiring highly trained performers in musical theatre. Resident companies doing repertory theatre are now rare, though some theatres still hire actors for several productions over a season. In the main, actors are hired for a specific show, whether in one theatre or on a tour. This may be a 'Number 1' tour, going to large-scale regional venues, or a village hall tour, with countless gradations in between. Fringe theatre takes place in pubs and small venues, often on a profit-share basis or for little or no fee.

The length of the tour and the rehearsal period vary depending on the budget, as do conditions and pay. Some tours require actors to take care of the set and costumes themselves. The company usually splits up and stays in several local 'digs', or basic accommodation. It is normal to perform six evening shows and two matinees per week.

Tours require discipline and energy, and can be a bonding experience for the company.

Commercials

Commercials tend to be lucrative and require a short period of work. However, casting is heavily dependent on whether an actor's look is marketable, and many performers are auditioned for each role. Well-known actors may also be paid to put their name to a brand and appear in its advertisements.

'Voice-overs' refer to the use of an actor's voice without their image. While many actors earn an income in this way, a small number of performers work exclusively as voice-over artists. This demands an innately interesting voice and time to build up a reputation and client base.

Films

Feature film work is rare for most actors, though many build up experience in short films. Depending on the budget, film can afford more time than television to explore, rehearse and experiment. The atmosphere of the set and style of camera work varies a great deal according to the director. Again, however, actors have scant control and may find themselves substantially cut in the final edit.

Entry requirements and training Drama schools are not rigid on academic requirements for entry. Acceptance at good drama schools depends on audition where talent is the primary criterion. At some schools, candidates considered most suitable will have qualifications at National Qualifications Framework Level 3 (A levels, BTEC National awards) or Scottish Credit and Qualifications Framework equivalent. A BTEC National Diploma in Performing Arts (Acting) is equivalent to three GCE A levels. It is important to contact individual schools as entry requirements vary.

Research indicates that the chances of success are best for students who have attended one of the established schools, whose acting courses are accredited by the National Council for Drama Training. Most of the schools with accredited courses also belong to the Conference of Drama Schools. Entry to good schools, however, is very competitive.

The majority of accredited courses are now in the maintained sector, with courses leading to a degree qualification. Students who are studying for their first degree and are applying for these courses should be eligible for a student loan and, if they meet the criterion, maintenance grants.

The government's Dance and Drama Awards (DaDA) were introduced in 1999 to provide help with fees and maintenance for students wishing to attend vocational courses in dance, drama and stage management at independent dance and drama schools (see *www. direct.gov.uk/danceanddrama*). Vocational drama courses last one to three years. Schools' curricula and ethos vary considerably but all accredited courses are seen to prepare the student for professional acting work upon graduation. Students unlikely to succeed are asked to leave, or leave of their own accord before the end of the course. Students who have already got a degree, or have substantial experience in acting, may take a one-year or two-year postgraduate course.

Academic drama courses at university normally focus on literary criticism, history and literature of the theatre, rather than vocational acting training.

Personal attributes Good health; distinctive features, but not necessarily beauty; the ability to learn lines quickly; a good memory; great self-confidence; imagination and sensitivity to interpret any part; resilience, to ignore or benefit from the constant and public criticism from teachers, producers, directors, colleagues and the critics; a good constitution; a sense of rhythm (preferably an aptitude for dancing and singing); outstanding acting talent; grim determination.

Mature entry and career change As already mentioned, there is stiff competition for drama school places. Increasingly drama schools are accepting more mature applicants, recognizing the value of their life experience, but most students commence their training aged between 18 and 25.

Work–life balance A career break is possible, providing contacts are kept up. The work is sporadic by its very nature and performers are strongly advised to have a second string to their bow. Most actors will find it necessary to find other employment at times, entailing a tricky balance between committing to the profession and earning a living.

DRAMA THERAPY

Drama therapy aims to use various dramatic techniques, including mime and improvisation, to provide therapeutic experiences for both adults and children, individually or in groups. It is practised either by specialist drama therapists or as part of a wider professional role.

Training A postgraduate training course in Drama Therapy leading to a qualification approved by the Health Professions Council, accredited by the British Association of Dramatherapists (BADth) and recognized by the Department of Health. Entry criteria are a first degree in drama or a psychological health-related subject or appropriate professional qualification, one year's full-time experience working with people with specific needs, experience of practical drama work and good interpersonal skills.

STAGE MANAGEMENT

The work Stage managers and their teams are responsible for implementing the director's instructions during rehearsals. This usually includes recording actors' moves and other stage directions in the prompt book; collecting props, sound effects, etc., for the director's approval; relaying the director's requirements to the scenic, costume and lighting departments; ensuring that the actors are in the right place at the right time for rehearsals, costume fittings, etc. During the run of the play stage managers are in charge of everything on stage and backstage, and are responsible for the health and safety of the company. Stage managers may also conduct understudy rehearsals. They often work very long hours. Stage managers are engaged by theatrical managements for one particular production, for a season, or occasionally on a more permanent basis.

There is a shortage of trained and experienced stage managers. Whilst in the past most gained their skills through experience, emphasis is now placed on professional qualifications. Some directors start as stage managers.

Training Training usually comprises a full-time stage management course at drama school for two to three years. Admission to the courses is by interview and only those who are interested in stage management in itself, or as preparation for work as a producer or director, are accepted. As with acting, those who have attended courses accredited by the National Council for Drama Training have the best prospects.

The subjects studied include history of drama and theatrical presentation; literature; the elements of period styles; stage management organization and routine; play study; carpentry; stage lighting; voice; movement; make-up.

Stage management training does not lead immediately to work in television and films, but, if supplemented with experience, it may do so.

Personal attributes Organizing ability; natural authority and tact; a practical approach; ability to deal with emergencies from prop-making to mending electrical equipment; calmness during crises; interest in the literary and technical aspects of theatrical production; the ability to speak well – both lucidly and concisely; visual imagination.

Mature entry and career change Should be fair opportunities for people with amateur dramatic experience or supervisory experience in other fields; maturity helps in a job which involves organizing others.

Work–life balance Live theatre requires stage management to work unsocial hours and many experienced staff look for alternative contracts – particularly when planning a family. Event management, festivals, trade shows and education/training providers can provide well-paid alternatives to the eight shows a week treadmill. A career break should be no problem if good experience is attained before the break.

Work may be sporadic rather than part-time. Long-term contracts are usually only offered by the major subsidized theatre companies, e.g. the Royal Shakespeare Company, National Theatre and larger regional repertory theatres.

Further information

National Council for Drama Training, 1–7 Woburn Walk, London WC1H 0JJ.
www.ncdt.co.uk
Conference of Drama Schools, PO Box 34252, London NW5 1XJ (publish *The CDS Guide to Professional Training in Drama and Technical Theatre*, single copies available free to UK addresses from French's Theatre Bookshop, 52 Fitzroy Street, London W1T 5JR, email *theatre@samuelfrench-london.co.uk* or downloadable from Conference of Drama Schools website).
www.drama.ac.uk
The British Association of Dramatherapists, Waverley, Battledown Approach, Cheltenham, Gloucestershire GL52 6RE.
www.badth.org.uk
Local theatre; drama schools

Related careers *leisure/recreation management – speech and language therapists – television, film and radio*

Driving Instructor and Examiner

Driving Instructor

Entry qualifications Minimum age 21. Four years' full (not provisional) car driving licence without disqualification. Registration as an Approved Driving Instructor (ADI).

The work The majority of instructors work on their own. This is more lucrative, but also more precarious, than working for one of the big driving schools. Hours are irregular and long: far more pupils want lessons at lunch time, after work or at weekends than during normal working hours. Most instructors teach between six and twelve pupils a day.

Being a good driver is not the only important aspect of instructing: instructors must like teaching and have the natural ability to do so; they must be able to put themselves into the position of a nervous, possibly not very talented, learner. They usually drive all day and every day through the same streets, which can be dull. The attractions of the work are, largely, being one's own boss; developing learners' road sense and driving technique; talking, during lessons, to a variety of people.

Business depends on area: it is essential, before investing in a dual-control car, to find out whether or not the area is already saturated with instructors.

Personal attributes Organizing ability; business acumen; ability to get on with all types of people and to put them at their ease; complete unflappability and fearlessness; some mechanical aptitude; teaching talent; endless patience; ability to criticize tactfully and explain lucidly.

Training Instructors must pass the Driving Standards Agency's three-part examination: a computer-based theory test (Part 1), a practical driving test (Part 2) and a test of instructing ability (Part 3). Parts 2 and 3 must be completed within two years of passing Part 1. Only three attempts at each of these two parts are permitted. The syllabus for Part 1 includes road procedure, traffic signs and signals, car control, pedestrians, mechanical knowledge, driving test, disabilities, law, publications, instructional techniques and also includes a hazard perception test. Part 2 is a stringent test at advanced level. In Part 3 the examiner plays the part first of a new learner and then of a pupil at about test standard. After passing Part 2, trainees are allowed to hold a six-month training licence and charge for instruction, but they must pass Part 3 before being registered as an Approved Driving Instructor.

Examiners

Driving Examiner
Entry qualifications and training A full, clean and unrestricted licence and at least four years' driving experience. Selection includes a theory and hazard perception test, a special driving test and a formal interview. The interview focuses on four key competencies: judgement and decision-making; customer service orientation; self-awareness; and change. Training begins with a four-week intensive residential course which covers some driving but focuses on learning the assessment and interpersonal skills required. On passing the course, examiners are allocated to a training centre to begin a nine-month probation period.

Traffic Examiner
Entry qualifications and training None specified but relevant technical qualifications and experience looked for. Initial training takes

place over a nine-month period and is based in the classroom and on practicals.

Vehicle Examiner

Entry qualifications and training City & Guilds Motor Vehicle Technicians Part 2 or BTEC/SQA equivalent and at least four years' experience in repair, maintenance or inspections of motor vehicles. Initial training follows a similar pattern to traffic examiner (see above).

The work *Driving examiners* are civil servants. They work as members of a team under a senior examiner, attached to one of over 400 test centres throughout the country. They test learner drivers of cars and other vehicles to ensure that candidates are competent to drive without endangering other road-users and that they drive with due consideration for other drivers and pedestrians. To do this the examiner takes drivers over an approved route and asks them to carry out various exercises. While doing this the examiner must take notes without distracting the driver's concentration and must make a fair assessment. The work is highly concentrated and, for work as responsible as this, can be fairly repetitive.

Traffic examiners, also civil servants, investigate, by observation on the road, by enquiry of operators and by examination of drivers' records, whether laws concerning operation of vehicles (such as the hours a driver may be in charge of a vehicle without a rest period) are being observed. Traffic examiners do not have to examine vehicles' mechanical conditions.

Vehicle examiners are employed by the Vehicle and Operator Services Agency to carry out a variety of mechanical testing and inspection tasks, including checking of HGVs; supervising the tachograph scheme; checking operators' maintenance arrangements; inspecting vehicles and preparing reports following road accidents. They may appear in court as expert witnesses.

Personal attributes Air of authority; friendliness; tact; ability to concentrate constantly; unflappability.

Mature entry and career change Most instructors and examiners have had some other job before; maturity is an asset.

Work–life balance *Instructor:* It is possible to have a small number of pupils, but it is never possible to work during school-hours only. Summer months are the busiest time. A career break might mean having to start up again and continued driving would be essential.

Examiner: The Civil Service is encouraging the introduction of flexible working in all departments. The DSA particularly welcomes driving examiners who are willing to work to a flexible pattern as driving tests take place on Saturdays and in the evening during the summer months and demand for driving tests is variable. Driving examiners can opt to work less than full-time, in which case their area office will contact them with an offer of work when available.

Further information
(*Driving instructors and driving examiners*) Driving Standards Agency, Stanley House, 56 Talbot Street, Nottingham NG1 5GU.
   www.transportoffice.gov.uk and www.dsa.gov.uk
(*Traffic and vehicle examiners*) Vehicle and Operator Services Agency, Berkeley House, Croydon Street, Bristol BS5 0DA.
   www.vosa.gov.uk

Related careers *teaching*

Economics

Entry qualifications *Degree in economics*: National Qualifications Framework Level 3 (A levels, BTEC National awards) or Scottish Credit and Qualifications Framework equivalent – A level or equivalent maths or statistics preferred, but not essential, for all courses.

The work Economics is concerned with the organization, utilization and distribution of productive and financial resources, nationally and internationally. This includes the study of political, industrial and social relationships and interactions.

Economics comes under the Social Sciences umbrella (but is not a 'science' in the same sense as physics or chemistry). Economic theories are 'applicable' or 'inapplicable' rather than 'correct' or 'incorrect'. Hence the variety of 'schools' of economists (e.g. Keynesian, monetarist), each with different answers to the same economic problems. Economics therefore involves making judgements, choosing to adhere to one set of principles rather than another.

Economists work in a wide variety of settings – in urban and regional planning, in industry, commerce, the City, the Civil Service (the largest employer), in financial and industrial journalism, as organizers or researchers in trade unions and in management consultancies and overseas in development programmes. They try to identify the causes of problems like inflation or traffic congestion and suggest courses of action which might solve or ease the problem. Economists research, analyse and interpret data and use mathematical modelling to identify trends and predict consequences of actions. Some economists specialize in, for example, the economics of energy resources, the car industry, agriculture, transport.

Extent of specialization varies enormously. Some economists become very knowledgeable about a particular aspect or part of an industry; others in an area of economics. One assignment required an economist with a background in the catering industry to suggest sites for and types of new hotels which a major company wanted to build. Work involved research: what makes hotels successful at home and abroad? in what proportion do food, accommodation, hotel location, service, pricing, affect a hotel's profitability? what constitutes 'good' food, accommodation, etc.? The economist spent a year asking questions in hotels – of guests and staff and management – analysing relevant companies' accounts, and then presented the report. Another economist who specialized in 'agricultural economics' prepared a report on measures to improve the productivity of an underdeveloped Third World country. New specializations emerge as society's needs, priorities and problems change. For example, economists in the Civil Service are concerned with all aspects of our lives, from energy conservation to services for the disabled, from monitoring the performance of the higher education system to cost/benefit analysis of a new motorway scheme.

Economists who take jobs as professional economists act as advisers, whatever type of employer they work for. They do not normally take or implement decisions, and they have to be prepared for their advice to be ignored. Economists who want to be involved more directly with the work of the organization that employs them may go into management in industry or commerce (see p. 43, p. 117 and p. 346, for example).

An economics degree can be a general graduate qualification; and it can be a 'specialist' qualification – for work in systems analysis, statistics, market research, investment analysis, cybernetics, operational research (see under relevant headings).

Training Most degree courses include, as 'core' studies, economic theory, micro-economics and macro-economics. Specializations to choose from include agricultural economics, monetary theory and policy, economics of less-developed countries, public sector management, econometrics, economic forecasting, economic geography, transport studies. Economics can be combined with almost any other discipline including accountancy, geography, computing, law, sociology, languages, maths, philosophy and politics. The content of individual courses and the emphasis given to the many aspects of the subject vary greatly from one to another, but quantitative methods are of increasing importance.

Employers now increasingly look for a postgraduate qualification.

Personal attributes Numerical and computing skills; interest in political and social affairs; analytical and problem-solving powers; ability to use statistical methods and to research and evaluate data; communication skills, e.g. ability to explain complex research findings to lay people.

Mature entry and career change Should be no problem for people with appropriate qualifications, who have commercial, financial or similar experience.

Work–life balance It is essential to stay in touch during a career break through reading journals, going to meetings and reading reports, etc. Freelance working is possible for established consultants.

Further information
Royal Economic Society, University of York, Heslington, York YO10 5DD.
www.res.org.uk
Study Economics (information on studying economics and career prospects).
www.whystudyeconomics.ac.uk

Related careers *accountancy – information science – information technology/information systems – journalism – management – management services: Operational Research – town planning*

Engineering

Engineering is not so much one career, more an expertise which opens doors into a vast range of jobs. Engineers probably have a wider choice of environment in which to work, and of type of job, than any other professionals. However, initially they usually specialize in one branch or discipline. The main branches or disciplines are:

Mechanical Engineering

Mechanical engineers have a vast choice of environments to work in: literally no industry is closed to them. They work in hospitals; in computer manufacture; robotics and all types of research establishments. Engineers who want to help humanity as directly as possible, who want to see the application of their efforts to the alleviation of suffering and discomfort, can work in medical engineering (see p. 216); engineers who want to go into technical sales or into marketing, or general management can take their mechanical engineering training into anything from mobile phones to agricultural machinery, oil extraction to food processing.

Civil Engineering

Civil engineering covers the design, planning, construction and maintenance of, first, the 'infrastructure': transport systems, water supplies and sewage plants; and, secondly, large-scale structures, ranging from oil platforms to power stations. Transport systems include roads, bridges, tunnels, ports and airports. Transport planning and management is another, growing, activity. Providing water supplies may involve building reservoirs, controlling the flow of rivers, ensuring safe drinking water and effective irrigation systems in developing countries, and the disposal and treatment of waste to prevent pollution.

Civil engineers work for local and central government, in industry and for international organizations. Many work as consulting engineers, called in by large organizations to design and carry out a project. Others work for civil engineering contractors supervising construction projects and dealing with building contractors; they may also do design work. Many British firms work on overseas contracts.

Structural Engineering

This is a specialized branch of civil engineering. Structural engineers are particularly skilled in non-traditional construction materials and techniques. Those working for civil engineering firms might design large-scale constructions such as grandstands and bridges. Those called in as consultants by architects might design the foundations and skeletal framework of large buildings such as skyscrapers and hospitals.

Environmental Engineering (Heating and Ventilating Engineering/Building Services Engineering)

Environmental engineers are concerned with heating, lighting, acoustics, ventilation, air conditioning, noise and air pollution and its control. They are called in as consultants by civil engineers and architects on building projects from hospitals to airports, office blocks to housing estates, chain stores to underground stations. This branch straddles mechanical, electrical and structural engineering.

Electrical and Electronic Engineering

The two overlap. Broadly, electrical engineering is concerned with the use and generation of electricity to produce heat, light and mechanical power. Electrical engineers work in generating stations, distribution systems and on the manufacture of all kinds of electrical machinery from tiny motors for powered invalid chairs to heavy motors for industrial plant. They are also concerned with research into the more efficient use of, and new sources of energy for, electrical power.

Electronics is mainly concerned with computers, telecommunications, automation, instrumentation and control.

Computers The electronic engineering industry is concerned with producing the machinery – the 'hardware' – which gives house-room to the software, i.e. the programs, and with producing the components and products which 'computer systems' need to perform their tasks. This includes microprocessors, visual display units, printers, etc. (For details of software/programming jobs see p. 280.)

The proportion of design, research and development engineers is greater in electronics than in other branches. (Mechanical, electrical and chemical engineers, physicists and computer scientists also work in computer manufacture.)

Telecommunications The range extends from voice-only and visual communication to voice-over-Internet and mobile and satellite systems. The trend is to ever more portable and flexible devices incorporating access to broadcast media and the Internet. The move of telecommunication technologies into homes as well as work environments and the increasing demand for faster connections and greater security makes this a very dynamic field.

Automation, instrumentation and control This is concerned with automatic control devices, from the operation of automatic flight control systems in aircraft to nearer-home gadgets such as automatic ovens and central-heating time clocks, and robotics.

Then there is the vast area of computer-controlled equipment which has become possible as a result of the development of microelectronics and nanoengineering: the design, development and production of scaled-down, minuscule electronic circuitry. The chip affects virtually every industrial, commercial, scientific and professional activity but it can do nothing by itself: electronics specialists develop its potential and 'program' (instruct) it to perform the precisely defined task for which it is intended.

Examples are electronic point-of-sale systems in supermarkets automatically linked to warehouse and distribution provision, document storage and retrieval systems (see p. 275), and manufacturing assembly robotics. Scientific applications include weather forecasting; computer-aided design in civil and structural engineering; dating archaeological discoveries; and photographic processing.

Medical or Biomedical Engineering

Medical engineering is a combination of electronic, electrical and mechanical engineering and physics, led by the development of ever smaller-scale applications. The health care industry is one of the world's largest industrial sectors and is expanding, creating a demand for new technology from improved hip replacements to an artificial retina chip which can partly restore lost vision. Medical engineers also design aids for people with severe disabilities, for example artificial replacement limbs or custom-built transport. They work in industry on the design and development of medical devices; in hospitals with medical staff providing non-clinical services; in research; and in government agencies.

Previously, medical engineers took a degree in either mechanical, electronic or electrical engineering combined with a postgraduate qualification or work experience, but there are now an increasing number of medical engineering degree courses. Medical engineering is a multidisciplinary subject which integrates a professional engineering course with a basic knowledge of anatomy, physiology and cell biology. Students may choose to study rehabilitation engineering, tissue engineering – the creation of biological substitutes for the replacement or restoration of tissue function lost through failure or disease – or medical imaging. Some courses have a foundation in mechanical or electronic engineering but others may be more focused on materials engineering or physics.

Medical engineering is often overlooked as an alternative to medicine for people who want to be closely involved with alleviating disabilities.

Chemical Engineering

Chemical (or process) engineers are concerned with the design and development of laboratory processes, and with their translation into large-scale plant, for the production of chemicals, dyes, medicines, fertilizers, plastics, etc., and increasingly for their subsequent recycling. Expertise in designing and managing plant in which chemical processes take place is also used in food processing, brewing, paper, textile and other industries. Biochemical engineers specialize in the design and development of industrial plant in which biochemical processes can take place (see p. 517), e.g. developing alternative sources of energy and converting noxious waste into useful by-products or at least into harmless substances. They are working with many different scientists on ways of producing a new generation of advanced medicines and similarly will work closely with others on the emerging use of human cells and tissues produced outside the body, for repair purposes. Chemical engineering has far wider application than is often believed: many chemical engineers do work in oil refineries and other heavy industry, but there is wide scope elsewhere, for example in textiles and electronics. 'Green' issues are of increasing importance.

Manufacturing Engineering

This branch covers all aspects of manufacture. It embraces knowledge of many aspects of engineering and ensures that labour, equipment and materials are used efficiently.

Manufacturing engineers need both technical and 'people management' skills, so that goods of the right quality are produced at the required time at the right price. They plan the production methods and systems (which nowadays often involve computer-controlled tools) and may modify machinery to suit a particular task. They liaise with other departments such as design, research & development (R & D), purchasing and sales.

Naval Architecture

Despite the title, the work is engineering rather than architecture. It is concerned with the design, repair, construction and economic operation of craft which float on or under or hover just above the water. Craft can be of any size from sailing dinghy to supertanker, hydrofoil to oil rig. Naval architects work for the armed services as well as for ship-building and boat-building firms.

Aeronautical/Aerospace Engineering

Concerned with aircraft design and construction and space and satellite research, as well as with planning, operation and maintenance of airlines' fleets of aircraft and aircraft components. Employers include aircraft manufacturers, airlines and the Ministry of Defence with organizations increasingly working across national boundaries. This is a small branch of engineering; a greater proportion work in R & D, fewer on production. People who want to work in this area can take electronics or physics degrees and leave more options open.

Agricultural Engineering
(see also *engineering in the land-based sector*, p. 71)

Other Branches

Some engineering specializations described elsewhere (or advertised) have different titles from all those mentioned here. They may be small branches or offshoots of, or options within, established engineering branches. Titles may describe jobs which can be done by people from various disciplines (e.g. in robotics). Or they may describe emerging new branches which are also still under the umbrella of an established branch.

Engineering can no longer be neatly categorized into the traditional disciplines. It is a fast-changing profession, developing as a result of scientific discovery (scientists discover; engineers exploit discoveries and make them work productively as well as in response to need). For example, new sources of energy are urgently being sought by governments: engineers working on the development of wind, wave and solar energy are *energy engineers*. Technological tasks are so complex now that people from various disciplines have to pool their expertise: at the same time, some disciplines are becoming so unwieldy that they subdivide. That applies especially in electronics and mechanical engineering. New titles do not have as precise meanings as have traditional engineering disciplines.

Here is a very brief (and superficial) guide to some of the current engineering job titles and the – probable – umbrella discipline, or function, which should be the first port of call for information on what knowledge is required and what work involved:

Computer systems, control engineering: umbrella discipline – Electronics.

Offshore, oil, fuel, energy engineering: umbrella disciplines – Mechanical, Electrical, Electronic or Chemical Engineering. (Energy engineering can also describe the energy-saving function in large organizations.)

Nuclear engineering: umbrella disciplines – Physics and Electronics.

Industrial engineering: umbrella discipline – Manufacturing Engineering, but can also be combination of Management and Engineering.

Process engineering: umbrella discipline – Chemical Engineering.

Plant, installation, test and commissioning engineering: umbrella disciplines – could be Mechanical, Production or Chemical Engineering, but also used for functions carried out by Mechanical or almost any other specialist engineer.

Professional Registration

Qualified engineers are registered in three categories on the Engineering Council's Register: Chartered Engineer (CEng), Incorporated Engineer (IEng) and Engineering Technician (EngTech). The UK Standard for Professional Engineering Competence (UK-SPEC), which was introduced in 2004, focuses on the skills and competences required at each level of professional engineering work. The emphasis is on competence, irrespective of the entry route. See the 'Training' sections below for more information on typical entry routes for each category of registration. Progression is possible from EngTech to IEng and from IEng and EngTech registration to CEng.

CHARTERED ENGINEERS (CEng)

(see also 'Incorporated Engineers' and 'Engineering Technicians', pp. 228, 229)

Entry qualifications For registration see 'Training'. Entry requirements for accredited degrees are usually at National Qualifications Framework Level 3 (A levels, BTEC National awards) or Scottish Credit and Qualifications Framework equivalent, generally including maths and a physical science (for Chemical Engineering usually maths and chemistry with another science). The grades required differ between universities. Courses with a built-in Foundation Year for applicants with alternative subjects are available at some institutions.

The work There is a range of engineering functions (see below), each appealing to different temperaments and talents. Engineers can concentrate on, for example, creative design; on developing ideas, seeing them translated into the end-product and sold at a profit; on managing people and/or resources and/or processes; on research.

Apart from the many aspects of practical 'active' engineering, there is the vital commercial exploitation of ideas and products. Technical sales and marketing (see below) are now often considered the sharp end of the profession, and engineers do well in both these areas.

It is estimated that most engineers spend about one-third of their time discussing work with colleagues, customers or clients, staff, bosses.

The 'transferable skills' gained through an engineering qualification are valued by a range of employers in other sectors, from marketing (see p. 362), industrial management (see p. 346), to public relations (see p. 484), television (see p. 597) and other graduate employment.

Engineering graduates' specific knowledge can be useful in an age when technology has a bearing on virtually any type of business; their analytical approach to problem-solving is invariably useful, even when the problem is not a technical one. So even young people who are not planning to spend their lives as engineers, but want to go into anything from investment banking to journalism, might well consider taking an engineering degree as a stepping stone. Engineering need be no more a vocational course than an arts degree.

There are postgraduate courses in business management, systems analysis, transport, etc., which can be taken either immediately after qualifying or a few years later (after a career break, p. 232). Courses in 'information engineering' (combining computing and electronic engineering) and 'mechatronics' (combining mechanical and electronic engineering) aim to train engineers to manage computer-based engineering systems.

Job prospects are good on the whole, because engineering is such an adaptable skill; the broader the areas of application of the discipline, the better the prospects; for example, mechanical and electronic engineers are needed in very many more areas of employment than are naval architects. Within electrical, electronic, mechanical and manufacturing engineering it is possible to switch from one branch to another. This usually requires taking a postgraduate course (possibly part-time, while working). Many engineers, from any discipline, go into industrial and commercial management (see p. 346) and into management consultancy (see p. 355). Others, especially electronics engineers, go into information technology (see p. 280). Chartered engineers can become maths, physics and engineering science teachers. There are opportunities in the EU and elsewhere abroad. The title 'European Engineer' (EUR ING) enables greater mobility and recognition for engineers working in Europe. To gain this title, professional engineers must show they have completed a package of degree, training and experience lasting not fewer than seven years. Competence in a second European language could improve employment prospects.

After training, engineers normally specialize in one function, or type of activity. The main functions within each branch are outlined below.

Design

This is the most creative of the engineering functions and is the core of the engineering process. Design engineers create or improve products which can be manufactured and maintained economically, perform satisfactorily, look good and satisfy proven demand. Looks matter more in consumer goods – microwave ovens, telephones – than, for example, in machine tools. Design engineers may also design a new, or improve an established, engineering process. Most designers work to a brief. For example, design engineers employed by a multinational manufacturer may need to incorporate energy-saving or safety requirements meeting a number of national standards.

Their job is to find efficient and economic solutions to a set of problems. They must investigate materials and processes to be used in the manufacture of the product, which means they have to consult experts from other disciplines; but it is the design engineer who specifies what goes into the manufacture of the product and what processes are to be used.

Because the work of design engineers varies so enormously, the job is impossible to define precisely. Designing an aircraft which is a team effort has little in common with adding a feature or two to an established type of machine tool or TV component. Most work is done in 'design offices', where several engineers assisted by technicians work under a chief design engineer. Some designing, in electronics for example, is done in the laboratory. CAD – computer-aided design – is now used extensively. An experienced design engineer can choose whether to be part of a team that designs, say, a whole new airport, or whether to work alone on simple, straightforward design.

Personal attributes High academic ability; an urge to put new technologies to practical use; creativity; imagination and interest in problem-solving; ability to coordinate the work of others; interest in marketability of product; ability to work as one of a team or to lead it.

Research and Development (R & D)

In some organizations research and development are two separate departments; in some the two, plus design, go together. But most typically, research and development form one department, with design separate, but very closely linked.

R & D engineers investigate, improve and adapt established processes and products, and they may create new ones. The work is essentially experimental, laboratory-based, but the 'laboratory' could be a skid-pan on which new tyre-surfaces are tried out, or a wind-tunnel in which to experiment with aircraft models.

While there is some extending-the-frontiers-of-knowledge kind of research, most engineering research is 'applied', i.e. aimed at maximizing sales and profits; or at saving precious resources; or at exploiting newly discovered materials or processes.

Work comes from several sources: *design engineers* may want to use a new material, but they need to know more about its 'behaviour' before using it; *manufacturing engineers* may ask R & D to investigate why there is a recurrent fault in a particular production process or product; the *marketing department* may complain that a particular aspect of a competitor's fridge or mobile phone makes the competitor's product sell better: R & D would investigate the better-selling product, and come up with suggestions. Research and development is very much teamwork.

Personal attributes Practical; high academic ability; imagination; perseverance; interest in following up ideas which have profitable application; ability to work well with colleagues from other departments; willingness to switch from one project to another if Marketing or Manufacturing have urgent problems.

Manufacturing

The manufacturing function broadly covers changing raw materials into all types of articles. This involves the selection of the most suitable material and the application of the manufacturing process and system in order to manufacture the products.

Products can range from pizzas to wind turbines, CDs to beer cans. The engineer must see that labour, equipment and materials are used efficiently and that the product is completed at the correct quality and cost, in the right quantity, at the right time. The work environment could be a huge (and noisy) heavy engineering plant; it can be a large, but very quiet, highly automated workshop.

As manufacturing processes become ever more sophisticated, and as industry has begun to recognize the need for greater efficiency and streamlining, this activity has grown in importance and status.

Production managers' work has much in common with human resources management: smoothing out problems on the shop floor before they flare up into disputes; dealing with unions and with staff problems which might affect the department's productivity.

Personal attributes Organizing ability; practicality; ability to get on well with people of all types at all levels in the hierarchy – from operatives to heads of research and managing director; ability to keep calm under pressure and in inevitable crises; liking for being very much at the centre of action and solving problems.

Technical Sales and Marketing

Sales engineers use engineering expertise in a commercial context. They spend most of their time away from the office, meeting people. Selling engineering products ('specialist selling'), which may be selling anything from machine tools to oil rigs, domestic freezers to road maintenance equipment and service, combines sales techniques with technical knowledge. Customers may be lay people to whom the virtues of a product have to be explained, or highly professionally qualified people (more so than the sales engineer, possibly) who ask searching questions about the product's performance and properties. Sales engineers also act as links between prospective customers and manufacturers, passing on criticism of and requests for products and changes. They must find out, for example, what features – design, after-sales service, cost – make a competitor's product sell better in other countries or at home. (See p. 362.)

Searching out new customers is an important part of selling. Some sales may take months of meetings and negotiating. Sales engineers may travel abroad a good deal, or they may have their own 'territory' near home – it largely depends on the type of product.

Personal attributes Outgoing personality; adaptability to use the right approach with different types of customers; perseverance, and indifference to the occasional rebuff; commercial acumen; interest in economic affairs; communication skills.

Consultancy

This function absorbs significant numbers in civil and structural engineering. Numbers in other branches – notably mechanical, electronic and manufacturing engineering – are increasing. Consulting engineers work in partnerships in private practice. A few set up on their own. Firms vary in organization and extent of specialization. Basically consultants provide specialist services for clients in charge of large projects who may be public authorities, architects, other engineers or quantity surveyors. Consultants advise, provide feasibility studies, design to a brief, and, sometimes, organize projects. They are not in the construction/manufacturing business but may be in charge of putting work out to contractors and, as their client's agent, may then be responsible for supervising contractors' work, including authorizing payment.

Consultants may specialize: for example, civil engineers may specialize in motorway or in sports stadium design, or in traffic management; electronic engineers may specialize in telecommunications or in medical electronics or in instrumentation and systems. Consultants are usually design engineers (see above), but as they move up the ladder they spend more time dealing with clients and getting business – i.e. on the commercial side of the job. Some go into or specialize in management consultancy (see p. 355). Civil and structural consulting engineers often work abroad, usually on contract for a fixed number of years.

Personal attributes As for design engineers, plus a confidence-inspiring manner, persuasive powers for dealing with clients and contractors; for senior jobs: commercial sense.

Other Functions

Apart from these specializations, there are many jobs which are, usually, carried out within one of the main functions. Titles and the work they describe vary. They include maintenance (work on employer's premises) and service (work carried out on customer's premises), test, installation, quality assurance, systems, control engineers. These functions may be carried out by graduates early in their career, they may be top jobs or they may be carried out by technicians (see p. 229).

Considering the need for precision in engineering, job and function titles are often surprisingly vague and can, therefore, be misleading.

Training Although not a requirement to practise in the UK, only engineers registered with the Engineering Council are entitled to call themselves Chartered Engineers. The route to registration has recently changed. In the past this involved meeting set academic requirements. As already mentioned above, Chartered Engineers now have to meet the UK standards for professional engineering competence, known as UK-SPEC, which has been introduced to place more emphasis on the skills and competences engineers have gained through their academic education and experience, rather than the entry qualifications specified for accredited degree courses. Skills and competences may be demonstrated through academic qualifications, experience and training, a professional review and membership of a licensed member organization. Two academic routes are accepted as exemplifying the required knowledge and understanding:

- An accredited BEng (Hons) degree, plus either an accredited postgraduate Masters or appropriate further learning to Masters level.
- An accredited integrated MEng degree.

Candidates for registration also have to demonstrate professional competence, either through an industrial placement as part of their degree course, through an employers' accredited graduate training scheme or through developing their own profile of competence. There is no set time requirement.

Applicants who do not have an exemplifying qualification can qualify for registration through submitting a technical report based on their experience and demonstrating their knowledge and understanding or by taking Engineering Council exams or by following an academic programme specified by the engineering institution to which they are applying. With any necessary additional learning and development, an Incorporated Engineer can also register as a Chartered Engineer through submitting a technical report.

There is a Graduate Apprenticeship Scheme for students wishing to integrate work-based learning and higher education study. It is open to students on degree and diploma courses, new graduates starting employment and engineers in employment who wish to raise their skill levels. Applicants without maths and physics A levels or equivalent can apply for courses which offer a foundation year after which they go on to study for a three-year or four-year degree.

Sandwich courses are particularly suitable for students wanting to enter industry, as they are able to sample the industrial scene. Some large companies sponsor students for all or part of their course (i.e. pay them while they are studying), who thus gain work experience in that organization. College-based students work for a range of employers during their course. 'Thin' sandwich courses include periods of work experience throughout the course, often over the summer vacation. 'Thick' sandwich courses involve a full year of work experience, usually the third year of a four-year course.

INCORPORATED ENGINEERS (IEng)

Entry qualifications For registration within UK-SPEC, see 'Training' below. Two or three GCE A levels or equivalent usually required for Accredited IEng degree or BTEC/SQA HND.

The work Incorporated Engineers take responsibility for a wide range of tasks: they take on many technical and commercial operational management roles, leading and supervising teams. They are involved in day-to-day decision-making and problem-solving. They manage current and developing engineering applications and they often have the key task of carrying through technology-led change across their industry. Their work is more practical and less theoretical than that of Chartered Engineers, who are more concerned with creative solutions and innovation such as within design and research. Chartered Engineers usually work at a more strategic level, often with overall leadership of projects involving teams of incorporated engineers and engineering technicians.

Training For registration as incorporated engineer with the Engineering Council (see 'Training' under Chartered Engineer, p. 226) the exemplifying qualifications are:

- An accredited BEng in engineering or technology.
- An accredited BTEC/SQA HNC/D or Foundation degree in engineering or technology plus appropriate further learning to degree level. Appropriate initial professional development (on-the-job experience and training) and Professional Review (assessment of competence based on UK-SPEC by a licensed professional engineering institution).

ENGINEERING TECHNICIANS (EngTech)

Entry qualifications In practice normally National Qualifications Framework Level 2 (GCSEs A*–C, BTEC Diplomas and Certificates) or Scottish Credit and Qualifications Framework equivalent, including maths and science. Technicians can also start by training as craftsmen/women through Apprenticeships.

The work Engineering technicians take responsibility for jobs in defined areas of technology. They use established methods and procedures for practical problem-solving. They usually work within teams, often with a supervisory role in relation to e.g. fitters.

Personal attributes A practical and methodical approach and an interest in technology are needed in all technician jobs. There is room for backroom types who like to get on with their work on their own, for those who like to work in a team, those who like to work in a drawing office or laboratory, and for those who enjoy visiting clients and customers. For some jobs (the minority) manual dexterity; for others, the ability to explain technical points in plain language and a liking for meeting people.

Training Advanced Apprenticeships developed by SEMTA, the Sector Skills Council for Engineering and Science, are a well-established work-based route for trainee technicians and craftspeople. Entry can be with appropriate GCSEs (see 'Entry qualifications' above), A levels, vocational A levels (A levels in applied subjects) or BTEC certificates or diplomas or SQA equivalents. Length of training depends on initial qualifications and eventual aim, but leads to an NVQ level 3 in a selected area and a technical certificate. Engineering Advanced Apprenticeships take a minimum of two years of combined theory and practical skills development, completed while working for an employer and studying part-time at college.

Many employers offer training programmes for technicians in manufacturing industry which combine theory with practical experience. Length of training varies according to the entrant's qualifications and ambitions. They will normally work towards NVQs/SVQs or BTEC National Certificate or Diploma or SQA equivalent.

Technicians who follow a work-based route to registration with the Engineering Council typically have a technical certificate achieved as part of an approved Advanced Apprenticeship or an approved level 3 NVQ or SVQ. Alternatively they can apply for an appraisal by their registering institution.

Full-time college route: Either a two-year full-time or a three-year sandwich BTEC National Diploma or equivalent approved vocational qualification (or SQA equivalent). With training and appropriate experience this can lead to registration as Engineering Technician (as above). Students can then take a two-year full-time or three-year sandwich course for a BTEC/SQA Higher National Diploma. Entrants with at least one relevant A level (usually maths or physics) and appropriate GCSEs (A–C) or equivalent can go straight into a BTEC Higher award course.

CRAFT LEVEL

Entry qualifications Average ability in maths, science, technical/practical subjects. Employers normally test applicants' aptitudes. Many ask for a GCSE pass in maths and relevant subjects.

The work Engineering craftsmen/women do skilled work and need sufficient theoretical knowledge to understand the principles behind the operations they carry out and to solve basic problems. They work in all branches and may be in charge of lower-skilled workers. Their work, and their scope, is changing as a result of new technologies. First, the distinction between craftspeople and technicians is narrowing, with craft-trained people becoming technicians more frequently than in the past; and second, as a result of automation in all engineering spheres, the distinctions between the specialist trades are blurring. Craftspeople may switch trades more easily than in the past, as well as learn new ones, but overall prospects are not as good as those for technicians.

Traditional crafts or 'trades' continue to be practised, including those below.

Machine-shop Crafts

Toolmaking: The use of precision machinery and tools to make jigs, fixtures, gauges and other tools used in production work. Apprentices may start in the toolroom, or they are upgraded from other trades.

Toolsetting: Setting of automatic (such as computer/tape numerically controlled) or semi-automatic machines for use by machine operators in mass production.

Turning: Operating lathes which use fixed cutting tool(s) to remove metal/material from a rotating workpiece.

Milling: Operating milling machines where metal/material is removed from a fixed workpiece by rotating cutter(s).

Jig-boring: Highly skilled work in which very heavy articles are machined to a high degree of precision.

Grinding: Obtaining a very accurate finish by removing small amounts of metal with rapidly revolving abrasive wheels. It is also used to sharpen tools.

Fitting

Fitters, whether working in mechanical, electrical or electronic engineering, combine the basic skills of the machine-shop craftsperson with the ability to use hand tools. In production work they may assemble cars, generators, TV sets, etc. They carry out maintenance and repair work on domestic appliances and office machinery either on customers' premises – private houses, factories, offices, etc. – or in workshops. Gas fitters install, service and repair gas-powered domestic appliances or industrial plant; marine engine fitters put together and repair ships' engines, etc.

Training Craftsmen/women increasingly train under the Advanced Apprenticeship programme, leading to NVQs/SVQs at level 3. There may be opportunity to specialize in one particular craft throughout or to train as a multi-skilled craftsperson, spending time in a number of different departments before specializing.

Mature entry and career change (general) Relevant background and appropriate qualifications/experience required.

Work–life balance Because of the pace of technological change, a complete gap of even a few years would be challenging, but support for women returners is improving all the time. There are various schemes for enabling people on a domestic break (mainly women) to keep in touch (see the UK Resource Centre for Women in Science, Engineering and Technology at *www.ukrc4setwomen.org*). These include encouraging women to visit their former employers regularly during the break and, on their return, for them to have a 'mentor' or 'industrial tutor' who, in an informal way, helps them to catch up.

There are few part-time jobs at present, but some opportunities for engineers who have specialized or can specialize in computing and related work. Others work on 'one-off' contracts. Job-sharing schemes do not seem to have been tried on any scale, but there is no reason why they should not work.

Position of women The proportion of women in engineering still remains very low. Despite two decades of initiatives to encourage young women to consider engineering careers, they still make up only a small percentage at all levels.

The Department for Innovation, Universities and Skills has a resource centre of information for women considering or already working in science, engineering and technology as already mentioned (see *wwwukrc4setwmen.org*).

See the Headstart Courses website at *www.headstartcourses.org.uk* for details of Insight courses for young women, offering team exercises, a one-day project and an industry visit plus other opportunities.

WISE, Women into Science and Engineering, produces a number of publications, provides speakers and runs campaigns to increase awareness of engineering careers among young women. (*The WISE Directory of Initiatives* is produced yearly and lists awards, courses, visits and other initiatives on offer to women – available on *www. wisecampaign.org.uk.*) WISE runs a scheme called the WISE Outlook programme giving girls aged 13–14 the opportunity to experience engineering.

Further information

(ECUK) The Engineering Council (for list of individual institutions as well as general information), 2nd Floor, Weston House, 246 High Holborn, London WC1V 7EX.
www.engc.org.uk

(ETB) The Engineering and Technology Board supplies impartial careers information about the SET sector; find out more at *www.enginuity.org.uk* and *www.scenta.co.uk.* For more information about ETB visit *www.etechb.co.uk.*

SEMTA, Sector Skills Council for Engineering and Science, 14 Upton Road, Watford, Herts WD18 0JT.
www.semta.org.uk

Related careers *agriculture and horticulture – art and design – construction: Construction Managers – information technology/information systems – science – surveying*

Environmental Health Practitioner

Entry qualifications An accredited degree or postgraduate qualification. A science A level or equivalent is recommended.

The work Environmental health practitioners ensure that people are protected from a wide range of hazards in the environment in its widest sense – houses, shops, workplaces, leisure facilities, the air we breathe, our water supplies. Increasing public concern about the environment is reflected daily in the news: a leak of toxic chemicals; an E. coli outbreak; contaminated water supplies; the effects of lead on children living near busy motorway junctions; housing unfit through damp for human habitation; noise pollution; the enforcement of smoke-free policies. Environmental health officers deal with all these problems.

The majority of environmental health practitioners work in local authorities. Their role is both to advise on safety and hygiene and to enforce legislation. This involves visiting a great variety of sites; a high proportion of EHPs' time is spent out of the office.

EHPs ensure that safe and hygienic standards are met in the preparation, manufacture, transport and sale of food. This can mean visiting high-technology plants or market stalls, restaurants or slaughterhouses, to check on the cleanliness of equipment and staff, storage facilities and handling procedures. EHPs have powers to enter and inspect housing if they 'have reason to believe that the premises are not fit for human habitation' or they may be called in by the residents. They advise on repairs, improvements and sometimes demolition. Responsibility for places of work overlaps with that of factory inspectors (see p. 249). EHPs check on working conditions, for example sanitary arrangements, overcrowding, temperature, ventilation, lighting and hours of work for juveniles.

Noise, pest control, water and waste, air pollution and communicable diseases are also the responsibilities of EHPs. They may also deal with caravan and camping sites, houseboats and leisure boats, swimming pools and leisure centres, and some aspects of animal welfare.

Some EHPs have a general role covering a wide range of responsibilities; others specialize in, for example, food hygiene, housing or atmospheric pollution.

Some work in industry, e.g. food manufacturing.

Training

- Three-year or four-year accredited BSc in Environmental Health. Syllabus includes the general study of science, technology, statistics, social science, public administration and law, and in greater depth, food, occupational health and safety, pollution, public health and housing issues.
- Accredited MSc for graduates with appropriate degree.

All EHP students are required to complete a period of practical training which can be achieved as part of the three-year or four-year BSc or follow on from the academic study. All candidates also take a two-part examination, consisting of a case study paper and an interview, leading to the CIEH professional qualification.

The degree courses can be studied part-time but even for those already working as environmental health technicians the requirement for practical training remains the same.

- *In Scotland*: Four-year degree in environmental health at Strathclyde University, in conjunction with a period of structured practical training in a local authority, which may be undertaken during university vacation periods, followed by a professional interview for the Royal Environmental Health Institute of Scotland Diploma in Environmental Health.

Personal attributes Interest in people's living and working environment; ability to take decisions; sufficient self-confidence to go where one is not necessarily welcome, to be firm when necessary and to discuss complicated problems intelligently.

Mature entry and career change There is scope for late entry, though the older one is, the more difficult it could be to get the necessary practical training. Degree courses may relax the academic entry requirements for mature entrants.

Work–life balance A career break should be no problem for those who keep in touch. EHPs' major employers, local authorities, are among the most forward-looking on flexible working.

Further information

The Chartered Institute of Environmental Health, Chadwick Court, 15 Hatfields, London SE1 8DJ.
  www.cieh.org
The Royal Environmental Health Institute of Scotland, 3 Manor Place, Edinburgh EH3 7DH.
  www.rehis.org

Related careers *health and safety advisers and inspectors – housing management – science: Food Science and Technology – trading standards officer*

Environmental Work

Entry qualifications Various but usually at least a first degree.

The work The popular image of environmental work is nature conservation or landscape preservation. But the sector encompasses the sustainable use of all natural resources, including the atmosphere and water. Most employment in environmental work involves supporting both the public and private sector in understanding and meeting increasingly stringent legislation and 'polluter pays' policies being introduced by government and the EU to protect the environment. It is indeed concerned with conservation but this heading covers a huge range of jobs, including the management of water resources, control of air and water pollution, waste management, decontamination of groundwater and soil, environmental risk management, modelling, impact assessment and auditing, energy supply, regeneration and the promotion of sustainable development. In addition there are those who formulate the policies on which much of this activity is based, and provide the research which underpins them.

Some environmental work is now becoming embedded in already established occupations, from farming and forestry to town and country planning. It is also increasingly a specialism within other professions. Major companies may employ specialist lawyers to advise them on environmental legislation or lawyers can specialize in prosecuting offenders against environmental regulations. Education for Sustainable Development is a statutory part of the National Curriculum but qualified teachers can also find employment outside school, for example setting up educational projects with companies or working with local communities to help them improve their environment.

Journalists, too, can specialize in writing about environmental issues, although regularity of work is dependent on the whims of the reading public.

Environmental work in practice is often a balance between enforcing regulations and promoting good practice, whether to a large corporation or to primary school children. The resource to be protected may be a local amenity such as a park or footpath or the very air we breathe and the water we drink. The ability to communicate well with people from all backgrounds is often as important to the job as scientific knowledge, as much of the work involves increasing public awareness, explaining the issues involved to groups and individuals, weighing up conflicting interests and making judgements.

The main single employer in the sector is the Environment Agency, responsible for overseeing air and land quality, the regulation of waste management, conservation and ecology especially alongside rivers and coastal areas, and the prevention of flooding. The Agency employs approximately 12,000 people across a huge range of specialist areas ranging from soil conservation to public relations. Local government, too, is a major employer, as is the voluntary sector. As the penalties for not complying with regulations can be severe, some large companies are starting to employ specialists to advise on their procedures and ensure that they are meeting legal requirements, though most depend on consultancies. Environmental work is an exciting new field, currently very much driven by legislation, which is changing and developing as new areas of expertise are needed. Much of it is overlapping, for example the management of water resources also involves the prevention of pollution and the protection of the natural environment. Below are some of the main areas of work (see also p. 52)

Nature Conservation

The number of jobs in environmental conservation is increasing year on year. The work is mainly concerned with retaining, restoring and improving habitats for wildlife. This includes ongoing work to preserve wildlife species throughout the world, many of which first have to be identified and recorded.

Closer to home, central and local government employ ecologists and conservationists at all levels, although, even with the expansion in demand, competition for jobs can be intense and many are academically over-qualified for their posts. Some will work on a variety of projects while others, employed as rangers or reserve officers, will be responsible for a single conservation area.

Competing pressures on the use of land mean that the work can often involve evaluating options and assessing the best use of the funds available. Many new developments require an Environmental Impact Assessment before planning permission is granted and this, along with the growing public interest in conservation and the increasing availability of funding from the National Lottery and the EU, has led to a steady expansion of jobs in this field. Few conservationists are employed in the private sector, although there are an increasing number of large consultancies offering a wide range of expertise who usually recruit experienced staff. The voluntary sector has openings for professional ecologists, often on short-term contracts, which may involve managing volunteers.

Waste Management

Waste management has become increasingly complex over the last few years. In the UK the traditional method of disposal has been to use landfill sites but the volume now involved and new directives from the EU are ensuring an urgent need to develop new approaches, for example creating demand for recycled products, recovering materials and harnessing the by-products of waste such as methane.

The waste management sector is increasingly employing people with scientific and technical expertise and managers with business qualifications. It is divided into three main sectors: those who regulate it (in England and Wales the Environment Agency and in Scotland the Scottish Environment Protection Agency (SEPA)); those who procure waste disposal services (usually county – or in Scotland local – councils); and those who provide the services. Industry is responsible for disposing of its own waste and often this may mean treatment on site. Finding suitable sites for waste disposal is a function of town planning (see p. 613).

Water Resources Management

Despite a drop in industrial use, there is still increasing demand for water and this, along with recognition of the requirement to protect the natural environment, is leading to the need for new approaches to managing supplies. *Water resources planners* may work for the Environment Agency or for water companies, investigating future demand and looking for ways to meet it. *Hydrologists* and *hydrogeologists* provide the technical support on which decisions can be made. *Abstraction licensing officers* process applications to abstract groundwater or water from rivers.

Drinking water treatment and wastewater management employ a range of people: engineers, analytical chemists, biologists and microbiologists as well as regulators and consultants.

Environment Protection

The main employers in this category who regulate emissions to air and water are the Environment Agency in England and Wales, and SEPA in Scotland. These agencies are responsible for monitoring the waste of some 7,000 industrial plants and ensuring that water and air quality is maintained. Farmers also have a duty to ensure that silage, for example, does not pollute local rivers or waterways and have to be supported and monitored. Environment Agency officers may work in multi-functional teams, with staff from related fields, and interpersonal skills and the need to be able to influence and negotiate are important.

Sub-surface – that is groundwater and soil – contamination is an area in which there has been enormous growth in demand for suitably qualified professionals. Until five years ago protection of this environment was largely voluntary but science-based regulations are now being introduced, resulting in a rapid expansion of consultancies in this field.

Training In a sector which overlaps with so many others and which is still developing it is still possible to enter environmental work from a variety of backgrounds. However, a degree in environmental science or geography or biology, usually including elements of ecology and biodiversity, is a good starting point. A list of accredited courses on the CIWEM website will give an idea of the more specialized courses available. Many entrants have postgraduate qualifications.

Some of the large consultancies may offer graduate training but ecologists taken on by organizations new to the field can find themselves defining their own jobs and responsible for gaining the knowledge and skills required.

There are a large number of Foundation degrees, reflecting the rapidly increasing need of employers for staff qualified in different aspects of environmental work. Course titles range from Wildlife and Countryside Conservation to Renewable Energy Technologies.

NVQs are also available in Environmental Conservation at levels 2 and 3. These can be completed as part of an Apprenticeship in Environmental Conservation or achieved through work-based training. A new 14–19 Diploma in Environmental and Land-based Studies will be available in some schools and colleges in England from 2009, and across the country by 2013.

The Chartered Institution of Water and Environmental Management (CIWEM) offers courses in practical environmental management, in partnership with Groundwork, an environmental regeneration organization, and online courses in partnership with the Open University. There are also a number of accredited university courses and details of these can be found on the CIWEM website *www.ciwem.org*

Additionally CIWEM has a comprehensive searchable website for environmental careers. This has case studies, profiles and includes a list of universities offering environmentally related courses (visit *www.environmentalcareers.org.uk*).

The Institute of Environmental Management and Assessment offers a number of short professional courses in environmental management systems and also a foundation course in environmental auditing.

In 2002 ten professional institutions with a focus on the well-being of the environment set up the Society for the Environment (SocEnv). The society has recently achieved chartership status and professionals with suitable experience and qualifications can now apply for the title Chartered Environmentalist. Further information can be found on *www.socenv.org.uk.*

Voluntary work is a recommended way to gain experience of dealing with people and to learn skills, for example the identification of species.

Identification Qualifications are offered by the Natural History Museum: these are not courses, but involve accreditation by examination of existing identification skills. However, a variety of courses on identification of plant and animal species is available (see *www. nhm.ac.uk/research-curation/postgraduate/idq/index.html*).

Personal attributes A committed interest in the care and conservation of the natural environment; an ability to work on own initiative; good communication and influencing skills; a willingness to seek and develop new approaches and solutions.

Mature entry and career change Relevant experience and background is important.

Work–life balance Career breaks and flexible working should not be a problem for those employed by central or local government. Part-time work should be possible in conservation but may be more difficult in environmental management. Short-term contract work may be possible and, for those with experience, consultancy is an option.

Further information

Chartered Institution of Water and Environmental Management, 15
John Street, London WC1N 2EB.
www.ciwem.org
www.environmentalcareers.org.uk

Institute of Environmental Management and Assessment, St Nicholas
House, 70 Newport, Lincoln LN1 3DP.
www.iema.net

Lantra, the Sector Skills Council for the Environment and Land-based
Sector, Lantra House, Stoneleigh Park, Nr Coventry, Warwickshire
CV8 2LG.
www.lantra.co.uk

Related careers *agriculture – environmental health officer – landscape
architecture – leisure/recreation management – town planning*

Fashion and Clothing

To offset global competition from low-cost producers, the UK clothing industry is changing and diversifying into ever more specialist areas; and although overall employment levels have dropped considerably, it is dependent on attracting new and talented people into all areas of the workforce. And British fashion design remains at the cutting edge. But even when designers achieve worldwide recognition, the industry is still about business, not art. Its focus is to produce garments that large numbers of people want to wear, at prices they can afford. Increasingly fashion and clothing is an international industry. Designs may be produced, patterns and lay plans developed, fabrics 'sourced' and garments made with each stage taking place in a different country; the finished garments may then be sold through shops in many parts of the world.

Entry qualifications Vary according to level and type of training.

Main Sectors of the Industry

In haute couture, garments to an exclusive design are cut and made up for individual customers almost entirely by hand. Up-market ready-to-wear follows couture trends but makes more garments in more sizes for sale through exclusive shops. These are the glamour end of the market, but are extremely small. They are fairly insignificant in employment terms, though not in influence.

Most employment opportunities are in the mass-production sector. It covers a huge variety of garments for different markets and for a multitude of purposes: womenswear; menswear; childrenswear; leisurewear and sportswear; workwear and specialist protective clothing; corporate wear.

The work Very few *designers* become 'names' in haute couture or up-market ready-to-wear (or in 'diffusion ranges', which are good-quality wholesale production of designer name garments and have successfully brought good design down market in the last few years). Some young designers set up on their own, designing and making clothes for boutiques (sometimes their own), perhaps occasionally getting orders from store buyers. Most work in wholesale manufacturing, where high fashion is adapted for the high street.

Designers do not work in isolation but as members of a team with fabric designers or buyers, marketing specialists, production specialists, buyers from retail outlets. Very rarely is design an artistic 'gut feeling'. It is marketing-led, based on research. The designer almost always works within a trend (e.g. an ethnic influence) and within a firm's particular 'hand-writing', incorporating both into garments which will sell to a given type of market (e.g. classic, young, elegant, country). The designer's skill is in adapting something for a new market, making it look fresh while retaining the features that made it popular.

Different kinds of garments present different kinds of design challenges. For example, the designer of uniforms for paramedics is not concerned with high street trends but with considerations like how the garment will stand up to the weather, how to make sure it will not get in the way of the wearer's work, how to make it as hygienic as possible.

Some designers do their own pattern cutting, or it may be the job of a specialist pattern cutter or technologist. *Pattern cutters* cut an accurate pattern from which the two-dimensional designer's sketch can be formed into a three-dimensional sample garment.

Garment technologists are the bridge between design and manufacture. They take the sample and plan the way in which the garment will be made. They decide on, for example, what thread will be used, what seam and stitch types, what machinery will be needed, the costs at every stage. Sometimes a design proves too complicated or expensive, so the garment technologist will work with the designer to reach a compromise, perhaps changing some details in a way which will reduce the number and complexity of the manufacturing operations but still retain the designer's concept.

When the design is finalized, it returns to pattern cutters, who will return it to a two-dimensional pattern suitable for mass production. A *pattern grader* then takes a standard size pattern and makes patterns to fit a range of different sizes. *Lay planners* work out how to place the pieces on the fabric in the most economical way. All these processes make extensive use of computerized systems.

The *production manager* is in charge of working out and managing production flow systems, ensuring that the manufacturing process, once it is broken down into a number of operations, will run smoothly, without bottlenecks, and keeping all the operators and equipment evenly busy.

The clothing industry invests very heavily in sophisticated machinery, so *engineers* are very important, ensuring that the machines are working effectively and advising on crucial investment decisions.

This industry is extremely varied. Job titles and functions are not clear-cut. People with different titles can be doing the same job and vice versa. People with different levels of qualifications can also be doing the same job. In smaller companies an individual may carry out several elements of the design/production process; in a larger company he or she may specialize in one particular function. There are also a number of liaison roles for retailers, designers and manufacturers.

Training There is a wide range of courses available at a number of levels. They include: textiles/fashion; fashion; clothing technology; fashion design with technology; design (fashion); fashion technology; knitwear design. Course title is little indication of course emphasis and content. Basically, most courses will include elements of design, pattern technology, garment technology, production management, business studies and raw materials. The balance and emphasis will differ, but most lead to a range of overlapping jobs. Some graduates start work at a lower level than their qualifications would seem to warrant, but they should be able to find a way up with experience. People who start with modest qualifications can also work their way up; prospects are better on the production than on the creative side.

Courses available

- Postgraduate degrees and diplomas: one to two years, full-time or sandwich; entry requirements – degree or equivalent.
- Degrees: three to four years, full-time or sandwich; entry requirements – two or three A levels plus supporting GCSEs or BTEC National Diploma or Foundation course or Scottish equivalent.
- Foundation degrees: two years. No entry requirements set and can lead on to an honours degree.
- BTEC/SQA Higher awards: two years full-time for the Diploma, two years part-time for the Certificate; entry requirements – one A level and four GCSEs (A–C) or Vocational A level or level 3 NVQ or National Diploma or Scottish equivalent.
- BTEC/SQA National awards: two years full-time; entry requirements – four GCSEs (A–C) or Intermediate GNVQ or level 2 NVQ.
- Engineering: a few specialist degrees but other engineering qualifications suitable (see p. 213).
- NVQs/SVQs are available at levels 1 to 3. No formal entry requirements.

Apprenticeships are available in areas such as manufacturing sewn products, garment technology and pattern cutting and grading. Local colleges may offer City & Guilds courses at craft and operative level.

Personal attributes Depends on particular job. For *top-level designers*, visual imagination, creative genius and exceptional business flair. For *other designers*, visual imagination and colour sense; adaptability; willingness to discipline creative flair to the technical and economic necessities of design for a popular market; self-confidence; some manual dexterity; ability to work as part of a team. For *production specialists*, interest in the technology of fashion; organizing ability; creative approach to problem-solving; eye for detail; ability to delegate and deal with people.

Mature entry and career change Depends on talent and drive. Competition from young college-leavers is very stiff.

Work–life balance Career break may be possible. *Designers*: Depends on how established before the break. *Production*: Probably no problem for those who have had good experience before the break. Changing technologies can easily be coped with by well-trained production managers. Part-time work not usual, except as freelance designer or, very occasionally, as relief (holiday) cutter, etc.

Further information

Skillfast-UK, Richmond House, Lawnswood Business Park, Redvers Close, Leeds LS16 6RD.
www.skillfast-uk.org

Related careers *art and design – journalism – photography – public relations – television, film and radio*

Health and Safety Advisers and Inspectors

Health and Safety Advisers

Health and safety advisers work in private sector companies and in local government.

Entry qualifications No specific requirements. Entry is at various levels (see 'Training' below).

The work Companies employ health and safety advisers, or managers, to ensure effective health and safety policies are in place, and that staff understand these policies and follow necessary guidelines. Their responsibilities may range from safety, fire and noise regulations to more complex occupational health and environmental protection issues.

Health and safety advisers in local government are responsible for ensuring that health and safety policies are in place, and that regulations are understood throughout the various departments of a council.

Training Relevant level 3 qualifications in occupational health and safety can be taken by part-time study and distance learning while working. Qualifications include N/SVQ awards, National Examinations Board in Occupational Health awards and British Safety Council awards. More advanced awards at levels 4, 5 and 6 can be taken after further study and employment experience.

Personal attributes Self-reliance; interest in technical matters and in people; diplomacy; ability to get on well with all kinds of people at all levels in the work hierarchy; fitness; initiative; ability to take responsibility; good report writing and general communication skills; ability to interpret legal issues; curiosity.

Further information

Institution of Occupational Safety and Health, The Grange, Highfield Drive, Wigston, Leicestershire LE18 1NN.
www.iosh.co.uk

Health and Safety Executive, Redgrave Court, Merton Road, Bootle, Merseyside L20 7HS.
www.hse.gov.uk

British Safety Council, 70 Chancellors Road, London W6 9RS.
www.britishsafetycouncil.co.uk

National Examinations Board in Occupational Health and Safety, Dominus Way, Meridian Business Park, Leicester LE19 1QW.
www.nebosh.org.uk
www.careers.civil-service.gov.uk

Health and Safety Inspectors

Entry qualifications Minimum National Qualifications Framework Level 3 (A levels, BTEC National awards) or Scottish Credit and Qualifications Framework equivalent, plus at least two years' relevant work experience, but entry is usually with a degree in any subject. Specialist inspectors usually require several years' relevant work experience plus appropriate professional qualifications.

The work Inspectors, who are civil servants, are concerned with the health, safety and welfare not only of workers, but of any of the public who may be affected by their work.

Health and safety inspectors are concerned with minimizing death, injury and disease stemming from work activities. They have a role in investigating major disasters where the public was placed at risk, but most of their work deals with prevention. They act as advisers, investigators, enforcement officers and sometimes prosecutors, collecting evidence and preparing and presenting cases. They deal with everything from a small workshop where people with disabilities may make toys to safety on offshore oil rigs.

Health and Safety Executive (HSE) inspectors are concerned with health and safety in the workplace. They cover a large range of industries and workplaces, not only factories but, for example, hospitals, construction sites, shipyards, offices and shops. There are also specialist inspectorates for agricultural, horticultural and forestry establishments, railways, offshore safety, nuclear installations, mines and explosives.

Generally the work may be divided into three types or levels. Inspectors are the 'GPs' who carry out the day-to-day work, visiting sites across the whole range of industry to ensure that conditions, machinery and equipment, procedures and safeguards meet the requirements of legislation. For particular problems inspectors may call on the advice of specialists (analogous to consultants in medicine) who may be experts in very narrow areas. When required, Health and Safety Laboratories provide sophisticated research, investigation and analysis. Inspectors are out of the office for as many as three days a week. They have considerable freedom to plan their work.

Further information

Health and Safety Executive, Redgrave Court, Merton Road, Bootle, Merseyside L20 7HS.
www.hse.gov.uk

Mature entry and career change Good opportunities. People with experience are needed, especially as the work is expanding. Track record may make up for lack of academic qualifications; each case is treated on its merit. Specialist inspectors always have previous experience.

Work–life balance Inspectors are civil servants (see p. 153).

Related careers *engineering – environmental health officer – science*

Health Services Management

Entry qualifications Entry is at all educational levels. There are formal training schemes for graduate entrants and for entrants at National Qualifications Framework Level 3 (A level, BTEC National awards) or Scottish Credit and Qualifications Framework equivalent. There is also direct entry with relevant professional qualifications and experience, and some managers move over from the clinical side.

The work The NHS is the largest single organization in Europe. With 1.3 million employees, and an annual budget of £90 billion, it is also the leading employer of managers. Health services managers provide the framework within which patients are treated by doctors and other clinical and paramedical staff. Their wide range of responsibilities includes: strategic planning; financial and human resource planning; the maintenance of buildings; the purchase and control of supplies and equipment; personnel management; contracting support services such as laundry, catering and other patient services.

Most jobs are with hospitals or community units, e.g. for the elderly or mentally ill. Work varies according to the size and structure of the unit as well as the individual manager's specific job. Thus one manager might be working on improving services to the ethnic community, arranging for translators and seeking advice on cultural expectations, while another works on the funding of a new consultant's position – what paramedical and other support staff will he or she need, when and where can an outpatient clinic be fitted in, what about extra equipment? Increasingly managers work in interdisciplinary teams (including doctors and other professional staff) to plan and develop new services, implement change (which is caused not just by legislation and reorganization but by medical and technological advances, changing population and so on), and manage staff, budgets and facilities. Negotiating skills are essential since resources are finite and various interests often conflict; for example, the cost of advances in one clinical speciality might mean a reduced budget in another.

Managers in the ten Strategic Health Authorities are responsible for long-term financial and manpower planning and helping to develop the role of the other tiers of the structure. Traditionally able, ambitious managers moved from unit to district to regional management, but the NHS changes have upset that pattern. For example, to head a Foundation Trust, with the new management freedom and demands, might offer a more attractive challenge. At local level responsibility for health provision is now devolved to Primary Care Trusts on which Health Authority representatives work with local health care and social care professionals.

New careers for managers are emerging in primary care. GPs employ practice managers to run their practices. This may involve managing financial systems and monitoring contracts.

Careers in health service management are not confined to the NHS. It is increasingly common for people to move between the private and voluntary health service sectors and the NHS, and there is also increasing exchange between the social services and the health services. The large pharmaceutical and health supplies companies also look to recruit managers who have a good understanding of the health service.

Training Training opportunities are both considerable in number and different in kind. They are multi-level and multi-mode. Schemes may be run nationally, regionally, by commissions and by larger trusts. Entry qualifications include degrees, A levels or equivalent and, for lower-level administrative work which can nevertheless lead to management, GCSEs or equivalent. Trainees can work towards postgraduate qualifications (including MBA and diplomas in management); relevant business/professional qualifications (e.g. in finance, personnel, purchasing); Institute of Healthcare Management award. There are an increasing number of undergraduate degrees in health studies.

Modes of study include full-time pre-entry courses, work-based training, day release, distance learning and open learning. A level 4 Diploma in Primary Care Management is awarded by AMSPAR. An individual's choice may be influenced not only by personal preferences and circumstances, but by what provision is available locally and the needs of a particular employer.

In-house training for supervisory posts or middle management may lead to an N/SVQ or an IHM award.

Entrants to the NHS Graduate Management Training Scheme spend the first two years in their choice of specialist role in finance, human resources or general management, while working towards professional qualifications in those fields. Further specialist training and support can lead to additional professional qualifications in subsequent years. Graduates with previous management experience in other organizations can apply to join the NHS Gateway to Leadership Programme, which may offer opportunities for accelerated promotion to senior management positions (see *www.come2life.nhs. uk*).

In Scotland: Scotland has introduced its own training scheme for health services managers (see *www.managementtrainingscheme. nhsscotland.com*).

The Institute of Healthcare Management provides continuing professional development to help managers adapt to the rapid changes and new developments going on in the health service.

Because so many qualifications are appropriate and training opportunities exist at many levels, anyone interested should contact NHS Careers.

Personal attributes Numeracy; flexibility; ability to discuss complex issues with specialists at all levels; organizing ability; ability to work as a member of a team; communication and negotiating skills; commitment to patient care.

Mature entry and career change Good opportunities for those with appropriate qualifications and experience – the NHS does recruit managers from outside, usually from other parts of the public sector.

Work–life balance The NHS has a commitment to flexible working, including part-time, job-sharing and term-time working. The NHS in principle encourages returners following career breaks but currently there is no specific programme for managers.

Further information

NHS Careers Helpline: 0845 60 60 655
www.nhscareers.nhs.uk

Institute of Healthcare Management, 18–21 Morley Street, London SE1 7QZ.
www.ihm.org.uk

The Association of Medical Secretaries, Practice Managers, Administrators and Receptionists, Tavistock House North, Tavistock Square, London WC1H 9LN.
www.amspar.co.uk

Related careers *chartered secretary and administrator – hospitality and catering – management*

Hospitality and Catering

Entry qualifications All educational levels. Considerable graduate entry. See 'Training', below.

The work The industry is traditionally divided into two areas of commercial hospitality services and catering services, although they overlap. Hospitality includes hotels – vast numbers of small ones, a small number of large and/or luxury ones, motels, clubs, pubs and restaurants. Catering services include what is traditionally called institutional management: the provision of meals in schools and colleges, hospitals, etc., as well as industry, local and central government, passenger transport. Contract caterers may work in either area. There is not necessarily any greater difference between jobs in commercial and in non-profit-making catering than there is between individual jobs within each area.

Catering skills are highly transferable and there is considerable overlap of the different sectors. But for senior hotel management, experience in food and drink services as well as in accommodation services is necessary; for non-residential catering, experience of accommodation services is not necessary.

Job titles vary: two jobs with the same title may involve totally different tasks and levels of responsibility. Much depends on the size of establishment and the level of service it provides. It is an industry in which it is still possible to start at the bottom and, with aptitude, hard work and willingness to gain qualifications, reach the top and/or start one's own business.

In senior management, work often overlaps with other managerial jobs and involves less contact with the public (the reason which brings most entrants into this industry). Senior managers in a fast food chain may, for example, work entirely at head office with visits to units where they meet customers; in industrial catering they may be responsible for a group of catering units, visiting individual managers and liaising with head office; or they may investigate the latest 'catering systems' (see below).

The majority of catering jobs involve working when customers are at leisure, as do so many jobs in service industries. This can make a 'normal' social life difficult at times, but there are compensations to be had in being able to shop, play sport, etc. at less crowded times.

Large industrial and institutional catering concerns and some chain restaurants increasingly use systems catering or catering systems instead of letting the chef decide what is for dinner and then getting the staff to prepare the meal. Dishes are partly or fully prepared, and sometimes even 'trayed up' in vast production kitchens. Then they are transported, frozen or chilled, to the 'point of consumption', which may be many miles away. Finally, at the point of consumption, food is 'reconstituted', perhaps in a microwave oven.

Managers must understand the technologies involved and their effects on ingredients, and they must be good organizers.

Hotel Manager

The manager's work varies enormously according to size and type of hotel. In large hotels, the general manager is coordinator and administrator, responsible for staff management, marketing and selling, financial control, provision of services, quality control and customer care. Departmental managers are in charge of specialist services: reception, sales, food and bar service, housekeeping, banqueting, etc. The manager deals with correspondence, has daily meetings with departmental managers and may be in touch daily or weekly with head office. Although managers try to be around to talk to guests (not only when they have complaints), most of their time is spent dealing with running the business side, making decisions based on information obtained from the accountant, personnel manager, sales manager, food and beverage manager, etc.

Managers do not normally have to live in, though they may have a bedroom or flat on the premises. Working hours are long, and often busiest at weekends and during holidays. They must be able to switch from one task to another instantly, and change their daily routine when necessary – which it often is. Among managers' most important tasks are:

- creating and maintaining good staff relations, as success depends entirely on the work done by others under their overall direction
- giving the hotel the personality and the character which either the manager, or more often the owner, intends it to have
- being able to make a constantly changing clientele feel as though each of them mattered individually. However, the extent of emphasis on personal service varies according to the type of hotel.

In small hotels the manager may have a staff of up to 30, and instead of several departmental managers, possibly one general assistant. Living-in may be necessary, and off-duty time may be less generous than in large hotels. There are far more small (and unpretentious) hotels than large or small luxury ones. Many small and medium-sized country hotels are owned by companies and run by couples.

General Assistant – Assistant Manager

The work varies according to the size and type of hotel. In small hotels, assistant managers help wherever help is needed most – in the kitchen, in the bar, in housekeeping. Although the work is extremely hard, it is the best possible experience – an essential complement to college training.

In large hotels, assistant managers may be the same as departmental managers (see above). They may take turns at being 'duty manager' available to deal with any problem that occurs on a particular shift. Trainee managers may spend some time as assistants in different departments before deciding to specialize.

Personal attributes *For top jobs*: Exceptional organizing ability and business acumen; outgoing personality; the wish to please people, however unreasonable customers' demands may seem; an interest in all the practical skills – cooking, bar management, housekeeping, etc.; willingness to work while others play; ability to shoulder responsibility and handle staff; tact.

For assistants/managers of small hotels: Partly as for managers, but exceptional organizing ability is not necessary; instead, a liking for practical work is essential, and willingness to work hard and get things done without taking the credit.

Receptionist/'Front Desk'

The reception desk is always near or at the entrance to the hotel and receptionists arc at the centre of activities. Since they are usually the first contact guests have with the hotel on arrival it is essential that they make a good impression.

Head receptionists are assisted in large and medium-sized hotels by junior receptionists. They check bookings and deal with enquiries over the telephone or by post. Steering a course between unnecessary refusal of bookings and over-booking is skilled work. Receptionists deal with correspondence; they must be able to do straightforward bookkeeping, compose and type their own letters: they notify other hotel departments of arrivals and departures, and keep the customers' accounts up to date. Almost all hotels have computerized reservations and accounts systems, which give instant information on a whole hotel group's vacancies, on guests' accounts, and possibly on the supply position regarding clean linen, beverages, etc. Reception also acts as general information office: staff answer guests' queries about, for example, train times, local tourist attractions or the address of a good hairdresser.

Receptionists work shifts, for example from early in the morning to mid-afternoon or from mid-afternoon to late at night. Especially in country hotels, they may live in; meals on duty are supplied free.

Head receptionists are usually responsible directly to the manager; theirs is considered one of the most important posts in the hotel business and can be a stepping stone to general management.

Personal attributes A friendly, helpful personality; an uncritical liking for people of all types; a good memory for faces – visitors appreciate recognition; ability to take responsibility and to work well with others; considerable self-confidence; a methodical approach; a liking for figures; meticulous accuracy; especially in tourist areas, modern language skills. For top jobs: Business acumen; good judgement of people; leadership.

Housekeeper

Except in small hotels, housekeepers do not do housework, but supervise domestic staff (mainly room-service attendants, formerly called chambermaids). Other duties include: checking rooms, seeing that they are clean, comfortable and that all the amenities are working (e.g. tea-makers and fridges); supervising laundry and ordering linen; pass-key control; room-service organization and supervision; liaison with other departments such as reception and maintenance; training and engaging staff and arranging work schedules. In a large hotel a head housekeeper may be in charge of a staff of 200.

In small and medium-sized hotels the housekeeper may be responsible for choosing and maintaining the furnishings, decoration and general appearance of bedrooms and lounges. In large hotels there may be one assistant or floor housekeeper to every floor, or every two floors; the executive housekeeper, who is immediately responsible to the manager, therefore has considerable overall responsibility.

Personal attributes Organizing ability; practical approach; an eye for detail; ability to handle and train staff.

Hotel Sales Management

A fringe hotel management career. Hotel sales managers work for large hotels and hotel groups. They sell 'hotel facilities' – efficiency, service, atmosphere, as well as conference and banqueting facilities. A hotel sales manager working for a group may approach large business concerns and try to fix contracts for business executives to stay regularly at the group's hotels. Jointly with tour operators (see p. 619) and airlines, etc., they build package tours.

Hotel sales managers come either via hotel management, or marketing or any other type of business experience.

Personal attributes Business acumen; numeracy; extrovert, friendly personality.

Restaurant Management

Eating places range from wine bars to large 'popular' and to exclusive haute cuisine restaurants. Restaurant managers must know how to attract and keep customers.

Catering for fluctuating numbers of customers with the minimum of waste is a highly skilled job, as is arranging staffing rosters to cope with busy periods without being over-staffed in slack ones.

Managers' responsibilities vary greatly according to type and size of restaurant. For example, if the restaurant is one of a chain, overall planning and ordering may be done at head office; in other places the manager may be given a very free hand to 'give the restaurant that personal touch', as long as menus keep within a given price range and reach the profit target. The responsibility for menu-planning is usually the chef's (except in chain restaurants), but the manager must have considerable understanding of food and also of wine.

According to type of restaurant, managers spend varying amounts of time on 'customer contact'. Chef-proprietors have to spend some time away from their kitchens talking to customers. Except in lunch-only restaurants, working hours, though not necessarily longer, are more spread out, with some evening and weekend work.

Professional Cook

Cooking always involves some physically hard work – the busier the kitchens, the tougher the job often is. Even with modern design and equipment, kitchens still tend to be hot, noisy and damp, and at times very hectic.

There is a variety of openings at various levels of skill and responsibility. For example, in large-scale haute cuisine, a chef heads a hierarchy of section chefs or *chefs de partie*, each responsible for one area of activity – larder, vegetables, pastry, etc. The chef may be responsible for budgeting, buying, planning – or this may all be done by a food and beverage manager, or at head office; responsibilities depend on type and size of organization worked for. In small restaurants, two or three cooks may do all the work. In simpler restaurants, convenience foods are used extensively and the cook's ability to produce palatable, inexpensive yet reasonably varied menus is the most important aspect of the work. It is no easier than, but very different from, haute cuisine. Production kitchens leave little scope for creative cooking; every dish is prepared to recipes specifying such details as the size, weight, colour and often even the position on the plate of meat or cucumber slices, of sprouts or strawberries. But in experimental kitchens where new dishes and technologies are tried out, the work combines creative cooking skills, an understanding of the effects on the ingredients of being prepared in these unorthodox ways and, above all, managerial skills. There is also scope for creativity in small proprietor-run restaurants.

In large kitchens there are many cooking jobs without managerial responsibilities, but anyone who wants to progress beyond the kitchen-hand stage must take systematic training; home-cooking experience is not enough.

It is important to distinguish between courses for professional cooks, largely run by colleges of further education and some universities, and for haute cuisine for home cooking, mainly found in private schools. Cookery classes and schools do not always make this difference clear.

Freelance Cook

Many people, both those professionally trained and gifted amateurs, make a living by freelance cooking. Clients range from company directors hosting lunches for a dozen clients to individuals wanting someone to cook for dinner or cocktail parties at their home. Some cooks specialize in party food for large or small gatherings. They need their own car or van to transport equipment and shopping. They must be able to budget and cook within various price ranges. Sometimes they cook for families on holidays abroad, or for travel agents' chalet-party package tours, working in ski resorts all winter, at the seaside all summer. This type of work usually includes general housekeeping.

Food and Drink Service – 'Waiting'

Food service can range from working behind a self-service food counter to highly skilled 'silver service' in a directors' dining room or luxury hotel. Beverage service includes working behind a bar in a hotel or public house and, as wine waiter, helping a customer choose a suitable wine. Like cooking, waiting is at times physically hard and hectic, although the working environment is usually much more pleasant. In a restaurant the quality of the meal service is often as important to the customer as the quality of the food and can help to make or break its reputation.

Fast Foods

The products of this expanding part of the industry range from fish and chips to curry, pizzas to hamburgers. Outlets may be independent businesses, part of a large chain or franchises (the parent company, or franchisor, supplies materials and services and the right to use a trade name, in return for which the franchisee invests capital and pays a levy). Some sell takeaway food only, others also provide table service; all resemble small food-factories with a retail counter. All operations can be learnt quickly and staff often take turns cooking and serving; most chains train in-house and in their own training centres. In what is very much a young person's environment, promotion from school-leaver entrant to supervisor level can be rapid. Management posts are filled either by very successful supervisors or by people with degrees or diplomas in catering, business studies or even arts subjects. The latter have to learn all the basic operations at first hand before undergoing management training. The fast food industry is highly competitive and requires considerable business expertise in order to maintain cash flow and to control stock. Success depends on high turnover, which in turn involves very long hours, but there are real opportunities for people to run their own business.

Pub ('Licensed House') Management

There are over 60,000 pubs in Britain, of which nearly a third are independent, half are owned by pub companies and the rest by breweries. Although the British pub has a traditional image, most now offer food, some with a separate restaurant; a few even have a theatre. Children are now allowed in parts of many pubs, while the loosening of licensing hours restrictions means that pubs can choose to open all day, including Sundays. Those who run pubs are proprietors, managers employed by the owner, or tenants or lessees, who rent or lease the pub for a given period. Many companies in the licensed trade now have graduate recruitment schemes and are keen to attract young people into the sector. It is a way of life rather than a job, as it means being tied to the bar during licensing hours, seven days a week. Work involves purchasing, stock-control and record-keeping as well as bar service. Thorough knowledge of licensing laws is essential. Interest in entertainment trends and more than just a 'liking for people' of all kinds are essential. Specialist training and experience in bar and cellar work is required by anyone hoping eventually to become a licensee.

An important area of employment for people working in the licensed trade is leisure and recreation: sports clubs, leisure centres, private clubs, racecourses and holiday centres nearly all have bars. Bar staff are the licensees and have their own 'franchise' – instead of working for a salary they 'rent' the bar on the premises and run it.

Industrial and Contract Catering

This covers the provision of meals at places of work. Service is provided either by staff employed by the organization itself, or, increasingly, by catering contractors. These run 'catering units' on clients' premises in factories, offices, old people's homes, hospitals, schools, colleges, and, with mobile units, at special/outdoor events. They may also operate vending machines. Contractors' staff can change the setting in which they work without having to change employers. Area and district managers are in charge of a number of units; unit managers and chef/managers work on the same premises regularly for a period.

Unit managers themselves usually only cook if fewer than about 50 meals are being served. Their main task normally is trying to achieve as even a flow of work as possible. Other tasks include: menu-planning – the complexity of this varies according to the range of meals to be provided, from a narrow range of standard dishes to a wide selection including directors' dining room 'specials', and according to the importance attached to nutritional values and tight budget control. Expertise includes being able to provide at least two weeks' changing menus within several given price ranges and at different grades of sophistication; costing – ingredients, labour costs, etc.; purchasing, which includes negotiating with suppliers and specifying, for example, the uniform size and weight of each lamb chop in an order of several hundreds.

Managers normally attend meetings with directors and/or personnel managers and also discuss improvements or complaints with staff representatives. They must keep up with technological developments and are usually responsible for, or for advising on, types of service, and purchase and maintenance of equipment. (That work may also be done by specialists.)

There is a wide choice of jobs: from preparing sophisticated snacks for a West End showroom, or a dozen haute cuisine lunches in a managing director's office with one or two assistants, to feeding 2,000 a day with a staff of 50 including two or three assistant managers.

In much contract catering, hours are more regular than in other parts of the industry, and staff often work weekdays only.

School Catering Services

These have undergone big changes in the last few years. Compulsory competitive tendering by local education authorities has meant that in many areas contract caterers, not the local authority itself, provide the service and, therefore, employ the school meals staff. Schools catering is basically the same as industrial catering, with special emphasis on catering for children's tastes, nutritional values and strict budget control. In some areas, only snacks are provided, in others much effort has gone into improving the standard and image of the service.

After training, caterers supervise the preparation of dinners, either at school kitchens or at centres from which up to 1,000 meals are distributed to a number of schools.

Promotion depends on the employing organization. Senior staff (who may be called school meals organizers) advise on buying, planning, staffing, kitchen management, nutrition, etc. They are also concerned with contract compliance, specifications and marketing. Cost control is very important. Organizers are responsible for geographical areas and do a good deal of travelling. Hours tend to be regular.

Hospital Catering

Hospital catering officers (now often called hotel services managers) organize provision of meals for patients, staff and visitors, which means meals for between 200 and 3,000 people, many of whom need meals round the clock. Some hospitals have opened up their conference/meetings facilities to outsiders. They usually prepare diets under the overall direction but not day-to-day supervision of dietitians. It is possible to enter as a school-leaver and train in-house. New entrants with vocational qualifications in hospitality and/or catering follow the NHS Hotel Services Development Programme.

Experience in hospital catering is very useful training for other specializations.

Hospital catering is also contracted out to specialist firms.

Transport Catering

This is often done by contractors using catering systems. Menu-planning in airlines involves taking into account climatic conditions at point of consumption; commercial facts such as air commuters' 'menu-fatigue' (business people travel the same routes regularly; frequent menu changes must be made or customers are lost to the competition); research into which dishes and wines 'travel well'.

Airline catering is very tightly cost-controlled; but in *marine* catering priorities are different: for passengers and crews at sea, meals are the highlight of the day. Proportionately more money is spent on food at sea than in the air, so seacooks and chefs have greater opportunities for creative cooking, and therefore for getting good shore-based jobs later.

Victualling ships – ordering supplies for trips sometimes several months long – is another catering specialization. Work is done in shipping companies' offices. Previous large-scale catering experience is essential.

Accommodation and Catering Management

This is management in non-profit-making, mainly residential establishments: halls of residence, hostels; the domestic side of hospitals; as well as, increasingly, in commercial conference and training centres. It also includes non-residential work: private school catering; meals-on-wheels; social service departments' day centres.

Managers may be called bursar, warden, domestic superintendent, catering manager. The range of titles makes it difficult to compare level of responsibility, status or duties. They may be wholly or partly responsible for all or some of the following aspects of community life:

- meals service
- budgeting; purchase and maintenance of kitchen equipment; planning additional building
- furnishings and decoration
- the use of the buildings for conferences or vacation courses
- dealing with residents' and staff's suggestions and complaints

- helping to establish a friendly atmosphere both among staff and among residents
- in small establishments, first aid and home-nursing (but not responsibility for sick residents)
- acting as host and as general information bureau; dealing with committees.

Most jobs are entirely administrative, but in small institutions the manager occasionally has to help out with housework or cooking. Many (by no means all) jobs are residential; accommodation varies from bedsitter to self-contained flat for couples (with partner not necessarily working in the organization concerned).

Training (generally)

The main choice is between a full-time college or university course and getting experience and training in-house, preferably as part of a formal training scheme, for example an Apprenticeship.

Main full-time college routes With two or three A levels or equivalent: three-year or four-year degree (titles include Hotel and Catering Management, Hospitality Management). These vary in emphasis on different catering aspects, but generally include supervision of food and beverage preparation (and some practical work); catering management principles and practice; catering technologies; specialist work such as airline catering; sales management and marketing; accounting; computer application; aspects of tourism, recreation and leisure industries; international catering and languages (some courses include opportunities to study in Europe or further afield).

There are postgraduate qualifications for people with a relevant degree or experience or any degree plus experience/interest in hotels and catering.

With one A level or equivalent: BTEC/SQA Higher National Diploma (titles similar to those for degree). Core subjects include study of the hospitality industry, customer service, food, beverage and rooms division operations and management accounting. Options may include conference and banqueting management, people management, sales and merchandising or e-business.

Main work-based routes With no set entry qualifications: NVQs/SVQs in a variety of catering subjects at levels 1–4. In order to gain these it is necessary to have training and support from the employer. The Institute of Hospitality awards provide flexible units of continuing professional development (CPD) which build up into fully accredited qualifications at levels 2, 3 and 4 on the National Qualifications Framework (NQF).

Apprenticeships programmes are available.

In-house management schemes may require a degree or HND/HNC.

A Foundation degree for employees in the hospitality industry can be studied on a flexible basis.

Training and qualifications for the licensed trade are also offered by the British Institute of Innkeeping and the Wine and Spirit Education Trust.

Personal attributes In varying degrees: organizing and administrative ability; outgoing personality; ability to motivate staff and to communicate with all types of people – from kitchen porters to managing directors, from salespeople to a coach-load of pensioners; interest in people and in their creature comforts; some practical skills; ability to work under pressure; stamina; flexibility; tact when dealing with 'difficult' customers; sense of humour.

Mature entry and career change No problem. Admission to courses depends on experience and motivation rather than age and qualifications.

Work–life balance Half the workforce is part-time, but there are still very limited opportunities at management level. Opportunities exist in cooking, housekeeping, junior reception, food service and bar work, and freelance catering offers possibilities.

Further information

The Institute of Hospitality, Trinity Court, 34 West Street, Sutton, Surrey SM1 1SH.
www.hcima.org.uk

People 1st, the Sector Skills Council for Hospitality, Leisure, Travel & Tourism Industries, 2nd Floor, Armstrong House, 38 Market Square, Uxbridge, Middlesex UB8 1LH.
www.instituteofhospitality.org

The British Institute of Innkeeping (BII), Wessex House, 80 Park Street, Camberley, Surrey GU15 3PT.
www.bii.org

The Wine and Spirit Education Trust, 39–45 Bermondsey Street, London SE1 3XF.
www.wset.co.uk

Related careers *consumer scientist – dietetics – science: Food Science and Technology – teaching – travel agent/tour operator*

Housing Management

Entry qualifications Various levels. Considerable graduate entry.

The work Traditionally housing managers are responsible for a wide range of functions relating to the administration, maintenance and allocation of accommodation let for rent. They may also be involved in the running of Housing Aid Centres; giving advice on rent and benefit schemes; housing research and the formulation of housing policy. Housing managers and housing assistants work mainly for housing associations and local authorities. However, as local authority housing stock has diminished, due to council houses being sold and not as many new houses being built, authorities have transferred their houses to housing associations and housing companies to manage. This means the number and scope of housing associations has increased, along with the number of people working for them. A small number work for building societies, property companies and voluntary bodies.

Day-to-day housing management adds up to an unusual combination of dealing with people, using technical knowledge and getting out and about. Duties may include interviewing applicants for homes; visiting prospective tenants in their homes to assess their housing needs; finding and monitoring bed and breakfast accommodation and trying as quickly as possible to move tenants into something more satisfactory; inspecting property at regular intervals and arranging, if necessary, for repairs to be carried out; dealing with tenants' complaints about anything from noisy neighbours and lack of play facilities for children to lack of maintenance. Rent collecting, which used to be the most important and time-consuming task, has all but died out: most tenants now take or send rent to the housing office.

Housing staff try to establish and maintain good tenant–landlord relationships and try to forge a conglomeration of dwellings into a community. To this end they may try to involve tenants in managing their block of flats or estate, or they may set up tenants' management committees. In Housing Aid Centres, housing staff advise on any problem related to housing, from how to cope with an eviction order or how to get a rent allowance, to where to apply for a mortgage.

At a senior level, the work involves top-level general and financial management using modern management techniques; the purchase of properties; the allocation of accommodation (which is the most onerous task); research into housing needs and into such questions as 'How can we retain neighbourliness in new developments?', 'What is a good environment?', etc.; advising architects and planners on social aspects of siting, design and layout of new developments.

The fact that there has been a considerable increase in owner-occupiers and a decrease in accommodation let for rent by local authorities has not diminished the importance of housing management, but it has changed its role. As stock for rent is reduced, and more tenants are poor and on benefits, so the welfare element has become more important. New problems emerge such as the shortage of affordable housing for key workers in central London and other areas. The emphasis now is more on efficient management, and on exploring innovative ways of coping with housing need. New approaches to the problem include shared ownership; rent-into-mortgage schemes; leasing short-life property from private landlords; more cooperation between local authorities, housing associations, and building societies and private property companies. There is also now more movement between housing associations and local authorities than there used to be. It is still easier, though, to move from local authority to housing association than the other way around.

In local authority departments which manage thousands of dwellings, staff usually specialize in one aspect of the work at a time. In housing associations, which manage a smaller number, one housing assistant or housing manager may deal with everything concerning a number of tenancies. Housing associations increasingly provide facilities for special groups, e.g. for the elderly, single-parent families, the disabled. Some run hostels for such 'special needs' groups as ex-prisoners or people who have been psychiatric patients and still need support while adjusting to living in the community.

The number of graduates moving into the profession is increasing. However, most housing associations will employ people with other transferable skills. These could be in general management, or accountancy, or with a degree in social science/administration or in surveying. As the stock of property increases, maintenance and conversion need more people with relevant knowledge.

A recent specialism is *housing consultancy.* Consultants are people with housing experience who set up as freelancers and advise on or help with state-of-the-art financial or general management, setting up rent-into-mortgage or other innovative schemes in which private and public sector organizations cooperate. They also help with in-house training.

Training There are qualifications in housing at all levels, from degree courses through N/SVQs at levels 2–4 to an Apprenticeship in Housing. Several routes lead to the Chartered Institute of Housing's Professional Qualification:

- Work-based route: First stage – entry with at least one A level and four GCSEs (A–C) or equivalent, for on-the-job training with day release or distance learning for the Higher National Certificate in Housing Studies, or the CIH's level 4 Diploma in Housing, or N/SVQ level 4 in housing. The next stage is a further two years' part-time or distance learning for the Institute's Professional Diploma. This route to the Professional Qualification usually takes four years.
- Graduates with a relevant degree take a one-year full-time or two-year part-time postgraduate Diploma or Masters course leading to the Professional Qualification. (Graduates with an unrelated degree are required to take a one-year conversion course.)

A Professional Diploma or BA/BSc in Housing leading to the Professional Qualification can be studied full-time or part-time or by distance learning. Before finally qualifying candidates must pass the Institute's APEX, which tests a candidate's practical housing experience. While housing associations often take graduates and do not expect them to train for the Professional Diploma, for career moves the Professional Diploma is increasingly required.

The CIH also offers a range of other qualifications which can be achieved at work, at college or through distance learning.

Personal attributes Ability to get on well with all types of people; an interest in social, practical and economic problems, and in planning; tolerance; ability to be firm; indifference to being out in bad weather; organizing ability and diplomacy for senior people.

Mature entry and career change Late entrants welcome. Aptitude and relevant work, as well as 'life experience', are often more important than qualifications.

Work–life balance Returners are welcome. The CIH has reduced membership fees for the temporarily retired. There are excellent opportunities for part-time work and job-sharing.

Further information
The Chartered Institute of Housing, Octavia House, Westwood Business Park, Westwood Way, Coventry, Warwickshire CV4 8JP.
www.cih.org

Related careers *environmental health officer – local government – town planning*

Information Science/Librarianship

It has been said that we live in an information society. The sheer weight of information available increases all the time and impinges on every facet of modern life. We need information on which to base decisions on a whole range of issues. The Year 11 student wants to find out where various A level combinations could lead him or her. A doctor needs to know the possible side-effects of a new treatment. An investor might look into the performance of various shares. A marketing manager wants to keep abreast of what the competition is up to. Information is vital to our education, our work, our leisure, our health.

Developments in technology have had an enormous impact on the 'information industry'. Not only has technology led to new ways of collecting, organizing and retrieving information, but it has also led to more information! The information specialist has to deal with a range of sources far beyond books and other printed material.

Entry qualifications For professional work, a degree; for assistant posts, nothing rigid, but four GCSE passes or equivalent, including English, may be asked for.

The work Distinctions between the librarian and the information scientist have blurred. Differences are often a matter of the emphasis of their work, rather than a fundamental difference of role or purpose. Job titles are not necessarily an indication of job content or emphasis. Information scientists may be Chartered Members of CILIP (Chartered Institute of Library and Information Professionals); a librarian in a specialist library may work with highly technical information. In information science, however, there is more emphasis on sourcing, analysis and presentation in formats for others to use. Information officer and research officer are other titles that may crop up in job adverts.

The common basic purpose of the librarian/information specialist is to see that relevant information is available and used effectively. For whatever purpose, the job of the information specialist is to acquire, organize and exploit information. This covers a vast range of activity. Acquiring might range from maintaining as broad and balanced a collection as possible to cater for a wide range of general interests, within a given budget, to trawling the international market to build up a highly specialist collection of academic or technical interest. Exploiting might mean inviting a children's author to read his or her stories to pre-schoolers or preparing a newsletter to keep specialists aware of developments in their field.

The public library service is vast and provides a wide range of services to the public. Librarians are responsible for the selection, purchase, cataloguing and arrangement of a wide variety of materials – books and periodicals, videos, cassettes, records, slides, CDs and information packs, for example. Many libraries run special services, such as 'books-on-wheels', children's activities, services to business or the ethnic community. All provide information, sometimes in specially produced packs, and answer inquiries. Many libraries have computerized information systems.

In a smaller library, and at early stages of their careers, librarians' work may cover several functions, but many jobs involve some degree of specialization. More senior positions involve managing staff and resources. As in most jobs, routine work is inevitable, but many of the routine tasks associated with libraries – issuing books, filling and tidying shelves – are not done by professional librarians but by library assistants. Most public librarians will be Chartered Members of CILIP (see below).

Academic libraries in universities and colleges offer a service to both staff and students, and sometimes to outsiders. In consultation with academic staff, librarians carefully select materials to support the teaching and learning going on in the institution. Many academic librarians are specialists in a particular subject area and often have a degree in that subject. Others may manage special collections, e.g. early printed books, manuscripts, music or computer software. Important aspects of the work in academic libraries are helping students to understand and use effectively the facilities available (including the latest technology) and helping academic staff to keep up to date with developments in their subjects. Many posts in academic libraries are open only to those who have a postgraduate qualification (see below).

Industry and commerce need good information to make good decisions. As in other areas, the information specialist is responsible for selecting material; this could demand considerable specialist knowledge of the organization's area of operations in, for example, science or engineering, as well as information skills. Information technology has had an enormous impact on the storage and retrieval of information, as well as on the range available, and information specialists will be expected to exploit this to fulfil their company's needs, whether it involves designing and implementing a system to catalogue all the company's information resources, or buying in the latest database. The provision of information for specific purposes is an important task and might involve, for example, researching and compiling a list or database of key references on a particular topic; exploiting a network of outside contacts, e.g. trade associations, learned societies, other company libraries; preparing summaries or abstracts of new information. A reading knowledge of a foreign language can be very useful.

Information specialists are also employed in government departments, museums, research and professional bodies, and the media. There are some opportunities to work as a freelance consultant.

In public and academic libraries, where services are affected by public-spending policies, openings are not increasing in numbers. In information departments and special libraries, particularly in health, the number of jobs is increasing. Graduates in physics, chemistry, computer studies and related science/technology fields are keenly sought; there is also a need for specialists in accountancy, economics, finance, law and management. (However, any degree subject can lead to work in this field.)

Training *For Chartered Information Professionals*: a CILIP-accredited three-year or four-year information degree or one-year full-time or three-year or four-year part-time postgraduate diploma/masters. To gain chartered status, an additional one year of professional in-post training. Candidates may also follow CILIP's ACLIP Certification programme (Certified Affiliate of CILIP) and then go on to Charter.

For library and information assistants: part-time courses leading to City & Guilds, BTEC and SQA National and Higher National Certificates in librarianship and information studies and CILIP's ACLIP Certification.

NVQs at levels 2 and 3 or SVQs at levels 2, 3 and 4 in Information and Library Services.

Employers' requirements and preferences can vary. For some jobs a relevant first degree can be more important than further qualifications. Some people take relevant postgraduate courses, but do not go on to professional membership.

Personal attributes Good communication skills; curiosity; an interest in a variety of related topics without the desire to delve too deeply into any one; a methodical approach; a high degree of accuracy; organizing ability; a retentive memory; staying power for long, possibly fruitless searches; resourcefulness; interest in electronic information systems; capacity to switch instantly from one topic to another; ability to cope with frequent interruptions when doing jobs requiring concentration; ability to anticipate users' needs. Because library and information work has so many different aspects, practitioners' relative strengths in these areas may vary.

Mature entry and career change Educational institutions may relax normal requirements for mature students.

Work–life balance A career break should be no problem if well qualified and up to date. Short courses can be used as refresher courses, though not intended as such. Formal schemes are increasing, particularly in the private sector.

Reasonable opportunities for part-time work at junior and up to middle-management level, but more difficult at senior levels. However, flexible working is becoming more common, including home working, job-sharing, term-time working and compressed hours, i.e. working more hours per day in return for a shorter working week.

Further information

Aslib (The Association for Information Management), Holywell Centre, 1 Phipp Street, London EC2A 4PS.
www.aslib.com

Chartered Institute of Library and Information Professionals, 7 Ridgmount Street, London WC1E 7AE.
www.cilip.org.uk

Related careers *archivist – bookselling – museums and art galleries – publishing*

Information Technology/
Information Systems

Entry qualifications This is mainly a graduate occupation, but exact requirements depend on job type (see below). For trainee programming jobs, in practice, at least two A levels or degree (any subject); for software programming/engineer, usually IT-related degree – computing science A level not required for most of these courses. An ability to think logically, good communication skills and attention to detail are important.

The work Information technology is an essential element of the nation's economic performance. Almost all UK businesses and professional organizations rely on some form of information technology system to help them function more effectively. IT applications make essential information easier to access, sort, interpret and present. The rapid expansion of Internet-based communications has further increased dependency on IT. The result is a continuing demand for specialists who design, develop, manage, maintain and support systems for others to use.

One recent estimate suggested that within ten years over a million people will be employed in IT occupations. An IT professional can no longer just be a 'techie'; to increase their employment chances they need to be able to offer management, sales, teamworking or customer sales skills.

The industry is also changing rapidly as technologies continually evolve and improve in terms of the ways in which information can be stored and processed.

A number of New Technology Institutes have been established nationwide. These involve universities, colleges and other training providers in developing information and communications technology (ICT) training opportunities for students and employers.

Computing and IT professionals are highly skilled practitioners and although qualifying routes are becoming more established, experience and potential can still be more marketable than qualifications. Demarcation between the various computer specialisms is constantly changing, and the emphasis is on teamwork, because devices are becoming ever more sophisticated, demanding new skills or newly combined skills. Teams of computer staff are headed by project leaders, who now have a well-defined planning and monitoring management role.

Job titles and functions vary considerably: the following descriptions are based on broad generalisations. With almost every sector of industry, commerce and government depending on IT, only a proportion of IT specialists work directly for an IT company.

Software Engineer/Designer/Developer, Computer Programmer, Systems Software Programmer (titles are interchangeable)

Software engineers produce the technology which drives the IT industry. There are two kinds of software: that which controls the operating system of a computer or other hardware and the software that runs the applications or programs used on computers. Some of them work at the cutting edge, 'pushing out new frontiers of science', but most now work on updating, refining or adding to systems already in use, or increasing the compatibility of different products.

The ongoing proliferation of increasingly sophisticated e-shopping and multimedia websites and other developments on the Internet is also increasing employment opportunities. Software engineers may be employed by software firms, or by consultancies who design and produce software for different clients, or by large companies to support in-house systems.

The work requires a high level of creativity and expertise and software engineers need to be familiar with different coding languages and applications. They usually work as a team but some do work alone. Nevertheless the work may involve consultation with clients or colleagues and where software is being written for a specific purpose, liaising with the end-users to acquire an understanding of the processes to be covered. They also implement and follow up new programs, testing them and correcting defects. They write the technical specifications and test plans for their programs and may liaise with technical authors in the publication of user manuals.

Depending on the type of organization in which they work, software engineers may become team leaders or project managers, responsible for managing staff, budgets and keeping to timescales. Software design is now a very competitive business and most software houses work to tight deadlines. These may mean long hours and a strong commitment to the work.

Network Specialists design and maintain the Local/Wide Area Networks (LAN/WANs) which allow computerized workstations to 'talk' to each other. Networking has become a means of integrating both computer applications and business functions. Jobs in this area cover network design, implementation, support and management. This is one of the most rapidly growing areas of IT and suitable staff are in short supply.

Systems Analyst/Designer

They identify the problem and design the solution to it. There are three stages to the job. First, they investigate and analyse the existing system – or lack of it – in the organization which is intending to install or update a computer system. In many organizations patterns of work have evolved haphazardly and, in the process, have become inefficient. The systems analyst spends several months getting to know the intricacies of the business, observing and talking to staff in all departments and at all levels – from junior clerk or packer to buyer or marketing and managing directors – to assess routines, bottlenecks, objectives. The work requires business acumen, knowledge of commercial practice and an ability to get people to talk freely about their work and to accept changes in long-established routines. When the old system has been translated into a logical sequence of procedures, the systems analyst writes a report on how the new system would affect the organization's staff, and how it would improve efficiency and profitability, and at what cost. If the report is accepted by the management, the systems analyst completes the analysis and design, using structured procedures, hands over the program specification to the programmers, and probably supervises the subsequent implementation, troubleshooting if necessary.

The systems analyst's role will often overlap with that of a business analyst, someone without a computing background, probably with a business degree, who analyses the problem from a business and financial perspective. They frequently work together.

Analyst/Programmer

In commercial computing – the vast majority of jobs are in this field, rather than in science or engineering – the jobs of analyst/designers and of programmers are normally merged into analyst/programmers. They see the whole project through, in teams under a project manager, until it is completed and validated. The vast majority of analysts and designers work for computer users; 'in-house' analysis and design used to be more usual than having the work done by software houses, i.e. consultancies which provide professional services for a number of clients. However, computing and IT skill shortages, downsizing and outsourcing have reversed this trend and many firms now employ consultants. Some analyst/designers (with ample experience) work as freelancers.

Analyst/designers' work also covers advising employers, or clients, on what systems to buy; so they must be knowledgeable about and critical of the various systems available. They must be very good at explaining complicated matters to lay people – the computer users.

The attraction and challenge of this computing job is the mixture of tasks and of talents required: applying highly specialized technical knowledge; improving an organization's efficiency; assessing competing computer manufacturers' claims for new products. On top of applying technical know-how, systems analyst/designers must be very good at dealing with people: communication skills are vital. They must make the computer acceptable to staff and design the interface to be acceptable to the clients; traditional working methods and hierarchies may have to change; retraining has to be arranged and accepted, and staff reductions may have to be faced.

Applications Programmer/Developer

Applications programming/developing covers various stages. Applications programmers/developers roughly assess the time needed to complete the program, break it down into separate components, and then break down each component into individual step-by-step sequences of instructions upon which the computer can act. All this needs logical, analytical reasoning, but not mathematical skills. Then comes the translation into an appropriate language, which is usually typed directly into a computer terminal. Applications programmers/developers may produce programs to instruct particular machines to perform particular tasks: for example, to enable a chain of hotels to keep a constantly updated record of vacancies, or a hospital group to keep a constantly updated record of the lengths of waiting lists within the various specialities and the various hospitals within the hospital group. In large organizations teams of applications programmers/developers would deal with a variety of programs – writing for new applications; updating existing programs. Applications programmers/developers with considerable experience, working for software/systems houses, manufacturers, consultancies, users and, increasingly, as freelancers, can also specialize in 'applications packages'.

Website Designer and Multimedia Specialist

Webmasters in large organizations may be employed as part of a team of IT specialists. There has also been a considerable growth in the number of small Web design studios and self-employed Web designers, who concentrate more on the visual design and content of the website. Some Web designers work for marketing agencies, providing services for their clients. Many have a multidisciplinary or an arts background. Good communication skills are essential as a major feature of the work is the ability to work with the customer and interpret their requirements. With increasing use of interactive features, many website designers are multimedia specialists, with skills in animation, video and sound technology. This is a fast-developing field and practitioners must be constantly developing and updating their technical skills.

Games Designer

With a video games industry now larger than the movie industry, games design is an important part of the IT sector. Most successful commercial games are created by large teams of specialist designers, animators and writers, working with technical programmers, testers and other specialists. There are numerous developmental stages between the initial idea and the final product. In a market where a mistake can cost millions of pounds, games publishers will usually look for applicants with proven experience and it is one of the hardest areas to break into.

Data Manager

Data is now viewed by most organizations as a valuable corporate resource. Database administrators design, manage and maintain the company's data and control access to it. This is a highly specialized and technical area. Considerable experience of database systems and business needs is required. Data architects design the data management systems.

Hardware Engineer

They design and develop computers and related products ('peripherals') for computer manufacturers (see p. 213). Various specialists are involved, mainly but not only electronic engineers, physicists, mathematicians. At the moment titles of relevant degree courses vary (for example, IT or Computers and Communications); computing hardware professionals of the future must carefully study degree course syllabuses. Terminology of job titles and specific functions varies too. Hardware manufacture is a declining industry in Britain; major companies that once concentrated on this are now moving into selling software instead.

Some 'Spin-off' Jobs With 'orthodox' (i.e. applications or software programming, systems/software design/analysis) qualifications and experience, there are a growing number of opportunities in rapidly changing and expanding computer careers, suiting individuals with various bents, abilities, expertise. Information technology, including as it does telecommunications (and office automation), is developing faster than any industry ever has done: new jobs are constantly emerging – but beware: the unskilled or semi-skilled ones may be short-lived.

End-user Support

Support staff provide a wide range of services to familiarize users with particular IT systems, and help them to resolve any problems associated with the software or hardware they use. Staff may work from a central call centre, providing telephone and email support, or they may work 'in the field' as service engineers, providing on-site support. Support staff may be employed directly by manufacturers and suppliers, or they may work for specialist support organizations. There are many opportunities for self-employment.

Technical Author

Authors – job titles vary – produce manuals and user guides for systems and applications. This requires the ability to put over complex information clearly, succinctly and unequivocally, and a thorough understanding of what the device described can and cannot do, and how it functions. Manual-writers have to know very much more about their subject than the people for whom they are writing.

Independent Consultant

Specialists from all aspects of the IT sector may develop their career by becoming independent consultants – advising prospective users on whether a system would be of use to them and, if so, which one. The work requires considerable experience plus specialist knowledge in a commercial, industrial or educational area. Many consultants are self-employed.

Training There is no standard training route. Many people at the top of the profession now have no formal computing qualifications, because when they started their careers there were no relevant qualifications. Others have succeeded with few qualifications because of the shortage of IT specialists, but new entrants must aim at a qualification. Training is also continuous, with the need for continuous updating (known as continuing professional development or CPD). Anyone joining the industry is advised to look for companies which participate in the British Computer Society's Professional Development Accreditation scheme. Small companies may not have the resources to do this, but instead may have an arrangement whereby the BCS will 'authenticate' the CPD undertaken by their staff (who keep a record of their training).

Courses are at all levels from postgraduate to those for people with few educational qualifications. Non-degree qualifications are awarded by a number of different organizations, some specializing in a particular branch of the industry.

The following are the main entry and training routes, but individuals should look very carefully at syllabuses to ensure that they choose a course to suit their particular interest and academic level. They need also to decide whether to take a full-time, part-time or distance-learning course (many can be taken by any of these methods).

- Degree (full-time or sandwich) in IT-related subjects (titles include Computing Science, Software Engineering, Business Computing, Computer Systems). Science A levels (physics and/or maths) are required for some, but not all, courses. Numerous courses offer an IT element in combination with another subject. NOTE: see p. 213 for introductory/foundation courses for people with arts A levels who want to take a degree normally requiring science A levels.
- Degree in a non-IT subject. The majority of IT entrants in the past have been from non-IT disciplines but as the sector develops this may change.
- Full-time and part-time Foundation degrees.
- Postgraduate or post-HND computing course following a humanities degree, particularly languages.
- BTEC/SQA Higher National awards in ICT systems support or software development.
- Specialist certificate level courses offered by independent training providers, often run as short intensive courses for existing staff in subjects such as information security. Degrees in many technology and business fields can also be combined with IT qualifications at certificate level.
- The British Computer Society (the main professional body) awards its own qualifications. The BCS Professional Examination has a modular structure set in three stages: Certificate – equivalent to the first year of a Higher National Diploma (HND); Diploma – equivalent to HND level; and Professional Graduate Diploma – equivalent to honours degree level. In addition, candidates undertake a Professional Project at either Diploma or Professional Graduate Diploma level, which aims to demonstrate professional competence in the development of a computer-based system. There are no formal entry requirements for the examination and both members and non-members of the BCS can enter for any part. NOTE: The British Computer Society also manages in the UK the European Computer Driving Licence (ECDL). This qualification involves seven modules covering basic concepts of IT, management of files, word processing, spreadsheets, database filing, presentation and drawing, and information network services. It is awarded following a period of

training recorded in a logbook and successful completion of a number of tests. An ECDL Advanced award is also available.

- Institute for the Management of Information Systems (emphasis is on business applications): offers, through part-time or distance learning, courses in information systems management at Foundation, Diploma, Higher Diploma and Graduate Diploma level.
- Edexcel BTEC National awards in systems support or software development or SQA Scottish Group Award.
- City & Guilds offers a range of vocational courses at different levels in applications programming/developing.
- The Open University has introduced a range of flexible programmes aimed at the continuing professional development of individuals working in IT.
- The e-skills Sector Skills Council oversees Apprenticeships in the IT and telecom industries, as well as NVQs at levels 1–5. Apprenticeships can lead to a higher apprenticeship which includes a Foundation degree and possibly an honours degree.

NOTE: Commercially provided training in IT is available in many forms, from full-time courses to computer-based training or through interactive learning systems. Major software providers such as Microsoft provide their own product-specific courses. If in doubt about the value of a qualification for a particular career aim check with the British Computer Society before enrolling.

Personal attributes *All professionals*: Communication skills, written and spoken; flexibility, willingness to adapt to new methodologies and to continue learning.

Systems analyst/designers: Well-above-average intelligence and powers of logical reasoning; numeracy; imagination to put themselves into the shoes of the people whose jobs they may be 'analysing away' or at least changing; tact and diplomacy; ability to get on well with people at all levels in an organization's hierarchy; a confidence-inspiring manner; curiosity; creativity to visualize how old-established methods might be changed; ability to explain complicated procedures in simple language; ability to listen; ability to take an overall view of a situation and yet see it in detail; business acumen, at least for many jobs.

Applications programmers/developers/programmers/analysts: Powers of logical thinking; numeracy; powers of sustained concentration; great patience and willingness to pursue an elusive problem till solved; liking for concentrated desk-work; ability to communicate easily with people in computing as well as with lay people. Programmers who hope to progress to systems analysis should note the different personal qualities required.

Systems programmers/software engineers: Very high intellectual ability; originality; research-inclined mind; imagination; interest in high technology and its implications and rapid developments.

Network managers: Practicality; liking for routine work; organizing/ administrative ability for those wanting to get promotion.

Mature entry and career change Good opportunities, especially for people with business or related experience and for mature students, who may take full-time or part-time degrees or other relevant courses.

Work–life balance Depending on the organization, as such a wide range of employers employ IT practitioners, including the Civil Service and the NHS, it should be possible to find flexible working. Self-employment through contracting is possible. Employers are willing to recruit career changers and returners with the right attributes. However, IT is a very competitive field and on the supply side the need to meet deadlines can mean a long-hours culture.

Further information
British Computer Society, North Star House, North Star Avenue, Swindon SN2 1FA.
www.bcs.org

Institute for the Management of Information Systems, 5 Kingfisher House, New Mill Road, Orpington, Kent BR5 3QG.
www.imis.org.uk

Institution of Analysts and Programmers, Charles House, 36 Culmington Road, London W13 9NH.
www.iap.org.uk

Institute of IT Training, Westwood House, Westwood Business Park, Coventry CV4 8HS.
www.iitt.org.uk

British Interactive Media Association, 4 Chase Side, Enfield, Middlesex EN2 6NF.
www.bima.co.uk

Sector Skills Council for IT and Telecoms, 1 Castle Lane, London SW1E 6DR.
www.e-skills.com

Sector Skills Council for the Audio Visual Industries, Focus Point, 21 Caledonian Road, London, N1 9GB.
www.skillset.org

Related careers *engineering – management services: Operational Research – science*

Insurance

Entry qualifications Entry requirements vary depending on the employer: insurance companies may take on recruits at a range of qualification levels. There are opportunities in some organizations for entrants at National Qualifications Framework Level 2 (GCSEs A*–C, BTEC Diplomas and Certificates) or Scottish Credit and Qualifications Framework equivalent, who are willing to study part-time (often with an employer's help). The best prospects are for entrants at National Qualifications Framework Level 3 (A levels, BTEC National awards) or Scottish Credit and Qualifications Framework equivalent, or higher level qualifications.

Growing numbers of graduates are being recruited to the sector; many large firms offer graduate training schemes. Degree courses in Insurance Studies and Risk Management are available and in addition business/management studies, economics, maths and law are among those considered useful. Foreign languages are also useful as insurance is an international activity and some jobs involve considerable travel.

The work Insurance is a method of compensating for losses arising from all kinds of misfortunes, from the theft of a video to an airliner crash, from a holiday cancelled through illness to the abandonment of a major sporting event. It is based on the principle that many more people pay regularly into a common fund than ultimately draw from it, and thus the losses of the unlucky few may be made good. The organizers of the system are the *insurers*, i.e. the insurance companies or Lloyd's. Lloyd's itself is not an insurance company, but a society whose individual members are grouped together into syndicates to accept and underwrite 'risks'. Each syndicate is administered by an agency which employs a professional underwriter (see below) to carry out the business. Banks and building societies (see p. 117) have also moved into insurance. It is usual to specialize in one of the main branches of insurance: marine and aviation, life and pensions, property, accident, motor and liability and reinsurance (where very large risks are 'farmed out'), although transfers are possible.

Underwriters are responsible for assessing risks, deciding whether they are insurable, and on what terms and conditions they can be accepted. Some underwriting decisions are routine and based on guidelines laid down by the company for dealing with standard cases (for example, ordinary motor insurance). Others are highly complex and/or unusual and demand specialized skill or judgement (for example, the Channel Tunnel or an art treasure on special exhibit).

In the case of buildings, industrial plant and other commercial operations, underwriters may call on the advice of *surveyors*. The surveyor prepares a factual report on any aspects that might affect the underwriter's assessment of the risks (e.g. fire protection or security arrangements). Some surveyors go into risk management, which is concerned with identifying, assessing and minimizing the risks a company may face in its day-to-day activities. Insurance surveyors are often selected from existing staff and trained internally; they are not necessarily chartered surveyors. When risks are very complex, science or technology graduates might be recruited for this work.

When a claim is received *claims staff* assess the loss and determine the amount to be paid. As with underwriting, some cases are straightforward (though you might be dealing with people whose loss demands your tact and sympathy), while others are complex and require technical, legal and medical knowledge. For large or disputed claims insurance companies may call in independent *loss adjusters* to examine the claim and help to reach a settlement. Some loss adjusters come from the claims department of an insurance company, but others have relevant qualifications, e.g. in law, surveying, accountancy, engineering.

Insurance brokers act as intermediaries, bringing together the insurers and those who wish to be insured. Jobs include finding new business, looking after and advising existing clients, and placing the risks in the market (i.e. finding insurers to underwrite the policy). Brokers may be small high street firms or international giants employing thousands of staff. Only accredited brokers ('Lloyd's brokers') are allowed to do business with Lloyd's underwriters.

Training Many of the larger firms offer structured training and the Chartered Insurance Institute's 'Pathways' also provides a clear career route. Flexible study through day release or evening study, distance or online learning leads to the Chartered Insurance Institute's qualifications. The CII's framework of qualifications is flexible, allowing candidates to choose a route that suits them. The Certificate in Insurance is suitable for those entering the industry; the Diploma is a technical and supervisory qualification for those working across all sectors of the industry; the Advanced Diploma is the professional qualification, leading to ACII (Associateship). Further professional options include Fellowship, an MSc in Insurance and Risk Management and Chartered Status.

Apprenticeships and Advanced Apprenticeships in Retail Financial Services are available for those aged 16–24 (see *www.cii.co.uk*).

Loss adjusters may take the Chartered Institute of Loss Adjusters' exams after insurance company experience if they already hold a previous professional qualification such as ACII.

Personal attributes Some mathematical ability; a liking for paperwork; ability to grasp the essentials of a problem; sound judgement; determination and a certain amount of push; tact; a persuasive, confidence-inspiring manner; ability to communicate with people, often in difficult circumstances. For brokers, extrovert manner and entrepreneurial flair.

Mature entry and career change Mature entrants, like younger recruits, would be expected to gain professional qualifications. Relevant experience, background and skills helpful.

Work–life balance Employers are introducing career-break schemes; details vary. Part-time, job-sharing and working from home are becoming more popular within the industry.

Further information

The Chartered Insurance Institute, 42–48 High Road, South Woodford, London E18 2JP.
www.cii.co.uk

The British Insurance Brokers' Association, BIBA House, 14 Bevis Marks, London EC3A 7NT.
www.biba.org.uk

The Chartered Institute of Loss Adjusters, Warwick House, 65/66 Queen Street, London EC4R 1EB.
www.cila.co.uk

Related careers *accountancy – actuary – banking and building society work – information technology/information systems – stock exchange and securities industry*

Journalism

Entry qualifications *Newspapers*: traineeship entry at National Qualifications Framework Level 3 (A levels, BTEC National awards) or Scottish Credit and Qualifications Framework equivalent. Majority of entrants are graduates. For pre-entry course: two A levels or equivalent in practice. *Magazines*: depends on editor; again the majority of entrants are graduates. Pre-entry experience is desirable.

The work Journalism covers a variety of jobs in a wide range of print, online and broadcast media settings. Broadly the main job groups are: reporter; correspondent or specialist reporter; feature writer; news editor; editor; freelancer. Division of duties depends on publisher's size and organization.

NEWSPAPERS

Reporter

Many newspaper journalists start as trainee reporters. Reporters cover any kind of event: from council or Women's Institute meeting to political demo, fire, or press conference for visiting film star or foreign statesman. Reporters 'get a story' by asking questions and listening to other journalists' questions and interviewees' answers at press conferences, or in one-to-one interviews with individuals. For such interviews, reporters have to do some preliminary 'homework' – to interview a trade union secretary or famous novelist, for example, requires some background knowledge.

Reporters usually compose stories quickly and meet tight deadlines. Accuracy, brevity and speed can be more important than writing perfect prose: reporting is a fact-gathering and fact-disseminating rather than a creative job.

Occasionally reporters may be on a particular story for several weeks, researching the background and/or waiting for developments. They work irregular hours, including weekends.

Specialist Reporter or Correspondent

'Hard news' is broadcast more quickly than it can be printed; to fight TV and radio competition, newspapers have developed 'interpretative' or specialist reporting. Specialists' titles and precise responsibilities and scope vary; the aim always is to interpret and explain news, and to comment on events, trends, causes and news behind the news. The number (and the expert knowledge) of specialists varies according to the type and size of newspaper. On the whole, only the nationals have specialists who concentrate entirely on one speciality; on other papers and in news agencies, reporters with a special interest in a particular field (or several) may do specialist along with general reporting. The main specializations are: Parliament and/or politics generally; industry; finance; education; foreign news; local government and/or planning; social services; sport; science and technology; agriculture and food; motoring; fashion; women's/home interests; theatre; films; broadcasting. Financial correspondents tend to be economics graduates, science correspondents are science graduates, but education correspondents are not normally teachers: there are no hard and fast rules about how specialists acquire their specialist knowledge (and how much they need).

News Editor

Journalists with organizing ability may become news editors, controlling reporting staffs, allocating stories to individual reporters and attending senior staff's daily editorial conferences. It is an office job and normally involves no writing. The title usually applies on daily papers; but titles and organization of work vary considerably from one paper to another.

Sub-editor

Sub-editors do the detailed editing of copy; they rewrite stories to fit in with required length, rewrite the beginning, and may 'slant' stories. They write headlines and, in consultation with the night or assistant editor, may do the layout of news pages. On large papers there are several specialist subs. Subbing is teamwork and entirely deskbound; it always has to be done in a hurry.

Feature Writer

Usually experienced journalists who can write lucidly and descriptively on any topic; but specialists may also write features. Reporters may combine reporting with feature writing.

Columnist

Like feature writing, a job for experienced journalists; there are specialists, e.g. financial or consumer affairs columnists, and general columnists. The work requires a wide range of interests and contacts.

Leader Writer

Leaders may be written by the editor, or specialist correspondent, or other experienced journalists.

Editor-in-chief, Assistant Editor, Deputy Editor

Editors (including departmental editors) are coordinators, policy-makers. The number of top jobs, and the amount of writing editors do, varies greatly: some editors write leaders on specific subjects, some write in crises only, some on a variety of subjects, others not at all.

The amount of freedom an editor-in-chief has to run the paper in the way they want depends on the proprietor; policies vary enormously.

There is no set promotion structure on newspapers. Some journalists do all or several types of newspaper work in succession in preparation for senior editorial jobs (subbing is a vital step on the ladder), others become heads of departments (finance, fashion, home affairs, chief sub, etc.) fairly quickly. Many remain reporters.

Titles, functions and division of labour are not consistent throughout the industry and often change with a change of editor-in-chief or proprietor.

Freesheets

Locally distributed 'giveaway' papers are the fastest-growing advertising medium. Free newspapers vary enormously in the proportion and variety of their editorial content. A few are much like small local weekly papers; some carry very little editorial matter. Some are published by established newspaper houses, yet others are run individually from tiny offices by one or two people. Jobs on free newspapers with varied editorial content may be acceptable as traineeships (see below), but generally are unlikely to lead to jobs on national or other prestigious local newspapers.

Training These are the most common methods:

Direct entry traineeship: two years, including six months' probation. Acceptance depends as much on paper's policy and candidate's suitability as on academic qualifications. Competition for trainee posts at any stage is fierce. Candidates must apply direct to editors of provincial (including suburban) dailies and weeklies. The London-based nationals rarely take trainees. (Previous experience in student or freelance journalism is essential. Candidates need to submit samples of work done: an article or report specially written for the particular paper, which shows the editor that the applicant has identified the paper's style, is important, as is work done for school or university papers.)

Traineeships include six to nine months' study for the National

Council for the Training of Journalists' preliminary examinations. Some employers run in-house programmes and trainees study by distance learning while others send trainees to accredited learning centres through day or block release. The preliminary examinations cover media law, public affairs (local and central government), newspaper journalism and trainees must achieve at least 100 wpm shorthand. In addition trainees serve at least an eighteen-month period of work experience while maintaining a logbook of their achievement, before being allowed to sit the National Council for the Training of Journalists' National Certificate Examination (NCE). Practical training should cover work in all departments. Quality and thoroughness of training schemes vary, so it is essential to find out as much as possible about them before accepting a traineeship. One or two groups now run their own training schemes independently of the NCTJ.

One-year full-time pre-entry courses: two A levels or equivalent required. The majority of entrants to newspaper journalism now take such courses, at colleges of further and higher education. Courses shorten subsequent traineeship by six months. A few candidates are sponsored by newspapers; the majority are accepted after having taken a written test and been interviewed by the NCTJ, to which applications must be made. Courses do not guarantee employment.

Postgraduate courses: eighteen to twenty weeks to one year. Graduates from these courses also have to start as trainees, but they take the NCE after eighteen months' training.

NVQs/SVQs: these are available at level 4. The NCTJ preliminary examinations can provide the necessary evidence of underpinning knowledge needed for NVQs/SVQs in Newspaper Journalism and Periodical Journalism. The Diploma in Newspaper Journalism is issued by the Newspapers Qualification Council on completion of the level 4 NVQ and six months' journalistic experience.

Foundation degrees and first degrees in journalism are available, many incorporating NCTJ training. These may appear to be an ideal entry route, but they may not give their graduates a significant advantage over routes outlined above for either newspaper or periodical journalism. The same applies to media studies courses. Editors may take candidates who have shown breadth of interest by studying disciplines other than journalism/communications/media. Vocational training then follows the degree.

MAGAZINES

More than 8,500 magazines are currently published in the UK in printed, online and other digital formats. Broadly there are two types: business journals and directories, geared to a particular profession, trade or organization, and consumer magazines catering for all types of leisure interests – including women's, teenage and hobby magazines and comics.

Journalists working on professional magazine, often liaise closely with experts in the particular field of which they must have/develop some understanding. They write features, report developments and rewrite experts' contributions. Magazine work, however specialized, can be a way into newspaper work – especially for graduates (particularly science or technology) with writing ability. It often requires broader skills than newspaper journalism: e.g. knowing about sub-editing and layout.

Consumer magazines employ feature writers, sub-editors and departmental editors more than reporters, but organization varies enormously. Consumer magazines use freelancers more than do newspapers. Editors' work includes originating feature ideas and selecting and briefing outside contributors, both freelance journalists and specialists who are not journalists.

Training The Periodicals Training Council (PTC) accredits a number of vocational courses for intending periodical journalists. A full listing of those courses which have achieved PTC accreditation is available on the Periodical Publishers Association website at *www.ppa.co.uk.*

The PTC Professional Certificate in periodical and electronic publications is for those new to journalism who want to show they have the core knowledge and skills needed to be a magazine journalist. This certificate combines on-the-job assessment with an external assessment and interview.

The NCTJ also has a scheme for magazine journalists covering media law, ethics, government, shorthand to 80 words per minute, news and feature writing, production and design, subbing and background to the magazine industry. Assessment is through exams and a portfolio. It also requires work experience on a magazine.

Magazine journalism training is much less tightly structured than newspaper training and entry is still largely with specialist knowledge (especially scientific/technical/computing, but also other expertise, from drama to sport, education to law) and with writing/editing ability. Quite a few arts graduates are editing technical journals.

Competition for trainee posts on magazines is fierce. Previous experience in student or freelance journalism is essential. Work on a journal dealing with one particular subject, whether electronics or municipal affairs, is good experience and can be a stepping stone to more general journalism. There is some scope in broadcasting (see p. 597) for experienced reporters. Science and engineering graduates have reasonable scope on the increasing number of publications which deal with various aspects of science and technology (especially information technology/computing) and which try to attract both specialist and lay readers.

NOTE: The NCTJ also runs distance-learning courses in magazine journalism and sub-editing, open to journalists and non-journalists: these can contribute towards NVQs in magazine or newspaper journalism (production).

FREELANCE JOURNALISM

Freelancers are either generalists – feature writers who write on any subject – or specialists. On the whole, only experienced journalists with staff experience, and particularly those with specialist knowledge which is in demand (technology, consumerism, child development, education, for example), succeed.

Specialists – teachers, engineers, lawyers, with writing ability and topical ideas – also do freelance journalism as a sideline, but this is becoming more difficult.

Personal attributes (generally) The different jobs demand different talents and temperaments, but all journalists need a feeling for words; the ability to express themselves lucidly and concisely; wide interests; an unbiased approach; a pleasant easy manner so that shy, inarticulate people will talk to them easily; a certain presence so that busy, important people do not feel they are wasting their time answering questions; powers of observation; ability to sift the relevant from the irrelevant; ability to absorb atmosphere and to sum up people and situations quickly; an inquiring mind; great curiosity; the ability to become temporarily interested in anything from apple-growing to Zen Buddhism; resourcefulness; resilience; tact; willingness to work very hard; punctuality; a fairly thick skin (interviewees can be rude). For senior jobs: organizing ability.

Mature entry and career change *Newspapers* – opportunities can be generated, particularly for those with specialist knowledge. Training is usually by arrangement with the employer. *Magazines* – quite normal for specialists.

Work–life balance Only well-above-average people who have proved their value to their paper before the break have much hope of returning after a career break. Many turn to freelancing or edit, on a freelance basis, small organizations' or professional magazines: this is almost a cottage industry and badly paid. Fewer problems for feature writers, sub-editors.

Few problems on magazines. Some job-sharing possibilities. Up to 80 per cent of magazine copy may be written by freelancers.

Further information
NCTJ Training, The New Granary, Station Road, Newport, Saffron Waldon, Essex CB11 3PL.
www.nctj.com

Newspaper Society, St Andrew's House, St Andrew Street, London EC4A 3AY.
www.newspapersoc.org.uk

The Scottish Newspaper Publishers' Association, 48 Palmerston Place, Edinburgh EH12 5DE.
www.snpa.org.uk

Periodical Publishers Association, Queens House, 28 Kingsway, London WC2B 6JR.
www.ppa.co.uk

Periodicals Training Council, Queen's House, 55–56 Lincoln's Inn Fields, London WC2A 3LJ.
www.ppa.co.uk

National Union of Journalists, 308–312 Gray's Inn Road, London WC1X 8DP.
www.nuj.org.uk

Related careers *advertising – information science – photography – public relations – television, film and radio*

Landscape Architecture

Entry qualifications No set requirements but usually a recognized undergraduate course accredited by the Landscape Institute. GCSEs or A levels or equivalent in subjects such as geography, art and design, geology, environmental science or ecology can be useful. See 'Training' below for more detail.

The work Landscape architects plan, design and manage our rural and urban landscapes and the outdoor environment. Their work is about shaping and making the best of open spaces: streets, squares, parks, promenades, waterways, shopping centres, business parks, housing developments, roads and transport networks, and a whole range of natural and built environments. A varied profession, landscape architecture could involve large-scale landscape planning or massive design projects, regenerating a run-down inner city area, or specializing in nature conservation, dealing with conservation of historical parks and gardens, or the complexities and intimacies of gardens.

Often working with architects, civil engineers and planners, landscape architects reconcile the demands made on the environment by developments such as industrial or housing schemes or new roads with aesthetic and environmental needs. Their aim is to create landscapes which are pleasing, and at the same time functional, environmentally sustainable, economic to build and manage, able to accommodate buildings, and that work with the people that use them. They must also take account of the natural environment and nature conservation. In urban areas the work is often concerned with regeneration schemes in almost any public space, including the layouts of housing schemes, roads and streets, public squares, shopping and pedestrian precincts, and urban parks and green spaces. In the countryside, landscape architects may plan how best to blend developments or industrial sites such as power stations and reservoirs into their surroundings so that they cause as little environmental and visual impact as possible. They may work on the restoration of derelict land caused by industrial processes, quarrying or mining, or be responsible for the long-term management of the landscape of National Parks, Areas of Outstanding Natural Beauty, World Heritage sites, or Sites of Special Scientific Interest.

Landscape architects may also specialize in landscape science or management. Landscape managers specialize in the long-term care and management of spaces while landscape scientists investigate and explore the geology, wildlife and natural features that make up landscape. They are predominantly concerned with the physical and biological principles and processes that are basic to landscape design and management.

Landscape scientists and managers might have specialist skills such as soil science, ecology, biology or geology. These skills are then applied to landscape design and management, for example by the ecological analysis of sites, working with the designers to ensure that land can be utilized and enjoyed by all plant and life forms now and in the future.

An increasingly important part of their work is concerned with environmental assessments. Landscape architects frequently act as expert witnesses at planning and other inquiries affecting the landscape.

About 50 per cent of landscape architects work for private practices – many of these are large multidisciplinary companies, working alongside architects, planners or engineers. Others work for the public sector, for local authorities or government agencies such as the Environment Agency or non-government bodies such as Groundwork. There are opportunities in EU countries, the USA and the Middle East.

Training Many landscape architects begin their career by undertaking a first degree accredited by the Landscape Institute. This can be followed by a specialist postgraduate diploma in subjects such as landscape architecture, landscape planning, ecology, landscape management. Entrants with a related, but not accredited, degree in subjects such as architecture, horticulture, can take an accredited postgraduate course, typically an MA Entry to an accredited course is not available with HND or Foundation degree qualifications alone.

A list of accredited courses, with further contact details, is available on the Landscape Institute website at *www.landscapeinstitute.org.*

On successfully completing an accredited course, graduates are eligible for Associate Membership of the Landscape Institute. After at least two years' qualifying work experience candidates can sit the LI's Professional Practice Examination leading towards Chartered status.

Alternative method of entry An alternative route to entering the profession may be available to those who have not undertaken a course accredited by the Landscape Institute but have a degree in an area relevant to landscape, and who have also gained relevant qualifications and experience, such as geography, geology, planning, soil science, plant sciences, environmental studies, art and design, architecture, garden design or horticulture (see p. 67).

Personal attributes Visual imagination; flair for or interest in design; a keen interest in the environment, ecology, human or physical geography; an appreciation of how people live in town and countryside; ease of expression, both in drawing and writing; the ability to work well in teams; a good business head (for private practice).

Mature entry and career change With the right initial qualifications it should be possible to make this a second career.

Work–life balance People who have kept up with developments should have no problem taking a career break. The Landscape Institute has a reduced subscription for members taking a career break. There are reasonable opportunities for part-time employment; possibility of running small consultative practice – but part-time work is likely to be sporadic rather than regular.

Landscape Architecture

Further information
Landscape Institute, 33 Great Portland Street, London W1W 8QG.
www.landscapeinstitute.org.

Related careers *agriculture and horticulture – architecture – art and design – civil engineering – town planning*

Languages

The British notoriously lack foreign language competence and the implications are likely to grow more serious with globalization and increasing European integration. In the European market, British companies could be at a real disadvantage compared with European competitors with a polyglot workforce. As one European businessman put it, 'We are happy to sell to you in English, but we like to buy in our own language.' Individuals could also lose out as increased labour mobility within the European Union will favour those with language skills.

Nevertheless it must still be emphasized that language skills on their own are of very little value to an employer looking for a rounded skill set. Saying that you can speak German or Japanese is, on its own, about as useful to an employer as saying that you can speak English. But in a context where the client is a speaker of German or Japanese, then the ability to operate in those languages can be as essential as being able to speak good English. What matters is the framework of technical, professional or practical skills within which you can apply your languages.

There are very few careers for which languages are the primary skill, and even these require other skills and qualities. For a growing number of careers, however, languages are a useful, sometimes essential, secondary skill. Demand is strong in finance, IT and legal services and is likely to increase in both tourism and the public service sector.

LANGUAGES AS A PRIMARY SKILL

Conference Interpreter

At international conferences interpreters may do either 'simultaneous' (the main type) or 'consecutive' interpreting. They must be exceptionally proficient in at least two major languages; an additional knowledge of one or more less common languages is a help. Simultaneous interpreters relay the meaning of a speech, often on complicated subjects, almost instantaneously. The technique can be learnt, but the talent and temperament are inborn. Consecutive interpreters relay a speech as a whole, or in large chunks, after each speaker. This requires as much skill as simultaneous interpreting. Interpreters are always under pressure to combine accuracy with speed as they work. The consequences of inaccuracy could be serious.

Conference interpreters invariably interpret into their own language. They need excellent command of their mother tongue, as nuance and tone are important in conveying meaning. English speakers are much in demand.

Some interpreters are employed by international agencies; others are freelancers and are booked for a particular conference. Most of the year is spent travelling to and from New York, Geneva, Strasbourg, Brussels and London, living in hotels. The life may be luxurious, but it is extremely hectic, with very long irregular hours. Most conference interpreters now are specialists.

Conference interpreting is an extremely small profession, represented by the worldwide association AIIC, which brings together professional conference interpreters in over 80 countries (see *www.aiic.net*).

Business and Specialist Interpreters

Business organizations of many kinds may need interpreters, for example when receiving trade delegations, negotiating international contracts and at trade fairs. Some of these interpreters may need specialist knowledge (such as engineering, information technology, computing, physical science or economics). Translators, both staff and freelance, may undertake this type of work. There are also opportunities working for conference organizers.

Freelancers are usually hired on a daily basis (of up to eight hours including breaks), with travel, accommodation and meal expenses paid by the client.

Public Service Interpreter

They are employed mainly by local authority social services departments to help members of ethnic communities whose first language is not English deal with officials in departments. For example, they help them to communicate with social security and housing officials, teachers and medical staff. They may also work in the courts. Employment is usually part-time and can be at short notice. Public service interpreters can work in trying circumstances and must adhere to codes of conduct, which include confidentiality and the duty to remain impartial.

Business, specialist and public service interpreters use ad hoc or liaison interpreting, in which they interpret into and out of two languages, for example in a conversation between speakers of different languages.

Additional interpreting opportunities include 'whispering' and telephone interpreting.

Translation

The work Translators must be able to translate idiomatically and to write lucidly and concisely – being bilingual is not sufficient. They translate into their mother-tongue, so the prevalence of English has increased rather than reduced work for English translators. Also with the use of ethnic community languages increasingly seen in the public sector as an equal opportunities issue, growth in demand for translators with these languages is expected to continue.

They need a very good education and specialist knowledge of preferably a range of related subjects, though this may be acquired on the job. Most translations have some specialist content – contracts require some legal knowledge; scientific articles some understanding of the subject matter; specifications (for construction work, of anything from ships to atomic power stations) need some technical knowledge. Translators often have to discuss phrases and technical jargon with engineers, scientists, lawyers, etc., to get the sense absolutely right; translating is therefore often teamwork.

Government departments, and industrial, commercial and research organizations, often have translating departments which employ specialists in particular fields, and sometimes non-specialists, who have, for instance, Chinese or Arabic, as well as one or two of the more usual languages.

Translating agencies employ specialists, and people who have unusual languages, often on a freelance basis. They like to have on their books a large number of people with widely different specialities and languages, on whom they can call at a moment's notice. There is increasing scope in translating instruction manuals for consumer goods manufacturers.

Much is rushed deadline work, especially for freelancers, who will spend a lot of time working in isolation. Advances in technology mean that good IT skills are important in the field.

Training It is increasingly important for interpreters and translators to have formal training and qualifications. The main courses and qualifications are:

- Postgraduate courses, usually lasting one year, in technical and specialized translation/interpreting. Candidates must normally have a degree in two languages at the same level. Different courses offer different languages; combinations may change according to market demand. Arabic, Russian, Chinese, Japanese, Greek, Portuguese and Polish are among options in addition to French, German, Italian and Spanish. Postgraduate diplomas and an MA in conference interpreting are also now available. A National Network for Interpreting will involve Leeds, Bath, Salford and Westminster Universities. The Network will be linked by a virtual learning system and will work to encourage study of languages.

- A few four-year degree courses include emphasis on translating and interpreting skills.
- The Institute of Linguists offers examinations (but not courses) including a Diploma in Public Service Interpreting in a large number of ethnic community languages and a postgraduate Diploma in Translating. (A number of institutions offer courses; distance learning is available (see the IOL website.)
- Currently there are no NVQs in translation and only one in interpreting (level 4 in British Sign Language/English Interpreting) but with the recent approval of occupational standards in both skills it is expected that more may be developed.

Personal attributes An agile mind; interest in current affairs; a knowledge of cultural and social structures not only of their own country but of any country in whose language they specialize; ability to concentrate for long stretches and to work under pressure; ability to work well with others.

Conference interpreters need a calm temperament and the ability to snatch a few hours' sleep at any time.

Teaching
(see also p. 586 for details)

Mature entry and career change Translating and teaching possible; interpreting: more opportunities likely in public service interpreting.

Work–life balance Theoretically, flexible working should be possible as translating and interpreting are so often done by freelancers. However, much of the work has to be done quickly – which means it may not be regular part-time work, but could be a few days' or weeks' rushed full-time work every now and then.

LANGUAGE AS A SECONDARY SKILL

There are a number of areas in which a knowledge of a foreign language can be a requirement or an asset, though it is not the primary skill and may not always be a day-to-day part of the work. They include broadcasting (p. 597); bilingual secretarial work (p. 531); librarianship and information science (p. 275); the Diplomatic Service (p. 159); travel and tourism (p. 619); patent agents (430); banking (p. 117); law (p. 316). In industry and commerce languages are undoubtedly becoming more important, but it is impossible to generalize about the roles in which they are most useful. Export marketing is an obvious example, but engineers, construction workers, computer staff, general managers could all, in some circumstances, need languages. Receptionists, call centre and switchboard operators are often the first point of contact with a foreign supplier or customer. You should not consider any of these careers simply as a way to 'use my languages'. Rather, you should recognize competence in a foreign language as a skill that can enhance almost any career, giving an entrée to more interesting prospects, at home and abroad.

General Language Training

There are many ways in which people may become proficient in a foreign language. Recent education initiatives aim to give more young people at least a starting point at school and to start teaching language at primary school. Under the National Curriculum all pupils have to study a foreign language until the age of 14. GCSEs in languages concentrate much more on oral skills than previous courses did and there is some excellent vocational training which includes a language component.

Post-16, there are many chances to further develop language skills. The Languages Work website gives an idea of the opportunities available and which are most suitable. Language degree course options include a traditional literature-based course, an 'applied' language course with emphasis on oral fluency and the economy, institutions and social climate of the relevant countries, or a degree combining languages with another subject such as law, engineering, business studies, marketing, computer studies and so on. There are also a number of college courses for A level entrants which offer languages for business, as well as language options in BTEC courses. Languages can often be studied as an extracurricular activity.

Examinations in languages at different levels, and for different purposes, are also offered by awarding bodies such as OCR and the Institute of Linguists. The National Centre for Languages (see below) has a post-14 table of language qualifications. As part of the Government's strategy to encourage language learning, the 'Languages Ladder' maps a scale of languages ability from beginner to mastery.

A spell abroad is an extremely useful way to refine language skills. Most schools run exchanges, and most language degree courses include a year abroad. The EU Lifelong Learning Programme includes schemes to encourage young people to work or study in other member states (*www.lifelonglearningprogramme.org.uk*).

Further information

Chartered Institute of Linguists, Saxon House, 48 Southwark Street, London SE1 1UN.
www.iol.org.uk

Institute of Translation and Interpreting, Fortuna House, South Fifth Street, Milton Keynes MK9 2EU.
www.iti.org.uk

CILT, the National Centre for Languages, 3rd Floor, 111 Westminster Bridge Road, London SE1 7HR.
www.cilt.org.uk

Languages Work – advice, information and case studies for using languages at work
www.languageswork.org.uk

Related careers *civil service: Diplomatic Service – secretarial, administrative and clerical work: Bilingual or Multilingual Secretary – teaching*

Law

Barrister (Advocate in Scotland)

Entry qualifications First- or second-class honours degree (any subject). Some universities require applicants to take the National Admissions Test for Law (LNAT), an on-screen test used as part of the selection process for entry to undergraduate law courses (see *www.lnat.ac.uk*).

The work Barristers plead in courts and give advice on legal matters. They advise on points of law and use their critical judgement in deciding what legislation and what precedents are relevant in any particular case. Their expertise helps clients, both organizations and individuals.

Barristers are normally consulted by solicitors on behalf of their clients and do not normally see clients without a solicitor being present. In some instances, barristers may be instructed by members of other professions, e.g. accountants, surveyors, architects and overseas lawyers.

Most barristers are self-employed, working from 'chambers', sharing overheads and administrative back-up with other barristers. Once in practice, a barrister must wait for briefs by *solicitors* or be given work by the *barristers' clerk* (see p. 321), who 'distributes' work which comes to the set of chambers rather than to a particular barrister in the chambers. However, many barristers are employed, e.g. by law firms or central government (see below).

Barristers normally specialize in areas of practice, which include common law (e.g. family, planning, personal injury litigation), criminal law, commercial law and chancery law (e.g. wills, trusts, estate duty, taxation, company law).

In criminal law there is likely to be an emphasis on pleading in court ('advocacy'); other areas of practice, e.g. chancery, may involve more work in chambers, drafting 'opinions' and advising. Appearing in court to represent clients involves presenting arguments, examining and cross-examining witnesses and it is important therefore to enjoy verbal battles and the court's somewhat theatrical atmosphere; other activities present the challenge of intellectual problem-solving.

Most barristers are based in London or in provincial chambers in cities and large towns or, in Scotland, in Edinburgh.

Barristers often work long hours and earn very little at first. Many barristers never attempt to practise at the Bar (others try to, but cannot get into chambers or get work); instead they become legal advisers in industry, or in local or central government.

The Civil Service offers a variety of work (see p. 513). Justices' Clerks advise the lay justices (JPs) in magistrates' courts, and have close day-to-day contact with the public.

The Crown Prosecution Service is responsible for deciding whether or not to prosecute cases in the criminal court; where they decide to prosecute it is the solicitors and barristers employed at headquarters or in one of the 42 areas who conduct the case, not, as previously, the police. In Scotland, Procurators Fiscal, assisted by Deputies, are the public prosecutors in the sheriff courts. Legal staff at the Crown office deal with more serious crimes.

Barristers, after at least seven years' practice, are eligible for appointment as Chairpersons of Employment Tribunals. These Tribunals deal with unfair dismissal, redundancy payments and other matters relating to employment generally. Under the Sex Discrimination Act they also hear complaints from individuals who believe they have been discriminated against in terms of equal pay, promotion, acceptance for a particular job and other employment matters. Other Tribunals involve mental health and social security. Chairpersons are appointed to regional panels and sit on Tribunals within a given area. Appointments can be full-time or part-time (i.e. some lawyers carry on with their practice as well).

It takes a good deal of determination to succeed at the Bar.

Training Training consists of an Academic Stage, a Vocational Stage and a Practical Stage.

- *The Academic Stage*: students take either a qualifying law degree, which is basically one that covers the foundation subjects (see Solicitor 'Training', p. 323), or a non-law degree followed by a one-year course for the Common Professional Examination (the CPE) at an approved institution or an approved Graduate Diploma in Law (GDL). Law degree courses vary greatly in emphasis on particular aspects of law. Students must make sure they will fulfil the requirements of the Academic Stage. It is also important to check content in relation to areas of interest. Consult the CRAC *Degree Course Guide*.
- *The Vocational Stage*: this consists of a one-year full-time or two-year part-time Bar Vocational Course (BVC) at one of the BVC institutions validated by the Bar Council. The emphasis is on the practical application of knowledge and advocacy skills. Students develop skills in, for example, negotiation, legal research, problem-solving, opinion-writing, drafting documents, oral and written communication, and presentation. Assessment is continuous and takes into account practical work, tests and examinations. On successful completion of this stage students are 'called to the Bar'. Applications for a BVC are made online at *www.bvconline.co.uk*. Before enrolling on the Bar Vocational Course all Bar students must join one of the four Inns of Court. By the end of the BVC year students must complete twelve qualifying sessions, with their Inn, before being called to the Bar by their Inn.
- *The Practical Stage*: Barristers wishing to practise at the Bar (or represent business employers in court) must serve one year's pupillage. During the first six months the pupil takes a background role, reading papers, drafting documents, attending court, helping to prepare cases, and becoming familiar with the rules of conduct and etiquette of the Bar. During the second six months a pupil, with the permission of the approved pupil supervisor, may take cases on

his or her own account. All chambers must now provide an income for pupil barristers of at least £5,000 per six months. Online applications for pupillage (OLPAS) can be made through the Bar Council's pupillage website at *www.pupillages.com*, where all pupillage vacancies can also be found. These may be in chambers or in other organizations authorized by the Bar Council.

Scotland: Scottish barristers, called advocates, must be members of the Faculty of Advocates in order to practise at the Bar. The procedures for qualification as an advocate are currently under review but at present, candidates, known as 'intrants', qualify in four stages:

- A law degree from a Scottish university, giving subject-for-subject exemptions from the Faculty examinations. (Many entrants take one or two Faculty papers because it gives them greater freedom to choose other subjects in their degree courses.) This stage is required for matriculation (the process of being admitted as an intrant to the Faculty of Advocates).
- A one-year full-time course at a Scottish university for the Diploma in Legal Practice (in common with Scottish solicitors).
- For those wishing to practise: 21 months' (reduced by nine months in certain cases) paid traineeship in a solicitor's office, followed by nine months' unpaid pupillage (known as 'devilling') with an approved member of the Bar.
- Pass the Faculty examination in evidence, practice and procedure. Admission to the Faculty follows successful completion of the scheme for assessment of 'devils'.

Personal attributes A confidence-inspiring personality; power of logical reasoning; gift of expression, e.g. communicating complex issues in a simple, easily understandable way; a quick brain; capacity for very hard work; tremendous self-confidence; some acting ability, or at least a sense of drama and relish for verbal battles in front of critical audiences; physical stamina; a good voice; resilience.

Mature entry and career change It is important for mature candidates to bear in mind the financial implications of training and the likelihood of low initial earnings. Mature applicants should highlight any relevant skills and experience they have gained. In Scotland the majority of those admitted to the Faculty of Advocates usually have two years or more experience of practice as a solicitor.

Work–life balance The Bar Council has recently revised the Equality Code for the Bar which now draws attention to work–life balance issues and includes new guidance encouraging better practice. Nearly 50 per cent of entrants to the Bar are female but there is a disproportionate drop-out among women barristers after about ten years and issues regarding their retention and progression to senior levels are now receiving attention. The Bar Council recently incorporated a new policy on Maternity, Paternity and Flexible Working into their Equality and Diversity Code. These guidelines ask chambers to have written policies permitting maternity/paternity leave, career breaks and flexible working arrangements. Anyone wanting a break of more than a year would need to keep well in touch if wishing to return. An advantage of self-employment is that barristers can accept cases to fit in with other commitments, for example only during term time. They can choose to work from home when possible and IT developments are making this easier.

Further information

The Bar Council/General Council of the Bar of England and Wales, 289–293 High Holborn, London WC1V 7HZ.
   www.barcouncil.org.uk
Faculty of Advocates, Advocates Library, Parliament House, Edinburgh EH1 1RF.
   www.advocates.org.uk
The Law Careers Advice Network.
   www.lcan.org.uk

Related careers *accountancy – civil service – Legal Executive/Solicitor* (see below)

Barristers' Clerk (England and Wales only)

Entry qualifications Entry is usually at National Qualifications Framework Level 3 (A levels, BTEC National awards).

The work Barristers' clerks 'manage' chambers and the barristers working in them (see p. 316). The job of senior clerk (or Clerk to Chambers) is a unique mixture of power-behind-the-throne and routine clerking, involving negotiating fees and other matters relating to briefs coming to chambers with solicitors (from whom the briefs come). Clerks play a particularly important role in 'building up' young barristers: many briefs come to chambers rather than to individual barristers and it is the senior clerk who decides which of the young barristers is to be given the brief.

Senior clerks usually have junior clerks who make tea, carry barristers' books and robes to court, type opinions and pleadings. Most new entrants start as junior clerks. Senior clerks get a commission on all their chambers' barristers' earnings and may often earn more than some of the barristers for whom they are clerking.

Training In-house, with seminars. Clerks can take the BTEC Advanced Award in Chambers' Administration recommended by the Institute of Barristers' Clerks, usually within the first five years of clerking.

Personal attributes Very great self-confidence and presence; tact; administrative and marketing skills; respect for tradition; interest in the law.

Further information
Institute of Barristers' Clerks, 289–293 High Holborn, London WC1 7HZ.
www.ibc.org.uk

Related careers *civil service – Legal Executive* (see below) – *secretarial, administrative and clerical work*

Solicitor

Entry qualifications A degree, or Fellowship of the Institute of Legal Executives (see p. 327) (most entrants are graduates). In Scotland non-graduates need good Highers grades, which must include English and either maths or science or a foreign language.

The work A solicitor is a confidential adviser to whom people turn for legal advice and information in a vast variety of personal and business matters. As everyday life becomes more complex, the solicitor is increasingly asked to help in matters where common sense, wisdom and an objective approach are as important as legal knowledge. Whenever possible, solicitors try to settle matters out of court.

Solicitors have full rights to represent clients personally in magistrates' and county courts and, with additional qualification, can appear as advocates in the Crown and High Courts (Scottish solicitors have somewhat greater rights in the equivalent courts). Increasing numbers of solicitors practise advocacy. When a barrister is briefed to appear for a client, the preparatory work and the liaison with the client is still undertaken by the solicitor.

The majority of solicitors work in private practices, ranging from large multi-partner departmentalized city firms to small general, or even sole-practitioner firms. Work content, conditions and remuneration are correspondingly wide-ranging. A city solicitor will generally specialize immediately, working for corporate clients in mainly commercial fields such as banking, taxation, company law and property development. Solicitors in smaller practices tend to handle a wider range of tasks, usually for individual clients, but everywhere there is a trend for earlier and greater specialization. Typical areas of work in smaller firms are crime, family law, personal injury, conveyancing, landlord and tenant matters, and smaller-scale commercial work. There are now small firms which concentrate on providing an expert streamlined service in just one or two areas, for example, medical negligence, entertainment law or immigration.

Much social welfare law, civil and human rights cases, and almost all legally aided cases, are undertaken by smaller firms and, to some extent, by publicly funded law centres, usually in inner-city areas.

Relaxation of traditional rules has enabled solicitors to become involved in financial services and estate agency and to advertise their services.

Solicitors are required to engage in continuing professional development (CPD). Since 1985 it has been compulsory to undertake sixteen hours per annum of black letter and professional skills training to keep abreast of developments in the legal field.

A solicitor with three years' experience can establish a practice but will need capital and contacts to succeed. More secure employment opportunities are available at all levels in local government and the Civil Service. For those interested exclusively in criminal work there are opportunities in the Crown Prosecution Service or the Procurator Fiscal Service in Scotland. Many commercial, industrial and other organizations employ legal advisers where the nature of the work will depend on the activities of the employer.

After substantial experience solicitors can apply to become registrars, stipendiary magistrates, recorders or circuit judges. There are also opportunities for appointments to chair employment and other tribunals.

Training There are three routes to qualifying in England and Wales:

- The law degree route (the majority of solicitors qualify this way): After successfully completing a qualifying law degree (one covering the foundation subjects – obligations including restitution, contract and tort, criminal law, equity and the law of trusts, law of the European Union, property law and public law including constitutional, administrative and human rights) graduates go on to take the Legal Practice Course. This lasts one year full-time and two years part-time. Successful completion of the Legal Practice Course is then followed by a two-year training contract ('articles') and a Professional Skills Course in three compulsory parts: advocacy and communication skills; finance and business skills; and client care and professional standards. Most people train in private practice, but there are some opportunities in the Civil Service, local government, the Crown Prosecution Service, the Magistrates' Courts Service, and industry and commerce. (The Solicitors Regulation Authority is moving towards the launch of a pilot scheme for a new work-based learning arrangement in 2008. This would be an alternative method of qualifying, without having undertaken a training contract.)

- The non-law degree route: Graduates take a one-year course leading to the Common Professional Examination (CPE) or a Graduate Diploma in Law (GDL) before proceeding to the Legal Practice Course and the training contract as above. Qualifying therefore takes one year longer than for law graduates.
- The non-graduate route: Candidates first become Fellows of the Institute of Legal Executives (see p. 327). They then take the Legal Practice Course. Sometimes the training contract may be waived.

NOTE: All routes are very competitive. Good grades are essential at all stages. Relevant work experience can be useful.

Routes to qualifying in Scotland:

Either an LLB degree at a Scottish university followed by a 26-week full-time course called the Diploma in Legal Practice followed by a two-year Post-Diploma Training Contract or a three-year training contract with a firm of solicitors leading to the Law Society of Scotland's professional examinations (called the 'Pre-Diploma Training Contract'), followed by the Diploma in Legal Practice followed by a two-year Post-Diploma Training Contract. The law degree route is the more popular route. The traineeship is undertaken under the supervision of a Scottish qualified solicitor, either in private practice or a public service or other organization.

The Law Society of Scotland is currently consulting on the routes to qualification for Scottish solicitors. These routes are subject to change. Further details can be found on the Society's website at *www.lawscot.org.uk/training/consult.*

Personal attributes Capacity for absorbing facts quickly; logical reasoning; ability to see implications which are not obvious; ability to come to grips with an intricate problem; a good memory for facts and faces; tact; patience; good communication skills; sound judgement of character; an understanding of human behaviour and a personality that inspires confidence.

Mature entry and career change (England and Wales) Mature entrants are advised to take the ILEX route (see p. 327) or take a law degree (most academic institutions make concessions for mature students). The ILEX route does not apply in Scotland.

Work–life balance Some firms of solicitors are now instituting formal career-break schemes. The Association of Women Solicitors runs a returner course aimed at those who have been out of the profession for five or more years. The BPP Law School has recently started offering courses for solicitors who wish to return to work after a career break or those who wish to re-train. Part-time opportunities are improving in private practice, the Civil Service, industry and commerce and local government. The last two also offer job-sharing, but it is very rare in private practice.

Further information
The Law Society, 113 Chancery Lane, London WC2A 1PL.
  www.lawsociety.org.uk
The Solicitors Regulation Authority (previously part of the Law Society).
  www.sra.org.uk
Law Society of Scotland, 26 Drumsheugh Gardens, Edinburgh EH3 7YR.
  www.lawscot.org.uk

Legal Executive (England and Wales only)

Entry qualifications Minimum entry is usually at National Qualifications Framework Level 3 (A levels, BTEC National awards).

The work A Legal Executive is normally an employee and currently cannot be a partner in a firm of solicitors, although it may be possible to become an associate in a law firm and Fellows of ILEX can go on to become advocates. Alternatively, a Legal Executive may be self-employed and run their own legal services business.

Legal Executives specialize in a particular area of law and thus the everyday work of a Legal Executive is similar to that of a solicitor. Depending upon which area of law they work in, Legal Executives may handle the legal aspects of a property transfer, be involved in actions in the High Court or county courts, draft wills, draw up documents to assist in the formation of a company, or advise husbands and wives with matrimonial problems or clients accused of serious or petty crime.

Legal Executives are fee earners. In private practice their work is charged directly to clients, making a direct contribution to the income of a law firm. This is an important difference between Legal Executives and legal support staff who tend to handle work of a more routine nature. Professional responsibilities increase with experience and Fellows of ILEX become one of the main points of contact for clients seeking professional advice on legal matters. Legal Executives may also run specialist departments in a legal firm.

Legal Executives are able to act as Commissioners for Oaths. With extended rights of audience in civil, criminal and family proceedings, those Fellows who train and qualify as Legal Executive Advocates can represent their clients in the County Court, Family Proceedings Court, Magistrates' Court including the Youth Court, Coroners Court and in most Tribunals depending on the area of law in which they practise. Fellows are licensed by the BarDIRECT committee of the Bar Council to instruct barristers directly without first going through a solicitor.

ILEX is authorized to award litigation rights to suitably qualified members. This will enable them to issue proceedings in their own name. Currently, ILEX is developing a framework for a litigation rights scheme; and Fellows are now eligible for judicial appointments for District Judges in civil and criminal courts and for Tribunal Chairman.

Legal Executives have the option to become solicitors in one or two years after becoming Fellows (see p. 322) and usually are exempt from the SRA's training contract. However, new emerging rights mean that the role and standing of Legal Executives and solicitors is becoming ever closer.

Training In-house, together with part-time training at day-release or evening classes, or by approved distance-learning courses, for the two stages of the Institute of Legal Executives' Professional Qualification. The syllabus includes general legal subjects and practice and procedure, and allows for specialization in one branch of the law. Training time varies from two to four years, but each stage normally takes two years when studied on a part-time basis (exemptions may also mean a short period of study). There are also a small number of full-time courses for the ILEX Level 3 Professional Diploma in Law. After five years' relevant employment (two of which must follow the ILEX Level 6 Professional Higher Diploma in Law) members can become Fellows.

Personal attributes Sufficient powers of concentration to detect relevant details in a mass of complex documentation; patience and perseverance; self-confidence and ability to discuss matters with all types of people from criminals to judges; common sense and good practical skills.

Mature entry and career change The ILEX route is suitable for school-leavers, graduates, legal support staff, career changers, mature students and those who already have family commitments, as the ILEX route means less debt, as students earn whilst they learn. It is possible to prepare for the ILEX professional qualification without being in relevant employment, although usually employers will pay for their staff to undergo ILEX qualifications.

Work–life balance Career breaks should not be a problem for people who keep up with legislative changes. Some opportunities exist for part-time jobs and also for training. Job-sharing should be possible.

Further information
The Institute of Legal Executives, Kempston Manor, Kempston, Bedford MK42 7AB.
www.ilex.org.uk

Related careers *Barristers' Clerk/Solicitor – Licensed Conveyancer – chartered secretary and administrator*

Licensed Conveyancer (England and Wales only)

Solicitors no longer have a monopoly in conveyancing property. Independent conveyancers may work on their own or in qualifying employment, i.e. licensed conveyancers, solicitors, financial institutions, local government departments, or property developers with in-house conveyancing departments.

Minimum entry is usually at National Qualifications Framework Level 3 (A levels, BTEC National awards) but is possible at National Qualifications Framework Level 2 (GCSEs A*–C, BTEC Diplomas and Certificates). Mature students over 25 and those in qualifying employment may be accepted with relevant experience only. Training is in two parts:

- Part-time study or distance learning for the Council for Licensed Conveyancers' Foundation and Finals examinations. Exemptions are available to those who have a recognized legal qualification.
- Two years' supervised full-time practical training, in qualifying employment, while studying for the examinations (can be completed on a part-time basis which extends the two-year period). Exemptions are available for those with conveyancing experience.

Further information
Information pack available from the Council for Licensed Conveyancers, 16 Glebe Road, Chelmsford, Essex CM1 1QG.
www.conveyancer.org.uk

Paralegals

Paralegals or legal professionals are non-lawyers with a variety of job titles who may work in a range of occupational sectors where knowledge of the law is required. ILEX's Paralegal Programmes can provide a route to legal executive training. The Institute of Paralegals in England, Wales and Northern Ireland (*www.instituteofparalegals. com*) and the Scottish Paralegal Association (*www.scottish-paralegal.org.uk*) are the relevant professional bodies.

Leisure/Recreation Management

Though we may not have become the 'leisure society' as predicted some years ago, people are spending more time and money on leisure activities. The leisure industry is enormous and at its broadest includes everything from hotels and catering to zoos and safari parks, taking in pubs, wine bars, cinemas, theme parks and heritage sites, sport and leisure centres, museums, art galleries and theatres, parks and playgrounds, even libraries. Though this may suit economists and industry analysts, it is not a practical starting point for career-choosers. Running a pub is almost certainly not what someone turning to this chapter has in mind; nor is the average librarian likely to consider themselves as part of the leisure industry. Many people who will find themselves in this broad-sweep leisure industry are likely to have interests and motivations that lead them to other chapters in this book. Nevertheless it is helpful for people who see leisure as primarily sport and physical recreation to recognize that the opportunities are very much wider than is commonly realized.

Entry qualifications None specified. In practice professional qualification and/or administrative experience.

The work The leisure industry has developed piecemeal, but it is characterized by growth, diversity and increasing integration. It is generally recognized that leisure and recreation are an important aspect of the well-being of both individuals and the community; it is also recognized that well-run leisure facilities can be profitable. So more facilities are being developed. They are increasingly sophisticated in response to market demand. Where once you had swimming pools you now have 'leisure pools' with waves, water slides, interior landscaping and probably a gym alongside.

Integration occurs on several levels. Local authorities (who used to be the largest employers of leisure management staff, though they have now been outstripped by the private and voluntary sectors) have established integrated, multidisciplinary departments to cover indoor and outdoor sports, parks and countryside, the arts, community and children's play facilities, entertainments and libraries and tourism. Large-scale complexes are being developed where people can, for example, shop, eat, swim, bowl, or take in a film or concert. Increasingly leisure facilities are a partnership of public and private sectors with, for example, an authority providing finance for a development, while a private concern manages it on a contract basis. In addition to local authority facilities there are opportunities in, for example, company sports and social clubs, countryside and theme parks, Sport England and governing bodies of individual sports, the Arts Council, arts centres, theatres and concert halls.

The work involved obviously varies a great deal and it is possible to give only a few examples. *Senior managers*, whatever their title, are responsible for financial management, marketing, promotion, and management and motivation of staff who might include those working in administration, catering and maintenance as well as specialists, e.g. coaches or instructors. *Assistant managers* generally look after a particular function (bookings and administration, for example), a facility (e.g. the swimming pool and all associated activities) or a range of activities (e.g. all outdoor sports or entertainments in an authority's parks). *Supervisors* are concerned with the day-to-day running of activities and the work of staff such as poolside staff, gardeners or entertainment centre staff. There are variations on this pattern: in a smaller centre a manager will have to take on a broader range of responsibilities, while in a larger facility there may be more specialized roles. Depending on the size and nature of the organization there may also be central roles in policy formulation, budgeting and planning.

By definition 'leisure' is when you are not working, so leisure staff at operational levels must work when most other people are not working.

The leisure industry is a very broad-based pyramid with many more jobs at basic than at senior levels. Its relative lack of structure, however, makes it a fairly easy pyramid to climb for those with the right motivation and qualifications. On the other hand entrants often have to start at a level lower than their paper qualifications seem to warrant: e.g. graduates entering the industry with sports-related degrees also often have to work their way up. It is possible to enter the leisure and recreation management sector at operational level, e.g. as a fitness instructor, lifeguard or leisure assistant, and work one's way up by taking training courses and gaining professional qualifications while in employment.

People with commercial skills from other areas such as retail are also crossing over into the growing 'sports industry'. In 2007 estimated market value in the sports industry in the UK was £3.6 billion and is growing year on year. This trend means there are more and more sports facilities, swimming pools and health clubs springing up, all of which need quality staff to service their customers.

Some areas of this vast field are obviously more specialized. Arts administration, for example, has a particular character and appeal, especially for graduates. It entails enabling artistic events (plays, concerts, etc.) to take place. This may involve planning, publicity, engaging performers, booking venues, handling ticket sales, finance (often including negotiating grants and sponsorship), maintenance of buildings and general administration. The actual range of tasks will depend on the size and nature of the organization – in a small company, managers might have to sell tickets at the door, at the Barbican they will not! Many arts administrators are graduates and there are some relevant degrees and postgraduate courses, as well as options on more general leisure courses (see 'Training', below). There is still, however, a foot-in-the-door element in this field and people develop careers from spare-time activities and voluntary work.

Training It is becoming increasingly necessary to have relevant higher educational or professional qualifications. Nevertheless, particularly in commercial leisure centres, successful managers may have few qualifications but lots of flair and entrepreneurial skills. Generally speaking, however, and certainly for local authority posts, systematic training is advisable.

The new Institute for Sport, Parks and Leisure was formed in January 2007 from two previous professional bodies: the Institute of Leisure and Amenity Management and the National Association of Sports Development. The Institute offers training courses and from March 2009 a new Professional Qualifications Scheme.

The Institute of Sport and Recreation has three levels of qualification in Sport and Recreation: a certificate in operations, in supervisory management, and the ISRM/City & Guilds Higher Professional Diploma. Apart from the diploma these can be achieved through work-based learning or via a full-time course. The diploma is for those working in management positions in the sport and recreation industry and can be studied by day release or distance learning.

SkillsActive, the Sector Skills Council for Active Leisure and Learning, has developed a National Qualification Framework which includes a growing range of N/SVQs, currently from entry level to level 3, covering aspects of work in the leisure field. Apprenticeships may be available.

Personal attributes Good organizing ability; practicality; ability to make different specialists work as a team; interest in the needs of all sections of the community; confidence in dealing with members of the public (even when they are impatient or boisterous).

Mature entry and career change Relevant experience and skills helpful.

Work–life balance Opportunities for career breaks and flexible working will differ depending on employer – they should be readily available if working for a local authority. There is considerable shift work in some jobs.

Further information

Institute for Sport, Parks and Leisure, The Grotto House, Lower Basildon, Reading, Berks RG8 9NE.
www.ispal.org.uk

Institute of Sport and Recreation Management (ISRM), Sir John Beckwith Centre for Sport, Loughborough University, Loughborough LE11 3TU.
www.isrm.co.uk

SkillsActive, Castlewood House, 77–91 New Oxford Street, London WC1A 1PX.
www.skillsactive.com

Sportscotland, Caledonia House, South Gyle, Edinburgh EH12 9DQ.
www.sportscotland.org.uk

Related careers *agriculture and horticulture – local government – museums and art galleries – public relations – sport – teaching*

Local Government

Local government is not a career but an employer. More precisely it is more than 400 employers throughout England, Scotland and Wales. Together they employ more than two million people in hundreds of occupations providing services, many of which are required by law, to their local communities.

In recent years there have been great changes in the way local services are managed. Council services are subject to competition and scrutiny to ensure they provide 'best value' for the taxpayer. Some council departments are run as external consultancies, selling their services to other departments.

Entry qualifications Most local authority employees hold qualifications relevant to the work they do. Some openings for those with a good general education, usually in administrative posts.

The work This varies enormously. Local government is enabled or required by law to provide a wide range of services. The larger employers of staff include: education, which includes schools, colleges, the youth service; social services; public protection, which includes the work of the police and fire services, consumer protection and environmental health; leisure services, which can include sports and community facilities, libraries, museums, theatres and the promotion of tourism; highways, housing, buildings and planning, which ranges from strategic planning to provision and maintenance of a range of community buildings. Obviously the scope of such activities involves a large number and wide range of people doing different things.

Among the scores of careers in local government are a number which can be pursued both inside and outside local government. These include accountancy, law, engineering, computer work, librarianship, public relations and human resources management. Local government is one option within these career areas. For another group of careers local authorities are the exclusive or major employers. These include teaching, social work, town planning, environmental health and trading standards (consumer protection). Another large group is involved in general administration, advising on policy formulation and procedures and coordinating the implementation of policies agreed by the elected councillors. Their work may include servicing committees, research and report-writing, as well as the day-to-day administration ensuring the smooth running of departments and services.

Many of the professionals employed by local authorities provide services directly to the public, e.g. teachers and librarians. Others, however, are part of the vast, essential support structure. IT and for the most part legal services, for example, are not offered direct to the local community, but they are essential to the provision of education and social services. In fact departments and services are not self-contained and projects usually involve multidisciplinary teams. For example, the building of a new school would involve not only the education department, but architects and surveyors, lawyers, planners, finance, possibly the fire services, even the leisure department if, say, it were intended that the school's sports facilities be used by the community outside school hours.

People may be promoted within a department and authority, but it is common to move among employing authorities, and being willing and able to move can aid rapid progress. It is also becoming increasingly easy, especially for those with good management skills, to move across departments.

Training Local authorities provide extensive training for all levels of staff, with opportunities to study for appropriate qualifications in a range of areas. The entry point, length and structure of training may vary. In some cases local authorities offer graduate entrants the opportunity to gain the practical training and experience necessary for professional qualification; in others they offer A level (or equivalent) entrants sponsorship on an appropriate degree course. Other entrants may be sponsored for day release for relevant qualifications. Among the fields in which training schemes are offered are: personnel (human resources management), IT, environmental health, town planning, trading standards, accountancy, engineering, surveying, social work, leisure management, architecture, housing management, law.

The Improvement and Development Agency for Local Government (IDeA) operate a national graduate development programme (NGDP) for local government, which recruits recent graduates with the potential to become senior managers onto a two-year management training scheme. Competition is intense.

For individual professions: see individual entries. (Some professionals train with local authorities; others join after qualifying.)

For general administration: entry qualifications vary. An increasing number of administrative officers are graduates, with some authorities running special graduate-training schemes. The professional qualification for senior administrators is membership of the Institute of Chartered Secretaries and Administrators, for which day release may be available. A level or equivalent level entrants may also study for this qualification or for a BTEC Higher award in public services. Those with four GCSEs (A–C) or equivalent can begin work and study for National awards in public services; those who are motivated and able can continue on to a related Higher award, a degree and/or ICSA membership. (It is probably best for those who are ambitious to aim for educational qualifications that will take them to the highest entry point possible for them.)

It is difficult to draw lines about who is an administrator and who is not. Many of the professionals mentioned above are part of the administrative structure (for example, personnel), and many qualifications can lead to senior management. In some departments it is very common for the senior management to have grass-roots experience; for example, senior education administrators commonly have teaching experience.

NVQs/SVQs and/or Apprenticeships are available in many occupational areas such as amenity horticulture, business administration, health and care, customer service, IT, sport and recreation and vehicle maintenance.

Some authorities also offer Foundation degrees in partnership with local universities in subjects such as community governance, early years care and education and housing.

Personal attributes Depends on the particular type of work, but generally interest in local affairs; good written and oral communication skills and ability to deal with people; good organization skills; ability to work as one of a team. *For senior management*: willingness to carry into effect decisions taken by councillors, whether or not one agrees with them.

Mature entry and career change Good for those with relevant experience and, as seen above, so much is relevant. Authorities' policies and practices vary.

Work–life balance Local authorities have been among the most forward-looking employers on flexible working arrangements. Increasingly they need to investigate different ways of working, not only to deliver more cost-effective and competitive services, but also to meet the demands of employees who want to achieve a better balance between their work and other priorities. Arrangements vary from authority to authority but among the flexible options are flexitime, job-sharing and part-time work, term-time working, working at home, secondments and career breaks.

Further information
Local government careers information
www.lgcareers.com
National Graduate Development Programme
www.ngdp.co.uk
Improvement and Development Agency for local government (IDeA)
www.idea.gov.uk

Local Government Employers
www.lge.gov.uk

Related careers *civil service*

Logistics, Distribution and Transport Management

The work Logistics is concerned with the management of the 'supply chain' for goods, from raw materials right through to the end-user. It is a vital part of manufacturing, retailing, local and central government departments and the armed forces. The final product could be anything from a loaf of bread on the breakfast table, a car in a high street showroom, military supplies in a front-line soldier's hands, a pint of beer in the pub, petrol in a car's tank, or a pair of surgical gloves in an operating theatre. Some estimates show that over a quarter of the UK population works in a logistics-related job.

There are two main reasons why logistics has become a specialist function, both concerned with giving companies a competitive edge. The first is the rapid development of IT systems, and their applications to logistics and distribution. For example, when the checkout operator's scanner 'reads' the label on a tin of dog food, a message is sent by computer to the supplier to say that the item has been sold and needs replacing. Similar systems enable a car manufacturer to monitor the exact level of stock of components and to order more to arrive 'just in time' – storage space is costly, so this system saves money. The second is the drive to provide better customer service: customers not only want basics, such as the right amount of raw materials arriving at the right time, but may be attracted by extra services, for example after-sales support or recycling of packaging.

The aim of all those involved in logistics is to ensure that the right resource is in the right place at the right time in the right quantity, the right condition and at the right cost. All managers need an understanding of the issues involved but, increasingly in larger organizations, logistics specialists are employed to oversee every link in the chain. Companies and organizations may have their own logistics department or they may use outside logistics services. These services may manage the whole supply business or may deal solely with transport or storage.

Job titles in logistics and distribution management vary between employers. Logistics manager, transport manager, supply officer, operations manager, warehouse manager, materials planner, inventory controller, commodity manager are some of the most usual. Associated disciplines and functions are marketing and selling (see p. 362), purchasing and supply (see p. 494), retail management (see p. 501), management (see p. 346) and finance.

Logistics Planner/Strategist

Planners analyse the various links of the supply chain and try to find ways of making the whole work ever more smoothly and efficiently. The key is the flow of information at every stage and this is where sophisticated computer systems can be so effective. Planners working in logistics consultancies will work with managers in the client's organization to look at logistics issues such as warehousing, supply, materials handling, transport and IT systems.

Road Transport Manager (Freight)

The vast majority of goods in Britain (and only slightly fewer in Europe) are carried by road. Movement of goods can be carried out by suppliers/manufacturers/retailers' own transport fleets (known as 'own account' operations) or by 'third party' operations. These specialists include small local hauliers and huge national and international carriers whose lorries are a common sight on motorways and at ports. A transport manager will oversee a fleet of vehicles and their drivers, making sure that deliveries reach customers on time and in good condition. The many aspects of running a transport business include finance, purchase and maintenance of vehicles, recruitment and training of drivers, safety (both of vehicles and in the loading and unloading of dangerous substances), looking for ways of making lorries more environmentally friendly (for example by changes in design and limiting of noise and other forms of pollution). Movement of lorries needs to be planned to ensure the lowest mileage and, wherever possible, 'backloading' – collecting a load for the return journey.

Warehouse Manager

Many manufacturers and retailers own and operate their own warehouses. Others use specialist distribution companies who may offer both transport and storage services. Warehouse managers may operate a warehouse dedicated to one customer's goods or provide storage, packaging and handling services to several different customers. The efficient use of space, the use of sophisticated systems for the checking in and out of goods means fewer people are employed in warehouses than in the past, but managers still have to oversee people, vehicles and systems.

Freight Forwarder

Freight forwarders arrange transport of all types of freight to and from anywhere in the world. They search out the most efficient method or combination of methods of transport in each particular case, evaluating respectively the need for speed, security, refrigeration, the type of goods, legal and commercial constraints, etc. Goods may be sent by rail, road, air or sea, or by a combination of several modes of transport. Freight forwarders must be well acquainted with the advantages and disadvantages of the various methods of transport (which they are likely to learn by experience and from colleagues rather than from the transporters themselves), and with the intricacies of freight handling and storage and the different techniques and arrangements in the various ports and airports all over the world. They must make it their business to find routes which, though possibly longer in mileage, may be more efficient because turn-round arrangements in some ports and airports are quicker than in others.

They are also responsible for documentation, such as Bills of Lading, import and export licences, and for specialized packing and warehousing. Some freight forwarders specialize in certain commodities or geographical areas; others in certain methods of transport and/or types of packing or warehousing.

Shipbroker

Shipbrokers match up empty ships with cargoes and negotiate terms on behalf of their clients. This process is known as 'fixing', and is rather like solving a giant jigsaw puzzle. Shipbrokers may use a regular cargo run or charter a ship for a single voyage or a series of voyages, or a part of a ship's freight space. They also act as agents for shipowners when their ships are in port and deal with customs formalities, loading documentation, arrangements for the crew and any problems that may crop up. Shipbrokers also buy and sell ships for their clients. Some specialize in one activity, others are involved in several. Shipbrokers often work long and irregular hours, as they have to be in telephone contact with people all over the world during their working hours.

Training Entry to trainee management posts is either with a degree in transport/logistics, or with a degree in another discipline with or without a relevant postgraduate qualification, or into a junior post as a school-leaver (A levels or equivalent in geography or economics useful) followed by study in-house for professional qualifications. People working in this area may not have formal qualifications, but these are becoming more important, especially where recognition by other European countries is necessary. Many of the larger employers now offer graduate training programmes and Foundation degrees have also been developed.

The main professional organization is the Chartered Institute of Logistics and Transport. It offers modular programmes leading to its Introductory Certificate, Certificate, Professional Diploma and

Advanced Diploma qualifications which can be followed at an approved centre or through distance learning. It also offers a three-year distance-learning degree course leading to an MSc in Logistics or Passenger Transport Management, validated by Aston University.

Freight forwarders may train through the Institute of Export Certificate, Advanced Certificate and Diploma in International Trade scheme. Study is part-time at an approved college or by distance learning or self-study. The British International Freight Association offers a range of modular programmes leading to its certificate, diploma and advanced diploma qualifications which can be followed at an approved centre or through distance learning.

Shipbrokers may take a correspondence or part-time course leading to membership of the Institute of Chartered Shipbrokers. For the Foundation Diploma in Shipping they take one compulsory subject, Introduction to Shipping, and one other. For the Qualifying examinations, in addition to compulsory subjects including Shipping Business, they take three specialist subjects of their choice: these include Ship Sale and Purchase, Marine Insurance, Tanker Chartering, Dry Cargo Chartering and International Through Transport. Partial exemptions may be given to entrants with relevant qualifications.

Third-party transport providers have to have someone in control who has a Certificate of Professional Competence awarded by the OCR examining body, or an exemption certificate issued by one of the authorized professional bodies on behalf of the Department for Transport.

Personal attributes Practical, analytical mind; interest in problem-solving; ability to see the large picture as well as attending to detail; independence and willingness to take responsibility; good communication and negotiation skills; for many jobs, willingness to move from one function to another; ability to cope with pressure and frequent changes; ability to motivate and lead others.

Mature entry and career change Many people have moved sideways into logistics functions or moved up from clerical or operational roles (many transport managers started as drivers). This may become less common as graduate entry grows, but it will depend on whether or not the candidate has relevant previous experience.

Work–life balance Opportunities for career breaks and flexible working will depend on employers, but some in this sector, such as large retail companies, have a good record in this area.

Further information

Institute of Logistics and Transport, Logistics and Transport Centre, PO Box 5787, Corby, Northants NN17 4XQ.
   www.iolt.org.uk

Institute of Export, Minerva Business Park, Lynch Wood, Peterborough PE2 6FT.
   www.export.org.uk

British International Freight Association, Redfern House, Browells Lane, Feltham, Middlesex TW13 7EP.
   www.bifa.org

Institute of Chartered Shipbrokers, 85 Gracechurch Street, London EC3V 0AA.
   www.ics.org.uk

Skills for Logistics (Sector Skills Council), 14 Warren Yard, Warren Farm Office Village, Milton Keynes MK12 5NW.
   www.skillsforlogistics.org and www.careersinlogistics.co.uk

Related careers *management – marketing and selling – purchasing and supply – stock exchange and securities industry – travel agent/tour operator*

Management

Entry qualifications Nothing specific (see 'The work' and 'Training', below), but a degree or professional qualification is advisable.

The work Management is a vast and sometimes confusing field, with vague terminology. It is not so much one structured career as an activity, the purpose of which is to make the best use of available resources – human, money, material, equipment, time – in order to achieve a given objective. It has become largely professional, with specific, though varied, theories, techniques and training leading to various qualifications (or none). It is also a 'transferable skill': managers now often take their expertise from one type of organization to another.

Any system which provides a product, or a service, has to be managed. Someone has to see that things actually happen and that policies are carried out effectively and economically. Traditionally this has been implemented through a hierarchy of managers sandwiched between the policy-makers at board or equivalent level and the 'doers'. Now, however, the pattern is less one of rigid hierarchies with policy emanating from the top. Companies cannot afford to carry the costs of too many 'non-productive' managers; instead they are beginning to 'empower' staff at all levels and encourage them to create and act on their own initiative. Many companies have removed levels of management to 'flatten the hierarchy' (which can be as few as four levels from top to bottom in a large international company), giving managers considerable autonomy. At all levels, managers must enthuse their subordinates into doing things as efficiently as they – the managers – would wish to have done them themselves.

Routes into management There are basically two routes into management – either by first becoming a specialist in something, or by starting as a 'management trainee' in an organization with a management training scheme. But trainee schemes which give broad-based, systematic training are not easy to get for people without qualifications, so pre-entry training for a qualification is advisable (see 'Training', below).

Levels of management There is no clear-cut distinction between junior, middle and senior management. Designations vary between organizations. Rising from one level to another does not necessarily depend on gaining further qualifications. However, qualifications are very useful and may be essential, especially when changing employers. Most people who choose a management career think of senior, and general, managers – but they are the smallest management section.

Junior managers are the easiest to define. They are often team managers, responsible for controlling a number of people who are all doing the same work – work in which the junior managers are themselves trained (or at least which they are able to do). Junior managers organize the flow of work, resolve problems and provide the link with middle management. However, there is a slow but growing trend to 'self-managed work groups', where there is either no manager, or the management element is a small part of the job. Some companies are experimenting with the concept of teams electing their own leaders on an annual basis.

Middle managers coordinate and implement policies; increasingly they also set policies. This level of management spans a wide range of jobs and levels of responsibility. The step from junior to middle management is the most crucial on the management ladder: while junior managers are usually responsible for people all doing the same kind of work, middle managers are responsible either for the work of a number of junior managers who are all doing different jobs, or for a larger group of people in the same field. Junior managers who want promotion must therefore broaden their experience and 'move sideways' before moving up. This experience-broadening is part of 'management development' and should be built into managers' training, but in very many firms young managers have to plan their own career paths rather than rely on personnel managers to do it for them. This is partly what makes 'management' such a difficult career to plan and to describe. It is not so much qualifications as varied experience, luck, drive and initiative that matter.

A vital and growing 'senior/middle management' area is 'management of change', which is often the outcome of the introduction of new technologies. There is as yet no single tried and tested way of tackling this development and its implications. In some companies consultants in 'organizational change' or 'organizational behaviour' (usual backgrounds: social or behavioural science degree and/or extensive business experience) may be called in to advise; more often managers (departmental, office, production, personnel – it varies enormously) have to cope. These managers may have to deal with employees' fears of new and unknown working practices; with the 'de-skilling' of some jobs and retraining staff for others; with 'slimming down' the workforce and with the search and training for new job opportunities for redundant employees. 'Planning for change' is evolving into a management specialism or at least a new management task (see p. 355). Change does not result only from automation. Companies also re-examine how they do things by looking at processes (a chain of activities that delivers value to a customer) rather than functions (bits of processes that represent the way a company is typically organized). This gives much greater scope for rationalization and avoidance of duplication, as well as brand-new ways of working. This is what is usually called 'business process re-engineering' or 'redesign'. Technology may enable this change to happen, but it is not the 'driver' and is only one component of the change. 'Planning for change' involves close cooperation with computer and other specialists.

Senior managers innovate and lead. They are concerned with strategy. They may plan far ahead and base planning and policy decisions on information and advice from specialist managers. The higher up the ladder, the more creativity, imagination and understanding of economic and social trends and the environment in which an organization operates are required. Senior managers also initiate changes in both the structure and the direction of an organization, and they are responsible for establishing effective lines of communication to ensure that policies are known and understood (and discussed) right down the line. They must also ensure that the effects of policy implementation are monitored.

There is, however, no strict dividing line between middle and senior managers. Anyone responsible to the board is definitely a senior manager. That usually includes heads of departments – personnel, production, finance, marketing, etc. And 'general managers', who do the coordinating, are usually considered senior managers.

Some terms used in management jargon

Line management: A line manager is the manager in charge of whatever the organization's principal activity and main purpose is. In a manufacturing industry it is the production manager; in retail it is the store manager; in an air freight charter company it is the person selling aircraft space. (The term 'line' is apparently derived from 'being in the firing line' – the line manager is the one who tends to get shot at when things go wrong.)

General management: General managers coordinate the work of several specialist departments (or functions), for example personnel, production, accountancy, etc. By training they are usually specialists in one of the functions for which they are responsible; which one is immaterial.

Executives and managers: The distinction is vague. Broadly managers are responsible for controlling other people's work, whereas executives are not necessarily: for example, a legal adviser is a senior executive, but not a manager. But middle or senior managers may also be called executives.

Managers and administrators: Again the distinction is vague. What is called management in industry is often called administration in the public sector. The terms are often interchangeable (in terms of activity), but 'administrators' are more likely to be concerned with the smooth running of a department or organization without making any changes; whereas 'managers' are expected to choose the most efficient (or 'cost-effective') of various alternative routes to achieve an objective. Management implies more decision-making. But as in the whole of the management field, different people mean different things by the same terms.

Management covers such a vast range of jobs that it is impossible to generalize about prospects. However, there is a shortage of good managers (especially with a technical background). Nevertheless entry to management trainee jobs is very competitive. Graduate and HND candidates on the whole stand a better chance than others. Over one-third of vacancies are for 'any discipline' graduates; where the discipline is specified, engineering/technological degrees are most in demand with IT subjects and then business/management studies next. First jobs are often in large firms' manufacturing (see p. 217), marketing and sales (see p. 362), purchasing and supply (see p. 494) departments, and in small and medium firms where specialisms are not so clearly defined. There are numerically more openings in small and medium-sized firms than in the large, household name 'first choice' companies and all-round experience in small firms can be very good training.

Employers usually prefer management trainee applicants who have had some work experience – if not on a sandwich placement, then in holiday or temporary employment. Having worked abroad – in whatever capacity – can also be an advantage. It follows that it may be advisable to take almost any job even if it is not a 'management' one, to gain experience of the 'real world' work environment.

Training Paths into management and progress once in are nothing like as clear-cut as they are in established professions – because of the diversity of management tasks, environment and objectives; of levels of responsibility and of 'management styles' (and because there is no precise, universally agreed definition of 'management'). What has become clear over the last few years is that getting in requires a very different combination of qualities and qualifications than getting on afterwards. That makes description and definition of training rather difficult. However, here are some guidelines and trends:

To be considered for a management trainee job, qualifications certainly matter in the majority of cases, but they must be accompanied by the right personal qualities (which vary from one employer to another – for broad guidelines see 'Personal attributes', below). Later, the balance and combination of requirements are different. For promotion, paper qualifications are less important; track record is more important. For example, a person with a degree but unimpressive work experience has fewer promotion/job-change chances than a person who proved managerial ability in a previous job, and somehow acquired the necessary theoretical knowledge.

For the majority of potential senior managers these are the usual ways of qualifying for management in industry, commerce and elsewhere:

- Degree in business or management studies (titles vary). Courses usually include practical experience in industry or commerce (or public authority) which gives students an insight into the real world of work. This enables those who do not enjoy the atmosphere, or find the pace too exacting, to change to some other graduate career. Employers welcome business/management studies graduates because they have had work experience, know what to expect, and have a basic understanding of business. Business/management degrees may be full-time or sandwich (i.e. with spells of work experience). There are also part-time business/management degrees, mainly for people in relevant employment, though people who have had previous relevant experience may be accepted. These courses are useful for people who want to return to work after a break or want to switch to a business career while still in other employment. Some 'mixed mode' courses enable students to combine one or two years' full-time study with two or three years' part-time study.
- A degree in any discipline or specialist qualification, e.g. in accountancy, or engineering.
- Postgraduate or post-experience courses. These fall into two main groups: (i) courses in general management; and (ii) courses leading to specialist qualifications such as personnel management, international marketing, transport, production, export management, etc. Both types of courses can be either full-time, part-time while in

relevant employment, or, possibly, while preparing to go back to work after a break. The best-known courses are at the graduate business schools in London, Warwick, Cranfield and Manchester, but there are a great number of others. Most courses last one or two years full-time or two to four years part-time. Some may be suitable also for people who have been working for a few years but have no academic or professional qualifications, and for people who have been out of employment for some time (women who raised families mainly) as well as for mid-career changers. These courses may lead to higher degrees (Master of Business Administration – MBA, MSc or MPhil) in management sciences, administrative management, industrial management, international management, etc. Titles vary and do not necessarily indicate a particular emphasis or content.

- Distance learning courses. The Open University Business School offers numerous open learning courses leading to Professional Certificate in Management, Professional Diploma in Management, MBA and other higher degrees by research. (Full details can be found at *www.open.ac.uk/oubs.*)
- BTEC and SQA Higher National Diplomas and Certificates. Higher National Diploma courses are usually two years full-time or three years sandwich. Higher National Certificates are usually taken by day or block release while in appropriate employment (see 'Employers' training schemes', below). These awards may lead to complete or partial exemption from relevant professional bodies' 'intermediate' examinations.
- A wide range of full-time, part-time and distance learning courses are available at junior or middle management level. Options include BTEC/SQA National Certificate and Diploma awards and the BTEC Advanced Professional Diploma in Management Studies.
- Employers' training schemes: Many firms (mainly large ones) and public sector industries run training schemes. Entry is at various levels either for training, with day release, for a professional qualification, or, for professionally qualified people – in whatever subject, but especially business/management, accountancy or

engineering – as 'graduate trainee' or 'management trainee'. Schemes vary enormously in content, quality and usefulness to the trainee. In some firms, trainees learn only how to be of use to that particular organization – and thus their future job choice is more limited; in others they get a thorough management training. Detailed research before accepting management trainee jobs is essential. Large organizations often take only, or mainly, graduates for training schemes likely to lead to senior or even senior/middle management. Some organizations consider HND and degree holders on an equal footing. Some large companies – sometimes as part of a consortium – run in-house MBA programmes tailored to their particular needs.

- NVQs/SVQs offer a framework of vocational qualifications appropriate to all levels of management. They are offered by Awarding Bodies including Edexcel BTEC, the Chartered Management Institute, City & Guilds and SQA. Some NVQs/SVQs are delivered by centres together with taught programmes. For example, a level 4 NVQ can be delivered with a BTEC Higher National Certificate. The Chartered Management Institute's own awards – Certificate in Team Leading, Certificate in Management, Diploma in Management, Executive Diploma in Management – lead to NVQs at levels 2–5.

Personal attributes Numeracy; business acumen; the ability to get on well with and be respected by people at all levels in the hierarchy; natural authority; willingness to take the blame for subordinates' misdeeds; self-confidence; unflappability in crises; organizing ability. *For senior management*: an analytical brain; creativity and imagination; ability to see implications and consequences of decisions and actions taken; ability to sift relevant facts from a mass of irrelevant information; enjoyment of power and responsibility; a fairly thick skin to cope with unavoidable clashes of temperament and opinion; resilience; courage; entrepreneurial flair; boundless ambition; ability to take snap decisions without worrying about them afterwards; physical and mental energy.

Mature entry and career change Some companies, so far mainly in retail and in catering, are encouraging women to become management trainees. Candidates are usually expected to have a degree, or professional qualification, or relevant experience.

Work–life balance A recent Chartered Management Institute survey found that one in five managers works fourteen hours more than they're paid for, effectively equating to a seven-day week. Almost half feel overloaded with work. One in three wanted flexible-working initiatives like compressed working weeks but fewer than 5 per cent believed that these will ever happen.

Opportunities for career breaks and flexible working vary greatly depending upon the level of management and type of employer. The Civil Service and local authorities are introducing flexible work schemes including part-time work and job-sharing at lower levels of management, but a long-hours culture may be the price to pay for climbing the management ladder whether in the private or the public sector.

Further information

No one specific information source: see specific careers; for higher education see UCAS website at *www.ucas.com*; for Edexcel BTEC and SQA awards see *www.edexcel.org.uk* or *www.sqa.org.uk*.

The Chartered Management Institute, Management House, Cottingham Road, Corby, Northants NN17 1TT.

www.managers.org.uk

Related careers *Virtually every career offers management opportunities*

Management Consultancy

Entry qualifications Degree and/or professional qualification and, often, management experience.

The work Management consultants are called upon to improve organizations' effectiveness, diagnose faults and suggest remedies. They provide objective advice and assistance relating to the strategy, structure, management and operations of an organization. They may, for example, be called in by a food manufacturer to investigate reasons for the company's declining market share. Before producing a plan of action to improve matters, they thoroughly research the firm's organization, its potential and the competition. They might then suggest the company should widen, or narrow, or completely change, its product range; or they might recommend changes in the company's marketing strategy, its management structure, its industrial relations policy, the introduction of new technology – or a combination of any of these and perhaps other strategies. But work is by no means confined to industry. Consultants are increasingly called in by, for example, charities and public authorities. A particular growth area is 'managing change' in any type of organization – i.e. helping to implement smooth transition from traditional to new working patterns – not only new technology-based ones but also such innovations as job-sharing.

Because the field is so wide and requires so many varieties of expertise, consultants tend to specialize. They may specialize in an aspect of management – for example in information technology (IT), financial, distribution, marketing, human resources (see p. 434), or information management. They may also specialize in working with

355

one type of organization – local authorities; charities; manufacturing industry or even one type of manufacturing such as light engineering, or one type of service industry such as catering or retail. Others specialize as consultants in 'change management'.

Training/experience Some management consultancies recruit new graduates – usually, but not always, people with technical or business/management degrees – and give them rigorous internal training, followed by on-the-job training while working for a client. But the vast majority of recruits have a few years' postgraduate or post-qualification experience. Many have an MBA. Consultancy firms may then provide in-house training and/or send staff on external courses. IT consultancies, for example, may be large accountancy firms or associated companies, major hardware suppliers who are taking on this role, or independents. There is a trend away from big consultancies to small specialist ones.

The Institute of Business Consulting offers certificate and diploma level awards through work-based study, plus the Certified Management Consultant award with further professional experience.

Personal attributes Ability to work as one of a team as well as independently; ability to cope with possibly hostile attitudes on the part of staff whose work is being scrutinized; adaptability to working in different environments; great diplomatic skill to deal with people at all levels and persuade them to change their ways; self-confidence and a confidence-inspiring manner; an analytical mind; an open mind to approach each new set of circumstances on its merits; curiosity; patience; willingness to work long hours; ability to put complex matters concisely and simply.

Mature entry and career change Maturity and experience are an asset.

Work–life balance Career breaks are possible but it is essential to keep up with developments and to keep the break short. Part-time work is possible theoretically by having small workloads or job-sharing. Few consultants work part-time. The Women In Consulting professional affiliation offers career development support and networking opportunities (*www.womeninconsulting.org*).

Further information

Chartered Management Institute, Cottingham Road, Corby, Northamptonshire NN17 1TT.
www.managers.org.uk

Institute of Business Consulting, 3rd Floor, 17–18 Hayward's Place, London EC1R 0EQ.
www.ibconsulting.co.uk

Management Consultants Association, 60 Trafalgar Square, London WC2N 5DS.
www.mca.org.uk

Related careers *accountancy – information technology/information systems – management – management services – personnel/human resources management*

Management Services

Entry qualifications For *work study* and *organization and methods*, nothing rigid, just appropriate work experience (although many practitioners do have a basic business degree qualification). For *operational research*, a degree, normally in a subject requiring numeracy.

The work Management services is the collective term for a number of functions concerned with the application of analytical techniques to problems concerning the efficient use of manpower, equipment, machinery or other resources. They provide objective information and analysis for improved planning and management decision-making. The core management services are work study, organization and methods and operational research, but some management services departments include other specialists such as economists (see p. 210), statisticians (see p. 368), or systems analysts (see p. 282), while some work might come under another department, for example human resources. Other words describing the results of management services activities are utilization, performance and productivity, and increasingly 'management services' comes under guises such as 'lean' thinking.

Work Study and Organization and Methods

Work study had its origins in manufacturing production, and organization and methods in the office (initially in central government) but the aims and principles are basically the same. There are two main aspects of the work: method study and work measurement. Method study is the analysis of how operations are carried out and how they might be improved. Work measurement means using specific techniques to measure the time and human effort involved in specific tasks so that standards of performance can be established for planning, control, payment systems and the introduction of new technologies, for example.

In addition to identifying problems, collecting the necessary data, evaluating and proposing solutions, management service practitioners often get involved in implementing the solutions, for example by training line managers or helping to design a new office layout or select new equipment. Tact, sensitivity and good communication skills are needed at every stage. People at all levels can be reluctant to admit there is a problem and can feel resentful at being 'measured' or threatened by the thought of change especially by somebody who appears 'external' to the function/activity to be reviewed. Your solutions may have to be 'sold' to a range of interested parties.

During the late 1990s and early 2000s, new application areas for management services' 'tools and techniques' were developed including such descriptions as: Business Process Re-engineering, Continuous Improvement, Change Management, Lean Engineering, Process Improvement, Process Management, Business Excellence Model, Supply Chain Management, Business Improvement, Business Performance, Six Sigma, Quality Improvement, Knowledge Sharing, 'Innovation' and Value Management.

Operational Research

Operational research (OR) is the discipline of applying appropriate analytical methods to help make better decisions. By using techniques such as mathematical modelling to analyse complex situations, OR can give executives the power to make more effective decisions and build more productive systems based on:

- more complete data
- consideration of all available options

- careful predictions of outcomes and estimates of risk
- the latest decision tools and techniques.

OR employs highly developed methods practised by specially trained professionals. It is powerful, typically using advanced tools and technologies that tend to be tailored to the needs of each client. An OR professional can help a client to define a specific challenge in ways that make the most of existing data and uncover the most beneficial options.

OR professionals draw upon the latest analytical technologies, including:

- simulation – giving managers the ability to try out approaches and test ideas for improvement
- optimization – narrowing down choices to the best, when there are virtually innumerable feasible options and comparing them is difficult
- probability and statistics – helping to measure risk, mine data to find valuable connections and insights, test conclusions and make reliable forecasts.

OR has been used to benefit organizations and experiences that are all around us in our everyday life: from better scheduling of airline crews to the design of queues at Disney theme parks; from two-person start-ups to FTSE100 leaders; from global resource planning decisions, to optimizing hundreds of local delivery routes.

Training For work study and organization and methods, largely in-house as an assistant. For membership of the Institute of Management Services distance-learning, day-release, evening or in-house training courses leading to Certificate and Diploma plus three years' experience.

For OR a postgraduate degree may be an advantage; a list of universities offering postgraduate OR courses can be found under 'Careers in OR' at *www.theorsociety.com*. Employers may sponsor students on these courses. On-the-job training is also provided, often supplemented by in-house or outside short courses.

Personal attributes Ability to get on with people at all levels in an organization; good communication skills; methodical approach; technical and analytical skills; tact; common sense; imagination; ability to understand and explain complicated matters clearly.

Mature entry and career change Prospects are good in work study and organization and methods, which are very much 'second careers', most people having gained some previous work experience. In operational research a suitable degree and industrial experience are required. It is estimated that some three-quarters of OR practitioners are under 40.

Work–life balance A career break should be no problem for those who keep in touch. Opportunities for returners and for flexible working are better in the public sector.

Part-time work can take the form of project or consultancy work rather than reduced hours in a regular job. Opinions differ on job-sharing; keeping in touch would be vital and home computer links could help. Given the problem-solving nature of the work, the 'two minds' argument seems persuasive.

Further information

Institute of Management Services, Brooke House, 24 Dam Street, Lichfield, Staffordshire ws13 6ab.

www.ims-productivity.com

The OR Society, Seymour House, 12 Edward Street, Birmingham b1 2rx.

www.theorsociety.com

For more information visit *www.scienceofbetter.co.uk*

Related careers *actuary – engineering – health and safety inspectors – information technology/information systems – management – science: Mathematical Sciences*

Marketing and Selling

Entry qualifications Nothing specific; for Chartered Institute of Marketing's Certificates see 'Training'. Considerable graduate entry.

Marketing

Effective marketing is the key to profitability and essential for Britain's trading position in the world economy. Marketing goods and services is as skilled an occupation, and as important, as producing them. But marketing is a rather vague term, often used loosely to cover a range of activities. Different establishments interpret the term differently, and titles include brand manager; product manager; development manager; marketing executive; marketing manager; export marketing manager, etc. Titles do not necessarily indicate any particular level of responsibility or scope.

The Chartered Institute of Marketing defines marketing as 'the management process responsible for identifying, anticipating and satisfying customer requirements profitably' – at home and, vitally important, abroad.

Marketing specialists find out what customers want or, more important, can be persuaded to want, at what price, and then relate potential demand to the company's ability to produce whatever it is, get it to the 'point of sale', and do all that profitably.

Marketing involves researching the market and analysing research results – which involves devising and organizing surveys and interpreting the results; discussing results with accountants, production, distribution and advertising people. Marketers may suggest the company adapt its existing products to cope with the competition's better products, or with changes in buying habits, or they may think up a totally new product and help to develop and launch it, or they may introduce a better after-sales service.

All these activities have always been carried out in business, but as business has become more complex and professionalized, with decisions being based on researched facts and, above all, figures rather than guesswork and experience, the 'marketing function' has become a 'business profession' and even an academic subject. Its importance in business has grown enormously in recent years. Poor marketing in the past is blamed for poor business performance. This applies particularly to international marketing. As exporting is becoming more and more essential for economic survival, international marketing is becoming a vital function in many more businesses. Marketing people have good prospects of going to the top in general management.

Marketing is often split into consumer goods and services marketing; industrial marketing; and international marketing (which could refer to either, and is part of the export business).

In all these activities, marketing involves several types of work: detailed research to establish customers', and potential customers', needs and potential needs: what type of customers, where, might buy at what price, with how effective an after-sales service, etc. Whether it is yet another washing powder or, in industrial marketing, a new piece of office machinery or computer, a new magazine or a food product, the procedure is basically the same. In industrial marketing, an engineering or science background is useful, but people switch from one area of marketing to another. In international marketing, a thorough understanding of other nations' cultural as well as social and economic set-up is vital (and, of course, speaking the relevant language). Perhaps the most crucial among several other marketing activities is sales forecasting. How many cars with what particular features will country X be willing to buy in two, five, ten years' time?

Marketing people must always base their conclusions on researched social and economic trends, which include statistics. Marketing has a glamorous image, but the basis of it is the correct interpretation of information.

Selling

Selling is both a career in itself and an essential part of (and sometimes the best way into) marketing. The two are closely linked: marketing finds out what customers want and helps to put the goods/services on the market; selling is concerned with finding and dealing with customers for the product/service.

There are different kinds of selling – and various ways of categorizing sales staff. A useful division is between consumer goods selling and specialized selling. In consumer goods selling (this totally excludes retail and door-to-door selling), sales representatives, or reps, sell to wholesalers and/or, more usually, to retailers. Selling to retailers involves 'merchandising', which means helping the retailer to maximize sales, by promotion campaigns, suggesting ideas for improving shop display, etc. Reps may also advise retailers on new sales techniques, etc. There is a hierarchy in consumer goods selling, with the field sales supervisors and area sales managers in charge of reps, and sales managers and sales directors at head office directing the whole sales operation.

Speciality or technical or industrial selling is usually done by staff with a technical background and perhaps manufacturing management experience. An engineering background is particularly useful (see p. 213). The speciality selling process differs totally from consumer goods selling: purchasing decisions are made not by shopkeepers or store buyers, but by technical and financial experts. To effect one sale may take months of negotiations, and extensive after-sales service. Speciality sales staff do not necessarily sell only standard products – whether they are large pieces of machinery or machine tools – but they may agree for their company to modify a product or produce a 'one-off' piece of equipment.

Sales representatives may form part of a team, or be the only rep in the firm. They may have a 'territory' in this country which may require them to be away from home for several days most weeks, or it may be a territory near home – it depends on the kind of product and on how many potential buyers there are within an area.

Exporting

Many different companies have export departments and some staff move into the export function from another department, most obviously from sales within the UK. However, companies frequently recruit staff from outside who have particular experience and expertise in dealing with overseas markets. Job titles and functions vary, but examples are:

Export clerk in manufacturing company: checks and acknowledges orders; liaises with production and packing departments; lets customers know of any delays; organizes necessary paperwork.

Export sales correspondent: prepares quotations, tenders and delivery schedules for customers, often within a geographical area or product range; supervises the work of the export clerk; takes part in sales promotions and deals with overseas agents.

Export area sales or product manager: responsible for reaching sales targets within a market or product area; visits and looks after existing customers and agents and researches openings for new business; arranges overseas promotions/exhibitions; negotiates new contracts.

Export manager/director: in charge of all aspects of export function; visits customers and agents in all the company's markets and product areas; appoints new staff; sets sales targets; liaises with UK sales and production managers.

Training There are various ways into marketing. It is possible to enter employment at any level and train while working or to transfer into marketing within an organization. Most graduates go straight into marketing as trainees on management training schemes; entry to these schemes can be extremely competitive and often requires a minimum of a 2:1 honours degree, in any discipline.

While working as a trainee, marketing staff can study for the Chartered Institute of Marketing's examinations. These are at three levels: the Professional Certificate in Marketing, requiring two A levels or equivalent; the Professional Diploma at graduate level; and the Professional Postgraduate Diploma in Marketing for which a postgraduate degree with significant marketing content from a CIM-approved university or equivalent or at least six years' management experience is needed. The Professional Diploma offers modules in research and information, planning, communications and marketing management in practice. Courses in arts marketing and e-marketing are also available through CIM.

The CIM also offers three levels of qualification in professional sales: Certificate, Advanced Certificate and Intensive Diploma. Most of the CIM's courses can be studied in a variety of ways, through full-time or part-time courses, e-learning, workshops and residential training.

Pre-entry training for marketing is either by business studies degree with marketing option or by specialized marketing degree. These degrees either link marketing to a specific area such as chemicals or textiles or engineering; or concentrate on international marketing and export. An engineering or science degree is a good way into speciality selling. HND and Foundation degrees in aspects of marketing are available.

There are also BTEC/SQA Higher awards with export marketing and distribution options.

For export marketing some trainees work for the Institute of Export's examinations, by day release or distance learning. The syllabus adds export procedure and principles of export management to marketing methods, principles and procedures.

The Institute offers a Certificate in International Trade at two levels, leading to examinations on the practical aspects of international trade. Students then go on to take the Diploma in International Trade.

Personal attributes *Marketing*: A high degree of business acumen and of numeracy; a little risk-taking instinct; self-confidence; ability to assess the effects of economic, social or political events; ability to stand perhaps unjustified criticism when forecasts turn out wrong, due to unforeseeable causes; social awareness and interest in social and economic trends; ability to communicate easily with colleagues and clients, whatever their temperament and their degree of expertise; ability to cope with change.

Selling: Numeracy; extrovert personality; ability to establish instant rapport with people; judgement; sensitivity for gauging right approach to customers; indifference to the occasional rebuff; enjoying being alone when travelling; willingness to be away from home a lot; good listening and communication skills.

Mature entry and career change People with technological or business qualifications can switch to marketing.

Work–life balance In this competitive field it will not be easy for any but the best and most determined people to return after a career break to what is essentially still a young person's career. Those with technological or science degrees or experience stand the best chances in industrial marketing. There are very few openings for part-time work, unless able to work for oneself as a consultant.

Further information

Chartered Institute of Marketing, Moor Hall, Cookham, Maidenhead, Berks SL6 9QH.
www.cim.co.uk
Institute of Export, Export House, Minerva Business Park, Lynch Wood, Peterborough PE2 6FT.
www.export.org.uk
Market Research Society, 15 Northburgh Street, London EC1V 0IR.
www.mrs.org.uk

Related careers *advertising – logistics, distribution and transport management – management – public relations – retail management*

Mathematics and Statistics

Entry qualifications Entry is usually at mathematically based degree level, and often at postgraduate level. Some entrants have first degrees in sciences, engineering or economics, plus mathematics- or statistics-related postgraduate qualifications.

The work Mathematicians work in science-based industries and scientific research (see p. 507), in financial management and actuarial work (see p. 53), in software programming (see p. 281), in operational research (see p. 359) – and in many commercial, industrial, public sector and research roles where they are in demand for their analytical skills. They may analyse data produced by engineers and scientists, usually working in interdisciplinary teams, making calculations which enable adjustments to various process. They frequently translate problems into mathematical terms – making 'models' – working out solutions and then express the results in non-mathematical form. Sometimes the mathematical models are so complex that a special technique called numerical analysis is used to solve them. The Government Operational Research Service provides analytical support and employs nearly 400 operational research analysts across 25 departments.

Statisticians, including mathematicians who have specialized in statistics, work in industry, medical, social and agricultural research, and in the Civil Service (the Government Statistical Service is the UK's largest employer of statisticians, with more than 900 in 30 different departments and agencies nationwide). They are concerned with the design of experiments, questionnaires and surveys and with the collection, analysis and interpretation of results. They process and interpret data, and help design and improve systems. In a government department they provide information on which policies can be based; for example they predict the effect of changes in the tax system or possible future demands for particular services. Statisticians also work in marketing and market research, where they design surveys to establish demand for goods and services, and in manufacturing quality assurance where they evaluate the quality of incoming raw materials and final products. The majority of statisticians need a scientific background; some need social science expertise (it is easier to switch with a science background to statistics in social sciences than to switch with a social science background to statistics in science).

There are also numerous teaching, research and consultancy opportunities for mathematicians and statisticians within higher education.

Training Various in-house and external training opportunities exist, leading to further professional and academic qualifications in all specialist fields. Appropriate degree qualifications plus subsequent practical experience can also qualify for membership of professional bodies such as the Royal Statistical Society or Institute of Management Services.

Personal attributes Mathematics and statistics graduates are generally valued throughout industry, commerce, science and public service for transferable skills such as problem-solving and logical thinking in addition to their specific numerical and analytical skills.

Mature entry and career change Refresher and other preparatory courses in mathematical skills are available, and there are numerous part-time and distance learning degree courses in mathematics and statistics. The Royal Statistical Society provides information for people looking for a career change.

Work–life balance Opportunities exist for flexible working and career breaks, particularly in public sector posts. Experienced practitioners in fields such as operational research and statistical analysis may work as self-employed consultants.

Further information

Institute of Mathematics and its Applications, 16 Nelson Street, Southend-on-Sea SS1 1EF.
www.ima.org.uk and *www.mathscareers.org.uk*

The Royal Statistical Society, 12 Errol Street, London EC1Y 8LX.
www.rss.org.uk

Operational Research Society, Seymour House, 12 Edward Street, Birmingham B1 2RX.
www.orsoc.org.uk

Government Statistical Service, Office for National Statistics, 1 Drummond Gate, London SW1V 2QQ.
www.statistics.gov.uk/recruitment/gss

Government Operational Research Service
www.ims-productivity.com

Related careers *actuary – information technology – sciences – operational research – management*

Medicine

Entry qualifications Entry to medical school is usually at National Qualifications Framework Level 3 (A levels, BTEC National awards) or Scottish Credit and Qualifications Framework equivalent – three good A levels or equivalent are normally required, including chemistry and increasingly biology: some medical schools will accept two science AS levels, one being chemistry, in place of one A level. A small number of medical schools run a one-year pre-medical course for candidates without the usual science background. An increasing number of medical schools are offering shortened courses for graduates, including a few for graduates in any subject. Most medical schools require applicants to take a pre-admissions test such as the BioMedical Admissions Test (BMAT) or the UK Clinical Aptitude Test (UKCAT).

General Practice (Family Doctor)

General practitioners are the front line of primary health care. As self-employed practitioners, GPs are responsible for their own premises and staff and have considerable autonomy in deciding how best to provide the services to patients required under their NHS contracts. Under the recent NHS reforms GPs now work with colleagues and other health service professionals in Primary Care Trusts. In Scotland primary care is managed by NHS Boards and contracts are practice-based rather than with GPs.

All family doctors are involved in:

- acute disease management, i.e. diagnosing, treating or referring for specialist treatment a range of ailments presented by patients
- preventative medicine, i.e. helping patients to understand how to prevent, look for and deal with problems
- counselling, i.e. dealing with patients' fears and feelings, both those that have a medical basis and those that lead to physical symptoms.

General practitioners may also get involved in community issues through involvement in their local Primary Care Trust. There are opportunities for GPs to work in hospitals, for example as a clinical assistant.

Most family doctors work in partnership with other doctors. Some practices organize themselves along specialist lines with, perhaps, one partner particularly experienced in obstetrics and gynaecology, while another may have a special interest in stress, and another in heart disease.

A typical family doctor's day might consist of a morning surgery from, say, 8.30 a.m. until 11 a.m.; routine office work, dealing with telephone inquiries, signing prescriptions, reading the post, dealing with letters to and from hospital consultants; home visits; lunch; visits or clinics (e.g. antenatal, minor operations, diabetic, child development); more office work; evening surgery. Most GPs have now opted out of providing 'out of hours' cover, that is cover for nights, weekends and public holidays, but they have to ensure patients have an alternative.

Recent years have seen enormous changes in general practice. New drugs are continually available; practices have direct access to investigation facilities and new equipment enabling them to provide care over a wider range of conditions; practice nurses handle routine procedures, health education and preventative work. Computerization is used for repeat prescription control, for the maintenance of registers (e.g. of all women due for cervical screening, or all under-5s due for immunization) and for the compilation of data that enables the doctors to measure and assess what they are doing for their patients as a whole. However, all these developments are merely aids to improve and monitor service. They do not replace the family doctor's traditional role of caring for patients largely by listening to and talking with them. There is currently a shortage of GPs.

Hospital Service

All doctors gain experience in hospitals, whether or not their intention is eventually to enter general practice. Doctors who remain in hospital medicine become specialists. There are more than 64 specialties. These specialties fall broadly into four main groups: medicine, surgery, pathology and psychiatry. Within each group are many sub-specialties ranging from general medicine and general surgery to smaller fields such as audiological medicine or paediatric surgery. Major specialties include accident and emergency, obstetrics and gynaecology, and anaesthetics.

Both the nature and pattern of work in different fields can vary considerably. For example, general medicine and surgery and obstetrics have far more emergency work than psychiatry or dermatology, while pathology has very little. The nature of the round-the-clock demands on anaesthetists means they have evolved a more predictable shift system than other doctors.

Many years of hospital doctors' careers are, though paid employment, technically training posts. As they progress through jobs in foundation training to more specialist posts at registrar level, they take on more and more responsibility under the supervision and guidance of more senior doctors. The most junior doctors take responsibility for practical, routine day-to-day care and administration (keeping records, communicating with families and other members of the medical team), progressing to more advisory work and greater clinical responsibility. Junior doctors' hours have traditionally been long and irregular but the European Working Time Directive has applied to doctors in training since 2004 and the maximum number of working hours will be gradually reduced to 48 per week by 2009. The more senior doctors become, the less they are likely to be called to an emergency, but they will be called for more complex diagnosis or treatment.

At the head of hospital teams are consultants, who have continuing responsibility for patient care. It can take from eight to twelve years of specialist training to reach this level, although recent changes are shortening this period.

Doctors' choices of specialty are determined not only by interest and inclination, but often by opportunity. Some fields are very much more popular and competitive than others, and it can take some time and experience before a final choice is made.

Research and Teaching

Research into new forms of treatment and new drugs and their effects is done in hospitals, research establishments and drug firms. Doctors can, and usually do, combine clinical and scientific work, but there are also research appointments, often including some teaching, for those who are interested in the scientific side of medicine rather than 'patient contact' (see p. 507).

Training UK medical students are required to take a five-year under-graduate course recognized by the General Medical Council leading to a Bachelor of Medicine and Surgery – depending upon the university an MBBS; MBBS/BSc; MBChB; MBBCh; BMBS – all of which are normally referred to as a 'first MB'. Most medical schools offer integrated courses which combine academic study and clinical experience throughout the five years. This is part of the ongoing change to medical education, implementing recommendations that courses concentrate less on the acquisition of factual knowledge and introduce greater emphasis on, for example, communication skills and practical clinical tasks. Medical schools have responded differently to the recommendations and as a result courses can differ greatly. It is important to look closely at their content as some still offer traditional lecture-based study while some have a more clinical setting-based approach. Some courses include study for an intercalated BSc degree while for others this is optional.

Accelerated courses (usually four years) for graduates are offered by some medical schools. Some require applicants to hold a science degree, whereas others will consider candidates with a broad range of degrees.

In 2005 a radical change was introduced to postgraduate medical training as part of the Modernizing Medical Careers reforms. Now after graduating, all doctors are required to follow an integrated, planned two-year Foundation Programme of general training, designed to act as a bridge between undergraduate medical training and specialist and general practice. This training, undertaken while working full-time (and usually very hard) in a variety of health care settings, gives junior doctors the opportunity to develop their competency in clinical skills and to sample a range of specialisms before making their final choice of area of medicine in which to specialize.

Doctors register with the General Medical Council (GMC) at the end of Foundation Year 1.

After completion of their foundation programme doctors begin their postgraduate medical education. This is in a chosen specialty or in general practice and the length of time depends on the specialty and training school chosen. Having achieved a Certificate of Completion of Training, doctors are qualified to apply for a post as a consultant or a GP principal.

Entry to both foundation and postgraduate medical education programmes is currently through open application.

Personal attributes The ability to communicate with people, take responsibility and to make vital decisions after weighing up all the relevant factors; patience with people unable to express themselves clearly; sympathy without emotional involvement; understanding of and liking for all types of people and tolerance of human weaknesses; self-confidence; conscientiousness; resourcefulness; the energy and stamina to work hard for long and often irregular periods; great powers of concentration; above-average intelligence; good health.

For research: Patience for long-term projects and an inquiring mind.

Mature entry and career change All applicants to medical school need to demonstrate that they have the ability to cope with the demands of the course, as well as commitment to a career in medicine. Candidates should take into account the number of years they would have after qualifying to work in medicine, before retirement.

Work–life balance The recent reforms to the NHS have included a significant increase in the support given to doctors combining practice with caring responsibilities. The NHS Improving Working Lives standard has required all NHS employers to introduce more flexible working and childcare support and to measure their practice against set requirements.The NHS has also introduced NHS Professionals, a new national staffing agency to provide temporary staff to NHS organizations.

Further information
British Medical Association, BMA House, Tavistock Square, London
  WC1H 9JP.
  www.bma.org.uk
Modernizing Medical Careers website
  www.mmc.nhs.uk
NHS Careers, PO Box 2311, Bristol BS2 2ZX.
  www.nhscareers.nhs.uk
Books that can be recommended include:

- *Learning Medicine*, by Rosalind Foster, Elizabeth Ingall, Peter Richards and Simon Stockill, available Hammicks BMA Bookshop: *www.hammicksbma.com*
- *The Insider's Guide to Medical Schools*, compiled by BMA Medical Students Committee, available Hammicks BMA Bookshop: *www. hammicksbma.com*
- *So, you want to be a Doctor?*, by Professor Sydney Nade, published by Careerscope
- *Getting into Medical School*, by James Burnett and Joe Ruston, published by Trotman.

Related careers *animals: Veterinary Surgeon – dentistry – medical or biomedical engineering – nursing – occupational therapy – optical work – osteopathy – pharmacy – physiotherapy – science – social work*

Merchant Navy

Entry qualifications *Undergraduate officer trainee*: (two routes). Entry to first route at National Qualifications Framework Level 3 (A levels, BTEC National awards) or Scottish Credit and Qualifications Framework equivalent. Entry to second route at National Qualifications Framework Level 3 (A levels, BTEC National awards) or Scottish Credit and Qualifications Framework equivalent, including awards in maths and/or physics. *Graduate officer trainee*: science, technology, engineering or similar degree. *Alternative schemes*: for those without the above qualifications entry may be possible on alternative training schemes.

All candidates must be in good health and pass a statutory medical examination, with a good standard of eyesight required for prospective deck personnel.

The work Ships carry over 90 per cent of world trade and seaborne trade is forecast to increase substantially by 2015. British shipping is technologically advanced and committed to respecting the environment, and includes a varied range of vessels – container ships, bulk carriers, supertankers, deep-sea tugs, naval support ships, ferries, marine mining vessels, cruise liners, specialist vessels and others. Life on board a ship is a 24-hour-a-day operation, seven days a week, 52 weeks a year. This work is divided into shifts – called watches, which are typically four hours on watch, followed by eight hours off watch, increasing to six hours on watch and six hours off watch at busy times. Leave time is generous, to compensate for time spent on board and away from home. For example, a voyage of around four months could be followed by as much as two months or so off at home.

The Engineering Department

Engineer officers are responsible for the provision and maintenance of all technical services on board, including the propulsion and auxiliary machinery in the engine room. They are responsible for the work of engine-room staff, so managing people is part of the job, as with all ships officers. An Engineer officer may progress to Chief Engineer officer. Engineer ratings are involved in routine maintenance, engine operation and machinery repairs.

The Deck Department

Deck officers are responsible for controlling the navigation of the ship, communications, cargo handling and ship stability. A Deck officer is a step on the way to becoming Master or Captain. Deck ratings assist with the navigation of the ship and are involved in operating deck machinery such as winches and cranes and carrying out maintenance tasks.

There are also some dual officer roles, covering both departments.

Communications

Electro-technical officers are responsible for the maintenance and efficient operation of complex electrical, electronic and control systems on board ship. This more specialized role is only required on certain types of ship.

Hotel and Entertainment Services on Cruise Ships and Ferries

This includes pursers/receptionists, restaurant and bar staff and chefs, housekeepers, cruise directors, entertainments team, etc., hairdressers, beauticians, photographers, retail staff, etc. Recruitment is usually based on those who are qualified and experienced within their own specialism.

Training Entry is by application to shipping companies or group training organizations that provide training as well as sponsorship to cover training costs and course fees (see 'Further information', below). Training consists of planned and progressive programmes of learning and experience based on a pattern of alternating periods at college and at sea and leading to nationally recognized qualifications and professional maritime certificates of competency.

Entry routes have a deck or engineering option. Each provides progression opportunities to the next stage and, through the ranks, to Master (Captain) or Chief Engineer officer, depending on ability and ambition.

Undergraduate Officer Trainee (two routes) Both routes provide structured learning for those aiming to progress to Master (Captain) or Chief Engineer officer and achieve degree level qualifications in addition to professional certificates of competency. Knowledge and skills are developed while serving aboard ship in a supernumerary capacity under the direct supervision of qualified officers. All of the time at sea and at college ashore is devoted to training and development. Entry standards may vary from company to company.

The first route provides a three-year training programme leading to a Foundation degree in either Nautical Science (or equivalent) for the deck department, or Marine Engineering for the engineering department, and professional Certificates of Competency. College and sea time are integrated throughout the three years. In Scotland, this training route leads to the Scottish Professional Diploma award.

The second route provides training for the honours degree, and lasts approximately four years, of which three are spent at university/ college. The other year enables development of seafaring skills, to complete the sea-service needed for the professional Certificate of Competency, and to provide shipboard experience. It can be undertaken at various stages throughout the programme, depending on the sponsoring company and the university/college, and will be either as a sandwich-based model or as the final year of a four-year programme.

Postgraduate entry Programmes have been developed for new entrants with suitable science, technology and engineering-based degrees, or similar. Provides a programme equivalent to undergraduate officer training but recognizes prior qualifications and maturity of applicants.

Alternative entry Programmes are available for suitably motivated candidates who have GCSEs only, or equivalent. Training is available at both rating and officer level, and consists of college and sea phases to gain the professional Certificates of Competency in either the deck or engineering departments.

Mature entry and career change There is no age limit for entry to Merchant Navy training programmes, and sponsoring companies will recruit onto training programmes based on their needs.

Work–life balance Opportunities for career breaks are available, as the professional Certificates of Competency provide the qualifications to work on board any type of ship anywhere in the world, and can be re-validated as required over time. In addition, seafaring skills and experience are in great demand in a wide range of jobs in the shore-based sector of the shipping industry. These include ship management, marine superintendents, maritime surveyors, port operations.

Position of women Women officers, trainees, cadets and ratings sail on modern ships, and are currently under-represented in the workforce. Shipping companies welcome applications from women.

Further information

Merchant Navy Training Board, Carthusian Court, 12 Carthusian Street, London EC1M 6EZ (for general information on all merchant navy careers and list of shipping companies providing sponsorship).
www.mntb.org.uk and www.careersatsea.org
Individual shipping companies
www.mntb.org.uk for listing of companies

Related careers *armed forces – engineering*

Museums and Art Galleries

Entry qualifications Various (see 'Training', below); for most jobs in museums and galleries, especially at curator level, a degree or equivalent is essential. In theory, the degree subject does not matter; however, if applicants want to specialize in a particular area – such as fine art, social history or education – it helps to have a relevant degree. A postgraduate qualification may also be needed.

The work The scope of museum work has widened greatly in recent years. Established museums and art galleries have shed their image of solemn shrines devoted to earnest study of art, artefacts and history. They are now a part of the leisure industry, wanting to entertain as well as inform, thus attracting a wider public. The term 'museum' is now used rather loosely and covers a more varied range of establishments than it used to. The term 'heritage centre' or 'heritage site' is increasingly used instead. Museum and heritage sector establishments overlap in terms of the work, which is basically selecting and organizing exhibits and attracting and organizing visitors.

Over half of Britain's roughly 3,000 museums were started in the last twenty years, and it is these museums which have transformed the museums scene. Museums fall into four main groups:

- *National museums* – such as the British Museum, the National Gallery and the National Museums and Galleries on Merseyside. These establishments receive their funding directly from central government and offer the greatest scope to the traditional academic specialist type of curators who chose the job because of their interest in pursuing their specialism. These curators may or may not combine collection management with general departmental management. National museum curators are normally graduates in subjects relevant to the department concerned. They usually start as assistant curators. Science/technology graduates are as likely to get a job as arts graduates. Competition is very keen indeed.

- *Regional and local museums* – such as Reading Museum, Bedford Museum and Roman Baths and Pump Room, Bath. They are funded by local authorities and range from a few large and prestigious ones to hundreds of small museums of local history or industry. Employment prospects vary; few jobs are research-based; most involve coping with everything. Entry is usually with a degree or comparable qualification (which could be non-specific management experience).

- *Independent museums* – such as the Galleries of Justice, Nottingham, and Dove Cottage and the Wordsworth Museum, Grasmere. These are the largest and fastest-growing group and are self-funded, either by sponsors and entry fees or entirely by entry fees. They are 'market led'. Their success depends on a commercially viable idea, and management, marketing and communication skills. The group also includes sophisticated tourist attractions like the Jorvik Viking Centre in York and the Museum of the Moving Image in London, as well as hundreds of small special-interest museums such as the Silk Museum in Macclesfield and the Freud Museum in London. Jobs go to applicants with commercial and communication skills; academic qualifications are not required, but as competition is very keen, academic qualifications in addition to the required skills help.

- *University museums* – such as Pitt Rivers Museum in Oxford, the Barlow Collection in Brighton and the Petrie Museum in London. This group offers a large range of size, type and function. The Ashmolean and Fitzwilliam Museums are important tourist attractions for Oxford and Cambridge while the Scott Polar Museum in Cambridge is a couple of rooms in the Scott Polar Research Institute.

Both local authority and independent museums use volunteer labour fairly extensively; such volunteer experience is very useful when applying for 'real' jobs. As there are always more applicants than vacancies, applicants are unlikely to get a foot on the career ladder without some work experience. Some museums, galleries and heritage organizations have well-run volunteer programmes on offer.

There is a broad range of career opportunities in museums and galleries – the larger the museum the more specialist the role is likely to be. Large national museums have separate departments to look after marketing, publicity, fundraising, human resources, finance, conservation, education work and individual collections. In smaller museums curators have to be able to undertake a variety of responsibilities. There can be crossover with other jobs too – such as education workers and outreach workers or collections managers and registrars.

Apart from traditional curators (in larger museums curators can also be called keepers), who are concerned with collection management and research, there is a range of many other museum jobs, including a few 'museum-specific' ones:

Exhibition designers. A growing number of museums are appointing in-house designers, but the majority are self-employed or work for exhibition design consultancies; their expertise is 'bought in' by museums. The work now often includes using audio-visual and interactive video equipment. Designers work closely with *interpreters*. Interpretation means showing objects in their context and imaginative presentation. It overlaps with *education workers* and may involve role-playing; perhaps dressing up as a 1920s chauffeur when showing transport from that period, or as a Roman shopkeeper when interpreting shopping in ancient Rome. Interpreters also help visitors use the high-tech equipment. The National Curriculum's emphasis on hands-on experience has increased the scope for museum–school collaboration. *Education workers* work with all ages – primary and secondary school groups plus adult learners and teachers – using a mix of formal and informal teaching.

Designers usually have an art-training background at Higher National award or degree level; interpreters and education workers are usually graduates (no particular discipline), and may or may not have teaching experience. However, experience of working as either a teacher, youth worker or community worker is invaluable. Many museums also employ *outreach workers* to work outside the museum with local groups and communities. Good outreach work draws on similar skills to museum education and often comes under the education department's remit.

Collection managers ensure that objects are properly cared for, often managing storage, conservation and record keeping associated with objects. They will also be involved in developing policies and standards for acquiring and disposing of objects.

Registrars usually work in national and larger regional museums. Their job is to record information about objects – what it is, where it has come from and where it is. This is a specialized activity in museums with international collections and large exhibition programmes requiring the movement of exhibits. *Documentation managers* maintain records about the objects in a museum's collection, usually through inputting information and images onto a database although the job may involve some research as well. Good multimedia and IT skills are essential.

In smaller museums titles and job roles may be less specific.

There is often movement between independent and other staff; experience in an independent museum may lead to work in a traditional one. Work in a heritage sector establishment or even a pure tourist attraction is useful experience in exhibit and visitor management.

Conservation is a profession in its own right and is a growth area. The national and a few local authority museums and art galleries use in-house conservators, but most are self-employed or work for private firms and collectors as well as for museums and art galleries. They do not by any means deal only with paintings or other traditional exhibits; anything from agricultural machinery to dresses or first-generation computers needs conserving. Conservators see their job in three stages: examination to assess the object's properties and need for repair; preservation to arrest or prevent deterioration; and restoration. Most conservators specialize by material and/or type of object: textiles, paintings, machinery, furniture, etc.

Other museum work, not museum-specific, includes marketing, public relations, visitors' services, shop management.

Training

The route into a museum or art gallery career is primarily an academic one; however, training has now become much more flexible to take account of changes in the work. NVQs at levels 3–5 are available and a Creative Apprenticeship programme is in development. The Sector Skills Council (Creative and Cultural Skills) is also developing a Graduate (all age) Apprenticeship.

There are three main routes to Associate Membership of the Museum Association (AMA) which, in addition, requires a specified period of continuing professional development over at least the following two years:

- a degree or NVQ/SVQ level 3 plus five years' experience or a postgraduate qualification plus an NVQ/SVQ level 4 plus three years' experience
- NVQ level 4 or 5 plus three years' work experience (no previous qualifications required)
- a recognized museum study qualification plus three years' work experience.

There are a small number of postgraduate courses available in museums studies or heritage management. These may be full-time or part-time and lead either to a Diploma or to a Masters degree. The Museums Association website has a list of recognized courses. It is also possible to include heritage management in some first degrees and Higher National Diplomas. There are also a few work-based training schemes available. The Victoria and Albert Museum runs what is effectively a graduate training programme. Recruits are taken on as assistant curators for five years.

On the conservation side, there is a variety of courses providing specialized training in a vast range of artefacts and materials, from plastics to stained glass, paper to antique clocks. Courses are at many levels from college certificate to postgraduate degree and may be full-time or part-time. NVQs/SVQs have also been introduced.

Personal attributes Intellectual ability; commitment; a love of knowledge for its own sake; visual imagination; a lively curiosity; organizing ability; an understanding of lay people's interests and tastes; communication skills; patience and determination in waiting for the right job and promotion.

Mature entry and career change Competitive career area: competition from young postgraduate candidates is very strong. Relevant skills and work experience helpful.

Work–life balance Career breaks may be available. In national and local authority museums, Civil Service (p. 153) and local government (p. 335) conditions apply; in independent museums and the heritage sector the situation varies greatly. Part-time work and job-sharing are beginning to be widely accepted.

Further information
Museums Association, 24 Calvin Street, London E1 6NW.
www.museumsassociation.org
Creative and Cultural Sector Skills Council (Creative and Cultural Skills), 4th Floor, Lafone House, The Leathermarket, Weston Street, London SE1 3HN.
www.ccskills.org.uk

Related careers *archaeology – archivist – art and design – information science*

Music

Entry qualifications Acceptance at music colleges depends on performance at audition. For most performers, except for singers, intensive musical training must have started by their teens at the latest. For degree courses, entry at National Qualifications Framework Level 3 (A levels, BTEC National awards) or Scottish Credit and Qualifications Framework equivalent, including A level or equivalent in music. For teaching, see p. 586.

The work Music covers a very wide field: performing, composing, recording, video-making, administration, teaching, criticism and journalism. Some of the traditional boundaries between what are loosely called 'serious' and 'pop' music and musicians are breaking down and fashions come and go as in any arts or entertainment area. In 'pop' and other 'non-traditional' music it is possible to reach the top without a proper musical training; success depends on many other factors. This section is concerned only with those parts of the profession that need formal training.

Performing

Some symphony orchestras and opera houses employ orchestral players on a full-time basis. Others, including smaller ensembles, are made up largely of regular but freelance musicians who may, or may not, work for other orchestras as well. Singers may be salaried members of a chorus or freelance.

Most freelance musicians, however devoted to serious music, are glad to work as 'session players' on TV commercials, film incidental music and other light music recording sessions, etc. A violinist may play in a concert at the Barbican on one evening and the following day in a TV jingle recording session.

A freelance musician has to fit in work as it comes. The work may fluctuate from three daily sessions (three hours each) over a long period, to no work for many weeks. Long practice at home is always necessary. Live concerts or recording sessions are arranged well in advance, but some lucrative TV or film sessions are booked at short notice, and accepting bookings requires careful judgement. Once a date is booked, it is unwise to break it, even if a better engagement is offered.

The musician's work is physically exhausting, and may include travel over long distances, combined with rehearsals and nightly performances, often in cold or overheated halls. An engagement for a season with a ballet or opera company may involve five performances a week with as many rehearsals, and practice at home. The atmosphere among musicians is usually friendly, although the competition is keen.

Part-time teaching, either privately or in schools, gives many freelance musicians a supplementary income. However, it may be difficult to fit in performing engagements with teaching.

Prospects in music are very competitive. It is estimated that only about one in ten music students who finish their full training (itself restricted to the good students) eventually makes a living as a performer. Of those, only a few become soloists. Good luck is almost as important as talent.

Composing

Making a living from composing concert repertoire is very difficult; it takes many years for composers to have a body of their music regularly performed. They normally need another source of income, mainly within the profession, sometimes outside. Some fortunate composers make a good living from writing music for different parts of the media, for example TV, films, commercials and corporate videos.

School Teaching

As the main job this is quite a different career. Teachers are employed in primary and secondary schools. They teach music either full-time in one school, possibly with a second subject, or part-time in various schools and/or youth clubs and evening institutes run by the local education authority.

There is scope for imagination and initiative. Music teachers' main job is to promote interest and enthusiasm, as only a minority of pupils take music examinations. They may start a choir or an orchestra; organize CD libraries, visits to concerts, etc.

There is currently a shortage of music teachers, particularly at primary level, now that music forms part of the National Curriculum.

Private Teaching

Many people go straight into full-time private teaching after leaving music college or university. They may prepare children, and sometimes adults, for graded examinations in an instrument. Because of its nature, this work is mostly done after school hours, in the evenings and at weekends. Some teachers prefer to do this rather than work in schools, as they have more control over what they do.

Sound Engineering/Music Technology

For broadcast sound engineering see p. 597. Sound engineers (not to be confused with professional engineers) in recording studios are responsible for the overall recording quality and for interpreting the producer's ideas. They need a grasp of basic physics and electronics in order to understand how to work their equipment, but they do not need great technical knowledge to start with (most enter as assistants or assistant engineers). Some highly qualified and experienced sound engineers may be called music technologists. They apply advanced technology to the creation and reproduction of sound. They work on the design and manufacture of equipment, as well as in recording studios and broadcasting.

It is difficult to enter this area; really good engineers, however, are always in demand and a few become producers.

Musical Instrument Technology

There is some limited scope in musical instrument technology, which means making or repairing musical instruments – anything from harpsichords to clarinets, organs to synthesizers. The electronics side, involving the manufacture and repair of musical equipment, probably offers the best prospects. There is a steady demand for piano-tuners.

Music Therapy

This is a small but growing field. Music therapists work with children and adults with physical disabilities or learning difficulties and in the field of mental illness in both the health and the education services. Music can contribute to the development and treatment of people with a range of learning, emotional and behavioural difficulties in various ways as a medium of non-verbal communication – by helping to relax their bodies and minds, as a mental stimulus, and as an emotional outlet. Autistic children, for example, and severely withdrawn adults, who do not respond to any other form of activity and cannot form relationships, often benefit greatly from listening to, and making, music.

Training – performers This has been gradually changing. Most courses at music colleges/conservatoires now lead to a degree, whereas in the past many led to graduate status diploma. The choice is between a three-year or four-year full-time course at a college of music or a university-based degree. Traditionally university music degrees were largely academic and were not intended primarily for performers. Graduates who wanted to join the profession would (and still can) go on to a postgraduate performers' course at a music college. However, there are now many university courses which do emphasize performance; they may lead to a degree in music or in performing arts. There are also now a couple of degrees taught jointly by universities and conservatoires. Applications to practice-based courses at a number of conservatoires in the UK can be made through the Conservatoires UK Admissions Service (CUKAS) at *www.cukas.ac.uk.*

Degrees may last three or four years, they may lead to an ordinary or an honours degree and this may be called a BA Music or Bachelor of Music (BMus). Where a college or university offers both degrees, the BMus is intended for those students who want to concentrate almost entirely on performance, while the BA Music contains more academic studies.

The syllabus of any performers' course (degree or diploma) normally includes a principal subject and a second study subject. Instrumentalists may sometimes play two instruments although resources are often scarce and instrumental tuition may be limited to the first study instrument. Singers may take either an instrument as second study or they may take speech and drama. Other subjects included are aural training, theory and history of music, analysis, orchestral experience, choral and opera study, contextual studies and, often, a language. In addition many colleges offer a wide selection of specialist options, such as composition, contemporary or early music, electronic music, music therapy, music administration, aesthetics, community music and conducting.

For people interested in non-classical music, there are now a number of HE courses in popular and commercial music, jazz and band studies.

Training – composers The most common route is to take a music degree at university, followed by a postgraduate course in composition at either university or a conservatoire.

Training – teachers Music teachers in schools must gain Qualified Teacher Status (see p. 586) by taking either a music degree (or graduate diploma) followed by a one-year course of professional teacher training or a BEd with music as a main subject. Teachers who give instrumental lessons in or out of school are not required to have Qualified Teacher Status. Some take education options within performers' courses; some take postgraduate teaching courses at music college (for example the Licentiateship of Trinity College London (Music Education)). A number of short or part-time courses exist for practising teachers. For example the Associated Board has a one-year part-time Professional Development Course for Instrumental and Singing Teachers; the ISM (Incorporated Society of Musicians) has also created a distance-learning diploma for music teachers in private practice in conjunction with Reading University.

Those wishing to be listed in the ISM Register of Professional Private Music Teachers must have suitable professional qualifications and experience.

Training – sound engineering /music technology Traditionally this has been in-house. Competition to get into the recording industry is now so great that some pre-entry training or experience is necessary. There are various ways to train: short introductory courses, evening courses, occasional day release. Recording companies often look for people with some kind of technical or engineering background, not necessarily electronics. There are now a number of degrees, Foundation degrees and HNDs available with titles such as Music and Audio Technology, Music Technology, Electronic Music, Music Acoustics, Music Production, or Electronics. For classical music recording sound engineers normally need a music degree.

Training – musical instrument technology There are full-time (usually two years) courses leading to City & Guilds, as well as BTEC/SQA and degree courses. Piano-tuners can study full-time or by day or block release.

Training – music therapy There are one-year and two-year full-time and part-time postgraduate courses in music therapy. Courses must be approved by the Health Professions Council and therapists are required to register with the HPC. Candidates must have had at least a three-year full-time usually musical education and some experience of working with disabled people. Some work full-time in one hospital, some do 'sessions' in several centres. The work is extremely demanding and needs maturity and sensitivity.

Other courses For those wanting to go into music administration or management there are one or two relevant courses. Otherwise openings tend to be for people with experience in some aspect of the music business or with specialist qualifications in, for example, accountancy or marketing.

Personal attributes *For performers*: Apart from outstanding talent, perseverance, resilience, courage and self-belief in the face of setbacks, the ability to work as one of a team; a pleasant manner; good health; very wide musical interest; good sight-reading speed; willingness to work outside the musical field between engagements. *For teachers*: as for teaching (p. 586), plus creative imagination and initiative.

Work–life balance It is unlikely that performers can resume orchestral playing after a long gap unless they keep up with serious daily practice; but there should be no problem returning to teaching after a career break.

Performing: work as freelancer is possible in many areas – but work tends to be sporadic rather than regular part-time. *Teaching and music therapy*: part-time or job-sharing should be possible, but not necessarily exactly where one wants it.

Further information
For early training: Local education authority music adviser.
For general information: Incorporated Society of Musicians, 10 Stratford Place, London W1C 1AA.
www.ism.org
For music courses: *Rhinegold Guide to Music Education* (Rhinegold Publishing), available at most libraries.
For sound engineering and record companies: The British Phonographic Industry (BPI), Riverside Building, County Hall, Westminster Bridge Road, London SE1 7JA.
www.bpi.co.uk
For music therapy: Association of Professional Music Therapists, 61 Church Hill Road, East Barnet, Herts EN4 8SY.
www.apmt.org

Music

Related careers *dance – leisure/recreation management – teaching – television, film and radio*

Nursery Nurse

The early years and childcare sector is expanding rapidly in response to demand. The government's Sure Start programme aims to recruit the new childcare workers required to meet that demand. The Childcare Act 2006 requires all local authorities in England and Wales to provide sufficient childcare provision for working parents. Working with local private, voluntary and independent sector providers, they are expected to meet local need, particularly in relation to families on lower incomes and those with disabled children.

Entry qualifications None laid down, but usually at National Qualifications Framework Level 2 (GCSEs A*–C, BTEC Diplomas and Certificates) or Scottish Credit and Qualifications Framework equivalent. Some entrants have A levels or equivalent.

The work Nursery nurses look after children from birth to 7 years. Their roles cover very much more than physical care and supervision of young children. Young children learn through play and through communicating with other children and with adults; they need adequate stimuli and individual attention to ensure their healthy intellectual, emotional and social development. When nursery nurses read to children, talk to them individually, discuss, say, their painting efforts, and generally help them to enjoy nursery activities they are, in effect, teaching.

Nursery nurses work in various settings:

- Nursery classes and pre-schools (for 3–5-year-olds) and infant schools (5–7-year-olds), run by local education authorities

(LEAs). Nursery nurses help organize play activities, read to and play with children. Usually one nursery nurse is responsible for a small group of children. A qualified nursery or infant teacher (see p. 587) is normally in charge.

- Day nurseries and family centres, run by social services departments for under-5s (mainly 3–5-year-olds) who are at risk socially, physically or emotionally; and for children whose parents have to go out to work or for other reasons cannot satisfactorily look after them during the day. There are now very few places for children whose parents merely think that nursery is a 'good thing'. A proportion of children in day nurseries have special needs, so work can be very demanding. Occasionally staff involve parents in the nursery's activities – largely to help parents understand the children's needs and development. Staff may also do unofficial 'casework' (see p. 538).

- Private day nurseries, workplace nurseries and crèches: there is an increasing number of these, catering for parents who want their children to have the benefits of nursery experience, especially in areas where there are few LEA-run nursery places. Most cater for working parents by being open all day, and some are, in fact, attached to one or more companies and open only to their staff.

- In hospital, nursery nurses help to look after babies in maternity wards, and on children's wards they play with and care for children. Actual nursing is done by registered nurses (see p. 403).

- In private family homes as 'nannies', mainly, these days, in homes where both parents go out to work. Unlike in the past, most nannies expect to share the care of the children with the parents. There is a variety of working patterns: some live-in nannies take charge of a young child or two or three children all day; in addition, in between the end of the school day and a parent's return from work (and perhaps during the school holidays), they may look after several schoolchildren whose parents share the nanny's salary. Other nannies work two days for one family, three days for another if the mothers concerned are themselves part-timers and need only part-week nannies. Work in a family differs from that outside the home in that nannies are on their own: nobody to ask for help in emergencies, and much of the time no other adult to talk to. The work is both more responsible and lonelier; it may also be less rigorous. Most nannies do some housework or at least cook for the children while the parents are at work.

- In their own homes as childminders, caring for children up to 8. Registration with the local authority is mandatory.
- A very small proportion work in hotels and holiday camps as children's hostesses. Experienced nannies can get jobs abroad.

Nursery nurses who take the Advanced Diploma courses have fair promotion prospects and may become managers in charge of nurseries of all kinds, at home and abroad. However, the ratio of senior to junior jobs is low.

Training – college-based route in England, Wales and Northern Ireland. A two-year full-time or longer part-time course at a college of further education, minimum age 16, leading to the Council for Awards in Children's Care and Education (CACHE) level 2 Certificate in Child Care and Education or City & Guilds or BTEC Certificate in Children's Care, Learning and Development or the level 3 CACHE Diploma in Child Care and Education or City & Guilds or BTEC Diploma in Children's Care, Learning and Development. The diploma course carries a maximum of 240 UCAS tariff points and may be used as a route into general nursing training or midwifery for those with a GCSE grade C or above in English and maths. Part-time courses are also available.

There are 18–24-month courses at the two private nursery training colleges. Students must be at least 18; to make sure they like the work, most look after children privately, in between school and college. Private colleges prepare students for the CACHE awards and for their own diplomas.

An Early Years Sector Endorsed Foundation Degree (EYSEFD) qualification at level 5 has been introduced leading to a new level of professional practice known as the 'Senior Practitioner'. Applicants will need to have a level 3 qualification in Early Years, Childcare or Playwork (or equivalent) and at least two years' experience of working in the sector. Students who do not hold a level 3 qualification may discuss APEL (Accreditation of Prior Experiential Learning) procedures with their intended institution of study.

Training – work-based routes NVQs/SVQs levels 2, 3 and 4 in Children's Care, Learning and Development are widely available and qualify candidates to work with children in a range of situations.

An Apprenticeship in Children's Care, Learning and Development is also widely available.

Training – in Scotland The most usual route is a one-year SQA National Certificate course followed by a one-year SQA HNC course in Early Education and Childcare. Alternatively SVQs in Children's Care, Learning and Development can be achieved either through full-time college courses or while in employment. Both routes lead to registration by the Scottish Child Care and Education Board. Apprenticeships are available.

Personal attributes A way with young children; patience; imagination; willingness to take responsibility and to work hard at routine chores; ability to work well in a team; interest in mental, social and physical development of children.

Mature entry and career change Entry is possible at any age.

Work–life balance A career break should be no problem. Opportunities for flexible working depend very much on type of employment. Local authorities usually have schemes in place.

Position of men Under 1 per cent of students are men; no reason at all why this should remain so – men welcome on courses and in jobs.

Further information
Council for Awards in Children's Care and Education (CACHE), Beaufort House, Grosvenor Road, St Albans, Herts AL1 3AW.
www.cache.org.uk

www.surestart.gov.uk
www.childcarecareers.gov.uk
Office G4, Scottish Child Care and Education Board, Unit G4, Stevenston Industrial Estate, Stevenston, Ayrshire KA20 3LR.
Local authority education or social services departments.

Related careers *nursing – social work – teaching*

Nursing and Midwifery

NURSING

Nursing and in particular nurse education has changed dramatically in recent years, and continues to change to meet the health needs of people in the twenty-first century. Changes in health care and nursing philosophy affect how nursing care is delivered. For example, increasing emphasis is put on health promotion and the prevention of disease; and where possible patients are increasingly being cared for in their own homes or other community settings. With scientific and medical advancements, patients in hospitals are receiving more sophisticated and advanced treatments; this requires the nurse to be more skilled than ever. This situation is true whichever branch of the profession a nurse works in.

Changes in the way that patients with mental health problems and learning disabilities receive health care have affected where and how care is given to these client groups. The emphasis is now on giving care in the community either in the person's own home or in small group homes. People with acute mental health problems may be cared for, for a period of time, in an acute psychiatric unit. These units are now often part of larger district general hospitals.

Nurses, no matter which branch of nursing they work in, form a crucial part of the multidisciplinary health care team. The team includes occupational therapists, physiotherapists and doctors. This closer working together includes joint decision-making about patient care. Patients and their families are also included in the decision-making; this ensures that patients receive more information about choices and have more control over the type of treatment they may be given.

'Nursing' covers a range of jobs which vary widely in terms of levels of functions, of responsibility, professional qualifications required, and environment worked in. There is, therefore, scope for people with widely differing aims, interests and abilities.

Opportunities for flexible and part-time working have increased considerably. Education is also available on a part-time, flexible basis; this makes it possible for people to qualify as a nurse who in the past may have been prevented from doing so.

There is also a need to attract more men into all areas of nursing. As nursing covers such wide-ranging client groups, the skills and attributes a person requires to be a nurse are very varied.

Nurses' work is much more difficult to define than other professionals' because there are so many, and some contradictory, facets to it.

Entry qualifications There are two main routes to becoming a registered nurse. Applicants may complete either a 'pre-registration' diploma or a degree in nursing, leading to registration with the Nursing and Midwifery Council (NMC).

There are no national minimum educational requirements for nursing courses, but applicants must be able to provide evidence of literacy and numeracy, good character and good health. Each university or college sets its own entry criteria, but as a guide most will expect National Qualifications Framework Level 3 (A levels, BTEC National awards) or Scottish Credit and Qualifications Framework equivalent for a degree. To encourage applications from a broad spectrum of society, there are now a number of different routes into nursing.

There is a range of access courses for people who do not have the traditional entry requirements for nursing. These courses must be Quality Assurance Agency (QAA) approved. Successful completion of the course meets the entry requirements for both the degree and diploma programmes.

People working as care assistants may be able to undertake an

NVQ/SVQ at level 3 which is usually acceptable as the minimum educational requirement for the diploma programme.

Foundation degrees/programmes are being developed which on successful completion normally allow a person on to the second year of either the diploma or degree nursing programme.

Applicants with a relevant degree can qualify by completing an accelerated pre-registration programme in nursing.

BRANCHES OF NURSING

There are four branches of nursing: adult, children, mental health and learning disabilities. All four branches require different types of people to work in them.

Adult nurse

This area of nursing is concerned with the care of people throughout all stages of adulthood, who are either healthy or have a wide range of health care problems.

Nurses use a systematic approach to assessing, planning and delivering patient care. Adult nursing is not just about delivering the physical care of patients; it is also about their psychological, sociological and spiritual needs. In order to fulfil this, nurses require extensive knowledge in nursing, biology, psychology and sociology, plus interpersonal skills and skills in research processes and methods and information technology. Patients are treated as individuals not as conditions.

Adult nurses work in a wide range of settings either within a hospital or in the community. As registered nurses they are responsible for the organization and delivery of patients' care, keeping records, listening and giving information to patients and relatives, liaising with other members of the health and social care team.

After initial registration, all nurses have a responsibility to remain up to date in the area in which they are working. There are a large number of courses available for continuing professional development (CPD) and these can help nurses to progress their careers in specific specialities such as accident and emergency nursing or care of the elderly. Further progression can lead to a nurse becoming a specialist practitioner such as a breast care nurse or diabetic care nurse. To carry out these types of roles, the nurse will have extensive experience in the speciality and will have undertaken further studies.

Personal attributes Common sense; practical skills; empathy for all people no matter what their age, ethnicity or religion; an interest in health and health-related issues; sensitivity coupled with a certain amount of resilience so as to be able to manage in a wide range of situations; organizing ability; patience; a sense of humour, in order to cope with inevitable encounters with aggressive and difficult people; ability to know when to be firm – and how to be firm but not rude; powers of observation; initiative; ability to assess and make decisions in the best interest of the patient.

Children's Nurse

Nursing sick children can be both rewarding and arduous. It requires a different range of skills from adult nursing, including the ability to work with the child's family and involve them in his or her care: mothers or fathers often stay in hospital with their young children. Many children stay only for a very short time, but may return to hospital on a regular basis for further treatment and follow-up; others stay for longer because they are very seriously ill and/or suffer from a rare condition which has to be assessed. Children's nursing is also concerned with detection and follow-up of physical and learning difficulties. Some children's nursing is highly specialized, with nurses having taken post-registration specialist training.

Children's wards are run to resemble home conditions as much as possible. Visiting is now normally allowed at all times with facilities being available for parents and other family members to stay. Children's nursing care is increasingly being delivered in the child's own home, therefore children's nurses are also employed in the community setting.

Jobs for children's nurses are many and varied and not just in general ward areas but also in specialist units such as children's operating theatres or paediatric oncology centres. Some children's nurses may decide to work out of the clinical environment and gain employment in schools and other areas where children may be.

Personal attributes The same as for the adult nurse, plus extra patience with children. A children's nurse must be able to talk to children on their own level while relating well to parents/carers and other family members. They form an integral part of the multidisciplinary team who care for children. Good powers of observation are essential, as small children cannot explain their ailments.

Mental Health Nurse

These days, caring for people with mental health problems takes place more frequently in the community than in the hospital setting.

In the community Many mental health nurses will work within the community even when they first register; if they decide to continue in this area they will be able to undertake further training to become a community psychiatric nurse (CPN). CPNs may be employed by a mental health trust or social services. This is in part because people with mental health problems frequently have social problems as well.

CPNs have, therefore, great scope to develop their own ideas and initiatives. Very broadly, CPNs combine three main, overlapping functions:

- They give practical help and counselling support (see p. 481) to patients discharged from hospital and now having to adjust to living with their families, in hostels or on their own; also, to patients who right from the start of their illness are treated as outpatients and/or attend day hospitals.
- CPNs provide a preventative service: they see people who may be referred by GPs, social workers, district nurses, health visitors, even relatives or neighbours, or they could be 'self-referred', i.e. people who realize they have problems which they cannot cope with.

- CPNs help to 'educate' the community to understand the nature of mental illness; they also help families and foster-families (even landlords) – anyone who has a patient living in their home – to cope with disturbed people's behaviour. Supporting patients' families and others is a very important part of community psychiatric nursing.

CPNs may also run clinics, do group-work (see p. 479) with patients and/or their families, and help run day centres. Because of the increasing numbers of patients with psychiatric problems cared for in the community, the profession is expanding greatly.

Training for community mental health nursing is not yet mandatory, but RNs (Mental Health) interested in this work are encouraged to take one of several full-time or part-time specialist courses.

In hospitals One adult in eight in this country at some time in his or her life needs help because of some form of mental or emotional problem. The majority do not need hospitalization, and even most of those who are hospitalized stay for only a short time, probably a few weeks, and possibly return for further brief spells in hospital in between leading normal lives. Only a minority are long-stay patients. The term 'mental illness' covers a wide spectrum. In severe cases sufferers may be unable to separate fantasy from reality and react to people and situations in unreasonable, even alarming, ways. Two groups of patients have increased in recent years: people of all ages who cannot cope with the stresses and strains of modern life and old people who suffer from dementia.

Over 90 per cent of patients are 'voluntary' or 'informal'. Many of them are able to go out to shop or visit friends or relatives, and when in hospital most are encouraged to undertake a range of activities. Occupational therapists, arts therapists, psychiatrists, psychologists, psychotherapists and mental health nurses work alongside each other to assist the patient. For most patients a vital part of their treatment is the contact with a friendly, skilled nurse; the inability to communicate with other people can be in part a feature of mental illness. Nurses help a great deal towards patients' recovery by talking to them and, above all, listening therapeutically.

In most psychiatric hospitals the atmosphere is relaxed and informal. Patients and staff live in a friendly so-called 'therapeutic' community. Patients are encouraged to share with the staff responsibility for running wards and for the active social life of the hospital. The aim is always to minimize the institutional atmosphere. Most wards are in small units of general hospitals.

At informal meetings with staff the patients are encouraged to discuss and even criticize treatment, to talk about their difficulties and to help each other with their problems. At staff-only meetings, after ward meetings with the patients, all nurses have a chance to discuss patients, treatments and new methods with consultants and senior staff.

Mental health nursing can, of course, sometimes be very demanding. Nurses must always remember that their patients' behaviour is often a symptom of their illness. Teamwork among the staff helps a great deal, and during their training nurses learn to recognize and handle the emotional aspect of their work.

Personal attributes Curiosity about what makes people behave as they do; emotional stability; patience and perseverance; the ability to listen well and to be genuinely concerned without becoming emotionally involved; outside interests to keep a sense of proportion; a sense of humour; good physical and mental health.

Learning Disabilities Nurse

In hospitals People with learning disabilities may have been born with a disability or acquired it after birth either through an illness or accident. Unlike mental illness, this condition is not normally curable, and some people may require residential care all their lives. However, the tendency today is to enable as many clients as at all possible to live in the community. This means that clients in hospital tend to be severely disabled, often both physically and mentally. Nurses help patients develop their potential as far as it is possible to do so. The extent of the disability in each client determines the degree of independence that can be achieved. It takes great patience and perseverance sometimes to enable a patient even to dress or feed him/herself. However, once the patient has taken even one small step towards independence, both patient and nurse feel they have achieved something. Some clients are prepared for life outside the hospital and learn to shop, use money, etc. This type of nursing is always a mixture of teaching, showing understanding, and establishing relationships of trust with patients. Nurses work in teams with doctors, psychologists, occupational therapists and physiotherapists. Like mental health nurses, these nurses attend meetings with other professionals to discuss patients and problems.

In the community Over 60 per cent of persons diagnosed as suffering from learning disabilities now live with their families, on their own, in shared accommodation or in group homes. Their need for continued care varies enormously from the occasional chat to regular care. A client or service user (terms now preferred to 'patient') may, for example, have a sleeping problem and the nurse may be able to suggest ways of improving the situation for the client and family. Follow-up would be required. The nurse may find that the extent of the client's learning difficulty is much smaller than the parents had assumed. Teaching relatives how to care for clients is an important part of the nurse's work. Some clients, perhaps those only recently discharged from hospital but able to live in a shared flat, may merely have to be encouraged to increase their independence: to learn such social skills as saying 'hello' to neighbours, and such 'living skills' as doing the shopping or using public transport. The aim of nurses is always to develop clients' potential as fully as their disability allows.

Nurses also hold 'information sessions' to help other community care and health professionals, as well as the community at large, understand developments and changes in the treatment of people with learning difficulties. Most learning disabilities nurses work in the community.

Personal attributes Personable nature; a practical approach; teaching ability; patience; gentleness; interests unconnected with the work; ability to be genuinely concerned without becoming emotionally involved.

Training (general) There are two routes leading to registration (with the Nursing and Midwifery Council (NMC)) as a nurse:

- Three-year Diploma of Higher Education in Nursing. Students are based at a higher education institution (HEI) where they will study theory and knowledge-based elements of the course. Half of the course will be spent in supervised nursing practice in hospitals or other environments.
- A Bachelor (Hons) degree in Nursing Studies. These are normally three years although a few four-year courses are available. Again, half the course is spent in studying theory and half in supervised nursing practice in a range of settings.

On both diploma and degree programmes, the first twelve months cover a Common Foundation Programme. The remainder of the course follows a programme in the chosen branch – adult, mental health, children or learning disability nursing.

Some NHS hospitals employ nurse cadets who are trained through practical experience and theory to be eligible for entry to a diploma course. Many HEIs offer diploma and degree courses on a part-time basis.

All students start at the same level. Diplomates can top up their diplomas to degree level by undertaking further studies once they are registered.

In some NHS Trusts, staff employed as health care assistants may be able to work towards qualifications (e.g. NVQs) which will enable them to meet the minimum requirements for entry on to a pre-registration course at a local HEI.

The NHS has introduced a nine-level career framework. Nurses achieving the diploma or degree, for example, start at level 5 ('practitioner' level) and are encouraged through supported continuing professional development to progress to level 6 – senior or specialist practitioner, or level 7 – advanced practitioner level.

In England, eligible students on the diploma course receive a non-means-tested bursary and eligible students on degree courses may receive a means-tested bursary, but are entitled to a student loan. Different arrangements exist elsewhere in the UK. Some students who have worked for the NHS may be seconded to do their training, in which case they receive a monthly sum almost equivalent to their previous NHS salary.

OTHER NURSING IN THE COMMUNITY

Nurses who work outside the hospital, where there is always someone more highly qualified to discuss problems with, may have much more independence in terms of decision-making and organizing their working days. District nurses, health visitors, community psychiatric nurses (see p. 404), school nurses, practice nurses and community midwives all come under what is now often loosely called community public health nursing. They are all examples of specialized 'nurse practitioners', a term increasingly used. They are part of the multi-disciplinary community care team, working closely with GPs, social workers and other colleagues from related professions. The proportion of community nurses is growing, as more and more patients live in the community but still need nursing care and support. Community nurses, like their hospital colleagues, are increasingly taking on more responsibilities including prescribing certain medicines.

District Nurse

District nurses provide skilled nursing care for patients in their home. They give acute care and ongoing care to patients. They may also help permanently disabled patients to learn to use new aids, and help relatives to learn to carry out routine nursing care. When necessary they put people in touch with social workers or with other members of the health care team. District nurses work closely with local GPs, who advise on whom to visit and, often, the treatment required. District nurses perform most of the skills that would also be performed in hospital such as changing patients' dressings and giving intravenous drugs. They also give moral support, helping patients and their relatives to come to terms with their situation. District nurses get to know their patients and families well; they also play an important role in the wider community. Experienced nurses often lead teams that include several district nurses and health care assistants. To provide a 24-hour service, nurses work shifts. Because of the close cooperation between hospital and community services, district nurses may on occasion visit their patients in hospital if they have been admitted. This means they have both the independence of community nursing and enjoy companionship and the chance to talk shop. Some district nurses specialize, e.g. in work with diabetics, the disabled, the elderly, terminal care.

Health Visitor

Health visitors are professionals in their own right. They organize their own work.

The important difference between health visitors on the one hand and nurses and social workers on the other is that the latter usually meet clients when something has gone wrong. The purpose of health visiting is the promotion of health and the prevention and early detection of physical and mental ill health. Health visitors give health care advice, identify the need for and, if necessary, mobilize other sources of help.

They are responsible for monitoring children's health from the time midwifery care ceases (ten days after birth usually) until the school nurse (see p. 414) takes over checking children's development. They advise mothers on childcare, health hazards and health care both by regular home visits and in clinics. Routine home visits may act as an 'early warning system', and health visitors often notice signs of stress or disorder before these develop into problems. For example, a young mother who gave up the companionship at work just before the child was born may feel lonely and guilty for not being a radiant mother; the health visitor helps by discussing her feelings and by suggesting ways of coping with the problem. Other matters which might develop into problems, but for the health visitor's early advice are older children's health or behaviour, or marital difficulties.

Health visitors also play an increasingly important role in the care of the elderly, in particular in health monitoring and health education and promotion. Health visitors work very closely with other members of the health care team, in particular GPs, CPNs and social workers. They may visit patients recently discharged from hospital; mentally ill or disabled people who are cared for at home; the elderly; anyone who may be referred to them by social workers, doctors, a neighbour even. They are very much involved with health education and may lecture in schools and other organizations.

When visiting, health visitors are concerned with the family as a whole, not only the ill member of the family. They may be based in doctors' practices, or work from health centres.

Occupational Health Nurse

Occupational health nurses (OHNs) work in factories, stores and wherever else there is a large number of employees, with the aim of promoting health in the workplace. They are also involved in health screening of staff, in particular in areas where the work environment may be hazardous. The work is about health promotion as well as preventative work.

OHNs also deal with accidents and sudden illness and give minor treatments, such as injections, changing dressings. They advise both on health problems generally and on those peculiar to a particular industry, e.g. skin or respiratory diseases caused by certain types of work. They are now very much involved, at least in most large and/or progressive organizations, with research into the effects of the intro- duction of new technologies and/or working patterns on employees' health and on their job satisfaction. This may involve discussing the arrangements of desks in word processing stations, or checking noise levels in tool shops, as well as shift and night work arrangements and canteen facilities. An important aspect of their work is the identification of health hazards, and initiating whatever measures are necessary to eliminate or minimize such hazards. They work closely with factory inspectors (see p. 249).

They also work closely with occupational health doctors. They usually keep medical records of all employees and assist at the medical examination of prospective employees. They often arrange for related services such as chiropody, eye-testing and physiotherapy. They discuss health and safety measures on the shop floor and in the office with management, shop stewards and factory inspectors and work closely with the human resources department. For example, if an employee's work is deteriorating, OHNs help to find the psychological or physical cause. OHNs also help to find suitable jobs for the disabled and may discuss with management measures which should be taken in special cases.

In large concerns there may be a medical department; more often there is one occupational health nurse working for the personnel director and/or the visiting medical officer.

To become an occupational health nurse, further studies need to be undertaken at an Institute of Higher Education (IHE). Unlike other nursing jobs, normal office hours usually apply.

School Nurse

School nurses take over the monitoring of children's development when health visitors' work stops, i.e. when children reach school age. They may be employed directly by the school or local NHS trust and regularly visit a number of schools. Their routine checking of vision, hearing, growth, etc. is a preventative service: they hope to detect problems before they become serious and make appropriate referrals. Teachers and parents ask school nurses' advice when a child shows signs of not being quite 'up to scratch', physically or mentally. The school nurse may contact parents when that seems advisable.

School nursing varies very much from one area to another, according to local organization; for example as to how many schools one school nurse is responsible for; and also according to individual school nurses' initiative and interpretation of their role.

School nurses are also very much involved in health education. Again, the extent of involvement varies: in some areas health education officers (usually health visitors by qualification) are appointed and school nurses would work with them; in other areas health education is left to health visitors and/or school nurses. Increasingly school nurses take part in a programme of lectures/talks both to schoolchildren and at parents' evenings/meetings, on such issues as drug abuse, AIDS, etc.

In some areas school nurses hold a kind of 'surgery' on certain days in 'their' schools, when parents, children and teachers can come and discuss any problem that bothers them. School nursing is very much less structured in terms of specific duties than most other nursing specializations.

Practice Nurse

Practice nurses have worked in GPs' practices for some time, carrying out such routine procedures as taking blood samples, changing dressings, etc. However, recent NHS changes have greatly increased the range of tasks which GPs or their support staff are asked to undertake; practice nurses' numbers and their importance have therefore increased greatly. Most practice nurses now undertake such non-routine tasks as setting up and running health promotion and continuing care clinics (e.g. well woman, asthma, hypertension and diabetic clinics) and they may also be involved in screening, i.e. checking patients' health. All new patients who register with a GP must be offered screening, and all over-75s at least once a year. Practice nurses may do this screening and decide whether the patient needs to see the doctor. In the case of elderly patients this may involve home visits. Some practice nurses are able to prescribe a range of drugs.

Post-Registration Courses All nurses, wherever they work, must qualify initially as a registered nurse and may need to complete additional training depending on the area in which they wish to specialize. This training is usually provided in the form of post-registration courses offered at IHEs.

MIDWIFERY

The work Midwives look after mother and child from early pregnancy until usually ten days after the birth of the child (when health visitors take over). They give antenatal, perinatal and post-natal advice, support and instruction, taking full responsibility during the birth in straightforward cases, and calling a doctor in case of complications. They run hospital baby units including those for premature and sick babies. They are trained to a high professional standard and work closely with doctors. They also run clinics for pregnant women as well as training sessions for expectant mothers and their partners. As mothers' stay in hospital is often very short, midwives' home visits are vitally important. These may involve counselling women who suffer from post-natal depression, or who need advice on coping with a new-born baby without neglecting their other children. It also often involves family planning advice.

Midwifery is a unique combination of applying complex practical and high-tech skills, teaching parent craft and counselling.

There is today much more emphasis on the psychological aspects of pregnancy, childbirth and the post-natal period and their effects on the rest of the family than there used to be. The majority of births take place in hospital but an increasing number are occurring in mothers' own homes. To ensure continuity of care from early pregnancy until the health visitor takes over care of mother and child, the emphasis is on an integrated hospital and community midwifery service, with individual midwives working in both home and hospital. But there are also opportunities for midwives to work only in hospital or only in the community. A small number of midwives work in the private sector. There is at present a shortage of registered midwives.

Training There are two main routes to becoming a registered midwife (registered with the Nursing and Midwifery Council – NMC):

- Pre-registration midwifery programmes for registered nurses who wish to gain a midwifery qualification. These shortened courses take eighteen months full-time.

- Pre-registration courses for those who want to go directly into midwifery take three years, leading to a specialist degree. Midwives can – and are encouraged to – take various post-registration courses.

Entry qualifications There are no national minimum educational requirements for midwifery degree courses but applicants must be able to provide evidence of literacy and numeracy, good character and good health. Each university or college sets its own entry criteria, but as a guide most will expect National Qualifications Framework Level 3 (A levels, BTEC National awards) or Scottish Credit and Qualifications Framework equivalent for entry.

There is a range of access courses for people who do not have the traditional entry requirements for midwifery. These courses must be Quality Assurance Agency (QAA) approved. Successful completion of the course may meet the entry requirements for the degree programme.

Personal attributes As for registered nurses, plus, of course, special interest in babies, ability to act on own initiative, to remain calm in stressful and emotional situations, and to relate to people from all backgrounds.

Mature entry and career change (general) Excellent opportunities. Mature entrants of both sexes are very welcome because they bring a wider experience to the job.

Work–life balance Nurses and midwives, like other NHS employees, should benefit from the government's Improving Working Lives initiative, introduced in 2002 to aid the retention of staff by ensuring a better work–life balance for NHS staff. Every NHS Trust has to demonstrate its commitment to more flexible working patterns, which may include part-time working, job-sharing and term-time working, evening and weekend work, and supporting returners after a career break. Part-time training is available.

Opportunities for flexible work patterns are now available much higher up the promotion ladder than they used to be.

In recent times the restructuring of the nursing career pathway in all of the branches and midwifery has encouraged practitioners to stay within clinical practice up to the point of becoming a consultant nurse or midwife. These relatively new roles are for senior nurses who are involved in patient care as well as research and education.

Position of men Still fewer than 11 per cent of those entering nursing are men, with far fewer entering midwifery. There has been an increase in the number of men applying for pre-registration courses.

Further information

For further information about nursing, midwifery and other careers in the NHS in England, contact: NHS Careers, PO Box 2311, Bristol BS2 2ZX. Tel: 0845 60 60 655. Email: advice@nhscareers.nhs.uk
www.nhs.uk/careers

Scotland: NHS Scotland Careers Information Service. Tel: 0845 601 4647.
www.infoscotland.com/nhs

Wales: National Leadership and Innovation Agency for Healthcare (NLIAH) Tel: 01443 233 333.
www.wales.nhs.uk

Northern Ireland Practice and Education Council for Nursing and Midwifery, Centre House, 79 Chichester Street, Belfast BT1 4JE.
www.nipec.n-i.nhs.uk

Nursing Careers Adviser, Queen's University of Belfast Careers Service, Student Guidance Centre, University Road, Belfast BT7 1NN.

Careers Advice, Department of Life & Health Sciences, University of Ulster, Jordanstown, Newton Abbey BT37 0QB.

Royal College of Nursing, 20 Cavendish Square, London W1G 0RN.
www.rcn.org.uk

Royal College of Midwives, 15 Mansfield Street, London W1G 9NH.
www.rcm.org.uk

Related careers *medicine – nursery nursing – occupational therapy – physiotherapy – social work*

NOTE: Health care assistants (HCA) or auxiliary nurses are non-qualified staff who work alongside and under the supervision of nurses and other health care professionals; they receive on-the-job training to fulfil their role. They may also have the opportunity to undertake NVQ level 2 and level 3 which could then lead on to nurse training.

Occupational Therapy

Entry qualifications An approved degree or postgraduate diploma. One A level or equivalent should preferably be in a science subject. Registration with the Health Professions Council.

The work Occupational therapists work with people of all ages who have physical, mental and/or social difficulties from birth or as the result of an accident, illness or ageing, to help them live as full a life as possible by maximizing their abilities. This covers a very wide range of activities concerned with physical, psychological, social and economic well-being. Occupational therapists are concerned with all the things that 'occupy' people day-in, day-out – basic everyday self-care, work, leisure, family and social interaction.

Together with other members of the health and social care team and the client, the occupational therapist assesses the problems and devises a programme of action, based on the client's lifestyle and preferences, to help them develop, retain or regain as much independence as possible. The emphasis is on clients' ability, not disability, and looking beyond the most obvious needs to aspects that could go unnoticed. Action might involve strengthening exercises – or shopping expeditions. Occupational therapists devise new ways for people to perform old tasks, e.g. cooking from a wheelchair, dressing, getting in and out of bed and bath. They may take clients on a trial visit home from hospital so they can advise on how the environment may need to be adapted. The solution is sometimes as simple as rearranging a room, or as complicated as building an extension. Sometimes there is no solution but rehousing, so the occupational therapist may have to liaise with the housing department. They also assess patients for various kinds of aids and equipment, from those which open jars to sophisticated hoists. Developing social and support networks, identifying work interests and capacities, and self-management skills are also part of the role.

The range of clients and complexity of their needs means the work of an occupational therapist is challenging and varied. They have one-to-one contact with their clients and also work with groups and communities. They have the opportunity to work creatively in the way they apply their knowledge and expertise. It is important to develop a good relationship with both the service user and their family/carers, who may provide much of the day-to-day support and often need help themselves to come to terms with how their lives have changed.

Occupational therapists work with patients in NHS and private hospitals, local community services, schools, prisons and in their homes. The main employers are the NHS and local authority social services departments. There are also opportunities in charities and voluntary agencies, government agencies, industry and equipment suppliers, special schools, GP practices and residential homes. An increasing number of occupational therapists are in private practice. Many choose to work in a particular field of health or social care and there are excellent career opportunities in clinical, research, teaching and management posts.

Occupational therapy *support workers* are generally employed in health and social services departments. They work under the supervision of occupational therapists, who can provide in-service training. They can also work towards NVQs/SVQs, BTEC, HNC or Foundation degrees and other awards which can subsequently count toward a degree course.

Training routes

- Three-year full-time course or four-year part-time course leading to an honours degree.
- Two-year accelerated courses for graduates.
- Four-year part-time in-service courses: some require students to be

employed as occupational therapy support workers or technical instructors, and others allow part-time study irrespective of employment status.

All courses are approved by the Health Professions Council as meeting their minimum standards. Courses may also choose to be accredited by the College of Occupational Therapists as meeting their further standards. Courses are broad based and about a third of the course is spent on practice placements, getting experience in the main branches of occupational therapy, usually physical rehabilitation, learning disabilities, mental health and social care. The NHS provides financial support to eligible students on approved courses. After qualification, students may take a rotational post in a hospital where they can gain a breadth of experience in various areas, or they may go directly into working with particular groups, e.g. children, orthopaedic patients, stroke patients, alcoholics, drug abusers, older people, people with learning disabilities or mental health needs.

Occupational therapists are required to maintain ongoing registration with the Health Professions Council. They may also choose to be members of the British Association of Occupational Therapists and any of its Specialist Sections.

Personal attributes An ability to identify and solve problems; creativity; sensitivity; tolerance; tenacity; good humour; the ability to work both independently and as part of a team; good powers of observation; the ability to explain things clearly to all types of people including families, employers and other professionals.

Mature entry and career change The majority of OT students nowadays are not school-leavers. Many have previous degrees, but students are welcomed on all courses and will be considered even if they do not have the stated academic requirements. These students often have work experience or are able to demonstrate their ability to undertake degree level studies or have completed recent study (e.g. an A level, BTEC, NVQ/SVQ, Open University foundation course or access to higher education courses (see p. 2 for further information).

Specific entry requirements should be checked with the university concerned.

Work–life balance Occupational therapists usually work a 35–37½-hour week if employed within the public sector. More flexible working and weekend posts are becoming available. In local authorities, terms and conditions vary significantly between employers. There are good opportunities for entry level and more senior practitioner part-time positions as well as job-sharing, but this is dependent on employer requirements.

Refresher courses and financial support from local Strategic Health Authorities or other sources may be available to occupational therapists wishing to return to practice after a career break. A period of supervised practice, length dependent on the amount of time spent out of practice, is required before re-registration with the Health Professions Council. The College of Occupational Therapists offers members more specific support with their continuous development and return to practice.

Further information

British Association and College of Occupational Therapists, 106–114 Borough High Street, London SE1 1LB.
www.cot.org.uk
NHS Careers, PO Box 2311, Bristol BS2 2ZX.
www.nhscareers.nhs.uk

Related careers *mental health nursing – learning disability nursing – children's nursing – adult nursing – physiotherapy – social work*

Optical Work

Optometrist (Ophthalmic Optician)

Entry qualifications An approved degree. A levels or Highers should generally be in science-based subjects or maths.

Registration with the General Optical Council (GOC).

The work The main duties of an optometrist are: examining eyes; measuring vision defects with the help of optical instruments; and working out lens prescriptions for short/long-sightedness and astigmatism.

Some optometrists now test sight with the aid of computerized equipment. They are also trained to dispense ophthalmic prescriptions. The training is broad-based and is both scientific and medical. The work combines dealing with people and applied science; much of the work is clinically based and the optometrist has to see the patient as a human being, not simply as a pair of eyes. Optometrists are concerned with the correction and treatment of visual errors and the health of the visual system. They do not treat patients with diseased eyes. If they find any abnormality or signs of disease in the eye they refer the patient to his or her general practitioner.

Optometrists work either in general practice, doing mainly sight-testing, or in hospital, where they see more intricate eye conditions and assist ophthalmic surgeons with investigations and treatment of eye disease, and with research. In general practice it is possible to specialize in a particular field, such as children's vision, low vision or contact lenses.

General practice may mean managing and/or owning an optician's practice and doing all the dispensing work as well; frequently it means doing the ophthalmic work in a shop managed and/or owned by a firm of ophthalmic or dispensing opticians or chain with a number of practices.

There is a steady demand for optometrists.

Training Three years for an approved (by the GOC) degree in optometry (in Scotland four years) plus one year's pre-registration training in paid employment. The syllabus includes physical optics, optical instruments, anatomy and physiology, abnormal and pathological conditions of the eye, refraction. The British College of Optometrists is the examining body for ophthalmic optics. After passing the College's Professional Qualifying Examinations, students apply for Registration with the General Optical Council. Registration is obligatory for practitioners.

Personal attributes An interest in physics and maths; patience; accuracy and manual dexterity; interpersonal skills appropriate for briefly meeting a flow of new people; a confident manner especially with old people and children; good communication skills; business ability.

Mature entry and career change Up-to-date knowledge of science is important in applying to courses.

Work–life balance If one has kept up with developments, a career break presents no problem. Refresher courses available for optometrists. There are good opportunities for part-time work at all levels. Job-sharing is possible.

Further information
The College of Optometrists, 42 Craven Street, London WC2N 5NG.
  www.college-optometrists.org

Dispensing Optician

Entry qualifications Minimum usually National Qualifications Framework Level 2 (GCSEs A*–C, BTEC Diplomas and Certificates) or Scottish Credit and Qualifications Framework equivalent – including maths or physics, English, plus one other science subject.

The work Dispensing opticians do not conduct eye examinations. They interpret the prescription of the ophthalmic surgeon or optometrist (ophthalmic optician) using complex apparatus to measure for, fit and supply spectacles, contact lenses and artificial eyes. All such work requires calculations of distance and angles, etc. Equally important are the selling and 'cosmetic' aspects of the work. Dispensing opticians discuss with patients (a term opticians use in preference to customers) which type of frame is the most flattering in each case.

Most dispensing opticians also deal with other types of optical instruments, supplying apparatus to ophthalmic surgeons, opticians and laboratories, and selling sunglasses, opera glasses, microscopes, etc. to the general public. Many Dispensing Opticians continue their formal education to secure honours qualifications in Contact Lenses or Low Vision.

Dispensing opticians can also get managerial jobs in 'prescription laboratories' (firms which make lenses to prescription) and in firms of dispensing opticians which manufacture optical instruments.

Dispensing opticians usually start as assistants but later may manage a retail optical practice in which optometrists or surgeons conduct the eye examinations.

Training Either a two-year full-time course at an approved training institution, plus one year's practical experience; or three years' work as a trainee with a dispensing optician, plus theoretical instruction, by day-release, distance-learning or block-release course (which must be approved by the General Optical Council); or a three-year full-time course in optical management leading to a degree.

All methods of training lead to the qualifying examinations for

Fellowship of the Association of British Dispensing Opticians (ABDO).

The syllabus covers optical physics, the anatomy and physiology of the eye, the interpretation of ophthalmic prescriptions, the necessary measurements and adjustments for frames, and the recording of facial measurements. The full-time courses also include business practice.

ABDO now offers an access course for students without Maths, English or a general science qualification (see 'Entry qualifications').

Personal attributes Some manual dexterity; interest in salesmanship and in fashion; ability and enjoyment in dealing with flow of people; good communication skills.

Mature entry and career change Science graduates may be exempt from part of the course.

Work–life balance A career break should be no problem: refresher courses exist and are increasing. There are good opportunities for part-time work and job-sharing at all levels up to managing a high street practice (shop).

Further information
Association of British Dispensing Opticians, 199 Gloucester Terrace, London W2 6LD.
www.abdo.org.uk

Orthoptics

Entry qualifications National Qualifications Framework Level 3 (A levels, BTEC National awards) or Scottish Credit and Qualifications Framework equivalent, preferably including a science subject. A degree recognized by and registration with the Health Professions Council (HPC).

The work Orthoptists are responsible for the diagnosis, investigation, treatment and progress-monitoring of patients who have defects of binocular vision, e.g. squint, double vision or related vision conditions. The orthoptist's role is expanding. The importance of early diagnosis and treatment of children is increasingly recognized. Orthoptists therefore work on screening programmes for pre-school-age children. Special equipment and special skills enable orthoptists to assess the visual abilities of even very young children – some patients are under a year old. Orthoptists also deal with children who have reading difficulties. They must be able to build up relationships with children of all ages and with their parents.

Other patient groups include people with disabilities; people who have had accidents or strokes; multiple sclerosis sufferers; and the elderly who can be helped to achieve their maximum visual potential, for example in glaucoma clinics. This last client group is growing in size as the proportion of elderly people in the population is increasing.

Orthoptists thus deal with a very wide age range, with a wide range of conditions, and in a range of settings – in hospitals, schools, paediatric, geriatric and neurological clinics or departments. Patients are referred by ophthalmic surgeons, neurologists, general physicians, paediatricians and other specialists.

Equipment used for diagnosis and treatment is highly sophisticated. Its use requires great technical knowledge and skill. The need for getting clients of all ages to cooperate and do exercises – both in the clinic and at home – requires orthoptists to understand and communicate well with people of all ages and temperaments.

Most orthoptists work within the NHS. There are opportunities for experienced orthoptists to become clinical teachers of orthoptics, and to work in private practice. British qualifications are accepted in most countries and there is scope for orthoptists in the EU if they speak the relevant language.

Training This is via a three-year degree course offered by the universities of Liverpool and Sheffield. Syllabus includes general anatomy and physiology; child development; anatomy and physiology of eye and brain; optics; diseases of the eye and the principles of eye surgery; practice of orthoptics. Clinical experience is gained through block placements throughout the course.

The NHS funds most places on orthoptics courses and eligible students may have their tuition fees paid in full and be able to apply for a means tested bursary.

Orthoptists are registered through the Health Professions Council.

Personal attributes A scientific bent; powers of observation, deduction and persuasion; understanding of people of all ages and temperaments; ability to work as one of a team, and also independently; communication skills.

Mature entry and career change The British and Irish Orthoptic Society requires normal entry qualifications. Experience of dealing with children can be advantageous.

Work–life balance The Health Professions Council requires orthoptists returning to work after a break to undertake a period of supervised practice, the length depending on the length of time they have been out of practice, and to meet their Standards of Proficiency. Some refresher/returner training opportunities exist for individuals wishing to return to the NHS. The NHS Improving Working Lives standards include a commitment to flexible working.

Further information
British and Irish Orthoptic Society, Tavistock House North, Tavistock Square, London WC1H 9HX.
www.orthoptics.org.uk
NHS Careers, PO Box 2311, Bristol BS2 2ZX.
www.nhscareers.nhs.uk

Related careers *medicine – science*

Osteopathy

Entry qualifications See 'Training', below. Registration with the General Osteopathic Council.

The work An osteopath uses manipulative methods both in the diagnosis and the treatment for the correction of derangements of the bony and muscular structures of the body, and makes a special study of the spine in relation to health and disease. Osteopathy does not include the curing of organic disease but it covers the treatment of some organic functional disorders. The majority of patients need treatment because of stiff joints, slipped discs, etc. Patients are often referred to osteopaths by GPs who recognize the value of osteopathic treatment for certain disorders, but many patients come through personal recommendation.

The majority of osteopaths work in private practice, but increasingly some are working within a number of NHS settings.

Osteopathy was granted statutory recognition under the Osteopathy Act 1993. Only practitioners registered with the General Osteopathic Council are entitled to call themselves osteopaths.

The majority of new graduates tend to practise as associates with senior colleagues in order to obtain further clinical experience and support; this may be at the same time as starting their own practice, which they may eventually concentrate upon as it becomes more established. Currently more osteopaths work on their own in practice, but there is an increasing number of group practices.

Training The only means of entry into the osteopathic profession is through a recognized course, accredited by the General Osteopathic

Council. Currently the recognized schools offer a variety of full-time and part-time courses leading to a degree or an award in osteopathy. There is one course, run by the London College of Osteopathic Medicine, which is open only to qualified medical practitioners.

Entrance requirements vary from one institution to another, but there is generally a preference for a science background. Emphasis is also placed on individual suitability for entry into the profession drawing upon personal attributes. The average intake of students each year usually includes a mixture of school-leavers and mature students.

The syllabus for all courses includes a comprehensive grounding in the basic medical sciences, and osteopathic theory and practice, in both the lecture room and the training clinics attached to the schools.

Personal attributes Interest in science; sense of responsibility at personal and community level; self-discipline; a good communicator; concern and motivation to care for others; a degree of manual dexterity and coordination; skills in observation.

Mature entry and career change The number of mature entrants is growing. Depending on the validation arrangements with the relevant university, there may be exemption from certain elements of a course for people with relevant qualifications (e.g. physiotherapy, medicine).

Work–life balance All Registered Osteopaths, both non-practising and practising, have to undertake continuing professional development activities in order to enhance their own personal level of competency. The General Osteopathic Council offers support to registered practitioners returning into practice after a period of non-practising or a career break. Opportunities for part-time work are very good.

Further information
Osteopathic Information Service, General Osteopathic Council, Osteopathy House, 176 Tower Bridge Road, London SE1 3LU.
www.osteopathy.org.uk

Related careers *medicine – physiotherapy*

Patent Work

Patent Attorney (Agent)

Entry qualifications Entry is usually at science, engineering or mathematics degree level; working knowledge of French and German very desirable.

The work Patent attorneys (formerly known as patent agents) work in the field of intellectual property. Put very simply, intellectual property is the right which protects a product, process, trademark, design or written material that has been invented or originated by one person from being copied or developed by another for a certain number of years. It is a mixture of legal and scientific/technological work. A patent attorney advises inventors, and others concerned with inventions, on the validity and infringement of patents at home and abroad. Until quite recently only patent attorneys registered with the Chartered Institute of Patent Agents had the right to submit patents. A change in the law means that now anyone can do the work of a patent attorney but cannot be called a 'patent agent' or 'patent attorney' unless registered. (They may be called 'consultants'.)

Patent attorneys make 'searches' for clients to ensure that their inventions really are new, and prepare detailed specifications, descriptions and formulations of claims which 'cover' the invention. They file and negotiate the applications for patents on behalf of their clients at the Patent Office. Having assisted in the creation of a patent, they may deal with its commercial application. They deal not only with patents for processes and products, but also with 'Registered Designs', 'Registered Trade Marks' and Industrial Copyright.

The majority of patent attorneys work in private practice, or for industrial organizations, and specialize in a particular type of work, e.g. in chemical or mechanical inventions, or in electronics – a very important area – or in designs and trade marks. Many patent attorneys are also trade mark attorneys, but there are also independent trade mark attorneys.

Patent attorneys' work has increased in scope and complexity since the coming into force of the European Patent Convention. In addition to preparing and processing patent applications in this country and corresponding with patent agents abroad to obtain similar protection for clients' inventions there, patent attorneys who are suitably qualified draft patent applications for submission to the European Patent Office (EPO) in Germany. English, French and German are the working languages of the EPO. Many patent attorneys also work as European patent attorneys: lack of relevant language skills may limit future career development. There are reasonable opportunities for travel to Europe and other countries.

Although this is a small profession there is increasing scope.

Training The Chartered Institute of Patent Agents' examinations are at Foundation and Advanced level, with separate exams for the Patent Agents and Trade Mark Agents Registers.

Although it is not a requirement that candidates have prior professional training, it is usual to work as technical assistant in a firm of agents or industrial patent department before taking the exams. Preparation for examinations is mainly by private study; some firms sponsor trainees on a three-month full-time or one-year part-time course for the Foundation stage and other courses are available which give exemptions from Foundation papers. The Chartered Institute arranges lectures and tutorials. Some technical assistants never qualify yet nevertheless do very well, but they cannot become partners in private practice firms.

Some universities offer postgraduate courses in intellectual property which give some exemptions from professional examinations.

Trainees must have two years' professional experience before being registered. Most are expected to go on to take the exams of the

European Patent Office in order to qualify as European Patent Attorneys, eligible to submit patents to the European Patent Office.

Personal attributes Curiosity; an analytical mind; a good memory; scientific aptitude; the ability to assimilate facts quickly and to reason and speak clearly; ability to write clearly and unambiguously; liking for concentrated desk-work.

Mature entry and career change Entrance requirements may be waived for people with relevant experience, but there are difficulties getting training vacancies due to the length of training involved.

Work–life balance Return after a career break is possible only for those who have kept up with legal and technological changes/developments.

There are some part-time opportunities; it is also possible for experienced patent attorneys with good contacts to run a small private practice from home. Job-sharing should be possible.

Further information
Chartered Institute of Patent Agents, 95 Chancery Lane, London WC2A 1DT.
www.cipa.org
Institute of Trade Mark Attorneys, Canterbury House, 2–6 Sydenham Road, Croydon CRO 9XE.
www.itma.org.uk
European Patent Office
www.epo.org

Patent Examiner

Entry qualifications First-class or second-class honours degree in a scientific, engineering or mathematical subject; ability to read French and German is very important. Entry is not possible at HND or Foundation degree level.

The work Patent examiners work mainly in the UK Intellectual Property Office (Patent Office) in Newport, South Wales, and examine applications for patents. The Patent Office is an executive agency of the Department for Innovation, Universities and Skills. An examiner's work involves detailed examination of the description of an invention; making a search through earlier specifications to ascertain the novelty of the invention; classifying and indexing the features of the invention; writing a report embodying the findings; and, if necessary, interviewing the inventor or the inventor's agent to discuss any problems.

The work requires an analytical and critical mind. Each examiner works in a specialized field. Training is in-house and includes a two-year probationary period. There are few vacancies each year. There are also opportunities for patent examiners at the European Patent Office centres in Germany and The Netherlands.

Personal attributes As for Patent Agent.

Mature entry and career change Unusual, but occasionally possible for people with relevant (technological) degrees and industrial experience.

Work–life balance Civil Service conditions apply (see p. 166).

Further information
The UK Intellectual Property Office, Concept House, Cardiff Road, Newport NP10 8QQ.
www.ipo.gov.uk

Related careers *civil service – engineering – science*

Personnel/Human Resources Management

Entry qualifications No specific requirements but most entrants are graduates. Any discipline is acceptable but business studies, the behavioural sciences and law may be particularly helpful.

The work Personnel managers are part of the management team. Titles vary and are not necessarily any indication of scope and level of responsibility. The term 'human resources manager' is now often used. Their primary aim is always the efficient use and development of people's talents. The Chartered Institute of Personnel and Development says that personnel management is not a job for people who merely want to 'work with people'. A personnel manager's main job is 'to provide the specialist knowledge or service that can assist other members of the management team to make the most effective use of the human resources – people – of the organization'.

'Personnel' is a 'management function', like buying, marketing and production. Its challenge is to interpret conflicting views and objectives to people at various levels in an organization, some of whom have divergent interests.

Personnel managers are employed not only in industry, but also in hospitals, local and central government: the efficient use of human resources is equally vital to profit-making and to non-profit-making organizations. The range of jobs is very great indeed. In a large organization, employing say 70,000 people at several sites, a personnel director may have a staff of 70, some of whom specialize in one aspect of the work; in a small organization one or two people might do everything.

Main (overlapping) personnel specializations

- *Recruitment, training and management-development*: Devising, monitoring and applying selection procedures, possibly selecting the most suitable of various psychological testing and assessment methods for all levels of staff; identifying individuals' potential and planning their education, training and career development. This involves reconciling individuals' needs and aims with the employer's requirements for staff with specific skills at specific levels of responsibility. It is a very important specialization now because of the emphasis in the last few years on the need for a more highly skilled workforce at all levels from operatives to management.
- *Management of change*: Personnel people may or may not be responsible for masterminding this (see p. 346) but they are invariably involved. During the introduction of new technologies or structures personnel people work closely with systems analysts/designers, with, perhaps, technologists, occupational psychologists and other specialists and with union officials, ironing out problems arising when changes in traditional working patterns are proposed and implemented. This requires personnel people to have thorough understanding of individuals' present tasks, of their place in the hierarchy, and of how proposed changes will affect individuals' jobs.
- *Reward management*: Covers job evaluation and equal pay for equal work administration. It involves systematic study of the tasks that make up individual jobs within the organization, in order to establish their gradings. Reward management sounds misleadingly like a desk-bound routine job, but it can be one of the most non-routine and controversial specializations.
- *Employee relations*: Establishing and maintaining lines of communication between an organization's various interest groups. It involves discussing, with shop stewards and management, 'worker

participation' schemes; implication of new legislation (of which there is a constant flow); mergers; implementation of new technologies; dealing with consequent redundancies, and planning reallocation of tasks and retraining schemes.

- *Employee services*: Concerned with matters of health and safety and all welfare aspects. It may include personal counselling services; responsibility for canteens, etc., as well as sophisticated job satisfaction improvement schemes and cooperation with manpower planning, training and other personnel specialists.

Training The Chartered Institute of Personnel and Development's Professional Development Scheme (PDS) is divided into four fields: core management; people management and development; applied personnel and development; and specialist and generalist personnel and development. To complete the last field candidates undertake four modules from a choice of fifteen. Graduate membership of the CIPD is achieved on completion of all four fields. The PDS is offered at CIPD approved centres and can be studied full-time, part-time, or through flexible or open learning.

Those not qualified or experienced enough to follow the Professional Development Scheme may study part-time for one of the CIPD Certificate courses: options include personnel practice, training practice, recruitment and selection, employment relations, managing people.

Some NVQs/SVQs in the fields of management and personnel may be recognized by CIPD for membership.

Personal attributes A flair for seeing all sides of a problem and interpreting each side's point of view to the other; a good memory for names and faces; at least an absence of dislike for figure-work, preferably a liking for it; interest in profitable management and in change; lack of prejudice; tact; detachment; an understanding of people of all types, ages, races and backgrounds, and the ability to gain their confidence and respect; organizing ability.

Mature entry and career change Some opportunities for mature entrants who have had relevant experience.

Work–life balance Opportunities for flexible working should not be a problem if employed within the public sector. Personnel workers taking a career break will need to keep up with changes in legislation and other developments. The CIPD offers a flexible-learning option for those who need to combine study with other commitments.

Further information

Chartered Institute of Personnel and Development, 151 The Broadway, London SW19 1JQ.
www.cipd.co.uk

Related careers *careers guidance – health and safety advisers and inspectors – management – retail management*

Pharmacy

Pharmacist

Entry qualifications Four-year degree in pharmacy. Entry to degree course at National Qualifications Framework Level 3 (A levels, BTEC National awards) or Scottish Credit and Qualifications Framework equivalent: A levels or equivalent including chemistry and two chosen from a mathematical subject, physics and a biological science. The subject not offered at this level should be offered at GCSE or equivalent. In practice, English and maths GCSE (A–C) or equivalent are essential. Students with alternative qualifications are advised to check with admissions tutors.

Registration with the Royal Pharmaceutical Society of Great Britain.

The work Pharmacists work in three distinct fields: community, hospital and industry. Students do not need to decide which branch of pharmacy they want to go into until after qualifying.

Community Pharmacist

Pharmacists dispense or supervise the dispensing of prescriptions. They act as a link between doctors and their patients, by explaining the effects and the correct use of medicines.

Most medicines are now available ready-made but pharmacists still make up the occasional prescription in the dispensary. They are also responsible for the safe and correct storage of a variety of medicines and some chemical substances. They are legally required to keep records such as the 'controlled drug' registers.

Pharmacists may also deal with the buying and selling of cosmetics, toiletries, etc., and the training of shop staff. In larger pharmacies, and particularly in chains of pharmacies, the pharmacist has the choice of remaining involved with the dispensing and sale of medicines, or of becoming more involved with the commercial side.

The role of pharmacists is changing. As more and more new drugs come on the market, both doctors and patients are making more use of pharmacists' thorough knowledge of the composition, action and interaction of new drugs. Many doctors ask pharmacists' advice – or at least their views – on the best way to use new drugs for particular conditions. Pharmacists have more time to keep up with pharmaceutical developments than doctors. Also, patients increasingly ask pharmacists' advice for minor ailments and their opinion on whether they should consult their doctor. Pharmacists are well qualified to know when medical advice must be sought and when a simple remedy (which may be cheaper than one on prescription) is all that the patient needs.

Increasingly pharmacists are becoming more involved with community health care and offer basic health checks, such as blood pressure monitoring. Some also serve residential homes. They may also need to visit patients in their homes to deliver oxygen equipment or fit surgical appliances.

Pharmacists are now more often managers of pharmacies or of dispensing departments than owners of their own business.

Abroad: Qualified pharmacists can practise and get jobs fairly easily in some countries of the Commonwealth; harmonization of qualifications within EU countries has been agreed.

Hospital Pharmacist

Particularly suitable for those interested in the science of pharmacy. Hospital pharmacists dispense – and supervise the dispensing of – prescriptions for outpatients; they advise patients on the proper use of their medicines; they issue medicines for use within the hospital and they work closely with doctors and nurses to ensure that medicines are used safely, correctly and economically. They advise on doses and side-effects of drugs, evaluate new drugs for the hospital and may be involved in clinical trial work. Most medicines used in hospital are ready-made, but some preparations are made up in the hospital pharmacy. They also have a teaching role – they assist with the training of student pharmacists and student pharmacy technicians; and they lecture to doctors and nurses.

Some hospitals offer a 24-hour pharmacy service, provided by pharmacists who live in when on duty.

Pharmacists may work with individual patients and be consulted on the best drug to use in any particular case. Young doctors often ask pharmacists' advice and pharmacists may be asked to check patients' drug-charts to look for adverse reactions if patients take several different kinds of drugs; so there is more patient contact than in the past.

Hospital pharmacists have a definite career structure. There is work which involves contact with people, and backroom work. Hospital pharmacists work in a community, with the opportunity of meeting people in similar jobs.

Outside the hospital, pharmacists also advise staff and residents in residential nursing homes and local health clinics.

Industrial Pharmacist

They work in laboratories of pharmaceutical and related firms and on the production and development of new drugs and the improvement and quality control of existing drugs. As in other scientific work (see p. 507), pharmacists work in teams, often together with scientists from other disciplines. Some jobs involve mainly desk-work such as providing information to doctors and the preparation of data on new products for the Medicine and Healthcare Products Regulatory Agency. Those with an aptitude for salesmanship can become representatives, visiting doctors in their surgeries and in hospital, providing information on their companies' products (and they may become marketing executives, an expanding area).

There is therefore scope for the quiet backroom type content with semi-routine work, for the team leader interested in pursuing new lines of thought and for those who want to go into general management, marketing and pharmaceutical sales.

Training (generally) Four-year pharmacy degree course at a university school of pharmacy. Degree courses are accredited by the Royal Pharmaceutical Society of Great Britain. The syllabus includes pharmaceutical chemistry – the origin and chemistry of drugs; pharmaceutics – the preparation of medicines; pharmacology – the action and uses of drugs and medicines in living systems; pharmacy practice – dispensing and counselling skills, pharmacy law and ethics.

After graduating, students must complete one year's paid pre-registration training in a pharmacy workplace, and pass the Registration Examination of the Royal Pharmaceutical Society of Great Britain, before they are eligible to apply for registration as pharmaceutical chemists.

Personal attributes *For all pharmacists*: Good communication skills; a strong scientific bent; meticulous accuracy; a strong sense of responsibility; a calm, logical mind; ability to concentrate; organizing ability; a liking for people; ability to work with semi-trained and untrained staff.

For community and industrial pharmacists: A flair for business; ability to deal with semi-trained and untrained staff; a liking for people.

For industrial pharmacists: An inquiring mind; ability to work as one of a team; infinite patience.

Mature entry and career change No upper age limit for training or jobs, but there is no relaxation of entry requirements.

Work–life balance The Centre for Pharmacy Postgraduate Education runs return to practice courses to help returners update their knowledge and dispensing skills. In some cases the NHS will pay costs of refresher courses. Some large multiple pharmacy groups also offer retraining. There are also some distance-learning courses. Job-sharing and other forms of flexible working are becoming accepted in hospital and in community work.

Further information
Royal Pharmaceutical Society of Great Britain, 1 Lambeth High Street, London SE1 7JN or 36 York Place, Edinburgh EH1 3HU. *www.pharmacycareers.org.uk* and *www.rpsgb.org*

Related careers *medicine – Pharmacy Technician – science: Chemistry; Biochemistry; Biotechnology*

Pharmacy Technician

Entry qualifications There is no formal academic requirement but employers or colleges will usually ask for a minimum of National Qualifications Framework Level 2 (GCSEs A*–C, BTEC Diplomas and Certificates) or Scottish Credit and Qualifications Framework equivalent.

The work This varies according to whether the job is in community pharmacy which includes pharmacy departments of retail chain stores, industry or hospitals. In community, technicians may spend time on the selling side when not assisting the pharmacist with dispensing (but they work always under the supervision of qualified pharmacists who must check prescriptions, etc.). In hospitals and industry, technicians have more chance to do responsible and varied work. They assist with experiments, with interviewing patients, and they may liaise with other departments, etc. The role of the technician in the hospitals and in industry is changing: as in other science-based jobs (see p. 507) technicians now often do jobs which overlap with graduates', but there will always be a considerable difference between the project-leader type and level of work, and that of technicians who implement proven techniques. While using their judgement and expertise, they do not take ultimate responsibility or do original research.

Training Training is usually through a two-year trainee post in a hospital or community pharmacy. Pharmacy technician apprenticeships are also available. To register with the Royal Pharmaceutical Society of Great Britain it is necessary to gain the level 3 NVQ/SVQ in Pharmacy Services, or National Certificate award – registration may become statutory in the future.

Personal attributes Enjoy working with people; good communication skills; meticulous accuracy; methodical; a scientific bent; number skills.

Mature entry and career change Depends on local supply-and-demand position. Entrance requirements may be waived; but school-leavers may be given preference.

Work–life balance The NHS is favourable towards career breaks and flexible working. Elsewhere opportunities may depend on supply and demand.

Further information

National Pharmaceutical Association, Mallinson House, 48 Peter's Street, St Albans, Herts AL1 3NP.
www.npa.co.uk

Related careers *retail management – science*

Photography

PHOTOGRAPHER

Entry qualifications No definite educational requirements for photography as such, but some courses may have specific requirements.

Photography covers over 30 specializations, but many photographers combine several of these. Metropolitan photographers tend to be more specialized than those in more rural areas. Many freelance photographers take on any work which is offered, in order to earn a living. 'Bread and butter' jobs can help pay for more creative, but less well-paid, assignments.

General Photography

Approximately half of all photographers work in general photographic studios. The bulk of their work consists of portraiture, group photographs and commercial services. Portrait subjects include, increasingly, pets; some photographers specialize in children.

Photographers prefer their subjects to come to the studio to be photographed, because it is easier to arrange the lighting there. However, there is also demand for portraits in the home, garden or workplace, especially in the case of children's portraits. The 'natural' portrait is much more popular today than the formal one. To produce not just a good likeness, but a characteristic portrait, photographers must have considerable understanding of, and insight into, human nature; they must be able to put sitters at ease so that their expression is natural.

Weddings and other group photographs (e.g. sports and social clubs) form another important part of the work. Wedding photography now offers more scope for 'creative' pictures in a less formal style than it used to. Commercial work is mainly for publicity purposes – for local companies, estate agencies, architects, etc. who do not have enough work to employ a staff photographer.

Opportunities are reasonable. One way in for the keen amateur is to help a busy studio with Saturday weddings.

Electronic imaging, image manipulation and electronic transfer have changed the way in which photography is processed and new entrants need to be familiar with the technology.

Advertising Photography

Very varied. Although advertising photographers are often given exact instructions about what to photograph and what effect to aim at, they are also expected to suggest their own ideas for new angles. Many advertisements are records of everyday life – whether it is of a child eating breakfast, or a woman getting out of a car – and involve both work with models, and persuading ordinary people to agree to be photographed.

Advertising photographs are taken either by the photographic departments of advertising agencies, by photographic studios (i.e. several photographers working as partners, sharing darkroom and office facilities, or salaried photographers and assistants working for an employer) or by freelance photographers. Most do some catalogue work; some studios specialize in mail-order photography (and may be owned by the mail-order company).

This is a very competitive branch; success depends entirely on ability, efficiency and the right personality.

Fashion Photography

Although advertising includes fashion photography, some photographers specialize in fashion. Most fashion photography is done by specialist studios or freelancers who are commissioned by editors, fashion houses or advertising agencies; they usually work under the direction of a fashion expert. This is the most sought-after branch and hence very difficult to enter.

Photo-journalism (Feature Photography), Press and Editorial Photography

Photo-journalism is, essentially, telling a story in pictures, and therefore a journalistic sense is needed. Feature photographers may work with reporters as a team; they may be freelancers, or work for studios. Only a minority are on editorial staffs. It is very varied work, and leads to assignments at any time and in any place – photographing VIPs at home, or life in foreign parts, or schools at work – anything that makes a story. Hours are irregular.

Press photographers must be versatile in taking all kinds of subjects. They must know what makes a good news picture; be able to write accurate captions; work well with reporters; be very quick and often work under difficult conditions. Hours are irregular.

Editorial photographers work mainly for magazines, nearly always as freelancers. Work can be very varied, depending on the article or report which needs illustrating. It varies from shots of a TV star at home with children/pets to a travel feature; from contestants in a cookery competition to action shots of a parachute jump.

Prospects are fair, but competition is stiff. The market for photo-journalists is small. Most work as freelancers and may specialize, e.g. in travel. For press photography there are always more candidates than jobs. Some possibilities for photographers in other branches to sell work to newspapers or press agencies. Editorial photography depends on building up good contacts and a reputation for reliability.

Industrial and Scientific Photography

This is the most varied branch of photography and has the most openings. Clients include manufacturing companies, research organizations, government departments, higher education establishments, the police and the Armed Forces. Examples of the work: making photographic progress reports in laboratories; recording the various stages of manufacturing processes; photographing building sites. Industrial photographers also take pictures for house magazines, exhibition stands and instructional purposes. Most of these photographers are salaried employees; some work as freelancers or for studios (see 'General Photography', p. 444).

Medical Photography

Most teaching hospitals and medical research institutions employ medical photographers, sometimes as part of a medical illustration team with medical artists and audio-visual technicians. They may produce images using specialized techniques on which treatment can be based or make still and video records of work done in operating theatres and research laboratories, and of particular cases among patients. They also illustrate health care guides for patients and teaching material for student nurses and doctors. Medical photographers must not be squeamish.

Training (generally)

- *Work-based route*: There is no set route into general photography and many professionals start as an assistant and gain experience while working towards qualifications as required. N/SVQs are widely available at four levels and larger studios may offer structured training programmes or apprenticeships.
- *College-based route*: Qualifications may be studied part-time or full-time. City & Guilds awards in photo imaging are available at levels 2 and 3, with various specialisms. BTEC National awards require four GCSEs or equivalent and Higher awards two or three A levels or equivalent. A number of colleges offer the BIPP PQE (Professional Qualifying Examination), often linked with an HND or degree course.
- *Higher education route*: Courses in photography, imaging or photo-media at HND, Foundation degree and degree level are widely available. Some courses specialize, such as degrees in commercial photography. Photography can also be studied as part of a broader

degree in art and design. Prospectuses need to be studied carefully as content and emphasis differ significantly. After initial training photographers may work towards membership of the British Institute of Professional Photography, achieved through submission of a portfolio. BIPP offers foundation academy courses in different specialist areas for those working towards membership.

Medical photographers need an HND or equivalent, or higher, photographic qualification and follow an in-house training programme leading to a professional qualification or an undergraduate or postgraduate degree.

Press photographers work towards the National Council for the Training of Journalists National Certificate in Press Photography/Photo Journalism, or an NVQ/SVQ level 4 in Newspaper Journalism (Press Photography).

Photographic Technician

Photographic processing laboratories provide a wide range of services including developing film, converting images to digital formats, enhancing or manipulating images using advanced software and printing images. This is a major employment area of photography.

The various types of processing laboratory include those specializing in 'finishing' services for professional photographers, labs run by large 'photofinishing' companies providing postal services for amateur photographers, 'mini labs' in high street shops and supermarkets and labs that specialize in areas such as medical or scientific image processing.

This work requires considerable concentration and technical knowledge, especially of the complex chemistry of colour film; without these skills a photographer's assignment worth hundreds or even thousands of pounds could be ruined. Experienced technicians can learn more specialized skills, such as photo retouching and image manipulation.

Training Usually starting as a junior or trainee in a photographic laboratory, while working towards N/SVQs levels 2–4 in photo imaging or processing. City & Guilds offer assignment-assessed certificate and diploma awards in photo imaging, for those wanting to develop higher level imaging skills. Training can also be achieved as part of a Foundation degree. Apprenticeships/Advanced Apprenticeships have also recently been developed.

Personal attributes (generally) Visual imagination; eye for detail and composition; patience; good colour vision; artistic sensitivity; creativeness; good powers of observation; ability to work quickly, under pressure, surrounded by crowds – in all kinds of unfavourable circumstances; ability to work well with others while keeping to their own individual style; originality; unusual inventiveness (for advertising and fashion photography); expertise with photo imaging software; business sense (for arranging appointments, sending out bills, etc.), as very few can afford secretaries; willingness to 'sell' themselves; a manner which encourages people to cooperate.

Press photographers: News sense; ability to remain calm and unmoved, however tragic or unpleasant the circumstances.

Medical photographers: Scientific aptitude; tactful and reassuring manner; total lack of squeamishness.

Technicians: Scientific aptitude; an eye for detail; patience; IT skills.

Mature entry and career change A number of photographers have worked in other fields before taking up photography. Some colleges waive entry requirements for mature students. The main drawbacks are intense competition from college-leavers and poor salaries of trainee or assistant photographers.

Work–life balance Possibly difficult to return in the best-paid and most competitive fields, but it should be possible to return to some kind of photography and/or to do some freelance work even while raising a family. The BIPP may offer reduced subscriptions for women on a maternity break.

Further information

British Institute of Professional Photography, Fox Talbot House, Ware, Herts SG12 9HN.
www.bipp.com

City & Guilds of London Institute, 1 Giltspur Street, London EC1A 9DD.
www.city-and-guilds.co.uk

Institute of Medical Illustrators, Bank Chambers, 48 Onslow Gardens, London SW7 3AH.
www.imi.org.uk

Association of Photographers, 81 Leonard Street, London EC2A 4QS.
www.the-aop.org

Skillset, Focus Point, 21 Caledonian Road, London N1 9GB.
www.skillset.org

Related careers *art and design – fashion and clothing – journalism – television, film and radio*

Physiotherapy

Entry qualifications Honours or Masters degree in Physiotherapy and registration with the Health Professions Council (HPC).

The work Physiotherapists use exercises and movement, electrotherapy – the use of heat, high frequency currents and ultrasonics – manipulation and massage in an integrated way to optimize an individual's functional ability and potential. They are responsible for assessing and analysing patients' conditions and for planning their treatment. This involves treating patients with recovering conditions such as head injury and stroke, patients with deteriorating conditions such as Parkinson's disease, motor neurone disease, multiple sclerosis and some cancers, and managing patients with stable conditions such as spinal cord injuries and lower limb amputation. They are also involved in health promotion and injury prevention. Physiotherapists operate as independent practitioners as well as members of health care teams of doctors, nurses, occupational therapists, podiatrists and social workers. They are able to act as first contact practitioners, and patients may seek direct care without referral from another health care professional.

Patients too ill to be moved are treated in bed; others, such as postoperative patients, may have to be helped to walk properly again. Stroke patients are taught to make their healthy limbs or muscles do the work, as far as possible, of paralysed ones, and how to use paralysed limbs. Some patients do exercises in water and the physiotherapist works with them in heated swimming pools.

Some patients are treated in groups, but most individually. In all cases, physiotherapists must use their judgement. They must know how far to coax a patient into doing an uncomfortable exercise, and must adapt treatment to suit each patient. They use tact and encouragement together with specialist knowledge when, for example, explaining to a patient why it is important that exercises are done regularly at home, or when persuading children to cooperate, or when allaying patients' fear of treatment.

Many work in hospitals but a large number work in GP practices and treat patients in their homes. After usually about two years' work, gaining all-round experience, they may specialize, for example in work with the elderly; in orthopaedic, chest or neurological conditions; and, increasingly, in work with mentally and physically disabled children and/or adults. Work outside the hospital in the community is increasing. This may be giving treatments or preventative health education work; advising in factories, hospitals, etc. on how to deal with carrying heavy weights, for example. Physiotherapists also work with expectant mothers in clinics. There is also room for physiotherapists who want to do only preventative work: sports clubs employ physiotherapists (often part-time) to keep their members fit, and to treat minor injuries; large industrial and commercial organizations employ physiotherapists to see that office desks are the right height for comfort, health and therefore efficiency; to show staff how to sit without risking injury; to teach sales assistants to relax while standing; to teach porters to carry without risking injury, and so on. Health farms and, sometimes, keep fit classes also employ physiotherapists.

Although newly qualified physiotherapists in the UK have experienced problems in finding jobs in the last two years, worldwide there is a shortage of physiotherapists, and of physiotherapy teachers and specialists. Physiotherapy qualifications are recognized in the EU and in many countries abroad, but in the USA and some other countries physiotherapists may have to take additional examinations. Experienced physiotherapists often decide to set up in private practice, treating patients either in their own treatment rooms or in patients' homes. But this needs good contacts with local doctors and capital to buy equipment and see them over the first few months.

Training In order to practise as a physiotherapist it is essential to have an honours degree, or a Masters degree, in physiotherapy approved by the Chartered Society of Physiotherapy and recognized by the HPC. The three-year or four-year courses include lengthy clinical placements. For graduates in other relevant disciplines two-year full-time accelerated courses leading to a Masters degree are available. Degree holders are eligible for membership of the Chartered Society of Physiotherapy, and for registration as a physiotherapist with the Health Professions Council, which is essential in order to work as a physiotherapist in the UK.

The first year is mostly pre-clinical (theoretical); subjects studied include anatomy, physiology, physics, behavioural sciences, pathology and technical treatment skills. From the second year theory is combined with working with patients.

The NHS funds most physiotherapy courses and eligible students may have their tuition fees paid in full and be able to apply for a means-tested bursary.

There are a large number of post-qualifying courses which enable qualified physiotherapists to specialize in a certain field.

Personal attributes The ability to cope with the academic demands of an honours degree in science and a recognition of the need for continuing professional development throughout one's career; a sympathetic yet objective approach to disability; ability to work as one of a team and to take responsibility and use initiative; enthusiasm.

Mature entry and career change The profession welcomes mature students. Entry qualifications are not so rigidly enforced; applicants' work and life experience are taken into account; but for those who do not have the usual qualifications, evidence of ability to cope with degree-level study (including science) is required.

Work–life balance Opportunities for part-time work are excellent, increasingly even in senior jobs. Job-sharing is encouraged. Returners are welcome; refresher training can be arranged by hospitals or health authorities. Those who have not practised for some time are required to undertake some form of refresher training or return to practice opportunity before re-registration with the Health Professions Council.

Further information

Chartered Society of Physiotherapy, 14 Bedford Row, London WC1R 4ED (*A Guide to Becoming a Chartered Physiotherapist and Guidelines for Mature Entrants* available free).
www.csp.org.uk
NHS Careers, PO Box 2311, Bristol BS2 2ZX.
www.nhscareers.nhs.uk

Related careers *occupational therapy – speech and language therapy – teaching*.

Podiatry (Chiropody)

Following a change in title some years back chiropody is now widely known by the title podiatry, and the professional body is known as the Society of Chiropodists and Podiatrists.

Entry qualifications A BSc (Hons) degree in Podiatry.

The work Podiatrists assess, diagnose and treat lower limb disorders; they assess children's and adults' feet to prevent minor ailments from growing into major ones. They are unusual among the Allied Health Professions in that they diagnose and treat conditions without medical referral. Most can undertake invasive skin/nail surgery under local anaesthetic, and a growing number are qualified to perform minor bone surgery. Podiatrists can choose the environment in which to work:

- *Private practice*: This is the most remunerative work and scope is growing. Podiatrists may practise in surgeries in their own homes and visit patients in their homes. Private practice can be lonely work (even though patients are seen all day) but many work in group practices – partners renting premises jointly or using rooms in one of the partners' homes as a surgery.
- *Hospitals and community health clinics*: Podiatrists employed by the NHS work in a variety of settings from orthotics laboratories and diabetes clinics to patients' own homes.
- *Industry*: Companies where staff are on their feet all day often employ full-time or part-time podiatrists.

In the two latter situations podiatrists enjoy the companionship and social facilities of a large organization. Some combine part-time work with private practice.

There are also increasing opportunities in sports clubs and leisure centres.

Training Graduates with an approved degree in podiatry from one of the schools of podiatry are eligible for registration with the Health Professions Council (HPC), which is essential for all public jobs, and for membership of the Society of Chiropodists and Podiatrists. The courses are modular and much of the content is practical and includes treatment of patients under supervision. Theory includes the basic medical sciences, anatomy, physiology, medicine and surgery, and local anaesthesia.

Courses which do not lead to degrees do not lead to HPC Registration and Membership of the Society of Chiropodists and Podiatrists. Degree courses can be three or four years full-time, although some schools now offer part-time routes that can be anything from four and a half to five years in duration. Following a change in legislation, to practise as a podiatrist you must be registered with the Health Professions Council. It is illegal to use the title chiropodist or podiatrist if you are not registered with the HPC.

Personal attributes A high degree of manual dexterity; ability to get on with people greatly enhances chances of promotion and of having a flourishing private practice. However, unlike many other careers with patients, shy, retiring people may get on well.

Mature entry and career change Good opportunities, with some relaxations in entry requirements.

Work–life balance Returners must re-register if wanting to practise as a podiatrist. The Health Professions Council has a return-to-practice policy for practitioners. A period of mentorship may be required depending on how long a person has not been on the HPC register.

There is ample scope for part-time work and job-sharing is possible.

Further information

The Society of Chiropodists and Podiatrists, 1 Fellmongers Path, Tower Bridge Road, London SE1 3LY.
www.feetforlife.org
NHS Careers, PO Box 2311, Bristol BS2 2ZX.
www.nhscareers.nhs.uk

Related careers *nursing – physiotherapy*

Police

Entry qualifications Vary slightly from force to force. In general, candidates must be at least $18\frac{1}{2}$ and have good health and eyesight. There are no formal educational requirements for recruitment to the police service, but applicants attend an assessment centre and are tested on their written English, verbal reasoning, oral and mathematical skills. Competition for places in all forces is fierce, therefore applicants may find it helpful to join a voluntary cadet scheme if there is one in their area. There is also graduate entry.

The work The primary purpose of the police is to protect life and property and enforce law and order. Notions of how best to serve that purpose change from time to time as society becomes more complex and its demands change. The emphasis today is on community policing, responding to the demands of the public. Surveys have shown that the public want to see their police and expect them not just to solve crime, but to prevent it. On one level this is reflected in the traditional role of the police constable on the beat, getting to know the community, keeping an eye out not only for trouble but for potential sources of trouble. But there are also broader initiatives through which the police forge links with and respond to the community. Community liaison officers, for example, might work with a range of community groups from schoolchildren to the elderly.

The 43 police forces in England and Wales and eight in Scotland are run independently and their organization will vary. Within a force, too, different areas will have differing policing needs. The problems of the inner city are not the same as those of a rural area or middle-class suburb. Whatever the situation, the police need to establish channels of communication so that problems can be evaluated and means established to reduce and prevent crime. A serious drugs problem might involve links with the local youth and community workers, while tackling car theft and vandalism in a town centre car park involves liaison with town planners and other local authority officers.

Within a typical large station you might find: the uniformed officers who patrol the community, some on foot, some in patrol cars; crime prevention officers, who, for example, advise individuals on safeguarding their homes and property; community liaison officers; juvenile liaison officers, who enforce the policy on dealing with juveniles; the custody officer, responsible for ensuring that arrests are lawful; CID, who work together with uniformed officers on the detection of crime. In the control room, staff are responsible for the operation of the computerized command and control systems, sending the right officers to the right jobs. Flexible shift-working patterns enable the police to respond better to the community's needs, which are obviously not the same at 11 a.m., 11 p.m. and 4 a.m.

Other areas of specialization are traffic, with responsibilities ranging from planning and operating large-scale traffic control systems to dealing with major accidents, and mounted, dog-handling and river police, all very small. Within the CID, specializations can include fraud, special branch and serious crime. Underwater search units are vital for investigating crime and searching for missing persons, firearm units include specialist teams trained in the use of firearms, and many forces have or share full-time air support. Officers in drug squads work with operational officers and other agencies to target drug dealers and to tackle the drugs problem. Police do not specialize permanently; promotion often involves a move to a new area of specialization and/or a new force. Many specialist roles require higher standards of fitness or eyesight, for example, than those needed for joining the police service.

Promotion is through the ranks. Everyone starts out as a PC, gaining experience in various areas of police work, from communicating with the public to dealing with a traffic accident, from sorting out a domestic disturbance to dealing with a riot. Even those on accelerated programmes (see 'Training', below) spend at least two years at this rank. Those promoted to sergeant, after a qualifying exam and further assessment, take on a more supervisory role with responsibility for a team of PCs. An inspector's time is divided between operational and managerial roles. Chief inspectors, superintendents and assistant chief constables take on progressively more managerial responsibility and become more involved in strategic and policy issues. The chief constable's responsibilities include financial planning and budgetary control, training and recruitment policy, and development of the force within the community. Some constables choose not to go in for promotion because they enjoy grass-roots uniformed police work and the contact with the public which it involves.

Training

- Everyone who wants to become a police officer has to complete a two-year probationary period including working on the beat as a police constable. Training is organized on a local police basis; probationary training courses are usually non-residential and delivered at local colleges or universities rather than at national training centres. Further training is also organized by forces and includes a wide range of courses on specialist subjects.
- Fast track *England and Wales*: The High Potential Development Scheme (HPD) is open to new recruits and to serving police officers. It is not exclusively for graduates and there is no age limit. Graduates and non-graduates alike have the opportunity to study at HE level and many take the HPD MSc in Policing and Leadership. Development is tailored to individual needs. Anyone making a success of HPD can expect to reach at least chief inspector, and probably beyond.
- *Scotland*: The Accelerated Promotion Scheme for Graduates (APSG) provides a structured career path for the most promising and capable graduates entering the police in Scotland. The programme lasts five to seven years and provides a structure that allows career development from the rank of constable to inspector; a number go on to hold chief officer rank. Some graduates are selected for APSG on entry; others join the fast stream after standard entry.

Personal attributes Maturity; honesty; courage, both physical and moral; sense of humour; flexibility; reliability; real desire to help people; resilience; an observant eye and a cool head; understanding of and sympathy with human weakness; ability to accept both authority and discipline and a high degree of personal responsibility; good health.

Mature entry and career change No upper age limit although police constables and sergeants must retire at 55. Officers in higher ranks may serve for longer.

Work–life balance Police officers are already able to request part-time work or job-share and to have their application seriously considered. The police force is keen to hold on to experienced officers who might otherwise have to resign because of domestic commitments and in 2001 the Home Office published a report *Flexible Working Practices in the Police Service*. The British Association of Women Police has developed the Gender Agenda, addressing issues such as balancing work and family commitments, and has produced a guide to flexible working (*www.bawp.org*). Flexible work practices can be found in most police forces but at the present time it is still up to the individual to negotiate their own case. Police officers who have completed their probationary period may apply for a career break up to a maximum of five years. Refresher courses are arranged by some forces.

Further information
Any police force recruiting department.
England and Wales: Recruitment website: *www.policecouldyou.co.uk*
 www.policeuk.com/careers
Scotland: Scottish Police website: *www.scottish.police.uk*
Scottish Police College, Tulliallan Castle, Kincardine, Alloa FK10 4BE.
 www.tulliallan.police.uk

Related careers *environmental health officer – health and safety inspectors – prison service – social work*

Printing

Entry qualifications See 'Training', below.

The work The printing industry uses a variety of technological processes to create a product of visual impact; it is always a form of communication. The product may be books, newspapers, theatre tickets, posters, packaging, stamps, manuals, record sleeves, credit cards, or reproductions of old masters. The printed materials include paper, card, plastic, metal, textiles. Some printing processes are centuries old, but printing technology has changed enormously in the last few years and continues to change. For example, traditional letterpress is much less common than it was, having been largely replaced by lithography, especially offset litho. Screenprinting is widely used for non-paper materials. Most text is produced by computer-aided typesetting using desk-top publishing (DTP) software. This enables an operator to turn all the elements of text and graphics into complete made-up pages which are then put on film ready for the platemakers. Special typesetting programs can 'convert' different sorts of word-processing programs used by writers so they are ready for typesetting. Electronic scanners are used in the production of both black-and-white and coloured illustrations; and holograms can be printed on credit and identity cards. Electronic transmission of text and illustrations for printing in another continent is now common.

There are several main types of printing organizations: large and small general commercial printers, specialist packaging printers, high-quality book printers, magazine printers and the high street instant print shops. Newspapers now form a very small part of the industry, as changing technology has reduced the number of jobs. The production manager (or planner) decides with the client on the most advantageous and economic method of production for each item; this means weighing up factors such as efficient use of machines, materials, speed, cost, quality, eventual use and appearance.

Training

The industry recruits trainees at all levels, from school-leaver to graduate. Older entrants usually have related qualifications or experience though there are no longer many specific college or university courses in printing.

Print production: Trainees tend to specialize in specific skill areas: pre-press (which includes typesetting and platemaking); machine printing; print finishing (includes operating cutting, folding and binding machines). Training may be work-based, possibly leading to NVQs/SVQs at levels 2 and 3, and specialist training courses in a large number of printing skills are available; trainees work for these and/or the City & Guilds Printing and Graphic Communications Certificate. Apprenticeships have been developed for young people aged 16–24.

Instant print and small printing units train mainly in-house. Most recruit experienced people.

Production management: Some experienced production staff continue with further company-based training and specialize in managerial skills such as estimating and selling. This industry still includes many small businesses: there are relatively few company-based formal management training programmes.

Personal attributes Depends on type and level of work, but generally some visual imagination; interest in machinery; practicality; some dexterity. *For managerial jobs*: organizing ability; ability to work under pressure; being a self-starter.

Mature entry and career change Open to people with related experience at all ages but competition is intense.

Work–life balance Return to work is likely to be difficult because of technological changes and shortage of jobs. A few retraining courses exist. There are few opportunities for part-time work; possibly as freelance typographer.

Further information

British Printing Industries Federation, Farringdon Point, 29–35 Farringdon Road, London EC1M 3JF.
  www.britishprint.com and *www.jobsinprint.com*
Institute of Paper, Printing and Publishing, 83 Guildford Street, Chertsey, Surrey KT16 9AS.
  www.ip3.org.uk

Related careers *art and design – engineering – publishing – science*

Prison Service

Entry qualifications Minimum age 18. No specific academic requirement (but an entrance test must be passed) except in Scotland where
five standard grades 1–3 or equivalent, or three years' experience of
people management are required. Selection is by aptitude test and
interview. Also graduate entry to Intensive Development Scheme,
which may lead to senior management post within five years.

Private contractors may have their own requirements.

The work The work of a prison officer goes far beyond locking and
unlocking cells and patrolling corridors. One of the responsibilities of
the prison service as set out by the Prison Board is 'to provide for
prisoners as full a life as possible, to care for physical and mental
health, advise and help with personal problems, work, education and
training, physical exercise and recreation, and an opportunity to
practise their religion'. What this means in practice is maintaining
a community where prisoners eat, sleep, work, train, learn, play and so
on. Prison officers are concerned with care as well as control, well-
being as well as security. They are also concerned at senior levels with
the management of staff and resources.

Prison officers (detention custody officers with the private contractors who manage some prisons and undertake court escort services) supervise inmates in the activities mentioned above, escort
them to and from courts and hospitals, accompany visitors to the
visiting room, receive new prisoners. Whatever tasks they are involved
in, they must try to work through cooperation with prisoners. An
important part of their role is rehabilitation, helping to prepare
prisoners to return to the outside community as law-abiding citizens.

This involves helping them to develop skills, confidence and self-respect. Partly this is done through activities, but also through building up a relationship. Prison officers can be involved in motivating prisoners to improve their education, whether it be learning to read or studying for an Open University degree; providing a shoulder to cry on when someone gets a 'Dear John' letter; reasoning with someone threatening violence. They must recognize and know how to deal with prisoners who are having to cope with feelings of anger, anxiety or shame, with those who are troublesome and those who are extremely worried or depressed. It may be important to know how physically to restrain a violent and abusive inmate, but it is equally important to understand how such situations arise and how to re-establish communication and cooperation.

Many prisons are old and overcrowded; prisoners' frustrations can lead to tensions that sometimes result in violence. Most prisoners reoffend. Many are unappreciative, some abusive. Prison work can be frustrating, even depressing, but it offers more scope for personal initiative, individual responsibility and the development of interpersonal skills than is commonly realized. Like social work, it can be very rewarding and is a vital service to the community.

The demands and routines of prison work will vary according to the type and size of institution. These include local prisons for those awaiting trial or serving short sentences; prisons where high-security prisoners are 'dispersed'; open prisons for those requiring a lesser degree of security; Young Offender Institutions, which accommodate 15–21-year-olds (under-18s are held in juvenile wings). Prison officers must be prepared to serve in any kind of institution, in any part of the country, though preferences are taken into account whenever possible.

All prison officers begin 'on the landings' (the equivalent to 'on the beat' for police constables) as part of a team. On promotion, for which it is often necessary to move, officers take on increased responsibility – for a team, a wing, a function or service (e.g. inmate activities, staff training), ultimately a whole establishment. There is an accelerated promotion scheme (see 'Training' below) for experienced officers and graduate entrants with top management potential. There are also opportunities, after basic experience, to specialize as, for example, a hospital officer, a physical education officer or a trades officer (teaching a skill or trade).

Training Training takes place within prisons and at the Prison Service College or at one of nine local training centres. The course lasts eight weeks and depending where the training takes place may involve time away from home. There is an Intensive Development Scheme for graduates and other particularly able candidates which grooms them to reach an upper-middle management position in fewer than five years. Private contractors are responsible for training their staff to standards laid down by the Home Office.

Personal attributes Leadership; a sense of right and wrong, without being censorious; a genuine desire to help people in trouble and the ability to understand and sympathize with people's failings without necessarily condoning them; the ability to find the right approach to all types of people; immense patience with people at their most unbearable; interests entirely outside prison work to help keep a sense of proportion; a friendly, naturally happy disposition; sense of humour.

Mature entry and career change Entry up to 62 years.

Work–life balance Prison officers may be posted to any prison. They are expected to work shifts, including nights, weekends and some long days. Part-time work and job-sharing is available.

Further information
England and Wales: HM Prison Service, Cleland House, Page Street, London WC1P 4LN.
www.hmprisonservice.gov.uk
Scotland: Scottish Prison Service Headquarters, Calton House, 5 Redheughs Rigg, Edinburgh EH12 9HW.
www.sps.gov.uk

Related careers *personnel/human resources management – police – social work*

Probation Work

Entry qualifications

England and Wales: There is no age restriction for applicants, although candidates under 21 usually require qualifications at National Qualifications Framework Level 3 (A levels, BTEC National awards); candidates over 25 may be accepted without formal qualification but a written selection exercise is set. In practice many candidates have a related degree but appropriate life skills are the most necessary qualification. Detailed requirements may vary with probation district.

Scotland: Four-year honours degree course. All criminal justice social workers will have to register with the Scottish Social Services Council (SSSC) in order to practise in Scotland.

The work The National Probation Service (NPS) for England and Wales is organized into 42 areas and is responsible to the Home Office for ensuring a national approach to reducing reoffending and protecting the public. A National Offender Management Service (NOMS), combining the work of probation and prisons, aims to facilitate the management of offenders across both services.

A major part of the role of a probation officer is the continuous assessment of offenders and the management of risk to the public. Work with offenders begins before sentencing when the probation officer may be asked to prepare a report to help magistrates and judges decide on a suitable sentence. Probation officers build up a picture of individual offenders through interviews with him or her, the family, employers and so on, and try to establish any circumstances relevant to the offence, whether it might happen again, and what risks there may be to the public and the victim/s. Information is recorded on an assessment system to help with future risk management.

Offenders may be sentenced to a Community Order. Probation staff are responsible for managing these orders, working closely with partners in the voluntary and other sectors to ensure the offender is encouraged to stay on the order and 'breached' or sent back to court or prison if they do not comply with its requirements. Community Orders can last up to three years, and include specific requirements such as completing a special programme to target an individual's offending behaviour, residing in specified approved accommodation and completing unpaid work for the benefit of local communities.

Offenders who receive a custodial sentence of a year or more will spend some period on 'licence'. In all these cases (where the offender is 18 years old or over) probation officers supervise the offenders, making sure they understand the nature of the licence and comply with any conditions set.

All offenders sentenced to a custodial sentence are allocated a supervising officer in their home area who keeps in touch with them during their sentence and supports them in finding accommodation and training or employment on release. Some probation officers are based in prisons, working with prisoners before their release to deal with managing problems such as substance abuse.

Probation officers have a very difficult job to do, being firm and clear about what is expected of offenders while under probation supervision at the same time as trying to help them develop self-knowledge and self-discipline and regain self-respect. They might assist with accommodation, work, developing skills, getting treatment for a psychiatric problem or social adjustment. Some offenders welcome the attention offered by probation officers, but others are hostile to any figure of authority. Probation officers have to find the right way of gaining cooperation, but can always ultimately refer back to the courts.

Scotland: There is no probation service in Scotland. Criminal justice social workers, employed by local authority social work departments, perform a similar role to probation officers in England and Wales.

Training

England and Wales: The qualification for probation officers is the Diploma in Probation Studies. This is a two-year programme combining work-based training towards a level 4 NVQ in community justice with academic study for a degree in community justice and is very demanding. Many entrants have relevant degrees and all candidates go through an intensive selection process. Trainee probation officers are employees of local probation boards and are paid a training salary.

Scotland: Criminal justice social workers qualify through a four-year honours degree in social work.

Graduates with a degree in any discipline can apply to join an accelerated 16–24-month traineeship – combining study with practical work experience – to gain a social work degree. For further information see *www.sieswe.org*.

Personal attributes A willingness to work with people irrespective of one's own personal likes and dislikes; the ability to communicate with every level of intelligence, cultural or social background or emotional state; perseverance in the face of apparent failure when offenders show no sign of improvement or appreciation of efforts made for them or on their behalf; stability; a ready understanding of other people's way of life and point of view; sympathy and tolerance of human failings; belief in individual's potential to do better; good verbal and written skills to record and report; the ability to take an interest in other people's problems without becoming emotionally involved.

Mature entry and career change New entrants to the NPS over 25 may be accepted without formal qualifications but need to show evidence of ability to study, usually by provision of an assessed piece of written work.

Work–life balance The National Probation Service employs many 'returners' who may be able to work flexible hours.

Further information

National Offender Management Service, Abell House, John Islip Street, London SW1P 4LH.

www.probation.homeoffice.gov.uk (links to local probation areas throughout England and Wales)

Criminal Justice Social Work Centre for Scotland, 31 Buccleuch Place, Edinburgh EH8 9JT.

www.cjsw.ac.uk

Related careers *prison service – social work – youth and community work*

Psychology

Entry qualifications For registration as a Chartered Psychologist (not a statutory requirement but recommended) three-year (sometimes four-year) degree course, accredited by the British Psychological Society (BPS).

The work Psychology is the scientific study of how people think and act, and of the mental and emotional processes underlying behaviour. Psychologists study individuals' development and how individuals interact with one another. They use observation, experimental and other methods (e.g. surveys, intelligence tests) to assess and measure all kinds of cognitive (mental) processes, attitudes and emotions. (They must not be confused with psychiatrists, who are medically qualified specialists who give treatment to mentally ill patients.) Psychologists must understand the difference between 'normal' and 'abnormal' behaviour and use their knowledge and skills to solve (or alleviate) a wide range of cognitive and behavioural problems.

The British Psychological Society maintains the Register of Chartered Psychologists; people wanting to be Chartered Psychologists and who are eligible (i.e. have taken training accredited by the BPS) can belong to one of the following specialist divisions: clinical; counselling; educational; occupational; forensic; neuropsychology; sport and exercise; health; teaching and research (see 'Training', below, for need for postgraduate training for specializations).

There is a steady demand for psychologists. Although only a small proportion of psychology graduates become practising psychologists, a psychology degree is a useful preparation for a range of occupations including employee relations and other personnel functions and social work.

Clinical Psychology

Clinical psychologists help people come to terms with various problems. Therapeutic work is carried out with adults, young people and children in individual counselling sessions or in groups in many different settings, including hospitals, health centres and remand centres. They usually work as part of a team, for example with other medical specialists or with social workers. The wide range of problems they treat include learning disabilities, relationship problems, child development or age-related problems, phobias and serious mental illness.

Work with clients involves clinical assessment using methods including interviews, psychometric testing and observation. Treatment may involve therapy, counselling and advice or a programme of rehabilitation. This is a rapidly developing field and practice is based on and contributes to ongoing research.

Most clinical psychologists work for the National Health Service as part of a team with other health professionals though some are in private practice. There are opportunities to work as trainers and teachers and as researchers in universities.

Educational and Child Psychology

Educational psychologists advise teachers, parents, doctors and social workers on children's and young people's adjustment and learning problems. They are responsible for making formal recommendations for the education of children with learning difficulties. Assessment may involve sessions with the child as well as, usually, his or her parents and teachers, and a thorough study of the individual's background and environment. Various established techniques, such as ability tests and 'personality schedules', are used. Treatment (called 'intervention') may include individual counselling sessions with child and/or parents and advice to parents and teachers on the 'management' of the problem. Apart from helping individuals when problems have arisen, educational psychologists work with 'systems' or organizations: whole schools, families, groups of teachers or social workers, school classes, youth clubs. Running in-service courses for different groups is an important part of their work. They are largely employed by local education authorities and work in school/county psychological services and child guidance clinics, while a growing number work as independent or private consultants.

Occupational Psychology

Occupational psychologists deal with people as workers. They advise on how people can both enjoy and be efficient in their work by giving vocational guidance. They set up selection procedures for employers and develop training schemes; they help in the organization of work itself by devising new methods of doing jobs; and they advise on the design of tools and machines so that they are easy to use ('ergonomics'). They also research into and advise on psychological implications of organizational structures and proposed changes, aiming at improving both job satisfaction and the organization's effectiveness.

Occupational psychologists have developed techniques for collecting information from people about what they like doing and what they are good at, as well as what they find difficult and unpleasant. They match this information against that collected by detailed studies of the actual work involved in the jobs concerned. They are very much involved with 'managing change' of working practices in offices and manufacturing, e.g. when new technologies are introduced (see p. 346).

Other occupational/social psychology specializations are concerned with retirement: pre-retirement counselling and training and generally looking into problems connected with the growing proportion of retired people in the community; with mid-career changes necessitated by changes in job opportunities; with problems connected with women's changing career patterns and aspirations; with stress management.

The main employer of occupational psychologists is the Employment Service (Jobcentres). Opportunities are increasing in industry and commerce, especially in personnel/human resources departments.

Forensic Psychology

Psychologists are employed in the prison service, by health authorities and by social services to work both with prisoners and with those who look after them. They work in all kinds of prisons, including secure hospitals and rehabilitation units. They may run training courses for prison officers and therapy sessions for prisoners and their families, as well as carrying out casework with individuals and preparing psychological reports to help in risk assessment or to help judges decide on sentencing.

Forensic psychologists often collaborate with professionals in other related areas; police officers, probation officers and lawyers are turning more and more to psychology to aid their work. Forensic psychology is also the term used to refer to investigative and criminological psychology – using psychology as an aid in solving and preventing crime.

Health Psychology

This is a relatively new area of applied psychology. It covers a wide range of interventions, for example preventing damaging behaviours such as drug abuse, or encouraging healthy behaviour such as exercise. Health psychologists also investigate ways in which to explain, predict and change health and illness behaviour and work with the psychological effects of illness on individuals and their families. They also consider how health care delivery can be helped by improving communication or preparation for stressful treatment. Health psychologists work in hospitals, research units, health authorities and universities. They can also work with health service managers and clinicians in putting research evidence in practice to improve services.

Neuropsychology

Neuropsychology is concerned with the relationship between the brain and neuropsychological function. Its study and practical application help with the assessment and rehabilitation of people with brain injury, stroke, neurodegenerative or other neurological disease. Neuropsychologists may be researchers or practitioners or combine both roles. They require specialist knowledge of the neurosciences and may work with acute patients alongside neurosurgeons and neurologists or in rehabilitation centres providing assessment, training and support to prepare a patient as far as possible for return to normal life. Rehabilitation of neurological patients requires helping their families and carers too, and neuropsychologists often lead multidisciplinary rehabilitation teams.

Teaching and Research

Some psychologists teach in further and higher education; a few are involved solely in research, but most research is carried out by lecturers as part of their work. Newly appointed lecturers may be expected to take a postgraduate certificate in higher education and for research it is usually necessary to take a PhD in a specialist subject. Research may be commissioned by government departments, the police, industrial organizations, research institutes.

Sport and Exercise Psychology

Although since 2004 it has been possible to register as a chartered sports and exercise psychologist, this is another developing area in which there is no approved route to qualification. Most psychologists who have the expertise to offer a service in sports psychology have taken a postgraduate research degree or have trained in another area of applied psychology.

Training (general) Three-year (sometimes four-year) degree course, accredited by the British Psychological Society (BPS), and leading to their Graduate Basis for Registration. The composition of the courses varies: some lead to BA, some to BSc. Topics usually covered include: experimental study of such cognitive processes as thinking, perception, learning and memory; biological basis of behaviour; animal behaviour; individual differences; social and developmental psychology; personality and intelligence; applied and specialist areas (clinical, educational, occupational, health, etc.); statistics and research methods. Graduates from other subject fields can also gain eligibility for the Graduate Basis for Registration by taking a conversion course, accredited by the BPS, to gain eligibility for the Graduate Basis for Registration.

Postgraduate courses are essential: approved postgraduate training courses are listed on the BPS website (see 'Further information').

- Clinical psychologists take a three-year full-time Doctorate training course. Applications to clinical courses are centralized by the Clearing House for Postgraduate Courses in Clinical Psychology (*www.leeds.ac.uk/chpccp*).
- Educational psychologists must first achieve the Graduate Basis for Registration and demonstrate relevant experience of working with children within educational, childcare or community settings; they then take a three-year full-time professional training course leading to a Doctorate in Educational Psychology (in Scotland an MSc in Educational Psychology – two years full-time and one year's supervised practice).
- Occupational psychologists take a general psychology degree followed by a one-year full-time Masters degree and two years' supervised practice. Alternatively psychology graduates can take the BPS postgraduate professional training course as well as complete three years' full-time supervised practice.
- Forensic psychologists need either an accredited MSc (one year full-time) in Forensic Psychology plus Stage 2 of the BPS Diploma in Forensic Psychology (two years' supervised practice) or Stages 1 and 2 of the BPS Diploma in Forensic Psychology. Applicants for

the prison service are required to attend a national assessment centre (for further information see *www.hmprisonservice.gov.uk*).

- Counselling psychologists take an accredited course or an independent plan of learning leading to the Qualification in Counselling Psychology.
- Health psychologists need either an MSc in Health Psychology (one-year full-time) plus Stage 2 of the BPS Qualification in Health Psychology (two years' supervised practice) or Stages 1 and 2 of the BPS Qualification in Health Psychology.

Personal attributes Interest in individuals' development and behaviour; an interest in scientific method; the ability to work well on one's own, but also to work as part of a team and to cooperate with people from different backgrounds; patience; numeracy.

Mature entry and career change No problem for qualified late entrants to degree courses who have the required entry qualifications; maturity and relevant work experience can be an asset. Owing to competition, and the length of training, mature applicants without normal entry requirements may have difficulty finding a place. GCSE or equivalent in maths is essential. An Open University degree in psychology may be the best bet.

Work–life balance Returners may find competition from newly qualified people (particularly for academic posts). Some opportunities for part-time work and job-sharing.

Further information
The British Psychological Society, St Andrew's House, 48 Princess Road East, Leicester LE1 7DR.
www.bps.org.uk

Related careers *nursing: Mental Health/Learning Disabilities – personnel/human resources management – social work – sociology – teaching*

Psychotherapy and Counselling

Psychotherapy and counselling are included in this guide because of the interest in and confusion about these occupational areas. The explanations given do not fit into the format used in the rest of the guide.

PSYCHOTHERAPY

The term psychotherapy has two meanings: it is an umbrella term for various forms of treatment for patients with emotional or psychological problems through dialogue with a skilled practitioner. Its aim is to help patients change the way they manage their problems. In this context, psychotherapy covers several methods which differ in intensity and underlying philosophy. The term psychotherapy is also used to define an occupation, but one without agreed entry requirements, qualifications or career structure (except for child psychotherapy, see below). It is never a career option for school-leavers or college-leavers but invariably a 'second' or 'Mature entry and career change' career for people with relevant qualifications, work and life experience.

Persons with a range of qualifications (or none) practise psychotherapy:

- *Psychiatrists*: They are medically qualified doctors (see p. 371) who have subsequently qualified for membership of the Royal College of Psychiatrists. Psychotherapy is only one of a range of treatments they use (drug therapy is another). Most psychiatrists work in the NHS, some work partly or entirely in private practice.

- *Psychoanalysts*: They normally have a medical degree or comparable qualification (some are also qualified psychiatrists); they have undergone lengthy personal analysis and then taken an approximately four-year (part-time but very time-consuming) training in Jungian, Freudian or similar psychoanalytical method. Although not a registrable profession, it is generally agreed that in this country only people who have qualified for membership of the Institute of Psychoanalysis or the British Psychoanalytical Society, whose members are qualified to belong to the International Psychoanalytical Association, are entitled to call themselves psychoanalysts or analysts. Very few analysts work in the NHS; most are in private practice with, possibly, some sessional work for voluntary advice centres. Psychiatrists who practise psychotherapy, analysts and those clinical psychologists (see p. 473) who do some psychotherapeutical work are all sometimes called psychotherapists – which is the reason for the confusion surrounding the term.

- *Psychotherapists*: At present anyone, whatever their qualification (if any), may use the title 'psychotherapist', a fact which rigorously trained psychotherapists very much regret. There are so many psychotherapy organizations and philosophies that agreement on a common training or accreditation scheme is very difficult. However, there are now two self-regulatory and registration bodies: the British Confederation of Psychotherapists (BCP) and the United Kingdom Council for Psychotherapy (UKCP). Although registration has not yet been made mandatory, both bodies have been in discussion with the government. The mainstream organizations, however, base their treatment on psychoanalytical methods. Their professional bodies accept for training only candidates with relevant degree or comparable qualifications and experience; require them to undergo lengthy personal analysis or therapy and then train them much as do psychoanalytical organizations. Courses last a minimum of three years part-time. In fact, psychoanalysts' and psychotherapists' training and work shade into each other (though psychotherapists more often than analysts also treat people in groups – families, couples, fellow-sufferers such as addicts, phobics, etc.). About a dozen universities now run courses for psychotherapists. Some are broad based; some are run in partnership with professional associations.

There are some jobs for psychotherapists in the NHS (particularly for child psychotherapists, see below); mostly they rely on private patients and – very few – voluntary organizations' clinic sessions.

Because there is a growing demand for help for people with problems, a vast number of self-styled psychotherapy organizations have sprung up over the last few years. Some are experimenting with new methods of 'alternative psychotherapy' in good faith, but the methods and the credentials of some organizations are dubious. Before signing up for training (often expensive, and/or too short and not rigorous enough to be of any value) potential psychotherapists must thoroughly check organizations' claims.

The above refers to what is called 'adult psychotherapy'. Child psychotherapy is a recognized profession (though a very small one). Child psychotherapists treat children for psychological disturbances of behaviour, thinking and feeling. The work is focused on the relationship established between the psychotherapist and the child, through which insight into the problem is gained. Children, adolescents and parents are seen, usually individually, sometimes in groups. Child psychotherapists work in child guidance clinics, young people's advice and treatment clinics, and in private practice. To be accepted for training with one of the six accredited organizations, candidates must have a psychology degree or comparable qualification and experience of work with normal children. Training, a mixture of theory and practice and including extensive observation of young children, takes four to five years. There is a growing demand for child psychotherapists in the National Health Service, but to work in the NHS child psychotherapists are required to have registered with the Association of Child Psychotherapists.

COUNSELLING

This is a much over-used and therefore vague term. It is best defined as the skill of helping normal people, through discussion, to decide how best to cope in specific situations. By listening attentively and without passing judgement the counsellor gives clients the opportunity to explore, discover and clarify how and why they feel as they do; they (the clients, not the counsellors) may then be able to make choices and decisions about their situation which they were incapable of making before.

While psychotherapists may try to change patients' personalities, or at least their attitudes, sometimes over a long period, counsellors tend to deal with immediate, often practical problems, e.g. redundancy or alcohol addiction. Yet psychotherapists' and counsellors' work may overlap, as they use similar methods. Psychotherapists more often deal with severe psychological disorders, especially if working in hospitals, but in private practice both may see patients with similar problems.

Counsellors work in many settings – schools, colleges, GP practices, clinics, counselling centres, staff welfare departments, as well as in private practice. There are counselling services that specialize in particular groups, e.g. young people or ethnic minorities, or in specific problems, such as drug addiction or AIDS. The number of full-time posts is increasing, but there are more trained counsellors than there are jobs. Many combine part-time work with social work, welfare rights work and administration.

There are a few full-time training courses for teachers, social workers and others working in the field. There are many more part-time courses leading to a certificate or diploma. These mostly expect people to have a degree or a professional qualification. The British Psychological Society now has a counselling psychology division and accredits courses. For people hoping to do counselling as volunteers and not looking for a vocational qualification there are part-time introductory courses, courses in counselling skills, and specialist courses for example in bereavement, cancer, child abuse counselling.

Although there is no legal requirement for counsellors to be properly trained, people interested in the work are advised to contact the British Association for Counselling for advice (address below).

Further information

British Association of Psychotherapists, 37 Mapesbury Road, London
NW2 4HJ.
www.bap-psychotherapy.org

London Centre for Psychotherapy, 32 Leighton Road, Kentish Town,
London NW5 2QE.
www.lcp-psychotherapy.org.uk

Tavistock Clinic, 120 Belsize Lane, London NW3 5BA.
www.tavi-port.org

Association of Child Psychotherapists, 120 West Heath Road, London
NW3 7TU.
www.acp.uk.net

British Association for Counselling and Psychotherapy, BACP House,
35–37 Albert Street, Rugby CV21 2SG.
www.bacp.co.uk

UK Council of Psychotherapy, 2nd Floor, Edward House, 2 Wakely
Street, London EC1V 7LT.
www.psychotherapy.org.uk

British Confederation of Psychotherapists, West Hill House, 6 Swains
Lane, London N6 6QS.
www.bcp.org.uk

Society for Analytical Psychology, 1 Daleham Gardens, London
NW3 5BY.
http://jungian-analysis.org

Related careers *psychology – social work – teaching*

Public Relations

Entry qualifications Usually a degree, not necessarily in a related subject.

The work Public relations specialists advise on ways to develop relationships with sections of the public whose support and goodwill is essential for the success of an enterprise. Public relations is part of the marketing mix, but is specifically about protecting and promoting reputation. Public relations is more than a publicity tool – it is an essential part of successful management in an increasingly competitive environment. Public relations officers provide factual stories about clients or their product to newspapers, magazines and television, thus keeping the product or the service in the news and creating a 'favourable climate or image'. They answer journalists' questions about their client's product, views or services, and may take journalists to see the client's product or service. They arrange receptions, exhibitions and other projects to 'put over' a client or promote a cause, and give talks to interested groups – schools, women's organizations, etc. They deal with inquiries (and also complaints) from the public as well as working in areas such as community and stakeholder relations. In recent years they have begun to share (with human resource management professionals) and in some cases lead on internal communications.

Public relations specialists work either in public relations consultancies (between 2 and 30 partners each with their own accounts and a shared office and staff), in public relations departments of advertising/multi-service agencies, or in separate press and public relations departments of individual organizations. More and more organizations employ PR specialists to advise on and put into action ways of communicating the organization's functions and activities to relevant groups. Today, local authorities, employers' federations, charities and professional organizations such as the British Medical Association employ public relations or information officers. In the Civil Service they are called information officers and work in nearly all departments, where they usually specialize in either press or publicity work. Hospitals, schools and universities increasingly make use of PR. Other important areas include financial PR and public affairs; some sporting and TV personalities also use public relations officers to help further their careers.

Entry into PR is highly competitive; far more people want to do this sort of work than there are opportunities, although really talented people are sought after. There has been a growth in the number of small, independent consultancies in the last few years.

Training Competition for jobs is such that it is now very difficult to get into PR by working oneself up from a junior position, such as secretary. The following are all possible entry routes:

- A sideways move with a degree and work experience in a relevant discipline or industry (e.g. engineering or science). Traditionally many PR people moved sideways from journalism and this is still a possible route.
- As a trainee with a PR firm or in a PR department with a non-specialist degree. Useful degree subjects are business studies, economics, languages, communication, but employers will take promising people from any discipline.
- With a degree or postgraduate diploma/degree in PR. The Chartered Institute of Public Relations (CIPR) recognizes over 40 university and college courses as leading to awards which qualify the holder for associate membership of the Institute. (A list of these courses is available on the CIPR website.)

Work-based training is through intensive or part-time study, or through distance learning, and leads to CIPR qualifications at Advanced Certificate or Diploma level. The Advanced Certificate in Public Relations is aimed at graduates interested in pursuing a career in public relations or those who have been working in the business, at fairly junior levels, for at least two years. The postgraduate Diploma in Public Relations is for more experienced professionals or those without an industry specific qualification and provides advanced capability in management and practice. The CIPR Diploma is the major vocational qualification for membership of the Institute.

The CAM Foundation's Diploma in Marketing Communications includes a public relations module. Entry qualifications are a degree or relevant professional qualification plus two years' experience.

Personal attributes Ability to get on exceptionally well with people of all kinds, whether hard-hitting journalists or less confident members of the public; enterprise and initiative; good news sense; sense of salesmanship; a calm temperament; analytical powers; ability to write and speak well and persuasively; imagination; tact; ability to keep polite under provocation and/or pressure.

Mature entry and career change Possible for people with special expertise/experience. Approximately a quarter of CAM students are aged 30+.

Work–life balance Well-established PR professionals can work from home, perhaps having only one client for a year or so, then gradually increasing their workload.

Flexible working is usually possible in the public sector or larger companies and part-time work may be possible in small, non-commercial (i.e. usually voluntary) organizations.

Further information

Chartered Institute of Public Relations, 32 St James's Square, London SW1Y 4JR.
www.cipr.co.uk
CAM Education Foundation, Moor Hall, Cookham, Berkshire SL6 9QH.
www.camfoundation.com

Public Relations Consultants Association, Willow House, Willow Place, London SW1P 1JH.
www.prca.org.uk

Related careers *advertising – civil service: Information Officer – fashion and clothing – journalism – marketing and selling – secretarial, administrative and clerical work*

Publishing

Entry qualifications In practice a degree or comparable qualification and/or specialist knowledge/experience; design training for some aspects of production. In specialist publishing, such as educational, scientific or art, editorial assistants normally have a degree in a relevant subject. In general publishing, the degree subject is normally irrelevant.

The work This expanding, multi-media and multi-format industry, the UK's largest creative industry, requires business acumen and an interest in marketing (see p. 490) as much as creativity and literary flair. More than 100,000 new book titles were published in the UK in 2006. In the same year, UK publishers sold more than 750 million books, worth over £2.5 billion.

Book and magazine publishing are the two principal sectors in this industry: they differ in organization and approach, although there are similarities in job roles.

BOOK PUBLISHING

The function of book publishing has been described as extending the writer's idea into a finished book and getting it into readers' hands – in other words publishing involves the organization of production, marketing and distribution as much as (and in many cases more than) literary effort.

Publishing companies, or 'houses', vary greatly in size, from large ones with overseas branches and several 'imprints', producing hundreds of titles a year, to those run on a shoe-string with a handful of employees and a small yearly output. The trend is towards 'multi-national' companies with large houses buying up smaller ones, but keeping their identities fairly separate. Many are now owned by US companies. Some publishers specialize in educational, scientific, art books, or paperbacks. Desk-top publishing (DTP), in which editor, designer and production staff handle text and illustration on disk at different stages, is widely used. Many organizations use DTP to produce publications for their own use and also for books which have very limited sales. In some cases one person can carry out all the tasks from start to finish.

Publishers select and commission manuscripts, design the appearance of the books, have them printed and bound, and promote and sell the finished copies, but the internal organization of 'houses' varies. The process is usually divided into three main departments (apart from the usual commercial ones, such as accounts). The division of work is more rigid in some houses than in others; in small houses everybody may have to do anything that needs doing (a good way of learning). The increase in DTP has tended to break down demarcation barriers.

The three main book publishing functions are editorial, production and marketing.

Editorial

Main duties are identifying publishing opportunities and commissioning authors. Increasingly agents working for authors play a large part and fewer books are commissioned from scratch. Editors are responsible also for getting outside specialist readers' opinions; preparing typescripts (or disks) for the printer; liaising with authors, possibly suggesting changes; dealing with contracts, copyright, subsidiary rights (these may be separate departments). Editorial departments also deal with new editions of existing books.

An editorial director or chief editor (titles and responsibilities involved vary greatly in different houses) is usually in charge. Individual editors may each be responsible for books on a special subject, or for a range of subjects. They may initiate a book on a special subject, select the author and deal with the project right through. The number of books one editor deals with at any particular moment varies according to type of firm and type of book, and so does the amount of contact the editor has with the author.

Editorial assistants and 'copy-editors' deal with 'copy preparation'; checking facts and references, spelling, punctuation, and possibly doing some rewriting, proof-reading and correcting. Again, responsibilities and duties vary greatly. Increasingly this work is done by out-of-house freelancers under the editor's management.

Indexing is a specialist area within publishing and many indexers work on a freelance basis. For further information contact the Society of Indexers, Woodbourne Business Centre, 10 Jessell Street, Sheffield S9 3HY. Website: *www.indexers.org.uk*

Design and Production

In larger publishing houses there may be a separate art department. In others designers work in the production department. The production department receives the edited typescript and decides in consultation with designer and editor on the appearance of the book, on the shape, typeface, paper, illustrations, etc.; the production department deals with printers, paper merchants, binders, etc. Staff must understand all aspects of costing and marketing and of the various types of illustration and typography. But above all they must understand the new printing and production technologies which are drastically changing established production methods. Technical and textbook publishers may employ their own illustrators, but most artwork, including illustrations and book jackets, is commissioned from freelancers and outside studios.

Marketing and Sales

In some ways the most important publishing activity, marketing or 'promotion' is responsible for planning, researching for and preparing review lists, sales campaigns, writing 'blurbs', and for the representatives who call on bookshops, schools, libraries, etc. to give information on forthcoming books and to collect orders. Marketing staff make representations to key accounts and there is a heavy emphasis on public relations. In addition, marketing people in many houses now often initiate projects, based on feedback gained by the sales representatives when they visit bookshops. On the basis of a 'feasibility study' – mainly researching the market and costing – it is decided whether to go ahead and, jointly with editorial, get the book commissioned, or whether to abandon the idea. This is a good department in which to learn how publishing works.

There are many more posts in non-editorial than in editorial departments.

Book Packaging

This is a small, but growing development outside traditional publishing. Packagers are marketing specialists. They find an idea which is likely to be profitable, commission an author and artwork and produce a dummy copy of the book. They then offer it to publishers, usually in several countries. 'Packages' are usually highly illustrated; a 'bank' of pictures is printed separately and then overprinted with the translated text with the minimum production expense. Promotion, selling and distribution are done by the publishers who buy the packaged book. Packagers' overheads are lower than traditional publishers' and it is therefore easier to start up as a packager than as a publisher. Good contacts, publishing experience and ideas are essential.

MAGAZINE PUBLISHING

With more than 2,500 consumer and special interest magazines produced in the UK, this is an important part of the publishing industry. But the 'glossy' consumer titles are only one aspect of magazine publishing. Other expanding sectors include customer publishing ('brand-based' loyalty magazines given to customers by a wide range of companies), business titles and directories and the rapidly increasing production of online magazines (often produced in parallel with 'paper-based' publications rather than as a replacement).

The principal magazine publishing activities include: feature editors need to be able to write original copy; editorial assistants must be able to 'sub' (reword, shorten, etc.) other people's writing. They all need to know something about layout and production, as well as to understand the business side of magazines (including advertising). Most magazines have a 'publisher' responsible for the business side: the usual background is in advertisement selling, but some publishers are ex-editorial staff.

Other roles include production, with designers who may work as members of an art department in larger organizations (see p. 104) and advertising sales specialists (who must generate sufficient revenue to maintain the title in print).

There are very limited opportunities on the editorial side of magazine publishing, which attracts the most applicants, especially in general publishing; more scope in technical, scientific, educational. First editorial job is usually as editorial assistant ('assistant editor' may mean the same thing). Opportunities are slightly better in other departments, especially in sales, marketing and production.

Sector opportunities are often on a freelance or short-term contract basis.

Training (generally) There are a small number of pre-entry courses, some of which are for graduates, and a growing number of degree and diploma courses in publishing. There are training courses in book production and design, and some art and design courses include book design and production (see p. 104). Pre-entry training is recommended especially for these departments. A few firms run their own training schemes, but most rely on short in-service courses provided by, for example, the Publishing Training Centre at Book House. Some of these courses are also useful to prospective applicants. Some companies offer work experience opportunities – these are occasionally mentioned on specific company websites. Previous bookselling or other sales experience is useful.

Personal attributes Creative ability; interest in social and economic as well as literary trends; ability to see books as a marketable commodity; some writing ability; critical judgement; common sense; resilience; good business sense; willingness to take responsibility and make decisions; ability to get on well with a wide variety of types of people.

Mature entry and career change Difficult because of the competition from young graduates, but possible in technical and educational publishing for people with technical/scientific background.

Work–life balance A career break should be possible but it is advisable not to give up completely, even temporarily. Experienced proofreaders, copy-editors, editors may be able to do freelance work.

Further information
Publishers' Association, 29B Montague Street, London WC1B 5BW.
    www.publishers.org.uk
Scottish Publishers' Association, 137 Dundee Street, Edinburgh EH11 1BG.
    www.scottishbooks.org
The Publishing Training Centre, Book House, 45 East Hill, Wandsworth, London SW18 2QZ.
    www.train4publishing.co.uk
The Periodical Publishers Association, Queen's House, 28 Kingsway, London WC2B 6JR.
    www.ppa.co.uk
Individual publishing house websites: many organizations, such as Penguin Group, have a dedicated careers section (see *www.penguin. co.uk*).

Related careers *art and design – bookselling – information science – journalism – printing*

Purchasing and Supply

Entry qualifications For professional qualification: National Qualifications Framework Level 3 (A levels, BTEC National awards) or
Scottish Credit and Qualifications Framework equivalent. Also
graduate entry. No specific qualifications for mature entrants with
relevant work experience (see also 'Mature entry and career change')
but see 'Training', below.

The work A company's supply, or value, chain stretches from sourcing its raw materials, via the supply market into the organization,
then out through internal customers to the end-user. Purchasing and
supply management is the link in that chain which manages the
interface between the supply market and the organization. Its importance lies in the fact that a company can spend more than two-thirds of
its revenue buying in goods and services, so even a modest percentage
reduction in purchasing costs can have a significant effect on profits.

Essentially purchasing and supply management involves working
with the company's internal customers to identify their requirements
and then obtaining the necessary products and services by negotiation
and agreement with suppliers. The primary objective is to obtain
value for money. This does not always mean achieving the very lowest
price – sometimes other commercial considerations are more important.

A well-qualified purchasing professional can walk into a wide range
of environments where they can use their skills to buy a whole range of
products. For example, in a manufacturing environment such as a car
plant, the purchaser would be directly involved in buying components such as glass, shock absorbers or in-car entertainment for the

production line. In a financial services company, purchases might well be for telecommunications systems, catering services and marketing services including advertising and design. A less conventional case is retail purchasing where the role is slightly different. Here some purchasers within the organization buy goods for use by the company itself, such as office furniture, electricity, etc., whereas other buyers are more involved in merchandising because they are responsible for selecting products which are sold in the shops themselves.

The choice of jobs within purchasing and supply management is vast as it is a role which is carried out by all organizations, including central government, local councils, charities as well as commercial companies. A need to influence people and achieve targets means there is plenty of intellectual stimulation, but the working environment is highly competitive. The range of specialist areas within purchasing and supply management includes purchasing, contracts, materials management, production planning, logistics and distribution, and systems implementation.

Training The Chartered Institute of Purchasing and Supply has six qualifying levels, equating to specific job roles, beginning with the Introductory Certificate in Purchasing & Supply. To achieve full CIPS membership, candidates have to complete or be exempted from level 4 Foundation Diploma and level 5 Advanced Diploma, gain the level 6 Graduate Diploma and have three years' professional experience.

There are various methods of studying for the Graduate Diploma, including evening classes, distance learning through correspondence course, a self-study programme and modular training, which consists of a series of intensive tutorial days.

Graduates of the degree courses in purchasing and supply that are accredited by CIPS can gain full membership after three years' professional experience.

A non-examination route to CIPS membership is also available through NVQs/SVQs in Procurement at levels 2, 3 and 4.

Personal attributes Numeracy; organizing ability; practical approach to problem-solving; considerable business acumen; ability to establish friendly relationships quickly; judgement to gauge the right approach to individual suppliers; networking abilities; awareness of technological changes and their implications for purchasing.

Mature entry and career change Good opportunities. People with previous work experience are welcome. Graduates and others with relevant experience are granted substantial exemption from CIPS exams.

Work–life balance A career break should not present problems, but keeping in touch with world economic conditions and commercial law is vital. Short Institute courses can be used as refreshers. Temporarily retired individuals pay reduced Institute subscriptions.

Opportunities for part-time work are good and job-sharing is possible.

Further information

The Chartered Institute of Purchasing and Supply, Easton House, Easton on the Hill, Stamford, Lincs PE9 3NZ.
www.cips.org

Related careers *logistics, distribution and transport management – retail management – surveying: Quantity Surveyor*

Radiography

Entry qualifications Degree course requirements: one or even two sciences, at either GCSE or A level or equivalent, may be required; BTEC/SQA awards or other qualifications may be accepted in lieu. It is essential to check with individual courses. There are accelerated courses for graduates.

Registration with Health Professions Council (HPC).

The work Radiography has two branches: diagnostic and therapeutic.

Diagnostic Radiographer

They work in diagnostic imaging teams with radiologists, who are doctors with specialist qualifications. They are involved with the whole range of imaging techniques, including the use of ionizing radiation to produce x-rays, medical ultrasound, magnetic resonance imaging, nuclear medicine and others. Radiographers have to be skilled in the operation of complex equipment. They must understand not only how to use imaging techniques, but the theory behind them. In addition, they have to produce reports on the images obtained to aid their diagnosis. Radiographers, therefore, need a considerable knowledge of anatomy, physiology, physics and radiation science.

They work in hospital x-ray departments and on occasions use mobile equipment in wards. They may also be asked to produce x-ray images during operations, when it is particularly important to obtain fast, high-quality images.

Diagnostic radiographers normally see patients only once or twice, but often in traumatic circumstances. They must, therefore, be skilled in patient care techniques, especially in gaining patients' cooperation and explaining procedures.

Therapeutic Radiographer

They are a crucial element in the cancer treatment team. They work with oncologists, doctors with specialist qualifications in the treatment of cancer. They carry out treatment by means of high energy ionizing radiation and sometimes drugs.

Treatment is often given over a long period of time. Radiographers must be expert in the giving of the treatment and also highly skilled in dealing with seriously ill and often worried patients. Cancer treatment is increasingly being seen in a 'holistic' way, i.e. as treatment of the whole person, not just the illness, and this is affecting the way radiographers work, just as it does other members of health care teams. Specialist Macmillan radiographers work with patients in their own homes and take a leading role in the patient's all-round care, with responsibility for other issues such as counselling. They need extensive knowledge of human anatomy and physiology and of radiation physics.

Exposure to x-rays can be dangerous, but x-ray departments are equipped with safeguards which ensure that operators are not harmed in any way. The controls are operated from outside the treatment rooms so that the radiographer is never exposed to radiation; treatment rooms are lined with material which the x-rays cannot penetrate.

There have been shortages of radiographers, especially therapy specialists. The majority work in hospital. There are a few posts in private practice. Radiographers can earn their living in most countries of the world, provided they speak the appropriate language. There is a considerable number of post-registration courses and opportunities to specialize in the newer techniques of medical ultrasound, nuclear medicine and magnetic resonance imaging (used in both diagnosis and treatment of various diseases).

Training An approved three-year (four-year in Scotland and Northern Ireland) degree at university. About 50 per cent of the course is clinical, i.e. spent within the clinical environment working with patients. Students train as either diagnostic or therapeutic radiographers.

The NHS funds most radiography places and eligible students may have their tuition fees paid in full and be able to apply for a means tested bursary.

Before they can practise, both diagnostic and therapeutic radiographers must be registered with the Health Professions Council.

Personal attributes Strong scientific aptitude; a steady hand and a sharp observant eye; a genuine liking for people and a desire to help the sick; a cheerful, confident manner; patience; calmness; firmness; ability to take responsibility and to work well with others; good health.

Mature entry and career change The number of mature applicants is increasing. Entry requirements may be relaxed. See also p. 16.

Work–life balance There are limited opportunities for returning to the NHS but refresher training is often essential – extent depends on length of break (changes in procedures and equipment are drastic and rapid). Refresher courses are available. Flexible working arrangements should be available for NHS employees.

Further information
Society of Radiographers, 207 Providence Square, Mills Street, London SE1 2EW.
  www.sor.org and *www.radiographycareers.co.uk*
NHS Careers, PO Box 2311, Bristol BS2 2ZX.
  www.nhscareers.nhs.uk

Related careers *radiology – photography – science*

Retail Management

Entry qualifications No set requirements; all educational levels from National Qualifications Framework Level 1 to degree, or Scottish Credit and Qualifications Framework equivalent.

The work Retailing is one of the largest industries in the UK, which it is anticipated will create a further quarter of a million jobs by 2012. Tesco is the largest private sector employer in the UK. This is also one of the few career areas where getting on does not necessarily depend on passing examinations.

No industry-wide career structure exists. Titles, and responsibilities attached to titles, vary from one company to another, and so do recruiting and promotion procedures. The main types of 'retail outlet' are hypermarkets and supermarkets; department stores; chain stores; cooperatives; independents. These categories are not as clear-cut as they used to be and the sector is continually evolving. Supermarkets and multiples have diversified by selling more than one type of merchandise; some department stores give floor space to specialist shop units; some independents have joined for bulk-buying purposes; retail parks continue to prosper, many combine retailing, entertainment and leisure facilities.

Online, or e-retailing, is expanding significantly. A recent survey by the Interactive Media in Retail Group concluded that 15 per cent of all UK retail spending was made online in 2007, and that e-retail sectors such as electronics and clothing were expanding rapidly. Companies include specialist 'pure-plays' which trade exclusively online and the 'multichannel' high street retailers that have developed major retailing websites.

Other types of retailing include:

- *franchising*: a centrally controlled retail group, often in foods and fashion sectors, sells the right to use its name and image to individual 'franchisees', who then operate their own businesses
- *mail order*: typically in fashion and household goods, including traditional 'catalogue companies' which sell through part-time agents, and 'direct marketing' companies which sell through media advertising.

In traditional retailing, buying and selling organization varies from one company to another. For chain stores, hypermarkets and supermarkets buying is usually done centrally: identical merchandise is allocated to stores which are also given display and promotion guidelines. In department store groups, buying is also done centrally, but individual outlets still have their own distinctive character.

There are varying hierarchies from sales assistant, shelf-filler, checkout operator, warehouse clerk, via section, department, specialist (transport, staff, distribution, etc.), deputy to store manager, and after that perhaps area manager. Job titles, and job functions, vary from one retail concern to another. Speed, and likelihood of promotion, varies from company to company, and according to age and ability.

Retail Management

Many people going into retailing hope to become buyers or store managers. While these positions are still very popular, there are now other sought-after activities in retailing such as merchandising, personnel, marketing, new product development and IT. Nearly always these require people to have A levels or a degree. Specialists, such as fashion graduates (see p. 244), food technologists (see p. 520) and electronics experts (see p. 213) are sometimes recruited as trainee-buyers.

Managers coordinate the various retailing functions: stock control; security; staff deployment; maximizing profit per square metre of premises; dealing with customers' complaints and queries; liaising with head office, etc. Supermarket and department store work differ greatly; supermarkets are much more hectic places with emphasis on fast-moving goods; managers must make their own, quick decisions, whether they are dealing with a staff, delivery or customer problem. In department stores, managers have such 'support services' as personnel, distribution and complaints departments on the premises and there is more emphasis on personal service. Hypermarkets and chain stores again make different demands. Ideally prospective retailers should decide which type of atmosphere and work is right for them. In practice, there may not be much job choice, but one can switch from one type of retailing to another: basic retail expertise is a 'transferable skill', although it is easier to switch from supermarkets to chain stores than the other way around.

Staff management and training may have its own hierarchy, parallel with store management, and it may be a step on the store management ladder (see p. 434).

Buying and Merchandising

Major retailers employ teams of buyers and merchandisers. *Buyers* select from suppliers' existing lines and also, jointly with manufacturers, developing new ideas, and adapting existing lines and prototypes bought or seen abroad or at a competitor's at home. Buyers work closely with marketing and production specialists and with store managers. Buying policies are based on methodical analysis and interpretation of past sales figures; on economic forecasts; on demographic trends (the present ageing population and the reduction in the number of late-teenagers have important implications for buyers); on lifestyle changes (the trend for more casual than formal clothing; the growing interest in healthier lifestyles; increasingly exotic foreign travel and resultant interest in foreign food and drinks, etc.). The work involves complex decision-making. For example, a buyer may find a very efficient and inexpensive spin-dryer with an unsatisfactory after-sales service. 'Does good performance and competitive pricing outweigh less-than-perfect after-sales service?' is the kind of decision buyers have to take – and be able to justify later, if customers complain.

Merchandisers tend to work at a policy level, forecasting departmental sales and profits and determining the budgets within which buyers operate. The work of both buyers and merchandisers involves constant decision-making and assessment of information. While merchandising is usually a senior head office job, confusingly it can mean different things in different companies. It can also describe people employed by wholesalers or manufacturers who ensure that their employer's products are adequately displayed in retail outlets. And it can describe persons who, working closely with display specialists, are responsible for the display of goods in a store.

Head office roles

Major retail companies undertake planning and policy-making centrally. The work includes general management (see p. 346); marketing (see p. 362); design (see p. 105); food science and technology (see p. 520); personnel (see p. 434); store planning; and retail analysis. As retailing is becoming ever more sophisticated and professionalised, new specialisms emerge, or traditional jobs are being fined down into separate functions. For example, 'transport management' may be divided into 'vehicle and depot management' and 'operations management' with responsibility for the movement of goods from supplier or port of entry to depot or store (see also p. 340).

Retailing also offers good opportunities to systems analysts and other computer experts (see p. 280) as more companies adopt computerized 'point of sale' stock-control and 'electronic fund transfer' systems and introduce computer-based armchair shopping. There are openings for computer science graduates or other computer-literate graduates able to work well in a team designing and modifying databases and making systems more user-friendly.

Training Many employers, including most of the larger companies, train staff systematically. External courses and in-house training schemes produce 'retail professionals' with transferable skills (i.e.

trainees who can later use their training in all kinds of retail companies). Other companies give little career training, but teach people to perform specific jobs in their organization. While promotion up the retail hierarchy does not depend on having paper qualifications, the importance of expertise is growing enormously, as technological and management systems are becoming ever more sophisticated; such expertise can, in practice, only be acquired by systematic training. However, there are many ways of training. It is generally agreed that the best way of becoming a retail professional is to learn on the job, with additional off-the-job training and being assessed for NVQs/SVQs (see below). That means finding a job with day release or similar facilities for taking courses.

Individual company training schemes vary greatly. All retailers stress the flexibility of their training schemes and emphasize that no specific qualification or training scheme automatically leads to any specific point on the retail job ladder. Individual patterns vary not only from one company to another, but also from one year to another according to company plans for expansion or consolidation/contraction or change of emphasis, and also according to current views on which type of training (length, outside or in-house course, theory-and-practice mix) is the most cost-effective. Companies may recruit young people at National Qualifications Framework Level 1 and 2 (GCSE, BTEC awards), NQF Level 3 (A levels, BTEC National awards) or Scottish Credit and Qualifications Framework equivalent, or offer graduate training schemes. Candidates are strongly advised to look at several companies' recruitment literature, to read the small print and, at interviews, ask questions about promotion prospects, etc.

Qualifications are offered at different levels. Sales staff in many companies work towards NVQs/SVQs levels 1 and 2 during their training. Levels 3 and 4 are established at supervisory and management level.

Apprenticeships are sometimes available for young people wishing to enter retailing straight from school.

BTEC courses in distribution and retail management are also widely available, both full-time and part-time, for those already working in the industry. Candidates with four GCSEs (A–C) can take a BTEC National Certificate (or Scottish equivalent), usually two years full-time, or National Diploma, two years full-time or three years part-time, which are both recognized as an entry qualification for most junior management training schemes run by major stores. For those with the BTEC National or with an A level, BTEC/SQA offer Higher National courses in retail management for those aiming at senior-level jobs.

Degrees in retail management are available at a number of universities and are increasingly recognized and requested by large retail companies.

Graduates are often expected to be ready for their first junior management job within a year. Degree subject is immaterial, and Higher National Diplomas (BTEC or Scottish equivalent) are usually considered as of equal value to degrees. Many companies recruit applicants to management training schemes with A level, or equivalent qualifications. Training patterns are as varied, and as confusing, as this.

Personal attributes Numeracy; an outgoing personality; an interest in both people and things; organizing ability; communication skills; commercial awareness. For *store management*: leadership qualities; ability to delegate and take decisions quickly and to keep calm in crises; physical stamina. For *buyers*: interest in social and economic trends; negotiating skills; objectivity to be able to judge the relevance of one's own taste and gauge that of customers. For *buyers* and *merchandisers*: good mathematical and analytical skills.

Mature entry and career change Good opportunities. Most companies positively welcome people who have had work experience, and will train people of up to about 35 for management. BTEC/SQA courses also welcome mature students and distance-learning courses are available.

Work–life balance Most companies encourage returners and provide refresher training.

There are ample opportunities for flexible working up to supervisor level, and increasingly also at management levels. With lengthening shopping hours, several managers share store management anyway, so it is quite possible to organize part-time and job-sharing at management levels. Head office jobs, including buying and merchandising, can also be done at 'less than full-time'.

Further information

Skillsmart, the Retail Sector Skills Council, 93 Newman Street, London W1T 3EZ.

www.skillsmartretail.com

Individual retailing concerns.

Related careers *hospitality and catering – management – logistics, distribution and transport management – personnel/human resources management*

Science

Entry qualifications Scientists and technologists usually enter at first degree or postgraduate level, but the borderlines between scientist, technologist and senior technician are often blurred; many technicians are graduates.

Degree course entry is usually at National Qualifications Framework Level 3 (A levels, BTEC National awards) or Scottish Credit and Qualifications Framework equivalent. Precise degree course requirements vary from one course to another. A level or equivalent qualifications should include: for physics, cybernetics and applied sciences degrees – physics and maths; for chemistry degrees – chemistry and physics and/or maths are preferred, but other combinations may be acceptable: for biological sciences degrees – biology, a physical science (preferably chemistry) and maths are ideal but other combinations may be acceptable.

Major fields include physics, chemistry, biological sciences, cybernetics, materials science, nanotechnology, biomedical and healthcare sciences, food science and technology, environmental sciences. There are major developments in all scientific fields, particularly in newer interdisciplinary areas such as genomics, robotics, artificial intelligence, nanotechnology.

Main functions or activities include research and development; analysis and investigation; production; technical sales and service; technical writing; education.

Science practitioners

Scientists who use their scientific training and education directly in all kinds of science-related fields can be described as practitioners. In countless research projects, they extend the frontiers of knowledge – in space and astronomical investigations, bioengineering, nanoscale science, etc., there is a huge variety of research areas. Then there is work for scientists who want to solve problems thrown up by scientific developments: excessive use of energy requires alternative sources; chemical industries have led to pollution of the environment. Biotechnologists, chemists and other specialists investigate and try to alleviate undesirable but inevitable side-effects of innovation. And then there is, of course, the vast, mainly physics-based, information technology industry and its spin-offs, to give just a few examples.

Prospects in the various functions vary mainly according to economic climate. In research and development, cutbacks tend to bite much earlier than in manufacturing and analysis and investigation. Many scientists only specialize in a function after graduation, although some degree subjects are more likely to lead to one function – applied scientists are generally more likely to be in demand in manufacturing than, for example, botanists, and a broad-based integrated course is not likely to lead to research.

Scientists may start their careers in a research and development role, later moving into manufacturing, technical sales and service, or writing; or they may use their science background in marketing, information science, patent work or operational research. Teachers of maths and most sciences are much in demand in schools.

Career prospects are generally much better for graduates who have at least a reading knowledge of a foreign language. Anyone who wants to work in EU countries must be fluent in the relevant language and/or have specific experience. Short-term contracts are possible in developing countries.

Science as a Tool

Scientists can equally choose not to practise as scientists, but to use their understanding of science as a tool with which to do other kinds of jobs – in commerce, industry, the public sector – more effectively. People who have scientific curiosity but are not sure whether they want to be scientists, can choose a science qualification confident in the knowledge that their scientific background will be a 'door-opener' into a variety of jobs in many different settings. For example, a scientist who goes into stockbroking or merchant banking is likely to become skilled at market forecasting and better able to assess a new high-technology company's chances of success, or the advantages or disadvantages of a merger between two science-based companies, than someone without a scientific background who has to go by hunch, or someone else's advice. A senior civil servant with a scientific background is better at advising ministers on, for example, the implications of rapidly changing technology when discussing the future of, say, transport, or the health service, or defence expenditure, than someone without. There are dozens of similar examples.

In industrial and commercial management and in marketing, science graduates are usually welcomed. A scientist's analytical approach to problem-solving is invariably useful even when the problem is not a scientific one. Scientists with communication skills are above all badly needed to close the communication gap: to explain basic relevant scientific facts, trends and implications to their scientifically illiterate colleagues – many of them in senior roles.

The work of practising scientists can be divided in two ways: by the types of activities or 'functions' and by the various 'branches' or specialist fields:

THE MAIN FUNCTIONS OF SCIENCE

Research and Development

Research is the lifeblood of science, enlarging existing knowledge and stimulating the growth of new branches. Development translates research findings into new – or improved – products and processes. The two overlap.

The terms 'pure' and 'applied' are often used to describe the type of research undertaken. In this context 'pure' research means increasing knowledge for its own sake and 'applied' research is 'goal-orientated' – directed towards solving technical problems, improving national defence or prestige – or 'wealth creating'. Science research is very expensive to carry out, much of it is sponsored, by industry or government, and is goal-orientated. Some university departments may fund 'pure' research from their resources or through research studentships which lead to higher research degrees (MPhil or PhD).

Most research is teamwork, with several scientists, often from several disciplines, and technicians, working under a team-leader or supervisor. The work may be divided into projects; several scientists are then responsible for their own project within the overall framework.

Personal attributes include above-average intelligence; enthusiasm; willingness to work patiently for long hours (or even months) and persevere with tricky problems; creativity; ability to work in a team and to take decisions and stand up for them if things go wrong; ability to communicate findings effectively; great powers of concentration; stubborn persistence in the face of disappointing research results. Industrial researchers must be willing to change direction – at however interesting a point in their research – in the interests of the company's profitability.

Analysis and Investigation

Routine tests and investigations are carried out in all fields of science. In chemical research, for example, analysis of intermediate compounds enables scientists to keep track of chemical changes that are taking place. In manufacturing industry, the composition of both raw materials and products is monitored by analysing samples in quality control laboratories. In the food industry, regular checks are made on biological and chemical purity of foodstuffs. In pharmaceuticals the safety of drugs, beauty preparations and food additives is investigated. Before some products can be marketed, substances are tried out by tissue culture or on experimental animals to see whether there are any toxic side-effects. In the agrochemical industry, new fertilizers and pesticides are given field trials; the chemicals are used on experimental plots in various parts of the country – and sometimes overseas – so that scientists can determine how performance is affected by different soils and climates.

Many analytical techniques are automated; most routine testing is carried out by technicians. The professional scientist trains and supervises technicians, initiates, organizes and oversees projects and researches into new experimental methods.

Personal attributes Interest in applied science; methodical approach; patience; ability to organize other people and their work; ability to communicate effectively with highly specialized colleagues and with trainee technicians; observation to recognize the unexpected.

Manufacturing Production
(see also *engineering*, p. 213)

The central activity in industry is organizing production which involves supervising the people who operate the industrial plant. Production managers (titles vary) are a vital link in the chain of command from chargehand to production director, and between production and other departments. Their main function is to see that production runs smoothly and is as efficient as possible. That means they must keep up with technological developments and arrange for and supervise the installation of new equipment as necessary. Hours can be long and irregular, and may include some shift work – but this is by no means so in all plants. Production managers usually have a small office, but they spend little time in it. The work involves daily contact with other professionals and managers from other departments as well as with supervisors, etc.

Production professionals are equally concerned with managing people and with the exploitation of new technologies. The largest opportunities are for chemists. Production managers, or whatever the title of persons in charge, are normally graduates; technicians work under them. Production specialists can switch from one type of plant to another; and they can later go into marketing or general management.

Personal attributes Willingness to accept responsibility and take decisions; ability to keep calm in a crisis; leadership skills to motivate and organize plant operatives; practicality; ability to get on well with people at all levels in the industrial hierarchy; interest in the commercial application of science.

Technical Sales and Service

Two closely related activities: selling a science-based product and providing a technical back-up service for the customer. The product might be a sophisticated scientific instrument, an industrial chemical, a drug or a pesticide. The customer could be a research scientist, an industrial manager of a tiny or a large concern, a pharmacist or a farmer, i.e. a person with a lot of or no scientific knowledge. The technical sales executive or 'rep' needs a thorough knowledge of the product, its uses and limitations. The kind of technical service a company provides depends on the nature of its products. A technical service scientist representing a plastics manufacturer deals mainly with customers who mould plastics into containers and would investigate complaints and answer technical queries (and perhaps suggest new ways of using the material). It is part of the job to act as a link between the research laboratories and the sales staff.

Representatives for pharmaceutical firms visit doctors and pharmacists and inform them about new drugs and also provide feedback to the company on doctors' opinions of its products. In agricultural service industries reps may sell fertilizers, pesticides and animal health products to farmers and give advice about how they should be used (see p. 64). Reps are usually given a 'territory'; its size depends on what they sell and whether it is a country area or town:

some reps may be away from home all week; others come home every night. Many work from home and only go to the office occasionally.

Personal attributes Outgoing personality; liking for meeting a succession of people; a thick skin for the occasional rude customer; sensitivity to gauge the right approach (long-winded, brief, aloof, friendly, etc.); ability to communicate facts effectively to customers who may be much more, and may be much less, knowledgeable than the reps themselves; self-sufficiency for possibly long hours of lone travelling.

Technical Writing

A technical writer assembles a package of scientific or technical information for a particular readership. The work is often done on a contract basis; specialist firms hire out technical writers to client companies for the duration of a particular writing project. This may concern, for example, a set of handbooks and instruction manuals to accompany a complex piece of electronic equipment which is being marketed by an electronics manufacturer. Two 'packages' may have to be written: one in simple language for operatives or chargehands who have only to know how to operate the equipment; and another package aimed at technical managers who want to know more technical details and may need to be able to repair or adjust the equipment. In the pharmaceutical industry, writers prepare 'case histories' of new drugs (experiments done, etc.) for submission to the Committee on Safety of Medicines.

Technical copywriters (see Advertising, p. 56) may write promotional material for science-based products. This is an expanding field, particularly in electronics, engineering generally and pharmaceuticals.

Personal attributes Wide scientific/technological interests and knowledge; an inquiring mind; ability to search out information and sift the relevant – for the particular purpose – from the irrelevant; ability to explain complex matters lucidly and concisely; a scientific grasshopper mind, to switch from one type of subject to another; liking for desk-work.

SPECIALIST FIELDS

The classification of science into content areas is constantly changing. Most people are familiar with physics, chemistry and biology, but more detailed classifications have evolved as scientific investigation increases in complexity and application. Traditional disciplines frequently overlap into distinct specialist fields, such as biophysics or biochemistry, and other interdisciplinary areas have developed their own concepts and methods of study, including nanotechnology, cybernetics, materials science and biotechnology.

The following descriptions are intended to introduce some of the main career fields, although they rarely exist in isolation. Food scientists, for example, may be working in association with chemists and agricultural scientists on a crop project that also requires the expertise of materials scientists, who will develop an improved packaging method based on the work of nanotechnologists and molecular scientists.

Physics

The study of matter and energy is fundamental to science. It is closely related to maths and also quite closely to chemistry – chemical physics, or the study of materials and molecules, is a subject in its own right. Biophysics – the physical properties of living matter – has assumed greater importance as biological knowledge has grown. Many aspects of engineering and materials science are 'applied' aspects of physics. So the physicist, who always has a sound mathematical background, has a wide choice of occupations and settings in which to work.

Many industrial openings occur in engineering and related industries – especially in electronics, telecommunications, computing and transport; other opportunities exist in chemical and energy industries, e.g. oil, gas, electricity. In the Civil Service physicists work on problems ranging from research into navigation to recycling industrial waste.

The work of medical physicists is increasingly important to medicine. They form part of a team of specialists concerned with the diagnosis and treatment of disease, using radiotherapy and diagnostic radiology, radioisotopes, ultrasonics and many other physical methods to help doctors cure patients (see p. 497 and p. 216). In occupational hygiene, physicists help prevent damage to people's health by monitoring potential hazards from radiation, noise, dust and other sources in working environments (see also p. 518). There are very limited opportunities for physicists (who may or may not have taken a degree in astronomy or astrophysics) and for mathematicians to branch out into astronomy. Research into such aspects of astronomy as satellite communications systems or the structure of the universe is undertaken at government, university, and some commercial telecommunications research laboratories. In computer design and manufacture, physicists play an important part.

Chemistry

Chemistry involves the study of the composition of materials, their properties and how they change and react with other materials, and occupies a central position in the sciences. It forms the basis of, for example, the manufacture of metals, pharmaceuticals, fertilizers, paints, synthetic fabrics, dyestuffs, plastics, paper, cosmetics, herbicides, pesticides, foodstuffs and many other products.

It has links with all the other sciences, such as physics, biology and geology, and contributes to 'applied' science areas such as food science, forensic science, materials science, pharmacology and pharmacy, and textile technology. So someone with an interest in chemistry has a wide choice of employment. The major chemical manufacturers, oil and pharmaceutical companies are the principal employers of chemists. In the Civil Service, chemists may work on building materials, road surfaces, nutrition, pollution, and other research; others are employed as forensic scientists; in the general

Civil Service they use their expertise in an advisory capacity and as background knowledge. Others work in the public health field, e.g. analysing drinking water, food and drugs, and in hospital laboratories. A few chemists work on restoration and research in museums (see 'Biochemistry and Microbiology' and 'Biotechnology' below.)

Biological Sciences

Biology can be subdivided into four major disciplines – the study of: plants (botany); animals (zoology); micro-organisms (microbiology); chemistry of living matter (biochemistry). However, as the interdependence of plants and animals is increasingly recognized, more emphasis is being placed on biology as an integration of botany and zoology, e.g. ecology. More specialized biological sciences deal with particular groups of living organisms – viruses (virology) and insects (entomology) for instance – and with particular biological processes such as the functioning of the body's organs (physiology) or the mechanisms of heredity and variation (genetics).

The most marketable aspects of botany and zoology are those related either to medical and pharmaceutical research (such as parasitology and physiology), or to agriculture and horticulture (such as plant pathology and entomology). Opportunities in marine and freshwater biology and general ecology are limited. However, concern for the environment has meant an increase in jobs in industry for 'environmental' biologists. The Department for Environment, Food and Rural Affairs employs marine biologists to monitor fish stocks and pollution levels. A small number of biologists work in the public services, for water authorities and museums. In industry there are limited opportunities in pharmaceuticals and agrochemicals.

Biochemistry and Microbiology

Biochemists and microbiologists may appear to have better career prospects than botanists or zoologists; there is a steady demand from industry (mainly food, drink, pharmaceuticals and agriculture), from medical research and hospital laboratories, specialist research organizations and, to a lesser extent, the Civil Service.

Microbiologists often specialize in bacteriology and virology and become experts in plant or animal diseases. In the food industry and in environmental health laboratories they check samples for pathogenic microbes and investigate spoilage. In oil companies they explore ways of producing synthetic protein by feeding bacteria with the by-products of petroleum refining.

A biochemist working for a pharmaceutical company might study the mechanism of a new drug or (helped by a microbiologist) investigate biochemical aspects of the production of antibiotics by fermentation. Hospital biochemists work alongside medical colleagues and technicians as members of a team: they supervise routine biochemical testing, do research into, for example, the function of hormones or the body's defence mechanisms, and may also teach clinical biochemistry to doctors and nurses. Some use biochemical analysis in clinical diagnosis or in forensic laboratories, such as for genetic fingerprinting.

Biotechnology

This is a more recent academic discipline involving the use of living organisms to perform a useful task. The main uses are in manufacturing industry (particularly brewing and the food, fertilizer, animal feedstuffs and pharmaceutical industries), medicine, agriculture and horticulture.

Biotechnologists work in a vast variety of science-based jobs, for example on the development of synthetic proteins; of new strains of wheat; of hormones and drugs. They also work on pollution control (e.g. with biodegradable waste products), and on the generation of new sources of energy from such varied natural materials as plant tissue and animal waste products. The usual way into biotechnology is via a science degree – preferably chemistry, biochemistry or microbiology – followed by postgraduate study, or a biotechnology degree. Genetic engineering – the manipulation, using scientific techniques, of genes – is one aspect of biotechnology. It is increasingly used to produce varieties of crops which are especially resistant to disease or tolerant of poor weather. Molecular biology – the understanding of how genetic information is stored and passed on – has opened up vast new areas of research.

Biomedical and Healthcare Science

Biomedical scientists undertake laboratory investigations of body fluids and tissue samples to diagnose disease, monitor its medical treatment and research into its causes and cure. Their work ranges from cancer screening and HIV diagnosis to global infection control programmes. Specialist fields include clinical chemistry: the analysis of blood and other biological materials; medical microbiology: the isolation and identification of bacteria and viruses from patients with infections, or in water and foodstuffs; haematology and serology: the study of blood; histopathology and cytology: the study of tissues removed during surgical operations and at post-mortem examinations, and in investigations for the early detection of cancer.

Healthcare scientists in physiological sciences use advanced equipment to measure and evaluate the functioning of body systems and organs. Specialist fields include audiologists evaluating hearing and balance, cardiac physiologists evaluating mechanical and electronic functioning of the heart, perfusionists managing heart–lung machines during open-heart surgery, neurophysiologists monitoring brain activity and vascular technologists using ultrasound techniques to assess and treat artery and vein diseases. There are many other specialist fields.

Biomedical and healthcare scientists usually work as members of a medical team and may also be involved in treatment and long-term patient care. They work in hospitals, National Health Service and private sector laboratories, blood transfusion centres, public health laboratories, medical research organizations and commercial companies. Scientists may supervise medical laboratory assistants.

Biomedical scientists are a state registered profession. Entrants require a degree approved by the Health Professions Council plus successful completion of a period of training. Entrants with non-accredited degrees in related sciences can study for an accredited postgraduate qualification possibly augmented by further learning before working towards the Certificate of Competence.

Materials Science

Materials science is concerned with developments in a vast range of metallic alloys and non-metallic polymers, fibres, ceramics, glass, electronic components and textiles. Metallurgists work on the extraction, refining and fabrication of ferrous and non-ferrous metals used in products ranging from aircraft bodies to electronic components. Textile technologists work with domestic materials, such as clothing and furnishing fabrics, and with industrial products ranging from insulation to artificial veins. Polymer scientists and technologists work on all kinds of plastics and other polymeric materials used in products used throughout industry.

Materials scientists are crucial to the development of medical replacement part surgery, developing advanced materials that can mimic the mechanical functioning of body parts – from joint replacements to artificial heart valves and blood vessels. Others are creating ever more efficient ways to store, communicate and display digital information – from hand-held iPods to global communications systems.

It is possible to specialize early in metallurgy, polymers, textiles or one of the other non-metallic materials, but most entrants to these industries have followed a more general course in materials science, or have a broader background in physics, chemistry or engineering. Much of the work requires interdisciplinary skills.

Nanotechnology

Nanotechnology can be described as the science of manipulating atoms and molecules into new formations. It is an application that is expanding rapidly to become an essential scientific tool, particularly in fields such as agritechnology, biotechnology, materials science and food technology where it is creating new products that are lighter, smaller, stronger or more effective – often at lower cost. Altered molecular structures can provide the basis for manufacturing foods with improved nutritional value, taste and shelf life, 'smart packaging' that can detect and even counteract food deterioration, new construction materials that are stronger yet lighter than any existing products, ways of capturing solar energy more effectively – and countless further applications.

Nanotechnology fields are commonly entered at postgraduate level, following specialist research by graduates from a range of scientific disciplines.

Cybernetics

Cybernetics involves the structure of complex systems such as communication processes and control mechanisms, and is closely linked to computer science, electrical and electronic engineering, mathematics, neuroscience and psychology. Its principles can be used in robotics to create machines capable of imitating human behaviour, in neuroscience to help understand how information is moved and processed in the brain, and even in operational research to study how organizations can operate most effectively. Entry is from a wide range of scientific disciplines (see also 'Operational Research' p. 359, 'Mathematics and Statistics' p. 368, and 'Psychology' p. 472).

Food Science and Technology

Food science is concerned with the chemical and biological nature of food and its behaviour under natural conditions, during processing and during storage. Food technology is the application of relevant sciences, including engineering, to the processing, preservation and development of raw materials and manufactured foods. Food scientists and technologists work in quality control, product development and production departments of food manufacturers and retailers. They also work for equipment manufacturers, ingredient suppliers, public analysts, environmental health departments and the Civil Service. Some work in research and development on 'fast foods' and 'systems catering' (see p. 256), monitoring the behaviour of foods as new technologies are introduced. Some work together with bio-technologists. Some research jobs are for food scientists, production jobs tend to be held by technologists; but there is no clear-cut division between the two and both types of specialists are found in most job areas. There are jobs for technicians and for graduate scientists and technologists.

Entry to technician level training is usually at National Qualifications Framework Level 3 (A levels, BTEC National awards) or Scottish Credit and Qualifications Framework equivalent. Part-time day release, full-time, or sandwich awards in various aspects of food science or technology are available at National Qualifications Framework Levels 4 and 5 (Foundation degree, Higher National awards or equivalent). Apprenticeships are also available.

Entry at scientist level can be with a degree in food science. These courses vary in title; some courses are commercially orientated (combining food science and marketing for example) and others more science-based or technology-based. While food science and technology degrees are strictly vocationally orientated, science and engineering graduates can also enter the food industries and then take postgraduate qualifications, either by part-time or full-time study. There are postgraduate courses in food science; food analysis and composition; food and management science; food microbiology; food engineering; biotechnology.

Environmental Sciences
(See also *environmental work*, p. 237)

Concern with climate change, pollution, dwindling natural resources and threatened plant and animal species has given a fresh impetus to the scientific study of the environment. Conservation and ecology, the study of how plants and animals interact with their natural surroundings, together with meteorology, oceanography, geology and geophysics, are important environmental subjects.

Environmental science is often a postgraduate specialization: scientists take a first degree in a traditional subject and then either graft on an appropriate postgraduate course or are trained by employers in environmental aspects of their subject. Meteorologists and physical oceanographers usually have degrees in physics or maths; biologists normally take a specialist course (for example, in ecology or marine biology) before becoming conservationists. Geoscience graduates are the exception: they can go straight into professional work without further training. But there is an increasing number of first degree courses in environmental subjects – either joint honours (such as physics and meteorology) or broad-based integrated courses in environmental sciences. The most useful of these are probably those offering a placement year in which students get 'hands-on' experience. Even graduates with an environmental science degree often need to take a more specialized postgraduate course and/or gain voluntary work experience before applying for paid jobs.

Conservation
(See also *environmental work*, p. 237)

Nature conservation used only to mean protecting unusual plants and animals and their habitats. Now, many human activities have a wider environmental impact. Crop protection chemicals, for example, can upset the balance of ecological systems. If herbicides are used to control aquatic weeds, dead plants consume oxygen while decaying. As a result, fish and other organisms may die through lack of oxygen. A pipeline or bypass laid across country may disturb plant and animal life around it; a quarry may leave a permanent scar on the countryside. Modern conservationists, recognizing the importance of protecting flora and fauna, are concerned with the wider problems of preserving the countryside as a whole.

Conservancy bodies for England, Scotland and Wales between them manage over a hundred National Nature Reserves and several thousand Sites of Special Scientific Interest, and advise farmers, landowners, local authorities, industrialists and others on conservation matters. Scientists (mainly biologists, botanists, zoologists, geologists and geographers) are employed as Assistant Regional Officers. The Nature Reserves are run by wardens (not always graduates) who are experienced conservationists. Environmental research covering land, ocean and fresh water is carried out by the many institutes which come under the aegis of the Natural Environment Research Council (NERC).

Geosciences

Geoscience covers all branches of science concerned with the structure, evolution and dynamics of the earth and with the natural mineral and energy resources that it contains. It comprises geology, geophysics and geochemistry. Geoscience investigates the real world beyond the laboratory and is directly relevant to the needs of society. Its study develops a wide range of skills useful in a wide range of careers, with opportunities in the UK and abroad.

Activities carried out by geoscientists include geological mapping, geophysical prospecting, geochemical sampling, borehole logging, chemical analysis of rocks and minerals, rock testing of geotechnical properties, computer processing of data, computer modelling of geological processes and of subsurface geology.

Meteorology and Oceanography

Meteorology and oceanography, which are concerned with the atmosphere and the oceans, are closely related. The physics and dynamics of atmospheric and oceanographic processes have much in common; the oceans exert a powerful influence on the weather. At honours degree level, meteorology and physical oceanography are highly mathematical; numerical methods are widely used in modern weather forecasting.

The Met Office also carries out research into such topics as the physics of cloud formation and energy exchange between atmosphere and oceans. Scientists are usually involved either in forecasting or in research.

Research in physical oceanography is undertaken at the National Oceanographic Centre, Southampton (part of the Natural Environment Research Council). Topics include studies of waves, tides, currents and general circulation of ocean water. NERC also investigates the ecology of deep-water organisms, the composition of the sea-floor, marine biology subjects. Oceanographic work is done partly in the laboratory and partly at sea.

Scientists in the Civil Service

Scientists in the Civil Service may be involved in research and development; they may also provide scientific services, statutory advisory and inspection duties and scientific contributions to the formulation of government policies. Within these broad areas of work is a vast range of activity and interest covering aspects of life as diverse as the 'food we eat, the air we breathe and the weapons that defend us'.

Technicians in the Civil Service work as part of a team led by a scientist engaged in research in any of the scientific disciplines. In laboratories scientists carry out fundamental research, investigate new techniques and equipment, ensure that standards of safety are maintained. Technicians provide support to research and project teams. Their work includes making observations of experiments, logging data, summarizing results for interpretation (see p. 153).

Science Technician

Minimum entry qualifications are usually at National Qualifications Framework Level 3 (A levels, BTEC National awards) or Scottish Credit and Qualifications Framework equivalent. Some technicians enter at National Qualifications Framework Level 5 (Foundation degree, Higher National awards or equivalent) or Level 6 (Bachelors degree or equivalent).

With the complexity of modern scientific investigation, science technicians are key members of most research teams. They are essential team-members working under the supervision of a scientific team leader, often using advanced technologies and analytical techniques. Job titles vary considerably, from laboratory technician to research assistant or scientific officer. They may work in any of the functions and branches of science.

Opportunities in industry frequently include quality control (QC): during the production of chemicals, detergents, plastics, cosmetics and other manufactured goods and in the food processing industry, technicians test, for example, the purity or nutritional value of food-stuffs. In the pharmaceutical industry they help with tests on drugs and medicines.

Training in laboratory skills is available through a wide variety of in-house and distance learning schemes leading to a range of awards from National Qualifications Framework Level 3 (National Diploma or equivalent) to level 6 (Bachelors degree or equivalent). There are opportunities for more advanced specialist qualifications.

Technicians also work in education, helping researchers, teachers and lecturers. They work in higher education science faculties, in research institutes and medical schools, secondary schools and colleges. They may prepare specimens for demonstrations and lectures, assemble and maintain laboratory apparatus. In research they may specialize in various analytical techniques.

Training (generally) Normally a degree: science courses usually consist either of a detailed study of a single subject, with supporting ancillary subjects, or of a study of two distinct disciplines in a joint honours course, or of a cluster of several related disciplines, such as biological sciences. The question of whether a broad-based or a specialized degree leads to better prospects is impossible to answer in a general way: it depends on an individual's adaptability, motivation, specialization, on changing economic circumstances and on technological developments. There is a continuing need for specialists, but a 'generalist' scientific education possibly leads to a wider choice of jobs especially for 'non-practising' scientists; its built-in flexibility enables the scientist to change direction if, for example, that should be desirable or necessary after a career break, or because supply and demand in a specialization have changed.

For research a first or upper-second honours degree is usually required but research assistants who work part-time for a PhD are occasionally taken on with a 2:2. A first degree may have to be followed by a career-orientated postgraduate course. First-degree course emphasis varies greatly. Some courses are very much more practical and vocational in approach and structure than others, and prospective students need to do careful research before applying.

Many degrees are four-year sandwich courses, with a year spent at work. This may be an advantage to people who want to go into industry: their experience of the work situation during their training reassures employers that the applicant at least knows what a working environment is like.

An increasing number of full-time undergraduate courses extend to four years and lead to a Masters degree, for example MSc, MChem, MPhys. Anyone intending to do research would be advised to choose one of these.

National Qualifications Framework Level 5 awards (Foundation degree, Higher National awards) or Scottish Credit and Qualifications Framework equivalent may lead to senior technicians' rather than to professional scientists' jobs, but the distinction between scientist and technician is often blurred.

Once in a job, training, or at least learning, continues. This may or may not lead to a further qualification.

Mature entry and career change Degree course entry requirements may be relaxed, but candidates' knowledge of maths and science has to be up to date; many late entrants first take evening classes or other preparatory courses to freshen up their school sciences, etc. Opportunities limited.

Work–life balance Opportunities for flexible working and career breaks are more hopeful for those employed in the public sector as both the Civil Service and the NHS are encouraging all departmental managers to support applications for flexible working. The NHS in particular encourages returners, often providing refresher courses. A list of Workforce Development Confederations who can assist those wishing to return to a health care science profession is available on the NHS careers website: *www.nhscareers.nhs.uk*. For those in the private sector, it will depend very much on company policy and individual circumstances.

Further information

Biochemical Society, 16 Procter Street, London WC1V 6NX.
www.biochemistry.org

Royal Society of Chemistry, Burlington House, Piccadilly, London W1J 0BA.
www.rsc.org

Institute of Biology, 9 Red Lion Court, London EC4A 3EF.
www.iob.org

Institute of Materials, Minerals and Mining, 1 Carlton House Terrace, London SW1Y 5DB.
www.iom3.org

Institute of Biomedical Science, 12 Coldbath Square, London EC1R 5HL.
www.ibms.org

Institute of Physics, 76 Portland Place, London W1B 1NT.
www.iop.org

Geological Society, Burlington House, Piccadilly, London W1J 0BG.
www.geolsoc.org.uk

Institute of Nanotechnology, 6 The Alpha Centre, Innovation Park, University of Stirling, Stirling FK9 4NF.
www.nano.org.uk

Cybernetics Society, 3 Willow Grove, Welwyn Garden City, Hertfordshire AL8 7NA.
www.cybsoc.org

Institute of Food Science and Technology, 5 Cambridge Court, 210 Shepherds Bush Road, London W6 7NJ.
www.ifst.org

Civil Service Recruitment Gateway
www.careers.civil-service.gov.uk

English Nature, Northminster House, Northminster, Peterborough PE1 1UA.
www.english-nature.org.uk

Scottish Natural Heritage, 12 Hope Terrace, Edinburgh EH9 2AS.
www.snh.org.uk

Countryside Council for Wales, Maes-y-Ffynnon, Penrhosgarnedd, Bangor, Gwynedd LL57 2DW.

www.ccw.gov.uk

Natural Environment Research Council, Polaris House, North Star Avenue, Swindon, Wilts SN2 1EU.

www.nerc.ac.uk

NHS Careers

www.nhscareers.nhs.uk

Institution of Physics and Engineering in Medicine, Fairmount House, 230 Tadcaster Road, York YO24 1ES.

www.ipem.org.uk

Society for Cardiological Science and Technology, Suite 4, Sovereign House, 22 Gate Lane, Boldmere, Sutton Coldfield, Birmingham B73 5TT.

www.scst.org.uk

British Society of Gastroenterology, 3 St Andrews Place, Regents Park, London NW1 4LB.

www.bsg.org.uk

Electrophysiological Technologists' Association, Stag Gates House, 63/64 The Avenue, Southampton SO17 1XS.

www.epta.50megs.com

Society of Perfusionists of Great Britain and Ireland, The Royal College of Surgeons, 35–43 Lincoln's Inn Fields, London WC1A 3PN.

www.sopgbi.org

Association for Respiratory Technology and Physiology, Suite 4, Sovereign House, 22 Gate Lane, Boldmere, Sutton Coldfield, Birmingham B73 5TT.

www.artp.org.uk

Association of Anatomical Pathology Technologists UK, 12 Coldbath Square, London EC1R 5HL.

www.aaptuk.org

Association of Operating Department Practitioners, 197–199 City Road, London EC1V 1JN.

www.aodp.org

Institute of Medical Illustrators, 29 Arboretum Street, Nottingham NG1 4JA.

www.imi.org.uk

Royal Pharmaceutical Society of Great Britain, 1 Lambeth High Street, London SE1 7JN.
www.rpsgb.org.uk

The Institute of Science Technology, Kingfisher House, 90 Rockingham Street, Sheffield S1 4EB.
www.istonline.org.uk

Secretarial, Administrative and Clerical Work

Entry qualifications There are opportunities at various educational levels, including graduate level: minimum usually National Qualifications Framework Level 2 (GCSEs A*–C, BTEC Diplomas and Certificates) or Scottish Credit and Qualifications Framework equivalent, including English and maths, but see 'Training', below.

The work Office work consists largely of handling information – searching for, producing, passing on (verbally or in print) facts and figures, questions and answers, messages and instructions. 'Information technology' (IT), which broadly describes the equipment and systems used to process, transmit, file or otherwise handle information electronically, is an essential tool of office work.

The main jobs:

Secretary

Titles have no precise meaning: executive secretary, private secretary, personal assistant may be used indiscriminately. Some of the most high-powered secretaries prefer to call themselves merely 'secretary'; some 'personal assistants' just do typing and telephoning for junior executives.

Team secretaries (in another office they might be called 'administrative assistants') 'manage' a group of, say, several junior architects in an architectural partnership, or overseas marketing people in an export department. They organize appointments, travel schedules, etc. and keep track of the department's various projects and assignments. If the head of the department or partnership wants to know where X is, or how project Y is progressing, the team secretary knows the situation.

Both personal assistant and team secretary may in fact be junior/middle management jobs but they are not necessarily recognized as such (see p. 346). They may supervise junior staff.

The traditional secretary still usually works for one person or, increasingly, more than one. (This is of course the 'office' secretary, not the administrator in charge of an institution, learned society or similar organization (see *chartered secretary and administrator*, p. 137). It is the secretary's task to manage the boss's time and energy so that he or she can concentrate on whatever the job is at that moment.

Secretaries act as buffer between the boss and callers and phone calls, and take minor decisions on her/his behalf. They must understand their boss's work well enough to know when to act on their own initiative and when to ask for instructions. This is one of the most challenging secretarial skills.

Traditional secretarial tasks include dealing with correspondence (letters and other documents, emails); maintaining diaries; arranging meetings and sometimes taking minutes; organizing office systems and supplies; booking conference rooms; recording and instant dispatch of voice and text messages; maintenance of lists, e.g. personal addresses, business contacts, internal telephone directories; 'unstructured information', e.g. product descriptions; training records; filing and retrieval; travel arrangements. Shorthand may be a requirement – there are still executives who prefer to dictate to an individual rather than into a machine.

Bilingual or Multilingual Secretary

The work They translate incoming mail; they may compose their own letters in a foreign language from notes dictated in English, but most outgoing mail is written in English. They sometimes read foreign journals and search for and translate or summarize relevant articles. Occasionally they may act as interpreter. Their scope varies: some secretaries hardly use their languages at all; others are relied upon totally by their monolingual bosses. There are commercial opportunities abroad for truly bilingual secretaries with, occasionally, the relevant shorthand. International organizations usually require previous senior secretarial experience. Overall the greatest demand is for French, German, Spanish, Italian and Dutch, mainly in international marketing and in export. There is an increasing demand for Portuguese and the languages of new EU countries, as well as for Russian, Japanese, Arabic, Mandarin and Cantonese.

Entry requirements Entry at various levels, from National Qualifications Framework Level 3 (A levels, BTEC National awards) or Scottish Credit and Qualifications Framework equivalent, including appropriate qualification in the relevant language, to language degree. Prospective linguist-secretaries who intend to take a language degree should look out for a course including 'business' or 'studies' in its title – which means it should give background knowledge important for getting jobs abroad with commercial firms and international agencies.

Medical Secretary

The work Medical secretaries work in hospital, for one or several consultants, in consultants' private consulting rooms, or for general practitioners. They require knowledge of medical terminology and of health and social services organization. In hospital, secretaries have less contact with patients than in consulting rooms and general practice, but they have more companionship. In GPs' group practices the work involves organizing/administration.

Entry requirements With National Qualifications Framework Level 3 (A levels, BTEC National awards) or Scottish Credit and Qualifications Framework equivalent, a one-year or two-year full-time course leading to the Advanced Diploma for Medical Secretaries.

Legal Secretary

The work There is a steady demand for legal secretaries who work for solicitors, barristers, courts and legal departments in large firms. In addition to the usual secretarial and office skills they need a knowledge of law and legal procedures and the ability to prepare and process legal documents and forms. Some may specialize in areas such as conveyancing, matrimonial or corporate work, but those in small firms will handle all types of legal work.

Entry requirements The Institute of Legal Secretaries and PAs runs a diploma course which can be studied by distance learning and is assessed through tests and coursework. They also offer individual subject courses for legal secretaries wishing to specialize in one subject area. The Institute of Legal Executives offers distance-learning courses for legal secretaries at levels 2 and 3 which are assessed through assignments and an external test.

Farm or Agricultural Secretaries

The work They deal with the paperwork which modern farming entails. They fill in forms, keep accounts, keep and analyse records, and deal with correspondence, often on their own initiative. Only very big farms employ full-timers; most need part-time help. So farm secretaries either work as freelancers, spending a number of days a month on different farms, or they are employed by farm-secretarial agencies and are sent out to different farms. The work is varied, as it involves working on different types of farm. Specialist training is a great advantage.

Entry requirements Full-time or part-time course leading to the Level 3 Certificate in Rural Business Administration. The Institute of Agricultural Secretaries and Administrators runs a programme of continuing professional development.

Clerk/Clerical Assistant/Administrative Assistant

This may involve word processing and certainly a knowledge of a range of office software. Clerical work varies even more than secretarial work. Some clerical assistants work on their own all day; others are in constant contact with colleagues and/or the public. In a small office a clerk may do everything from answering the telephone and handling post and filing, to making the tea. In a large organization they may have just one or two specific tasks. In a mail-order firm, however computerized the system, clerks may check incoming orders to see whether correct money is enclosed; in a hospital or commercial office a junior may do nothing but photocopy. Clerks may work in post-rooms, collecting and distributing mail from and to various departments and individuals. In human resources departments, they may work on computerized staff records, entering details about absence, wage increases, etc.

Clerks may also become telephone operators/receptionists. The receptionist's job may be rather more complex than it appears – requiring a good knowledge of who does what in the organization so that they can direct callers to the right person or department. Hotel receptionists (see p. 256) may do behind-the-scenes accounts work as well as dealing face-to-face with clients and staff.

Training No set pattern. Training is often in-house, involving courses in specific skills/areas, available in-house or externally. The initial requirements to work in secretarial, administrative or clerical work at any level are what are now usually referred to as business skills – an appropriate level of IT literacy, i.e. to know how to use the latest office software (word processing packages, spreadsheets, databases, email and the Internet), as well as knowledge of how to operate in an office environment.

Most of these skills can be obtained at local colleges where courses including administration and office skills or office technology lead, for example, to certificates and diplomas awarded by Oxford Cambridge and Royal Society of Arts (OCR), the London Chamber of Commerce and Industry, or City & Guilds. Courses are often offered at National Qualification Framework levels and usually last a year. Private colleges also offer full-time courses or intensive courses in business skills which may be just for one day.

Qualifications at National Qualifications Framework Level 3 (A levels, BTEC National awards) or Scottish Credit and Qualifications Framework equivalent, followed by an intensive course in office skills, could be more useful than leaving school at 16 and taking a one-year course. A degree is not necessarily an advantage. Many graduate secretaries are arts graduates who, having acquired keyboard skills in the course of studying for their degree, drift into administrative or secretarial work because they could not find another job or have no clear career aim – not because many secretarial jobs are so intellectually demanding that only graduates could fill them.

Those with good keyboard skills and familiarity with the most popular office IT packages are at a distinct advantage in the job market in most fields, whatever their role. Many people these days teach themselves to touch-type, often at an early age, in order to be able to email or word process written work. However, there is still a difference between a skilled touch-typist and someone using two fingers, however expertly. It is worth looking closely at the syllabus of courses to find out how much time will be spent on these skills. There is a wide choice of typing or keyboard courses which can be studied online or bought on disk; the BBC offers a free typing course on its schools website.

Those seeking to work as high-level secretaries should still learn shorthand, at least at 90–100 words per minute, and audio-type at 50 words per minute. They must also be able to spell, know how to use, and where to find, sources of reference and have a good grasp of who does what in the commercial world, in the community, in government. They also need to be able to draft and summarize letters, reports, etc. – both verbally and in writing. Some personal assistants work in demanding environments, working closely with senior manager(s), in roles that involve considerable responsibility, including their own project work.

Personal attributes (general) Secretaries: Organizing ability, self-confidence and good telephone manner, determination and ambition; a logical brain; business acumen; willingness to take responsibility and willingness to work in a supporting role; ability to communicate easily with colleagues at all levels in the organization; willingness to work long hours.

Personal assistants: Willingness to work on own initiative alongside willingness to work in a supporting role and as part of a team; tact and discretion; strong written and oral communication skills; good time management, ability to prioritize workload and meet deadlines; resilience; business understanding and awareness; skills in research and presentation, as appropriate.

Mature entry and career change Relevant experience and appropriate skills helpful. Some courses geared to mature students are available.

Work–life balance A career break should be no problem for anyone with business skills. Numerous courses are available for those wishing to update their skills.

Good part-time opportunities in most office roles although not quite as good for secretaries, who are expected to be available whenever the boss wants them. However, even here part-time work and job-sharing are possible, but part-timers are never likely to have as wide a choice of jobs as full-timers. The fewer the hours they are willing to work, the more restricted the choice of job.

Part-time can be anything from six hours a week to four full days; two or three full, or three or four half days are the most usual. A flexible number of hours, varying week by week, is sometimes possible. There are a few jobs which can be done in term-time only, leaving parents free during the children's holidays; and occasionally some jobs offer one week (or fortnight) on, one week (or fortnight) off.

Temping is a kind of part-time work. It is particularly suitable for actors, artists, models, etc., people who have to 'fill in' while waiting for their own kind of work; for parents who cannot get a term-time-only job and for those who prefer a frequent change of environment to getting involved with one set of people and one type of work. It also gives the opportunity to try out different kinds of work, employers or sectors. Temps normally work for agencies which send them to employers on a weekly or daily basis; only those with very good contacts and experience can work as freelancers.

Further information

Association of Medical Secretaries, Practice Managers, Administrators and Receptionists (AMSPAR), Tavistock House North, Tavistock Square, London WC1H 9LN.
www.amspar.com

Institute of Agricultural Secretaries and Administrators, National Agricultural Centre, Stoneleigh, Kenilworth CV8 2LG.
www.iagsa.co.uk

The Institute of Legal Secretaries and PAs, 9 Unity Street, Bristol BS1 5HH.
www.institutelegalsecretaries.com

ILEX Tutorial College, College House, Manor Drive, Kempston, Bedford MK42 7AB.
www.ilex-tutorial.ac.uk

Related careers *civil service – health services management – hotel and catering: Hotel Reception – information technology/information systems – languages – management – personnel/human resources management – public relations – working for oneself*

Social Work

Entry qualifications Recognized degree plus registration with the General Social Care Council, in Wales with the Care Council for Wales and in Scotland with the Scottish Social Services Council.

The work Social workers help people to overcome or adjust to a wide variety of social or personal problems. They work in a variety of settings: in local authority social services departments, dealing with the problems of families and children, the elderly, those with physical and mental disabilities and the homeless; in hospitals and other health settings, dealing with those who are ill and their families; in education departments, with children who are having problems which affect their education; in voluntary agencies which supplement the work of statutory services, sometimes with particular groups, e.g. the elderly or disadvantaged children.

The training of social workers is 'generic', i.e. it equips them to deal with all kinds of social problems, in various settings, with all age and client groups. Nevertheless, on graduation and after a period of practice, there is scope to specialize in work with particular client groups, e.g. children or the elderly.

Fieldwork

Field social workers generally work with people who live in their own homes, as opposed to residential care. Most local authority social services departments (social work departments in Scotland) organize their field workers into area teams, providing a full range of services across the spectrum of client groups in a given geographical area.

Within the area team there may be specialist workers or teams dealing with particular groups. Organization and balance between 'generic' workers and specialists vary. Some generic workers become virtual specialists simply by the balance of their case allocation. The nature of the area also affects social workers' caseloads; problems occur in some areas (e.g. a large refugee population) which are non-existent in others.

The work is a mixture of counselling, liaison, mediating, monitoring and practical problem-solving. Some people who turn to social services for help have immediate problems which can be sorted out fairly quickly. For example, a family with a young baby might need a social worker to negotiate on their behalf with an electricity company so that their supplies are not cut off. Other problems require a longer-term relationship in which the social worker provides both practical assistance and counselling, helping individuals or families to identify both their problems, which are often complex and interrelated, and ways in which they might cope with them. The problems are very varied, from the stresses and problems of intractable poverty or long-term ill-health to the strains of caring for elderly relatives or children with disabilities.

Social work is very much more complex than simply offering a sympathetic ear and practical help. There is a great deal of legislation which gives social workers both responsibility and powers to act in cases where people are at risk. The most obvious example is child protection, which is a top priority at present and which can take up a large proportion of a social worker's time. Social workers must assess and monitor families at risk of neglecting or abusing their children, visiting regularly and giving support, keeping an eye on how they handle their children, perhaps referring them to a family centre to learn childcare skills and discuss their problems. Sometimes, of course, social workers decide that it is not in the children's best interests to remain with their families and must take the necessary action and provide the proper supervision. The mentally ill are another group over whom social workers have powers of removal if they become a danger to others or to themselves.

Social workers do not just sort out problems: they try to prevent them from getting worse or leading to other problems. For example, the isolation and poverty of young mothers can lead to child abuse. Social workers' preventative work can take the form of individual counselling and support, work with whole families or group work, where people with similar problems are brought together for mutual support.

The day-to-day work of a field social worker is very varied. Much time is spent visiting clients, listening to their problems, offering support and encouragement and monitoring those at risk. Most team members will have a day as duty officer, seeing clients who come into the office (e.g. seeking advice on benefits or without money to pay overdue bills) and taking calls (e.g. from a neighbour or teacher concerned about a child with unusual bruising). Time is also spent on paperwork, keeping detailed case notes, and writing reports, e.g. on a juvenile offender or for an adoption hearing. Liaison with other professionals or organizations is very important and time-consuming. For example, a social worker might have to arrange for an elderly client to have help at home, find residential accommodation for someone unable to cope alone, or track down additional complementary support from a voluntary agency.

Some field social workers within area teams specialize in, for example, adoption or child abuse cases. Others do more specialized work in a variety of other settings. Social workers in hospitals help with the problems that can arise through illness. For example, children might need to be looked after while their mother is in hospital; a family might need advice on financial assistance when the main breadwinner is unable to work; a pregnant teenager might need support and advice before, during and after the birth of her baby. Some social workers are attached to special units, such as clinics for the treatment of those dependent on drugs or alcohol, and some work in general practices or health centres alongside the family doctor, nurse, health visitor, community midwife and district nurse.

Social workers also work in day centres, adult training centres, social education centres, child guidance clinics and in the community with young people at risk. Community social workers (there is debate about to what extent they are a part of mainstream social work) work in the community to help people identify their common problems and work together to solve them, e.g. by setting up a mother and toddler group or establishing a community social centre. (With cutbacks in public expenditure this type of work has virtually disappeared in some areas.)

Social workers work with schools, dealing with the problems which prevent children benefiting fully from their education. The problems can be very wide-ranging, from inadequate transport in a country area to complex family problems leading to truancy or behaviour problems, to material or emotional deprivation. The social workers work with schools to identify the problems, establish links with the home and devise ways of overcoming the problems.

Residential Care

Some people have problems that cannot adequately be dealt with in their homes with their families, even with the other help available. These people may need residential care on a long-term or temporary basis. Residential homes vary in size, purpose and client group. They may be run by local authorities or by voluntary agencies. They may cater for the elderly, the physically or mentally disabled, single mothers or children.

The work varies greatly according to the type of home and client group. It can range from complex assessment and care in conjunction with other professionals to arranging birthday and other celebrations, to helping with basic day-to-day tasks such as dressing, feeding, shopping and so on. Counselling is also part of the job and may arise from many everyday occurrences. The aim is to help the residents to achieve as much stability and independence as possible, whether they return to their own homes or remain in care. Good residential care depends on developing good relationships with residents and effective teamwork with colleagues.

Residential care workers do not necessarily need to live in, but may be required to do so on a shift basis. Even those who live on site are not required to be on call all the time. A high proportion of workers in residential care are not qualified social workers. There are NVQs/ SVQs available for care assistants.

Training The professional qualification for social work in England, introduced in 2003, is an approved three-year honours degree course. The degree can be studied full-time, part-time, or through work-based, distance or open learning. Graduate entrants may achieve the qualification in a shorter timescale and in some cases this may be linked to a postgraduate award. As part of their degree students will be required to complete 200 days in practice settings to ensure they have the practical skills required of them before entering the workforce.

A non-means-tested bursary is available to students not supported through training by an employer.

In Scotland, since 2004, the minimum qualification is a four-year honours degree course. Wales and Northern Ireland also introduced their own degree level qualifications in 2004.

There are Apprenticeships in Health and Social Care and a wide range of NVQs/SVQs for social work support workers.

In England all social workers and social care workers are required to be registered with the General Social Care Council, in Wales with the Care Council for Wales and in Scotland with the Scottish Social Services Council.

Personal attributes The desire to help people irrespective of one's own personal likes and dislikes; the ability to communicate with every level of intelligence, cultural or social background or emotional state; perseverance in the face of apparent failure when clients/groups show no sign of improvement or appreciation of efforts made for or on behalf of them; stability; a ready understanding of other people's way of life and point of view; sympathy and tolerance of human failings; belief in individuals' potential to do better; good verbal and written skills to record and report; the ability to take an interest in other people's problems without becoming emotionally involved; a sense of humour; wide interests unconnected with social work (to keep a sense of proportion); patience and empathy.

Mature entry and career change Age is not necessarily important but maturity is essential. In 2002/03 nearly 50 per cent of entrants to social work training were over 35. Some programmes are specially designed for those with family commitments.

Work–life balance Social work returners are welcomed back. Some authorities may have formal schemes. Part-time work and job-sharing are available.

Further information

England: General Social Care Council, Goldings House, Hay's Lane, London SE1 2HB.
  www.gscc.org.uk and *www.socialworkcareers.co.uk*

Wales: Care Council for Wales, 6th Floor, South Gate House, Wood Street, Cardiff CF10 1EW.
  www.ccwales.org.uk

Scotland: Scottish Social Services Council, Compass House, Discovery Quay, 11 Riverside Drive, Dundee DD1 4NY.
  www.careinscotland.co.uk and *www.sssc.uk.com*

Related careers *careers work – nursery nurse – nursing – police – prison service – teaching – youth and community work*

Sociology

Entry qualifications Graduate entry.

The work Sociology is sometimes confused with social work, but there is a vast difference between the two. Social work (see p. 538) is a practical profession that deals with individuals and families, and the problems that they experience; sociology, on the other hand, is an intellectual discipline that tries to examine social life itself. Sociologists study the conditions that give rise to 'social problems' to understand the causes that lie behind them. Sociology is not bound by a concern for such social problems, however. Its theories and concepts are concerned with building an understanding of how societies actually work and how they change over time.

Sociologists research into the social relationships from which societies are formed. They look at the interactions between individuals, between groups, and within and among whole communities. They are concerned with how all of these change or remain constant over time. For example, sociologists who are interested in education will investigate a number of different issues. They may examine interactions between teachers and pupils in different settings (in class, on the sports field, in the street), the family backgrounds of different pupils and the inequalities that these involve, the gender and ethnic composition of pupil groups and the teaching profession, the organization of schools and local authority control over them, and government policies towards education. These various investigations allow sociologists to develop an understanding of and theories about the structure of school life, its importance in society and the problems that people may experience in the educational system.

Sociology covers every area of human social activity, including race and ethnic relations, sex and gender divisions, union–management disputes, doctor–patient relationships, crime and policing, illegal drug use, class inequalities, patterns of religious belief and practice, the organization of protest movements, sexual behaviour, family relationships and kinship patterns, the nature of the mass media, life in cities and communities, and such issues as homelessness, poverty and unemployment. Sociologists examine the institutions and inequalities of a society in relation to its changing position in an increasingly globalized world.

Virtually every aspect of modern life is of interest to sociologists, and they are usually concerned with highly topical issues. In recent years these have included the impact of new information technologies, the development of genetic and reproductive medicine, child sexual abuse, the spread and treatment of AIDS, and anti-capitalist protests.

Sociological understanding can often help to avert or alleviate social problems. Advice may be offered to employers, councils and government with a view to changing the conditions responsible for these problems. Policy-makers are not always prepared to listen to sociologists or to take their advice, and many sociologists have emphasized the critical task of sociology. By exploring the conditions responsible for the problems that are experienced by people, sociologists help to raise public consciousness about wider social issues.

Sociology is an empirical discipline: its theories are guided by the collection of information. This information is collected through a variety of research methods, such as the fieldwork techniques of observation and interviewing, the social survey, and the use of published documents and statistics. Sociological observation may involve participating in the work of an institution or an organization such as a factory, a church, or a gang, or it may mean moving into an urban or rural community and joining in the life of that community. A particular study may take many months or even years. Interviewing can sometimes be combined with observation, but is often carried out independently. This will generally involve using systematically prepared sets of questions, and many interviews take the form of an in-depth interview or life-history interview. Other kinds of interviewing are those that are carried out in large-scale surveys, using interview schedules or questionnaires. Many such surveys do not rely on interviews but involve the self-completion of a questionnaire. In much sociological research the data sources will be newspapers, government documents, television programmes, and other kinds of documents and media products. A great deal of research uses official statistics produced by government and other agencies.

Different kinds of study call for different styles of research, and sociological studies often combine two or more methods. After the information has been collected, it must be analysed, collated and interpreted, and it must be presented in sociological reports. Statistical methods are widely used, and computers are used extensively, but much research involves the qualitative and non-mathematical assessment of data. The development of theory and concepts through empirical research forms the starting point for new investigations.

Sociology is closely allied to and overlaps with other social sciences, especially social anthropology, social psychology, criminology, politics and economics.

There are far more sociology graduates than there are jobs or professional training opportunities as sociologists. Careers in research and higher education have become very scarce. However, sociology can be the basis for many other kinds of jobs, some of which involve further specific training. There are good opportunities for employment involving applied social research within health and the social services, in government departments and in voluntary agencies. Many sociology graduates go into industry, often working in industrial relations or other personnel specializations (seep. 434) and in jobs related to organizational and technological change. There are some opportunities in market research (see p. 58) and marketing (see p. 362). The police (see p. 458) welcome a sociological understanding of human behaviour, especially if a degree scheme has involved the study of crime and deviance.

Training Honours degree in sociology or in combination with other social sciences and humanities. There are courses that combine sociology with modern languages. On some business studies degrees sociology is a major option. There are also a few courses where sociology can be combined with, for example, maths, education, management or computer studies. Modularization of degree courses gives wider scope for students of all disciplines to study some sociology.

The choice of the right course is important, and complicated: the wording used to describe courses varies, and the combination of subjects covered and the emphasis given to the different aspects of sociology cannot necessarily be deduced from the title given to a particular course. It is essential to study up-to-date prospectuses. It can be useful to go by the experience of people who read sociology very recently, but be aware that changes and innovations occur very rapidly in this field.

In some universities, students begin their specialization in their first year and study the subject almost exclusively through their degree. In other universities, the first year may involve studying a number of different social sciences (economics, politics, social and/or economic history, psychology, geography, etc.), with specialization beginning only in the second year.

Personal attributes A deep but detached interest in how people live, think and behave; a rigorous and disciplined approach to contemporary social issues, rather than a purely emotional response; an ability to recognize one's own prejudices and biases, and a willingness to control them; an analytical, logical mind; the ability to discuss and write lucidly, and some basic mathematical ability.

Mature entry and career change Many mature students study sociology.

Work–life balance A career break should not cause any problems as long as would-be returners keep up with developments. There are occasional part-time research assignments. Job-sharing is possible.

Further information

British Sociological Association, Bailey Suite, Palatine House, Belmont Business Park, Belmont, Durham DH1 1TW.
www.britsoc.co.uk

Related careers *advertising: Market Research – economics – management services – nursing: Health Visitor – personnel/human resources management – police – psychology – social work*

Speech and Language Therapy

Entry qualifications Graduate entry. Some courses require specific GCSEs and A levels or equivalent. Some accelerated courses for graduates are available. Speech and language therapists are required to be registered with the Health Professions Council (HPC).

The work Speech and language therapists are specialists in communication disorders and eating, drinking and swallowing problems. They assess, diagnose and treat people with speech, language and communication problems. Around 2.5 million people in the UK have a communication disorder of some kind. Of those, 800,000 have a difficulty so severe that it is hard for anyone outside their immediate families to understand them. The aim of speech and language therapy is to help people to communicate to the best of their ability.

Speech and language therapists work with people who have difficulty producing and using speech, difficulty understanding or using language, a stammer, a voice problem, or difficulty with feeding and swallowing.

Clients may have a range of conditions including learning disabilities, physical disabilities, neurological disorders like Parkinson's disease, stroke, cancer of the mouth and throat, head injury, hearing impairment, cleft palate, dementia or psychiatric disorders. Clients can be any age, although around 60 per cent are children. Communication problems can make people feel isolated and depressed, so empathy and support are important aspects of the job. As well as working directly with clients, speech and language therapists advise and support their families and carers.

Speech and language therapists work closely with a range of other professionals from the health, education and social care sectors including doctors, nurses, psychologists, physiotherapists, dietitians, social workers, teachers and representatives from charities and voluntary organizations.

Work locations include community health centres, hospitals (wards and outpatients), mainstream and special schools, assessment units and day centres, and clients' homes. Some travelling can be involved in seeing clients, particularly in rural areas. Most speech and language therapists are employed by the NHS, others by education services or charities, and some work privately.

Qualified speech and language therapists are in demand so employment prospects are generally very good. Most newly qualified speech and language therapists work with a general caseload of clients for at least a year with appropriate support and supervision. They may then choose to specialize in the treatment of a particular group of clients or a type of clinical work. There are also opportunities to move into research, teaching or management.

Most speech and language therapists apply for more senior positions after around two years' work.

Training Speech and language therapists must successfully complete a degree or postgraduate course jointly approved by the Health Professions Council (HPC) and Royal College of Speech and Language Therapists (RCSLT). Courses are offered at eighteen higher education establishments across the UK. Degree courses last for three or four years. Postgraduate courses last for two years.

Subjects studied include language pathology and therapeutics, speech and language sciences, behavioural sciences, biomedical sciences, education, research methodology, psychology, sociology and professional issues. The practical component of the courses is very important and usually combines weekly clinical placements with periods of longer placements. These may take place in a variety of settings such as schools, hospitals and community health clinics, and are designed to develop skills in the assessment and treatment of communication disorders.

A number of degree course places are funded by the NHS and

students may be eligible to have their tuition fees paid and to apply for a means-tested bursary.

Personal attributes Good communication, listening and problem-solving skills; ability to relate to people of all ages, abilities and backgrounds – clients may suffer from behavioural or emotional problems, so sensitivity and understanding are vital; a creative and flexible approach to work with individual clients. Good negotiation skills and the ability to influence others are needed as therapists may have to advise families, carers, teachers and employers to change their behaviour, and often have to represent the interests of clients who cannot speak up for themselves. Teamwork is important, but so is the ability to work and take decisions as an individual.

Mature entry and career change Mature applicants to speech and language courses are welcome: evidence of recent study may be required.

Work–life balance Therapists who have not practised for fewer than five years and who wish to return to work must obtain two references from RCSLT members in order to register. Returners who have not worked for five years must work for a period under supervision.

Therapists who have been out of practice for more than two years need to undertake a period of updating their skills and knowledge before they can become re-registered. More details are available on the HPC website, at: *http://www.hpc-uk.org/registrants/readmission/index.asp*.

Opportunities for part-time work or flexible working depend on employer. Through its Improving Working Lives standard the NHS is committed to flexible working, including part-time, job-sharing and term-time working, as well as evening and weekend work.

Further information
The Royal College of Speech and Language Therapists, 2 White Hart Yard, London SE1 1NX.
www.rcslt.org

Speech and Language Therapy

NHS Careers Helpline: 0845 60 60 655.
   www.nhscareers.nhs.uk

Related careers *occupational therapy – physiotherapy – psychology –*
teaching: Special Needs Education

Sport

Entry qualifications No formal educational qualifications. For degree courses in sport or recreation studies: National Qualifications Framework Level 3 (A levels, BTEC National awards) or Scottish Credit and Qualifications Framework equivalent.

The work Sport can be divided into three main career areas, although many people combine two or more:

- Players or participants who are paid professionals. This guide is concerned only with those sports in which it is possible to earn a living, in particular football, cricket, tennis, golf and horse racing. However, there are also opportunities in other sports including athletics, boxing, cycling, basketball, rugby, hockey, ice hockey and snooker.
- Teaching or coaching children or adults.
- Administration (which overlaps with leisure/recreation management, p. 328).

PROFESSIONAL PLAYERS

In most cases those with sufficient talent will have been spotted well before they leave school. People whose job it is to find and nurture talent will have discovered potential players through schools, youth clubs, local and county teams. In general it is too late to start serious training for a sporting career after leaving school (exceptions are horse and motor racing which cannot be started while at school). For most people sport has to remain a recreation. Currently there are still more opportunities for men to participate professionally than for women. However, this is gradually changing as the number of women taking part in traditionally male-dominated sports, such as football and cricket, is increasing.

Recently there has been increasing regulation to ensure that young people training for a professional career in sport also receive a broad education, and new qualifications and routes which combine the development of sports skills with related vocational or academic study are being developed. An Advanced Apprenticeship in Sporting Excellence (AASE) has been introduced which leads to an NVQ/SVQ level 3 in Achieving Excellence in Sports Performance while also providing an opportunity to achieve academic or vocational qualifications. This is now available for football, rugby, golf, cricket, tennis, and aquatic sports and there are plans to extend it to other sports (see *www.skillsactive.com*). Sporting authorities now recognize that some trainees won't make it to professional level and even those who are successful can only expect a short career so all must have the basis for an alternative future.

The Talented Athlete Scholarship Scheme (TASS) is a government-funded scheme to assist and support talented athletes in their development both as athletes and students, through services and facilities provided by regional groupings of further education and higher education institutions. For more information visit *www.tass.gov.uk*.

Football

Almost all young professional footballers are now graduates of Football Academies or Centres of Excellence, where boys, from the age of 9, have access to training and support. As part of the Football Association's Charter for Quality programme all Premier League clubs must have academies and all Football League clubs must have Centres of Excellence. Scholarship programmes for 16–18-year-olds enable trainees to allocate more time to their academic education as well as developing their technical skills. There are also Centres of Excellence for women's football which develop the skills of girls aged 10–16.

In Scotland, professional footballers are encouraged and given financial help to continue with educational courses throughout their careers to prepare them for life after football.

Cricket

Most county cricketers are recruited straight from school, having already played trial matches. The England and Wales Cricket Board (ECB) licenses County Cricket Clubs to run Academies for young male players with potential to play at the highest level. Each academy supports and funds a squad of up to twelve players, between the ages of 13 and 18, each year. The non-residential intensive individual training programme covers technical, mental, tactical and physical development and lifestyle management. The ECB's National Cricket Performance Centre develops talented players for all of England's teams.

The MCC also supports six University Centres of Cricketing Excellence which provide an opportunity for potential first-class cricketers, both men and women, to study for a degree while developing their talent. Some county players each year find cricket jobs overseas during our winter, playing cricket or coaching. The rest have to find other employment in the close season. Most have stopped playing by the age of 40, although top players may stay in the game as coaches, umpires or managers.

Tennis

Most aspiring players will have started playing at age 7 to 9 (usually mini tennis at school, club or sports centre). The Lawn Tennis Association's National Performance Programme aims to identify and then develop talented players, providing a route from mini tennis to 'top player'. A training network includes nineteen High Performance Centres (HPCs), offering coaching and fitness to 'emerging players' aged 10–16. Satellite (county accredited) clubs, mainly for players under the age of 12, act as 'feeders' to the High Performance Centres. National Performance Programmes aim to balance education and tennis at junior level. The Advanced Apprenticeship in Sporting Excellence, mentioned above, is available at some HPCs. A National Competitive Framework is also being developed.

Golf

There are two distinct kinds of golfing professional: (1) the club professional (belonging to the Professional Golfers' Association); and (2) the tournament player (belonging to the PGA European Tour and, for women, the WPGA European Tour). Although some professional golfers have become successful in both areas, this is not recommended for newcomers, since intense competition within each branch requires single-minded dedication to one only.

Club professionals (around 4,000): Work at a club, running the shop, repairing equipment and giving lessons. The job requires a high level of playing ability (they have their own tournaments organized by the PGA), business flair and organizing ability. In golf there is a very clear distinction between amateur and professional status and aspiring club pros should first seek advice from the PGA before taking the plunge and forfeiting their amateur status.

The PGA offers a three-year Foundation degree programme which combines an annual five-day residential course and distance learning. Applicants should hold a handicap of four or better for men and six or better for women and at least four GCSEs or equivalent, and attend a two-day Admission Review Programme followed by an Ability Test held over 36 holes. Before being registered as trainees, potential professionals must be 18 years old and have been working on a full-time basis with a fully qualified member of the PGA.

Tournament players: Aspiring professional men players have to qualify their first season for a Player's Card by competing in a pre-qualifying school (tournament), then in the qualifying school held in Europe. To retain their Card they need to finish in the top 125 in the European tournaments that season. Only a handful of tournament players are successful enough to earn large sums through winnings and commercial sponsorship.

Women's golf is a growth area and women have their own association. Applicants for probationary membership of the WPGA European Tour must be aged 18 or over and, if amateur, have a current handicap of one (without star). Existing professionals may also apply, provided they are members of a recognized ladies' professional golf association tour. All applicants must be proposed and seconded by members of the tour.

Horse Racing

There are two kinds of races – flat and National Hunt (over jumps). Most training of stable staff for both kinds of racing stables is carried out at an approved centre such as the British Racing School, Newmarket, and the Northern Racing College, Doncaster, rather than by trainers themselves. Formal qualifications are not required; the emphasis is on personal qualities of commitment, dedication, determination, alertness, a desire to work outdoors and the confidence to live away from home. Previous riding experience is not essential but helps. Training is free to those who are EU citizens and aged 16–25.

Training, leading to NVQs in Racehorse Care, starts with a residential course at the approved centre and continues with a work placement in a racing yard. Courses cover riding, grooming, mucking out and basic care of horses along with lectures on racing topics. Training through the racing schools is open to applicants up to the age of 25. With experience lads progress to positions with more responsibility such as travelling head lad, assistant head lad, head lad, assistant trainer or trainer. A tiny minority with excellent riding skills and commitment become apprentice jockeys – the great majority remain as stable lads. Similarly, a very small number become 'conditional' jockeys (the National Hunt equivalent to apprentice jockeys). Flat jockeys are usually about 8 stone in weight. National Hunt jockeys are heavier (around 9 stone 7 lb).

There is a clear distinction between amateur and professional jockeys, with many more races for professionals. Jockeys who race on the flat or in National Hunt races must possess a licence or permit from the Jockey Club to ride. Full professional flat jockeys are aged 25 and above and are expected to achieve 25 winners per year to renew their licence for the next season. Trainers retain some, but most are self-employed. Full professional status for jump jockeys starts at age 27. Competition among jockeys is fierce and the lifestyle demanding, with most retiring by the age of 45, or younger for jump jockeys.

Women have done well over jumps and on the flat but their racing history is comparatively short. They have only been allowed to ride as professionals on the flat since 1975 and over jumps since 1976. The problem is that only those considered likely to ride winners are given rides; so until they have had success and proved themselves, they are unlikely to be chosen, which makes it hard for them to get started.

TEACHING, COACHING/INSTRUCTING
(for *PE teaching*, see *teaching*, p. 586)

Coaches and instructors in individual sports work at varying levels and in different settings, from national teams to youth clubs, from private sports clubs to local authority leisure centres. A great many coach part-time and/or voluntarily, while following another paid occupation. Full-time paid coaches are nearly all ex-professionals or leading amateurs. Some combine playing with coaching. As well as having great technical expertise they need the ability to get the best from players, to know when to sympathize and when to put on pressure. The relationship between player and coach is crucial to success.

All the sports' governing bodies run courses for coaches and instructors, e.g. the LTA Training of Coaches scheme. Colleges and universities also run courses at various levels and entry is decided on the basis of ability and commitment to sport as well as academic ability. Higher education courses include degrees in sports science, coaching, movement studies or physical education. A degree in a sports-related subject can be helpful but a coaching qualification is still essential. Sports Coach UK, the government agency which oversees sports coaching, is developing a new five-level flexible qualification, the UK Coaching Certificate or UKCC, which will endorse coach education programmes across 31 sports within the UK, against agreed criteria. For more information, including a list of sports that have been successfully endorsed, see *www.ukcoachingcertificate.org*.

A range of NVQs/SVQs and Apprenticeships are available under the umbrella heading Sport, Recreation and Allied Occupations.

SPORTS ADMINISTRATION
(excluding leisure/recreation management, see p. 330)

Most sports governing bodies have a very small paid staff. Apart from the usual secretarial and clerical posts, the administration of organizations such as the FA or Lawn Tennis Association is carried out by people with relevant expertise, either as former players or managers, or in business or public relations which could help to bring in sponsorship. There are occasional openings for people with degrees in sports science or recreation management.

Active sports careers are necessarily short. After this a minority manage to find work in some way connected with their sport (coaching, managing, promoting products), while the majority have to look elsewhere for employment. Therefore it is essential that those considering a sporting career should look ahead and reach as high a standard academically as possible while at school or college to enable them to take up another training later. This may mean combining a course of further or higher education with part-time playing (e.g. as some cricketers do). Skills in IT and general office procedure as well as in marketing are an advantage.

Personal attributes Total dedication and single-mindedness; strong competitive urge and will to win; high level of physical fitness and mental and physical stamina; ability to respond positively to criticism; resilience and willpower to cope with injuries and setbacks.

Mature entry and career change Very few sports professionals start their career in adult life. Most professional sportsmen and women begin training extensively at an early age. Successful amateurs, however, may turn professional at any point. Some sports offer more opportunities for mature entrants than others.

Position of women Sport is different from any other work area. Private clubs are not covered by all current equality legislation and, as most sport is organized by clubs, those who choose to can refuse women as members. Even the outstanding girl or woman who is good enough to merit a place in a male team and who may be the best available player can be barred and so is unable to experience the highest level of competition. A consultation paper published by the Government in June 2007 proposes that private clubs with mixed membership would no longer be able to treat women differently, but this would not apply to exclusively male organizations. Girls are often automatically assumed to be worse at sport whereas certainly at primary school sex differences are negligible (and it is at this age that serious interest and training in most sports needs to start). Men's events are generally more prestigious, better sponsored and carry higher prize money than women's. Very importantly, the media often still takes less notice of women's sporting achievements, whether amateur or professional.

However, the situation is improving and no potentially outstanding sportswoman should be put off. In certain sports the gap is narrowing between male and female achievements and each year sees a new 'first' for a woman. In 1997 the Football Association launched its Talent Development Plan for women's football as part of the FA's Charter for Quality, to provide a sound structure for the development of elite talent. An integral part of this plan is the establishment of a development structure for girls aged 10–16. Football and cricket are both examples of previously male-dominated sports where women are now able to play at county and national levels. Current UK initiatives in women's sport include the setting up in 2001 of a UK coordinating group. The strategy aims to encourage the full involvement of women in every aspect of sport, focusing on participation, performance and excellence as well as on leadership.

Further information

Sport England, 3rd Floor, Victoria House, Bloomsbury Square, London WC1B 4SE.
www.sportengland.org

The Central Council of Physical Recreation (CCPR), Burwood House, 14–16 Caxton Street, London SW1H 0QT.
www.ccpr.org.uk

Women's Sport Foundation, same address as Sport England.
www.wsf.org.uk

Football Association, 25 Soho Square, London W1D 4FA.
www.thefa.com

England and Wales Cricket Board, Lord's Cricket Ground, London NW8 8QZ.
www.ecb.co.uk

The Lawn Tennis Association, The National Tennis Centre, 100 Priory Lane, Roehampton, London SW15 5JQ.
www.lta.org.uk

Professional Golfers' Association, Centenary House, The Belfry, Sutton Coldfield, West Midlands B76 9PT.
www.pga.org.uk

The PGA European Tour, Wentworth Drive, Virginia Water, Surrey GU25 4LX.
www.europeantour.com

The British Horseracing Authority, 151 Shaftesbury Avenue, London WC2H 8AL.
www.bhb.co.uk

Sports Coach UK, 114 Cardigan Road, Headingley, Leeds LS6 3BJ.
www.sportscoachuk.org

Skills Active, Castlewood House, 77–91 New Oxford Street, London WC1A 1PX.
www.skillsactive.com

Related careers *leisure/recreation management – teaching*

Stock Exchange and Securities

The securities industry is part of the UK financial services sector which is often referred to as 'The City' and much of it is indeed based in the City of London. London is a major world centre for the trading of domestic and international securities – stock and shares – but the securities industry is truly international, with trading a 24-hour activity.

The London Stock Exchange (the Exchange) is the leading UK marketplace through which securities are traded. For UK companies to be traded on the Exchange they need to be approved or 'listed' by the Financial Services Authority and then 'admitted to trading' by the Exchange under its own rule book.

There has been significant change in the operations of the London Stock Exchange over recent years. Trading on the market floor was replaced by electronic trading via computers and telephone in 1986 and in 2001, after 200 years as a mutual, the Exchange became a Private Limited Company by listing on its own market.

All buying and selling of securities is carried out by London Stock Exchange Member Firms. These include merchant banks, clearing banks and investment banks as well as smaller private-client stock-broking and investment management firms. Since deregulation in 1986, all are brokers/dealers, able to act in both capacities. Prices for many securities are quoted on SETS (Stock Exchange Electronic Trading System), which is displayed in firms' offices, or via retail service providers, competing firms of market makers.

In addition, the City is home to the commodity markets, including the International Petroleum Exchange and the London Metal Exchange which still has a trading floor although the commodities market is now mainly computerized. LIFFE, the London International Financial Futures and Options Exchange, the exchange where derivatives (options – the right (but not the obligation) to buy or sell securities at a specified price on or by a future date; and futures – a contract to buy or sell securities or other goods at a specified future date at a predetermined price) are traded, offers a wide range of derivative products. The London Clearing House guarantees the integrity of these markets, keeps records of transactions and ensures the smooth transfer of the shares.

The financial rewards in the industry can be extremely high. But recent years have shown that the risks are also very high as firms have cut down or pulled out of trading activities – and shed large numbers of highly paid staff. Market movements are cyclical and employment can be as well.

In 2001 the Financial Services Authority was established to regulate the industry and this has brought about some changes to training and recruitment.

Entry qualifications Front-office roles: a good degree in any subject though a finance-related subject may be an advantage in particular areas such as economic analysis. Back-office or administrative roles: no specific requirements but usually at least National Qualifications Framework Level 3 (A levels, BTEC National awards) or Scottish Credit and Qualifications Framework equivalent, or a degree.

The work City institutions recruit specialists from many backgrounds, including accountants and lawyers. The industry offers a mix of roles and staff tend to work either in a front-office role dealing directly with clients, or in the back office or operations area, undertaking the administration of all the front-office transactions. The number of staff in clerical and administrative roles has fallen with the introduction of computerization but there has been an increase in demand for computer-trained staff to help in the design, development and running of the various automated systems.

The main roles specific to the securities industry are:

Traders/Market Makers

Traders buy and sell shares, bonds and derivatives. They work under a strict code of practice and may act on behalf of stockbrokers and their clients or on behalf of their own firm. For some clients they will be trying to make as much money as possible out of the transaction, for others to minimize the risk. Traders check prices on their screens, talk to other dealers, etc. on the phone and their working environment, even at quiet times, is very pressurized. Although they are fed information on which to base their decisions by researchers/analysts, it is up to them to know and make the final decision about the state of a market and to buy or sell accordingly. This is particularly true with derivatives, as traders have to predict the market at a future date.

Researchers/Analysts

Researchers provide the information on which to base advice to clients. They usually specialize in a particular industrial sector or group of companies. They develop a thorough understanding of their area by studying company reports, meeting managers, seeking out any information of relevance to the industry and keeping up to date on any news likely to affect it, analysing past, present and future indicators and forecasting future performance.

Brokers/Dealers

Brokers and dealers work for member firms, which may be based anywhere in the UK. They buy and sell shares on behalf of their clients. Some deal with institutional clients, developing long-term relationships with their fund managers. Brokers dealing with private clients may have to deal with many more clients and many more securities, since small investors may be interested in a range of companies too small to be considered by the institutional investors. Some clients follow the market themselves and require only an execution service. Others require advice on investment and brokers must thoroughly understand their clients' circumstances in order to give appropriate advice.

Fund Managers

Fund managers construct investment portfolios for their clients who may be wealthy individuals or institutions. The fund manager will have met with the client and agreed with them their investment objectives and attitude to risk. They will arrange to buy and sell stocks and shares on their clients' behalf to increase the value of the portfolios or to reduce their risk profile, or both. Because they handle large sums of money institutional fund managers are perceived to be more prestigious than their private client counterparts and will need to be highly numcrate, while private client fund managers will need to have strong interpersonal skills. Both will need to demonstrate confidence and credibility in volatile market conditions otherwise nervous clients may remove their funds. The client-facing role of fund managers may be taken by account managers whose technical expertise may be less practised but whose communication skills will be vital.

Settlement Staff

Settlement staff process the transactions arranged by the dealers. This is done through a paperless transfer system, CREST.

Compliance Officers

Compliance is an expanding area. Compliance officers ensure that their colleagues know the rules and regulations and keep to them. Since the Financial Services Authority was fully established in 2001, these have been increasing in complexity and compliance officers need the tact and confidence to be able to question colleagues about their practice and to investigate breaches if necessary.

Training On-the-job training has always been a feature of the securities industry and continues to be so. Trainees in investment business who plan to deal in securities or give investment advice normally have to pass a benchmark examination such as the Securities and Investment Institute Certificates, which meet the requirements of the Financial Services Authority (FSA) for 'approved person' status. Study for front-office roles is usually via intensive face-to-face tuition though there is a growing interest in courses delivered electronically. Operations staff tend to study using distance learning or in-company tuition. These exams are tests of the fundamentals needed by individuals to undertake their job; there are more specialized exams at the level of a Masters degree leading to, for example, the SII Masters Programme.

Staff employed in general clerical and administrative work can work towards the SII Introduction to Investment – The Foundation Qualification – and staff working in the Operations area of the business can take the SII Investment Administration Qualification.

The list of examinations taken by staff can be found on the Financial Services Skills Council's (FSSC) Appropriate Examination List for staff working with retail clients or the FSSC Recommended Examination List for staff working with institutional/wholesale clients.

Passing the examinations is not the only factor in gaining Approved Person status; firms have to apply to FSA confirming that the individual is 'fit and proper' and competent for their role.

Personal attributes For *researchers/analysts* – numeracy, ability to assess long-term trends, analytical skills; for *brokers/dealers* – affability, the ability to develop good relationships with clients and inspire confidence, stamina, willingness to take risks, ability to make quick decisions, high powers of concentration, exceptional self-confidence, memory for people and figures. For *fund managers*, both sets of skills apply.

Mature entry and career change Opportunities mainly for those with professional qualifications in, for example, accountancy, economics, computing, general management. Analysts often have previous experience in industry.

Work–life balance A career as a trader or researcher is not for those for whom work–life balance is important – normal hours are 7 a.m. to 5.30 p.m. or longer, and unpredictable. Career breaks may be possible and job-sharing, but not part-time work, may be accepted. Support staff from all specialisms work more regular hours. The London Stock Exchange operates a flexible benefits scheme which includes access to childcare support and part-time work may be possible for administrative staff.

Further information

London Stock Exchange, 10 Paternoster Square, London EC4M 7LS.
www.londonstockexchange.com

The Securities and Investment Institute, 8 Eastcheap, London EC3M 1AE.
www.sii.org.uk

Financial Services Skills Council, 51 Gresham Street, London EC2V 7HQ.
www.fssc.org.uk

Related careers *accountancy – banking and building society work – economics – insurance*

Surveying

SURVEYOR

Entry qualifications For membership of the Royal Institution of Chartered Surveyors: enrolment on an RICS accredited degree. For many courses, specific subjects at A level or equivalent or from a group of subjects are required. For example maths, or geography or economic geography, or a physical science may be asked for.

The work The work is not necessarily mainly technical: in many surveyors' jobs the commercial element is greater than the technical; but technical expertise may be essential background knowledge. The variety of jobs is very great.

The various surveying branches each involve a different mix of technical, commercial, practical and academic ingredients, and different amounts of time spent on dealing with clients, dealing with other professionals, and on office and outdoor work. Each branch, therefore, suits people with different temperaments, interests, aptitudes. For example, the urban estate agent-surveyor has little in common with the hydrographic surveyor charting oceanic depth, or with the planning surveyor doing research into shopping centres, although they do share core skills such as law, economics, valuation and management.

The profession is continually evolving and areas can overlap and merge but the main surveying specializations are, in order of size: general practice which covers valuation, estate agency, auctioneering and urban estate/housing management; quantity surveying; building surveying; land agency and agricultural surveying; planning and development; land and hydrographic surveying; minerals surveying.

General Practice Surveyor

Valuation surveyor (also called valuer, or simply surveyor)

They assess the value of any type of property at any particular time. It may be in connection with rating, insurance, death duty purposes, as well as for general commercial and, these days, for investment purposes. Some specialize as investment surveyors. There are various valuation methods; the most commonly used is the 'comparison' method. This is an intricate mixture of basing judgement on ascertainable facts – value of property in the neighbourhood or other similar property, quality, etc. – as well as on 'getting the feel'. Various factors have to be considered when assessing property values, such as possible future development in the area, amenities and facilities. Valuers may also value land, industrial machinery and house contents.

Apart from working for estate agents, local authorities, property developers and other commercial concerns, valuation surveyors also set up in private professional practice.

Estate agent

Valuation surveyors may be estate agents, but estate agents are not necessarily valuation surveyors. Within surveying, estate agency is the most commercially and least technically oriented specialization and probably the largest in terms of opportunities. Most firms of estate agents have at least one RICS-qualified partner. Estate agents negotiate the sale, purchase, leasing of property – not only of houses but also of industrial and commercial premises, agricultural and other land. They arrange and advise on mortgages and on implications of rent acts, and on relevant law generally. As managing agents they manage property for clients, which involves drawing up leases, collecting rents, responsibility for maintenance, etc.

Estate agents' clients may be property managers of vast commercial empires, or first-time house purchasers who need to be guided through the complexities of making the most expensive purchase of their lives. Estate agents may specialize in one type of property (residential, or commercial or industrial), or they may deal with a mixture of types of properties. Negotiators, who deal with clients, often specialize in dealing with one type of client, for example with house purchasers, helping them to sort out priorities: few can afford their dream house, i.e. what they want exactly where they want. Negotiators help weigh up advantages of, say, sunny garden or 'good neighbourhood'; solidly built but no garage; not-so-solid but near shops/school/transport/parks, etc. Or they specialize in dealing with industrial property: are there goods transport/loading facilities; planning restrictions? Is there a supply of skilled labour?

Estate agents advise vendors on the price to ask, so they have to understand something about valuation, even if they are not professionally qualified valuers. The work involves a lot of client contact, of getting about and getting to know an area and being aware of changes in type of locality and its effect on property values.

Home Inspector

Properties marked for sale in England and Wales require a Home Information Pack (HIP), which includes a home energy rating. They are produced by Home Inspectors, who examine a property and produce a report. Qualifications in home inspection at level 4 (degree equivalent) are offered by the Awarding Body for the Built Environment (ABBE) and City & Guilds. Length of training depends on previous surveying and property experience. Domestic Energy Assessors produce the energy performance certificate part of the Home Information Pack. Qualification is at level 3.

Auctioneer

Some estate agents are also auctioneers. (Normally estate agents employ different people as negotiators and as auctioneers, but in small firms everybody might do everything.) Some firms specialize in auctioning commercial, industrial, residential or agricultural property; others specialize in furniture, machinery, works of art. (The few well-known auction rooms where paintings, etc. are auctioned are staffed by art specialists, who have learnt about auctioneering, as well as by the estate agent-valuer-auctioneer.) An auctioneer outside London may well auction the contents of a house one day, cattle in the local marketplace the next, and a row of shops the day after that. Work varies according to whether done in country town or big city. The actual auctioneering is only part of the work: it also involves assessing value and advising vendors on 'reserve price', and it involves detailed 'lotting up' and cataloguing items to be sold.

While some firms of auctioneers, especially in the country, engage people specially for auctioneering and teach them the necessary skills and techniques, it is advisable to train as valuer (see above) as well.

Quantity Surveyor

Quantity surveyors are also called 'building economists', 'construction cost consultants', 'building accountants'. Quantity surveyors are essential members of the design team on construction projects of any size. They translate architects' or civil engineers' designs into detailed costs – of labour, materials, overheads; and they break down all materials and processes to be used into detailed quantities and timing. They evaluate alternative processes and materials and may suggest alternative design technologies and materials to those suggested on the original design. Their thorough and up-to-date knowledge of new construction technologies and materials enables them to find ways of getting work carried out in the most speedy, economical and efficient way, without impairing the design. The calculations involved may be very complex – for example, future maintenance costs have to be considered when evaluating the use of alternative materials and processes.

Quantity surveyors are normally appointed by the designer of the project, i.e. the architect or civil engineer. Because of soaring costs and constantly changing technologies, the quantity surveyor's status in the design team has risen enormously in the last few years. Although the architect/civil engineer still has the last word, the quantity surveyor's suggestions for modifications are taken very seriously indeed.

Quantity surveyors are responsible for cost control during the whole project. They advise on cost implications of any proposed variations to the design, make interim valuations of completed work, check contractors' interim accounts and settle final accounts. They are also involved with financial administration of contracts for mechanical and electrical engineering and similar services and may be responsible for overall project management.

Quantity surveyors' work is a combination of straightforward figure work, complex calculations and negotiating skills. They must be able to deal with colleagues from other disciplines, contractors, clients. They spend more time at their desks doing calculations or writing reports and at negotiations than on the construction site, but the time spent on the various ingredients of the job varies from project to project, and according to the type of employer and method of working.

Many quantity surveyors are in private professional practice; others work for contractors, consultant engineers, in government departments, local authorities, commercial and industrial firms.

Building Surveyor

Building surveyors make structural surveys of and diagnose defects of buildings of all types, for prospective purchasers, vendors, owners, building societies. They assess maintenance costs and control maintenance programmes; they prepare plans for conversion and improvements. They draw up plans and specifications, go out to tender, and may supervise contractors' work and check accounts. They advise on building, planning, health and safety regulations, and they may also be involved with restoration or maintenance of ancient monuments and historic buildings. They spend a good deal of time clambering about on buildings to check roofs, lofts, drains, fire escapes and general structural soundness, so their work requires agility.

Many work in private professional practice; others are employed by any type of organization which owns, sells, buys, builds, manages property. This includes housing associations, building societies, all types of industrial and commercial firms, local authorities and central government. This is the most practical specialization, with the least office work.

Rural Practice Surveyor (Land Agent/Agricultural Surveyor)

Terms are confusing as they have changed in recent years. Traditionally land agents (called factors in Scotland) were (usually resident) managers of farms or other rural properties. More usually now their work is done by firms of agricultural surveyors (also called rural practice surveyors), who manage a number of farms and estates on a contract basis. They do much the same work in rural areas as general practice surveyors do in towns. They may do valuation (including livestock and agricultural plant), estate agency, auctioneering, or they may concentrate on farm management (see p. 64). They also advise on alternative uses of land, for recreational purposes such as country parks, caravan and camping sites, country trails, long-distance footpaths, nature reserves. They would then also implement changes.

Rural practice surveyors may also conduct sales and auctions of country properties, contents of country houses, livestock, agricultural machinery, plant, forests and forest products.

Many are in private professional practice. According to the size of the practice, other specialist surveyors (valuers, building surveyors) may be employed. Rural practice surveyors sometimes do farm business management as well, perhaps employing specialists to advise on mechanization, diversification (see alternative land use above) and other ways of improving farm profits. They are also often involved with conservation issues, trying to reconcile landowners' and conservationists' sometimes conflicting interests.

They also work for Defra (see p. 64), local government, the National Trust and other bodies which own/manage land.

Rural practice surveying is an unusual combination of business, technical, environmental and agricultural work, and is one of the few professional jobs that include getting about the countryside.

Planning and Development Surveyor

The work overlaps with town planning (see p. 612).

Planning surveyors are concerned with the efficient allocation of resources in planning and with planning economics and planning law. The work is largely desk research (including statistics) and communicating with other specialists concerned with planning. A planning surveyor, for example, investigates the economics of a proposed shopping area. That would involve collecting facts and figures from various sources, assessing their implications and writing up the findings. Another project might mean having to find a suitable site for an industrial plant which has to be somewhere within a given area, must be near an inland waterway, near transport and must not be within an area of scenic value. That would not necessarily involve travelling, but consulting maps and relevant organizations.

The planning surveyor also advises clients on planning implications or proposals to buy and develop a property. This could involve visiting the site, taking photographs, and then appraising the proposal from a civic design point of view. They are also involved in marketing completed properties.

Planning and development surveyors work for planning consultants, local and central government, or as specialists in general practice surveying firms.

Land and Hydrographic Surveyors

Land surveyors must not be confused with land agents/agricultural surveyors. Their work is quite different and much more 'technical'. They use sophisticated technologies (including satellite positioning systems and laser alignment devices) to measure and plot the precise shape and position of natural and man-made features on land for the purpose of map-making, including large-scale maps which are used for engineering constructions. (Before motorways can be sited, for example, or bridges built, the minutest physical details of the area have to be plotted and mapped.)

Land surveyors do not draw maps; that is done by cartographers (see p. 134). Land surveyors work in private practice, or for the government (Ordnance Survey, Ministry of Defence mainly), or for consulting engineers and big contractors. A few go into archaeological surveying (see also p. 85).

Hydrographic surveyors are the smallest and most scientific branch, although the needs of off-shore oil and gas industries have widened their scope. They survey oceans, waterways, harbours and ports for purposes of producing nautical charts which show the precise shape, size, location of physical features of the seabed, etc. and hazards, currents, tides, sunken wrecks. They supervise the dredging of ports and channels. The information sent by hydrographic survey ships operating in most parts of the world to the Navy's Hydrographic Department is being continuously revised. Collecting and interpreting information is done with highly sophisticated electronic equipment. British Admiralty Charts are used by seafarers all over the world, and by North Sea oil and gas engineers.

Many hydrographic surveyors are also naval officers. This is fairly tough outdoor work, combined with high technology.

Minerals and Mining Surveyor

This is the smallest specialization. Mining surveyors are responsible for mine safety and for mapping mineral deposits, and are involved with the potential use, value, properties, management and exploitation of mineral deposits, which means combining technical, scientific, managerial and commercial aspects. They are also responsible for minimizing environmental damage to the countryside where mineral deposits are mined.

In this country, mining surveyors are concerned mainly with coal mining, but minerals surveying overseas covers a variety of other minerals.

Prospects for chartered surveyors of all kinds vary according to economic conditions, but are mostly reasonable, especially as a wider range of organizations now employ surveyors, for example financial institutions; best opportunities are for general practice, quantity and building surveyors. Some opportunities in EU countries (for those who speak the relevant language fluently), especially for quantity surveyors, who are also in demand in Africa and the Middle East.

Training (generally) For membership of the Royal Institution of Chartered Surveyors the majority take three-year full-time (or four-year sandwich) degrees in surveying; others study while in appropriate employment, which takes five to six years of part-time study (or four years for one of the distance-learning BSc courses run by the College of Estate Management). Details of RICS-accredited courses can be found on their website at *www.ricscourses.org*. This is followed by either two years, or, with five years' relevant experience, one year in a work-based professional training scheme working towards the RICS Assessment of Professional Competence (APC).

Personal attributes Practical approach to problem-solving; ability to inspire confidence in clients; ability to take complex decisions on own initiative and work as one of a team as well. For consultancy and estate agency: business acumen; liking for being out of doors.

Mature entry and career change Possible, but requires very strong motivation. No problem getting training, but first job may be difficult for over-30s. With sufficient related experience and study based on the final year of a RICS-accredited degree course, graduates with a non-accredited degree can qualify for RICS membership.

Work–life balance A career break should not be difficult in, for example, general practice surveying; possibly more difficult in areas where technologies change rapidly, but here keeping up with developments by reading journals and attending meetings should help. Part-time work is not very common. No reason why established surveyors should not suggest to their employers that part-time with flexible hours or job-sharing should work well.

Further information

Royal Institution of Chartered Surveyors, Surveyor Court, Westwood Way, Coventry CV4 8JE.

www.rics.org

College of Estate Management, Whiteknights, Reading RG6 6AW.
www.cem.ac.uk

Awarding Body of the Built Environment, Room A045, University of
Birmingham, Perry Barr, Birmingham B42 2SU
www.abbeqa.co.uk

Related careers *agriculture and horticulture – architecture – cartography – engineering – housing management – town planning*

SURVEYING TECHNICIAN/TECHNICAL SURVEYOR
(includes managerial jobs in the construction industry, see p. 169)

Entry qualifications At least National Qualifications Framework
Level 3 (A levels, BTEC National awards) or Scottish Credit and
Qualifications Framework equivalent.

The work Most specializations overlap very much with supervisory
and management jobs in the construction industry (see p. 169). Titles
vary: the term 'technician' may not be used, even when the qualification required is a technician qualification.

Individual technicians' work varies enormously: some are deskbound draughtspersons, some are out and about; all now use computerized procedures and equipment. Some have a great deal of client
contact, some have none. Almost invariably they are part of a team.

The majority work under the overall direction of surveyors, architects, civil engineers or planners. Some of their work is indistinguishable from that done by chartered surveyors: until some years ago,
chartered surveyors qualified almost exclusively by on-the-job plus
part-time training, and they had only slightly higher entry qualifications than technicians often have now. While chartered surveyors'
training is certainly much more demanding academically than technicians', many tasks are still the same as they always were and do not
require the chartered surveyors' in-depth training. Technician-level
qualifications are sufficient for the majority of those 'surveyors' who,

while wanting responsibility and professional training, do not aspire to initiate and take charge of complex projects.

Building Surveying Technician

Subdivisions cover construction and assessment of structures; administration of building regulations; preparations of plans; specification for and organization of work to be carried out by contractors; estimates of cost before projects start; dealing with tenders and contracts and checking and passing contractors' accounts; advising lay public on soundness of construction of property they consider buying (while ultimate responsibility for such advice lies with the employing chartered surveyor, the actual surveying on which surveyors' reports to clients are based is often carried out by technicians – the customer is not necessarily aware of this); advice to property owners on maintenance and repair. This may include drawing up schedules for redecoration, advice on eradication of damp, dry rot, etc. (see also p. 169).

Building surveying technicians work in a great variety of settings – and under a great variety of titles (for example building manager, building surveyor, building inspector). They are employed by virtually any type of organization which owns or is responsible for the building and/or maintenance of property, and by firms of consultants. When they work for building contractors, they may also be called planning or contracts manager, or contracts surveyor. Their work may be mainly organizational – ensuring that manpower and equipment are used efficiently; this means planning all the operations which are involved in completing a contract to build whatever it is. For example, if a firm of building contractors is engaged simultaneously on converting several houses into flats and building office blocks, the contracts planner or manager has to estimate for how long how many workers and which equipment will be required on each job and when the various specialists, such as heating engineers, plasterers, electricians, should be where.

While in the past only very large contractors had contract planners, now middle-sized firms often engage such staff (under various titles, and not necessarily only engaged on this type of planning).

Another job for building surveying technicians is as site managers. They are responsible for organization of the sequence and smooth working of operations on site.

Technicians who prefer desk-bound work can become CAD (computer-aided design) technicians, drawing up building and site plans, and may eventually be in charge of a drawing office.

Many building surveying technicians also work for estate agents, where they meet the general public.

Quantity Surveying Technician
(see also *quantity surveyor*, p. 571)

They form part of the surveying team concerned with the costing and financial management of all types of construction work. There are three main, but interrelated subdivisions (with rather quaint traditional titles).

- *Takers off*: They abstract and measure from architect's, surveyor's or engineer's drawings every item of labour and materials to be used on a project, and list them in recognized terms. The information is needed to produce a 'cost plan' or Bill of Quantities. The job is usually office-based, and involves liaison with architects and other specialists, often as part of a technician team.
- *Workers up*: They work out volumes, quantities and areas of all the items which have been measured by the taker off, and record them in a way which can be understood by all construction workers. These are then presented on the Bill of Quantities used by the quantity surveyor in deciding the most economical means of construction. Workers up are entirely office-based; they may be responsible for a part or whole of a project.
- *Post-contract surveyors and site measurers*: They divide their time between office and site. Work includes monitoring work done so that interim payments can be made to contractors. They may

discuss the implications of variations on the plans with subcontractors employed on the site and must understand contracts. Post-contract surveyors may be physically measuring work on site one day, attending a site meeting with a number of colleagues from different building-work spheres the same afternoon, and perhaps negotiating final payment with a subcontractor the following day. Usually they will have been workers up and takers off before becoming post-contract surveyors. Their job can overlap very much with that of chartered quantity surveyors.

General Practice Technician

This division covers the work done by chartered general practice and planning surveyors.

General practice technicians may specialize in valuation, estate agency, estate and property management, housing management, town planning (see p. 612). Openings are the most varied, ranging from suburban estate agency's or international property company's negotiator to HM Revenue and Customs or insurance company's valuation technician. This specialization offers scope both to those who are mainly interested in meeting members of the public and to those who want to do mainly drawing or other office work and are interested in combining technical and commercial work.

Land Surveying Technician

These work with chartered land surveyors. The work has changed considerably in the last few years with the use of electronic distance-measuring equipment and digital coding and modelling of land shapes. There are also opportunities in photographing and tracking man-made satellites, and in aerial photography. This is one of the most adventurous of technician specializations, with work for oil companies and air survey companies at home or abroad, including Third World countries.

Minerals Surveying Technician

This is a small division and involves the preparation of accurate plans in connection with safety, operation and development of mines, and plans of geological formations in connection with mineral deposits. Much of the work is underground.

Hydrographic Surveying Technician

Making and updating charts of seas and coastlines, and profiles of sea beds; 'sign posting', on charts, of shipping lanes. This can be arduous outdoor work on survey ships and requires practical seamanship; only few draughtsmanship, office-based jobs.

Agricultural Surveying Technician

This work overlaps with agriculture (see p. 64) and land agency. Main employers are local authorities and gas and electricity companies.

Surveying technicians generally are in demand but especially in quantity, general practice, land and building surveying where their work often overlaps with that of chartered surveyors. In these specializations there are often more opportunities for technicians than for chartered surveyors. Experienced technicians have some opportunities in EU countries if they speak the relevant language fluently. There is a 'bridging arrangement' which enables qualified technicians to attain RICS membership and become chartered surveyors.

Training (generally) A related HNC/HND or S/NVQ Level 4 – a list of RICS-accredited courses and N/SVQs can be found on their website. Membership (TechRICS) is through the Assessment of Technical Competence (ATC) and involves a minimum of two years' work-based training, written submissions and a final assessment interview.

Personal attributes Some mathematical ability; interest in finding practical solutions to technical problems; liking for outdoor work; ability to work as one of a team and also to take responsibility, coupled with willingness to work for people more highly qualified than oneself; meticulous accuracy; ability to supervise construction site workers.

Mature entry and career change There is no reason why people should not start in their 20s or 30s, especially if they have had some related experience or training, e.g. a geography degree or work experience in estate agency, on a construction site, with computers.

Work–life balance If returners have kept up with developments, there is no reason why experienced technicians should not return to work. It would probably be easier in general practice and quantity surveying than, say, in agricultural surveying. There is no reason why experienced technicians should not try to make their own part-time or job-share arrangements, especially in estate agency work.

Further information

Chartered Surveyors Training Trust, Downstream Building, 1 London Bridge, London SE1 9BG.
    www.cstt.org.uk
National Association of Estate Agents, 6 Tournament Close, Edgehill Drive, Warwick CV34 6LG.
    www.naea.co.uk

Related careers *architecture – chartered surveyor – construction – housing management*

Tax Inspector/Adviser

Tax Inspector

Entry qualifications First- or second-class honours or postgraduate degree in any subject or equivalent. The Civil Service sets entry requirements for its own specific courses. (Opportunities also for those starting as tax officer, see 'Junior Manager', p. 157.)

The work Tax inspectors work within HM Revenue and Customs. Their main duty is to investigate the accounts of business concerns in order to agree the amount of profits for taxation purposes. By examining accounts and interviewing individuals they aim to spot any cases of tax evasion or fraud. They also advise taxpayers on tax and business law. Their work brings them into contact with the whole range of Britain's industry and commerce in their own district. HM Revenue and Customs is now also responsible for National Insurance and Tax Credits.

They deal with many kinds of people – accountants, lawyers, industrialists, farmers, small shopkeepers – by personal interview as well as by correspondence. They also represent the Crown before an independent tribunal when they and the taxpayer concerned cannot agree on the tax assessment. There are District Offices in all areas. Promotion prospects are best for people willing to move to where there happens to be a vacancy.

Training Graduates are recruited through the Civil Service Fast Stream Graduate Programme (see p. 155) or through the HM Revenue & Customs Talent Recruitment Programme, a training and development programme that takes around four years to complete. Applicants can choose between a Management Fast Track or the Inspector Development Programme.

Tax Adviser

Entry qualifications Usually a degree in accountancy, law or management or related subject or the ATT qualification. Membership of the Chartered Institute of Taxation.

The work There has been an increasing demand for tax advisers. There are two main activities: tax consultancy, which involves helping clients to plan for the future in order to lawfully minimize tax liability; and tax compliance, which means preparing and submitting current tax returns. Tax advisers must keep on top of highly complex tax legislation, research and present information to clients and liaise with HM Revenue and Customs on their behalf where appropriate. Some tax advisers work for large accountancy or law firms dealing with corporate taxation while others set up in private practice and may combine the work with accountancy services. The work is usually office-based though tax advisers may visit clients, and it can be very pressurized towards the end of the tax year. Many tax advisers are becoming involved in international taxation.

Training There are three routes to applying for membership of the Chartered Institute of Taxation: qualification as an accountant or as a solicitor, or membership of the Association of Taxation Technicians, gained through work-based training leading to examinations in law, accounting and taxation and two years' practical experience. To qualify as a Chartered Tax Adviser (CTA) it is necessary to achieve membership of the CIOT through their CTA examinations and three years' relevant experience. Some larger tax consultancy and accountancy firms offer graduate training scheme entry.

The CIOT offers an advanced diploma in International Taxation.

Personal attributes Common sense; judgement; good communication skills; administrative ability; keen intellect; the ability to sum up people and situations; impartiality; equanimity; enjoyment of responsibility.

Mature entry and career change Tax advice is a field where maturity can be an advantage (see also p. 153).

Work–life balance Tax inspectors are civil servants (see p. 166). Part-time work and career breaks are possible in tax advisory work, and with experience tax advisers can be self-employed.

Further information

The Chartered Institute of Taxation, 12 Upper Belgrave Street, London SW1X 8BB.

The Association of Taxation Technicians – address as CIOT above.

www.tax.org.uk
www.att.org.uk
www.hmrctalent.co.uk
www.careers.civil-service.gov.uk

Related careers *accountancy – actuary – banking and building society work – civil service – insurance*

Teaching

There are more than 400,000 teachers in service in maintained (state) schools in England and Wales alone, making teacher training one of the biggest graduate recruiters in the UK, and teaching one of the most varied career paths. Amid considerable competition to recruit good graduates, teaching remains a popular choice for graduates. Teachers are required to work in a demanding, stressful and continually changing environment, and the image of the profession has suffered in recent years. Nevertheless, the challenges and rewards are still attracting a rising number of recruits and in 2006/07 39,600 people started teacher training.

It is vital that first-class teachers are recruited and retained, but supply and demand does vary from subject to subject. There is great competition among the professions to recruit graduates with backgrounds in maths, science, technological subjects and modern foreign languages. Various financial incentives are available. A training bursary of £6,000–£9,000 is paid to eligible postgraduate trainees, depending on when their course starts, where they are training and on the subject they are being trained to teach. (From August 2008 the training bursary for eligible postgraduate trainees starting primary courses in England will be £4,000.) Additional 'Golden Hellos' are paid at the time of writing to eligible newly qualified teachers of English (including drama), maths, design and technology, science, modern foreign languages, ICT, religious education and music at the end of their induction year. Postgraduate trainees in England may be eligible for a grant of £1,230 and to apply for an additional means-tested grant of £1,535. For up-to-date information on funding and financial incentives for teaching see *www.tda.gov.uk/ Recruit/thetrainingprocess/fundinginengland.aspx.*

Entry qualifications All those who wish to teach in state-maintained schools in England and Wales must hold Qualified Teacher Status (QTS). This is awarded to students who successfully complete an initial teacher training (ITT) programme. A degree and GCSEs or equivalent at grades C or above in maths and English are also required; those born on or after 1 September 1979 who wish to teach in the primary or middle phases must also hold GCSE or equivalent qualification at grade C or above in a science subject. (For Scotland see 'Training'.)

Primary Schools (including Nursery)

Primary schools are generally organized into infant and junior schools but there are also first and middle schools for pupils of pre-secondary school age. Most children go on to secondary school at 11, but some remain at their primary/middle school until 12 or 13. Sometimes the younger and older primary children go to separate schools; in other cases a single school deals with the whole primary range. Some schools have attached nursery units, taking children at 3 or 4. (NOTE: To teach in a state-maintained nursery school you must be a qualified teacher, though there may be unqualified assistants.)

The precise organization of primary education varies from one local education authority (LEA) to another. Schools also vary greatly in size, location and catchment area. Some schools will have as few as 2 teachers, others as many as 30. In the former case each teacher will teach several age groups; in the latter several teachers will share responsibility for an age group, sometimes through 'team teaching'.

Nursery and lower primary children learn largely through play and activity, which are planned and supervised by the teacher to achieve certain goals and develop children's skills. For example, a listening game might be devised to improve children's concentration skills. The teacher observes all the time to recognize which areas need working on for each child. Children of this age are extremely demanding; they are only able to work independently for short periods of time, and demand a high level of attention, reassurance and encouragement.

The introduction of regular, dedicated sessions on literacy and mathematics and end-of-key-stage assessments (sometimes known as SATs) has brought a more prescriptive approach to primary education. The teacher has to plan schemes of work, relating them to the age group; make sure all the necessary resources are to hand; check National Curriculum attainment targets in the appropriate subjects are met and record them; and be prepared to constantly evaluate and rethink strategies.

One of the most important skills for a primary teacher is effective classroom management. This includes timetabling, the grouping of children and the organization of the classroom. Learning time is wasted if, for example, the most boisterous child sits with those of his or her peers least able to cope, or if children involved in a messy activity need to move among children quietly engaged in other activities in order to get to their materials.

Primary teachers normally take their classes for all subjects, all day. The demands of the National Curriculum and the introduction of new subjects have led many teachers to take additional in-service specialist training to enable them to act as advisers or coordinators for a particular subject within their schools. Lesson preparation can take up a good deal of time, as can assessment and record-keeping, extra-curricular activities and maintaining good relationships with parents.

Secondary Schools

Usually at the age of 11, but sometimes at 12 or 13, children transfer to secondary school. Most children go to comprehensive schools, which cater for all ranges of ability. Some authorities, however, have retained a selective system where the more academically able children go to grammar schools. In some authorities children remaining in full-time education at 16+ go to sixth-form colleges, some of which offer a traditional sixth-form curriculum, while others offer a more diverse range of courses.

Unlike primary teachers, secondary teachers teach a limited number of subjects that are usually closely related to many different age and ability groups, throughout the day and week. Within the framework of their specialist knowledge, they need the teaching skills to establish working relationships with a diverse range of pupils: the unmotivated, the slow learners, the young pupils who look to the teacher for everything, the sixth-formers who test them with profound questions. They must try to stimulate the interest of all pupils and help them to achieve the best they can, whether it be two hard-earned GCSEs or three top-grade A levels. This demands enthusiasm and flexibility.

Secondary teachers obviously need a good grounding in their subjects, but they do not need to know it all. Modern education is about learning how to learn, handling data and developing thinking and problem-solving skills. These are skills and challenges for teachers as well as pupils.

Secondary teachers spend a good deal of time (much of it out of school hours) on preparation and marking. They must be clear what they are going to achieve in each lesson, following the scheme of work as planned in the syllabus, and have the necessary material ready at each point, in each lesson, every day of the week. Good organization is vital. Formal assessment and recording have, in recent years, involved teachers in a good deal of additional administrative work, but assessment is also an intuitive and continuous process which occurs as teachers build relationships with their pupils.

Most teachers have responsibilities in addition to their subject teaching. Personal, social and health education, for example, is often a shared responsibility. Time is taken up in registration, form time and assemblies; administration, departmental and other meetings with colleagues; and contact with parents. Many teachers get involved in a range of extra-curricular activities, from sport to drama, chess or other special interest clubs. These can take up considerable time. Some plan and accompany children on trips. In addition, everyone on the staff shares responsibility for standards and so is effectively 'on duty' throughout the day, watching out for, preventing and dealing with problems.

Teachers can never rest on their laurels; year by year, new subjects are introduced, old subjects develop and are approached in new ways, and teaching and examining methods change. In addition, each class and each child is unique and will require different teaching methods. Good teachers need to update and evaluate their work constantly, deciding what to change and what to repeat, and finding the right method for a particular pupil or group.

Special Needs Education

Children may have special educational needs for a variety of reasons ranging from emotional or behavioural difficulties, through specific learning difficulties, to complex multiple physical and/or learning disabilities. Increasingly such children are, whenever possible, educated in mainstream schools. Depending on circumstances, a child might be integrated into an ordinary class but receive special help, or be in a special unit or class attached to an ordinary school. Some children still need to go to special schools, sometimes for the whole of their schooling, sometimes only for short periods.

Working in special needs education is emotionally and physically demanding. The teacher is involved not only in teaching academic subjects but may also be required to help pupils manage a range of day-to-day activities such as eating and playing. The teacher needs to build up a good relationship with a child, but also with the others concerned with the child's welfare and development, such as doctors, social workers, speech and language therapists, physiotherapists and psychologists.

Apart from teachers of children with sight or hearing impairment, special needs teachers do not need additional qualifications, though they may take up in-service training courses. The usual route is to gain a teaching qualification (see below) and experience of teaching children with no special educational needs before moving into special needs work.

Independent Schools

Independent education covers a very wide range of institutions, from the renowned public schools to Montessori nursery schools. Some are based on a traditional academic approach while others are very 'progressive'. Many have outstanding records in preparing their pupils for external examinations and higher education, while others compare unfavourably with good state schools. Some pay their teachers considerably more than the scale for teachers in the maintained sector while others fall far short.

There are courses and qualifications of interest to particular sectors of independent education (e.g. Montessori and Rudolf Steiner), but these do not qualify one to teach in state schools.

Further Education

Many of the courses offered in the further education sector have a vocational bias. Some colleges are devoted to one particular field, e.g. agriculture. However, colleges also offer a broad range of other courses, from GCSEs and A levels (which many students take in conjunction with vocational studies) to leisure interests such as painting, foreign languages and keep fit. Increasing numbers of school-leavers are continuing their education in FE colleges and some local education authorities are making them the focus of 16+ provision. In addition some colleges in partnership with local schools teach students aged 14–16 who are taking work-related subjects.

Since 2001, further education lecturers have been required to hold or be working towards a recognized qualification. In September 2007 new initial teacher training qualifications and routes were introduced. The Preparing to Teach in the Lifelong Learning Sector (PTLLS) award is an introductory course. The Diploma in Teaching in the Lifelong Learning Sector, which leads to Qualified Teacher, Learning and Skills (QTLS) status, is for full teachers. This includes specialist Skills for Life routes. The Certificate in Teaching in the Lifelong Learning Sector, which leads to Associate Teacher, Learning and

Skills (ATLS) status, is for associate teachers, who take on less than the full range of teaching responsibilities. Further information is available from the Lifelong Learning UK website: *www.lifelonglearninguk.org*.

Higher Education

In higher education, a higher degree is normally required for teaching. Academic qualifications are more important than certified teaching skills, but a formal postgraduate teaching qualification for higher education (HE) lecturers has now been introduced. The PG Certificate in Learning and Teaching (HE) is accredited by the Higher Education Academy (see *www.heacademy.ac.uk*) and is required for new staff on permanent contracts by many institutions. The role of higher education institutions is not merely to pass on knowledge, but to extend it, so research is an important element of work in this sector. Administration is another key task.

Training (generally) The two most popular initial teacher training (ITT) routes leading to Qualified Teacher Status (QTS) are:

- *The undergraduate route.* This can be a Bachelor of Education (BEd) or a BSc or BA with QTS. Most undergraduate courses require a minimum of two A levels or equivalent (with at least one in a National Curriculum subject) and GCSEs (or equivalent qualifications) at grade C or above in maths and English language. Additionally those born on or after 1 September 1979 who wish to teach primary or Key Stage 2/3 (age 7–14) must also hold GCSE (or equivalent qualification) grade C or above in a science subject. Courses last for three or four years and include experience in the classroom, professional practice (such as theory of education and child development) and subject study. Students normally specialize in the teaching of particular age ranges and subjects, but they are not restricted to those in their subsequent careers. Many primary teachers qualify by this route. Most secondary teachers qualify through the postgraduate route described below.
- *The Postgraduate Certificate in Education (PGCE).* This is the most

popular route into teaching for those who have already completed their first degree. Entry qualifications are normally a degree in a subject related to the chosen teaching specialism and GCSE or equivalent in maths and English at grade C or above. Additionally those born on or after 1 September 1979 who wish to teach in the primary or middle phases must also hold a GCSE (or equivalent qualification) grade C or above in a science subject. PGCEs can be studied as a one-year full-time course, or over two years part-time. Some providers now offer two-year PGCE courses to develop subject knowledge and professional training. Courses for primary teachers must include eighteen weeks of teaching practice in schools; secondary courses must include 24 weeks. Eligible postgraduate ITT trainees currently receive a £6,000–£9,000 tax-free bursary while they train (see above).

ITT providers offer flexible (or 'modular') training programmes which allow candidates to fit teacher training around other commitments, for example, a job or family. These flexible routes take into account any previous experience of teaching, for example, voluntary work abroad, or teaching in the private sector.

A number of other initial teacher training routes operate, including the SCITT (School-Centred Initial Teacher Training) scheme, where consortia of schools organize school-based training for graduates which leads to QTS. For those who wish to train through a paid, employment-based route, the Graduate and Registered Teacher Programmes (or GRTP) are competitive programmes which offer a number of funded places for training in schools. The Graduate Teacher Programme (GTP) offers training to graduates for up to a year (depending on previous teaching experience), which leads to QTS. Candidates must first find a school which is willing to take them on as a trainee teacher. Candidates' training needs are assessed and the training programme drawn up by a designated recommending body (DRB) or recommending body (RB). Training is mostly delivered in schools. The Registered Teacher Programme is for candidates who have completed two years of higher education and wish to complete their degree studies alongside teacher training in schools. The candidate's training needs are assessed and the training programme drawn up by an RB. Training programmes last up to two years and require a sound foundation in the chosen teaching subject for entry. The GRTP is organized by the Training and Development Agency for Schools. 'Teach First' is an employment-based route for new graduates, offering teacher and leadership training in challenging secondary schools (see *www.teachfirst.org.uk*).

All those training to be teachers in England and Wales are required to pass skills tests in numeracy, literacy and IT in order to gain QTS. The award of QTS is followed by a mandatory induction year. Financial incentives, in the form of 'Golden Hellos', are available to some teachers on completion of their induction year (for details see *www. tda.gov.uk/Recruit/thetrainingprocess/fundinginengland.aspx*).

Notes on the Scottish system To be eligible for permanent teaching appointments in maintained schools in Scotland, teachers must hold a recognized teaching qualification and must be registered with the General Teaching Council for Scotland. Registration confers eligibility to teach a particular age range, either in primary, secondary or further education, and, in the case of secondary education, a particular subject or subjects. Primary teachers may take either a four-year BEd, for which the normal entry requirements are three Higher passes (one must be in English or a National Course award at Higher level at C or above in English and Communication) and two Standard grade passes (one must be maths at credit level or intermediate 2), or a one-year postgraduate course for which a degree plus Higher grade English and Standard maths are required. Secondary teachers usually take a one-year postgraduate course in specific subjects following first degrees with sufficient specified achievement in the relevant subjects. There are secondary BEds in physical education, music and technology. A combined or concurrent degree includes study of a main subject and of education, plus some school experience.

As in England, alternative equivalent qualifications may be acceptable for entry. Mature students may get some concessions, but acceptable qualifications in maths and English must be held. Teachers who have trained outside Scotland and who have suitable qualifications may be admitted to the register, in some cases after additional training.

Teachers in further education do not need to be registered. The course for registration is open only to serving teachers seconded by their authority.

Personal attributes To be a teacher you need: to enjoy working with children and young people; patience; a sense of humour; enthusiasm; flexibility; fairness and consistency; confidence; optimism; good organizational and time-management skills; sensitivity; good communication skills; and the ability to work alone and as part of a team.

Mature entry and career change There are good prospects for mature candidates wishing to enter teaching, for career changers and those seeking to return to the profession. The Training and Development Agency for Schools' recruitment figures show that one-third of those entering teacher training are over 30. The introduction of flexible, modular style routes and the expansion of the GTP have improved access to ITT for candidates with life commitments such as work or a family, which would normally preclude full-time, institution-based study.

Work–life balance Supply work, part-time and job-sharing are all options, dependent on local availability and practice, and subject specialisms.

Schools and education authorities are keen to attract teachers back from the 'PIT' (pool of inactive teachers). Initiatives include special courses for returners and the encouragement of flexible working arrangements such as supply work, part-time work and job-sharing. The Training and Development Agency for Schools operates a 'Returning to Teach' programme (0845 6000 993) and can provide a directory of courses and other useful information for those wishing to return to teaching. Their figures indicate that 12,000 people return to teaching each year.

NOTES ON CLASSROOM SUPPORT STAFF: Teachers are assisted in their work by teaching assistants for whom a wide range of qualifications is now available. A new role of Higher Level Teaching Assistant has recently been introduced. HLTAs undertake training which permits them, under the direction of a teacher, to assess, record and report on pupils' progress and also manage other classroom-based staff or supervise a class in a teacher's absence. For further information see *www.tda.gov.uk*.

Further information

The Teaching Information Line offers information and advice to those interested in becoming teachers – 0845 6000 991. This service is run by the Training and Development Agency for Schools, 151 Buckingham Palace Road, London SW1W 9SZ.
www.tda.gov.uk

Scottish Government, Education Department, Area 2A North, Victoria Quay, Edinburgh EH6 6QQ.
www.teachinginscotland.com

Related careers *careers guidance – nursery nurse – personnel/human resources management – social work – youth and community work*

Television, Film and Radio

Entry qualifications Very varied but mostly graduate entry. IT skills are almost essential. This whole area has been going through a period of unprecedented change, both technological and organizational, with a dramatic impact on career and training opportunities. It is in the independent, non-broadcast sector that there is likely to be most growth. Whole programmes and/or particular expertise are bought in from small production companies. The industry relies heavily on freelance staff. Most 'career' opportunities lie in management/administration/sales.

TELEVISION

The industry includes 'terrestrial' and satellite broadcasting companies, independent companies producing for broadcast, the corporate sector (e.g. training and corporate image promotional film and videos), commercials, music promotion and feature films. There are also production facilities in educational establishments and community-based units. Satellite and cable companies produce mainly news and sport items, but buy in most of their other programmes and offer most job opportunities in sales and marketing and on the technical side. The boundaries between the sectors of the industry are becoming increasingly blurred. Independents commonly work in more than one sector, e.g. both making programmes for broadcast and doing corporate work. The broadcast companies are also diversifying into, for example, corporate work or making programmes for satellite and cable. Broadcasters are investing more in identifying audiences, and the rapid development of interactive media is increasing the feasibility of targeting ever narrower groups of viewers, opening up more opportunities for small companies. The range of jobs is wide and evolving and Skillset, the Sector Skills Council for the audio-visual industries, now does an annual census of employment within the industry (*www.skillset.org*). Terminology and job content can vary considerably. Job titles are not clear-cut. In addition, there is an industry-wide trend towards 'multi-skilling'. Sometimes this is the result of technical development when, for example, one piece of equipment and operator can do what previously took two pieces and two operators. Another impetus is the need for a more flexible workforce; film editors learn video editing in order to survive.

Put simply, activities can be divided into pre-production, production and post-production. Each has a range of different jobs involved, but people tend to be employed (as freelancers) not until, and then only while, they are needed. Also, distinctions between jobs are blurring as people need to do more to keep employed.

Below are some of the programme-making jobs involved in broadcast TV. They are based on the BBC, but similar jobs are needed elsewhere in programme production, including the growing independent sector. Where possible, indications of the kind of qualifications and training normally needed are given, but see 'Notes on entry and training' p. 608.

Production Staff

Producer/director

Exact functions vary. Producers are usually responsible for initiating, budgeting, casting, and the shape or 'treatment' of programmes. Directors are responsible for interpreting the idea and actually making the programme. These top jobs are very responsible and are done by specialists in particular fields, such as current affairs, drama, education, science or technology, who have long, often technical experience in the medium. Many work on contracts for particular projects.

Production assistant

They provide organizational and secretarial support to a programme. They may do some research, make bookings, arrange meetings, sit with the producer in the gallery checking on timing, cue the inserts of film or tape and are normally responsible for continuity. They have considerable contact with people both inside and outside TV. They see to it that the right instructions about make-up, costumes, sets, rehearsal times and studio bookings go to the right people. Production assistants perform any secretarial duties including typing (and often retyping) the shooting script.

Floor manager (known as 'stage manager' in outside broadcasts)

They may be involved at the planning stage in advising on design, sound and props. During recording they control the studio floor. They are responsible for discipline on the floor and for safety of staff and artists. Duties include relaying the producer's/director's instructions to actors and presenters, using headphones to keep in touch with the gallery. They are responsible for cueing the actors, which can be a complicated task as they are often working on different sets and cannot see each other. The floor manager has to move around the sets while keeping out of camera shot. A diplomatic, pleasant personality is essential. In outside broadcasts they have to liaise with the general public.

Entry Nearly all from the ranks of assistant floor managers or other production posts.

Assistant floor manager

Similar to assistant stage manager in the theatre. Work varies according to size and type of production, but usually includes making sure that all the props are available, taking charge of the prompt book and mark-ups during rehearsals. Assistant floor managers usually start their on-the-job training with the easier talks and discussion programmes before going on to drama series, etc.

Entry Candidates are expected to have experience in professional stage management, in theatre, film or TV.

Researcher

The majority of researchers are freelance. Research may be anything from looking through newspaper cuttings and finding a suitable person to be interviewed – not by researcher but by interviewer/presenter – on a news programme, to spending several months researching the background for a documentary or drama series. Researchers must be good all-rounders, able to pick out relevant facts from a mass of material. They usually write 'briefs', which may range from a few questions which an interviewer is to ask on a programme, to exhaustive background material for a documentary scriptwriter. Researchers in current affairs must also be able to think up programme ideas and to work under tremendous pressure. Specialist researchers, for example for scientific or medical programmes, are often freelancers.

Entry Usually graduates and/or ex-journalists, or by promotion from within.

News staff, presenter, interviewer

Newsroom staff compile and write scripts for the presenters; reporters and correspondents 'get the stories' and present some themselves. The essence of broadcast news is brevity. TV and radio journalists (there is a trend for all journalists to have to work in both media) must be instant fact-selectors and decision-makers. They may be sent anywhere at any time. Editors are senior staff responsible for piecing a programme together.

Entry Entrants are almost invariably graduates (any subject) with keen interest in current affairs, but 'general education' plus proven journalistic ability (i.e. good job on a good paper) can also lead in.

Design

Set designer

They are responsible for designing the sets down to the smallest accessories in accordance with the producer's concept. The producer calls in the designer when the idea is beginning to take shape. The designer's interpretation of the atmosphere the producer has in mind and their own suggestions are vitally important to the success of the production. They must have a good grasp of the technicalities of production. Design assistants work with the designer on the technical, rather than creative, tasks. They draw ground plans and make working drawings; draw up specifications; make models of sets; and make or search for props.

- *Graphic designers* and their assistants create credit titles, 'linking material', captions, maps and general illustrations. This is now usually done using specialist software, but nevertheless it is still essentially creative work.
- *Scenic artists* and assistants paint backcloths and decorative features such as curtains, carpets and portraits.
- *Visual effects designers* and assistants devise, make and operate a wide variety of visual effects and 'illusions'.

Entry Whatever the level of entry qualifications, all first appointments are to the post of assistant. Generally speaking, progress to designer is from design assistant. All design assistants need degree level qualification in relevant art disciplines. Additionally graphic design assistants normally need commercial art experience (e.g. advertising) following a degree or diploma; scenic artists need wide knowledge of painting, history of art and architecture, and interior design; visual effects staff need to be able to work in all kinds of materials, make models and have a basic grasp of physics. Most design is 'outsourced', i.e. done by freelancers or those working in facilities houses. Some companies employ designers as project managers.

Costume designer (also called 'wardrobe')

They are in charge of hiring, designing and adapting up-to-date and period costumes. They are called in on new productions at an early stage to discuss the costumes and to advise on whether to hire, make or adapt, and to arrange for this to be done. Later they liaise with other designers and make-up staff. They need a thorough knowledge of period styles, but further research is often needed to make certain of representing the exact year or season. Assistants help designers in all aspects of their work and may stand in for them, e.g. when filming on location.

- *Dressmakers* make up costumes under the supervision of designers and make alterations to costumes which are hired or from stock.
- *Dressers* work on last-minute ironing and maintenance of costumes and help actors to dress for performance.

Entry For *costume designers*: preferably a theatre or textile design degree and considerable experience in theatre or film costume. All entrants start at assistant level, from which designers are promoted. Assistants must be at least 19 with an A level standard of education and a good knowledge of costume design and history (a degree or diploma is essential for promotion to designer). Virtually all work is done on a freelance or short-contract basis. For *dressmakers*: a degree or diploma recommended plus previous experience of work with a costumier. Knowledge of history of costume an advantage.

Make-up artist/designer

Television make-up is highly skilled. It requires the ability to understand and defeat the camera's often unkind effects on faces. It also requires a thorough knowledge of period hairstyles. An experienced senior assistant is usually in charge of each dramatic production and makes up the star actors. Juniors see to the rest of the cast and also look after the simpler make-up required for non-dramatic productions. Tact and diplomacy are essential.

Entry Most make-up artists train privately, which is expensive.

Technical Operations

These concern the technical interpretation of the director's instructions and producing the required sound and vision effects which are finally seen and heard. Most TV programmes are pre-recorded. When recording a programme as well as during 'live' transmission, previously recorded and/or filmed material may be slotted in. The operational and technical sides of creating programmes and getting them on to TV screens are highly complex and require creativity, technical expertise and an unflappable temperament.

- *Camera operators* help in setting up and operating electronic cameras and associated equipment in studios and on outside broadcasts. Promotion is to assistant and later cameraman/woman, vision supervisor, vision controller and ultimately possibly to technical manager responsible for lighting (various titles).
- *Sound assistants* help in setting up and operating sound recording and reproduction equipment; they 'collect sound effects', and may eventually become sound supervisors responsible for control and balance of the various sound sources which are combined for final transmission.
- *Audio assistants* do similar work to sound assistants but they work in the regional (smaller) centres, and are also involved in the operation of radio sound equipment in joint radio/TV centres.
- *Recording operators* control the increasingly sophisticated digital, videotape or telecine (the film equivalent) equipment. They set up and run the recorders and must respond instantly to the producer's requirements. Recordings may be for instant replay or later transmission.

Entry and training Applicants for training courses should have a keen interest in, and some 'hobby experience' of, sound reproduction, recording music, colour photography or lighting for amateur dramatics, and, for sound operators, ability to read a musical score. A strong interest in current affairs and IT skills are also very useful.

Vision-mixer

A number of cameras may be in operation during a production. The producer in the control room decides which camera's picture to send out to the audience, and tells the vision-mixer, who switches to the selected camera as the order is given. This needs concentration and quick reflexes.

Training Mostly in-house for existing TV staff.

Engineering

Some TV engineers work in studios or outside broadcasting, coping with emergency repairs and sudden equipment failure, generally acting as technical 'back-up'. Others are responsible for operation and maintenance of equipment used to route, control and distribute signals from various sound and vision programme sources. All this work can be hectic and needs quick decision-making and a cool head. Other departments are concerned with research, development, planning, installation of a variety of complex equipment (see p. 213 for engineering functions). In a time of changing technology they must be prepared to update their knowledge and assimilate new ideas quickly. Currently this is one of the areas being reduced, with a blurring of distinctions between traditional engineering and IT skills.

Entry and training Increasingly employers are favouring some specialist degree courses.

Filming for TV

Film camera and sound staff are quite distinct from TV camera and sound staff. A considerable amount of television material is filmed (although most is on videotape and digital media); whole programmes are filmed, e.g. schools broadcasts, documentaries; film is also used as an important ingredient in all kinds of programmes – light entertainment, current affairs, children's programmes, plays and series. Camera crews travel a lot and at short notice. There are three basic jobs: editing, camera, sound (titles may vary).

- *Film editors* work entirely in the cutting-room, 'editing down' material shot in the studio or on location. A great deal of their work is done on their own initiative, as directors do not have time to be with editors all day. The job is highly creative as it is the editor who shapes and fashions the final programme which audiences see. Editing can lead to directing.

- *Film camera crews* usually consist of two to four people. The head of the camera crew is in charge of lighting; works in close cooperation with the director; knows the script thoroughly and arranges the all-important lighting and camera angles for each individual shot, so as to achieve the atmosphere the director wants. Lighting camera-man/woman can be an important step to directing film.

- *Assistant camera crews* load and change magazines, make sure the right equipment is available at the right time and place and in working order, and they learn how to operate cameras and lighting equipment. Promotion is pretty slow – it takes about ten years to reach lighting cameraman/woman status.

- *Rostrum camera crew* record on film, tape and digital media the artwork produced by the *graphic designers* (see p. 601).

- *Film sound recordists/sound technician*s are concerned with dubbing, sound-transfer and above all with mixing sound from various sources. This may include location recordings on tape, and sounds produced by effects machines. Achieving the correct balance, controlling the 'input' from various sources, is a highly skilled job, requiring great technical skill and musical creativity.

- *Assistants* manipulate microphones and other recording equipment and learn by watching. Far fewer apply for sound than vision jobs so chances of acceptance are better.

- *Projectionists* (or *film assistants*) operate projection equipment and may also work on dubbing.

Entry qualifications and training Interest and 'hobby experience' are crucial. There are a number of film/TV courses at art schools, either as part of an art and design degree course, or two- to three-year BTEC Diploma courses, or at postgraduate level. Course emphasis (and entry requirements) vary enormously: for example on closed circuit educational television films; on feature or instructional films; with technical or creative bias, etc.

FILM INDUSTRY

Recently there has been greater investment in feature film making in Britain. The future demands of cable TV and the home video market should provide greater opportunities than the recent past. However, entry into cinema film making will remain very highly competitive. The only real job prospects lie with the growing number of often very small production companies which combine TV film making and, very occasionally, cinema, with the whole range of other productions, e.g. training and advertising films.

Video and digital recorders, while not offering the same 'creative' scope as film cameras, have very wide and growing applications: sales promotions (e.g. for pop records and at 'point of sale' in shops), training of all kinds, recording ballets for a dance company's repertoire, monitoring the performance of racehorses during meetings. Many companies use only freelance staff as and when they need them and many of these specialize, e.g. in making wildlife or travel films. Studio facilities and sophisticated equipment are often hired from 'facilities houses' which do not themselves make programmes.

Entry and training There is no essential difference between filming for TV and making non-broadcast films. Similarly people employed in video production do much the same work as those in films. There are no jobs which can be done straight from school. Entry is normally via one of the following:

- TV training and experience.
- An appropriate diploma, degree or postgraduate course at film school or art college (titles and content vary, so it is essential to study prospectuses carefully).

- An electronic engineering course (all levels) plus in-service training.
- Training through one of the Film and Television Freelance Training (FT2) Screen Firsts Schemes (supported by all sides of the film and TV industry). Separate schemes specialize in design, grips, production and technical fields.
- Specialized knowledge leading to making videos on a particular topic.
- Very occasionally, extensive amateur experience.

There is more scope for versatility in video than in film making: people tend to work 'cross-sectorally', i.e. move from one type of work to another fairly easily. Technicians need to be able to work in both film and television. There is always room in this expanding industry for really good technical people.

RADIO

Independent radio has more than 50 per cent of the listening audience. They therefore account for the bulk of jobs – and most of those are in sales or advertising.

Entry routes differ between BBC network, BBC local (which is largely journalism-based) and independent local radio. Once trained it is possible to move from one to another. Below are some examples from network radio.

Production

- *Producers* are responsible for initiating and developing programme ideas. They need an interest in the creative use of radio, a journalistic approach, some experience in relevant subject areas, e.g. the arts, science, medicine, social issues, drama, comedy, popular music, etc., and good technical skills. Work formerly done by studio managers is now done by producers. Producers are recruited from within the BBC – from local radio, researchers, studio managers and radio production assistants, for example; by direct advertising in the press.

- *Radio production assistants* help producers by providing all-round administrative back-up for a programme, varying from typing scripts to helping in the studio. They may be recruited from secretarial and clerical staff or direct.
- *Researchers* work on individual programme strands. They will have specialist knowledge and skills. They may be recruited by direct advertising in the press and work mainly on short-term contracts which can vary from one month to one year.
- *Continuity announcers/newsreaders* are recruited from existing broadcasters in local radio or from other employees with good, clear voices. They work on their own and need to be good at problem-solving. Occasionally jobs will be advertised in the press; previous broadcasting experience is generally required.
- *Sports assistants and correspondents* often come from local radio, or have experience as sports journalists on newspapers. They need a good broadcasting style, an all-round knowledge of sport and more detailed commitment to one or more sports.
- *Reporters* who work on all the main 'magazine' programmes from *Woman's Hour* to *Front Row* are freelancers who generally started their careers on local or independent radio.

NOTES ON ENTRY AND TRAINING (TO THE INDUSTRY GENERALLY):
The uncertainty in the industry in recent years has meant that training schemes in independent television have virtually ceased. The BBC occasionally offers training schemes which are an excellent way into the industry but they are intensely competitive (see *https://jobs.bbc.co.uk/fe/tpl_bbc01.asp*). As far as the numbers entering are concerned, they have only ever been the tip of the iceberg; permanent jobs tend to be in administration, finance, law and personnel.

Currently over half those working in the industry are freelance. Competition to enter the industry at any level is intense. A recent report from the Audio Visual Industries Training Group acknowledged that a key issue within the industry is that it does still survive on recruiting through networking or entrants able to afford to do unpaid work experience when they first start and that this is not helpful to those unable to follow these routes. It is still very much a foot-in-the-door industry. However, a number of initiatives are being introduced to change this; for example the BBC has opened up opportunities for work experience by advertising openings on its website: *www.bbc.co.uk/jobs/workexperience.*

Clearly the 'take-any-job-do-anything' strategy can work. But it is not easy to get these first jobs. On the operational side you need to get skills and that means you need to be enterprising. Hospital and local radio often need volunteers and can offer 'hands-on' experience. Get involved in amateur theatre or make your own videos or recordings. Watch television and become aware of companies' output.

Independent production and facilities companies, corporate in-house production units, major educational and franchise workshops are likely to be growth sectors and can provide experience that can take you into the broadcast companies as permanent staff or on a freelance basis (all sectors increasingly use freelancers). They are also career outlets in themselves. Most are very small. Probably about three-quarters of them have ten or fewer employees. Recruitment and training patterns are haphazard, but a small organization can often offer all-round experience. Corporate in-house production units offer employment to only a very few people, but they often have state-of-the-art equipment. Many entrants take a first job as a 'runner' (most of whom are graduates in their 20s) – the person who makes the tea, does deliveries, deals with the post and answers the phone can really find out how the industry works and who does what, which is vital.

Increasing numbers entering the industry, especially on the production side, are graduates. Media studies degree courses will not necessarily give a head start. What employers are looking for is a lively interest in current affairs and broadcasting, and evidence that you have got practically involved in a way to complement your interests. Nevertheless some courses are favoured by employers. Before taking any 'relevant' course, question in what ways it will stretch your mind and help you to develop wide interests. Ask to see details of what previous graduates have done and whether NVQs are available.

Once in, most people develop their own careers. They may pick up new skills informally, by following around someone more experienced or experienced in a different area, or formally, as through the BBC's system of 'attachments' whereby staff can try out other jobs. The industry recognizes the need for more structured training, especially for freelancers. Vocational qualifications cover every level up to senior technical, production and management grades.

Even when particular training is useful or essential, getting that training does not guarantee a job. Good team skills are essential; this is not an industry for prima donnas. Specific skills, for example the ability to speak Welsh or highly developed IT skills, can give you a head start. But, as ever, much depends on being the right person in the right place at the right time. The more you know about the industry, the nearer you are to being the right person – and the better able to find the right place.

Skillset is the Sector Skills Council for the audio-visual industries. It is vital that anyone considering working in this complex and rapidly changing field contacts them. The Skillset website at *www.skillset.org* includes extensive background information about the film industry.

Personal attributes Creative imagination; wide interests generally, a special interest in a particular subject; a clear, quick, logical mind; appreciation of what audiences want; a strong constitution; the ability to work as one of a team and to take responsibility; a sociable nature; a fairly thick skin; tact; calmness in crises; speed of action; self-confidence; determination and persistence; desire to communicate ideas; ability to take criticism; temperament and skills to be self-employed.

Mature entry and career change Scope mainly for people with relevant experience and qualifications, especially for experienced journalists and engineers. In general, people in this insecure, heavily freelance industry are getting younger.

Work–life balance In an industry dependent on freelancers and short-term contracts career breaks are often a matter of individual choice. Skillset offers a specific range of help to established freelancers, including advice and guidance on career direction and a range of short courses for those wishing to renew or expand their skills for which funding of up to 60 per cent may be available. The BBC offers a range of flexible working arrangements, including career breaks, part-time working and term-time-only contracts.

Further information
Skillset, Focus Point, 21 Caledonian Road, London N1 9GB.
www.skillset.org

Related careers *advertising – art and design – drama – journalism – music – photography*

Town Planning

Entry qualifications Degree or postgraduate qualification accredited
by the Royal Town Planning Institute (see also 'Training', below).

Town Planner

In a world of increasingly complex, interrelated and rapidly changing
urban and rural environments, town planners play a key role in the
process of promoting and guiding physical, social and economic
change and in mitigating its impact. The core of the work is based
on developing an understanding of the environmental, social, economic and political factors which have shaped towns, cities and the
countryside, and which are prompting change in them.

Working with a wide range of associated disciplines, including
architecture, landscape architecture, estates surveying, transportation, sociology and economics, planners prepare, evaluate and
respond to proposals ranging from a small house extension to a
new airport runway. The variety of issues with which they may be
involved is such that, whilst many planners are generalists, a growing
proportion specialize in particular aspects such as economic development, social regeneration, conservation and management of historic or natural environments, urban design or renewable energy and
sustainable development.

Historically most planners worked in local and central government.
However, the employment picture has become more complex. Private
practice consultancy has grown substantially and planners now act as
in-house advisers to companies and agencies, including property

developers, major retailers, and organizations such as the National Trust and the utility companies.

Even within local government work roles are varied and range from core activity in the statutory planning processes such as preparing structure and local plans to guide future development and the assessment of individual applications for development through to roles with chief executives and service departments contributing to advice on issues such as transportation, recreation or housing policy, and to across-the-board corporate policy.

Career paths are very varied and a high proportion of the wide range of employing organizations now recruit new graduates who do not have initial experience gained in work on statutory planning processes in local and central government.

Training A degree course accredited by the Royal Town Planning Institute, usually a three-year undergraduate course followed by one-year postgraduate study leading to a Diploma or Masters. The route to Chartered Town Planner status is the Assessment of Professional Competence, which with mentor support involves two years' relevant work experience, a professional development plan, keeping a logbook, and written submission.

Sociologists, geographers, economists, architects, landscape architects and other specialists concerned with the various aspects of planning also work in planning departments, particularly in counties and big cities. For work concerned with overall strategic planning issues and policy, i.e. for senior posts, however, a planning qualification is essential (see also 'Training', p. 89).

Personal attributes A keen interest in other people's priorities and way of life; social and community concerns; powers of observation; excellent communication skills at all levels; ability to differentiate different needs and demands; creative imagination; patience for painstaking research; the ability to work as one of a team as well as to take responsibility; interest in social, economic and environmental developments.

Mature entry and career change An RTPI accredited distance-learning course offers a route for graduates or non-graduates who want to switch to planning from related careers (architects, geographers, engineers, etc.) in mid-career. It should also be useful for people returning after a career break.

Work–life balance Local authorities and the Civil Service are introducing flexible working practices. Planning priorities and legislation change constantly, so planners taking a career break must keep up with developments. There are 'mid-career' updating courses and seminars for all planners, which could be useful as refresher courses. Returners can also take distance-learning short courses. The RTPI offers advice on career breaks. Experienced planners increasingly do consultancy work.

Planning Support Staff

Support staff carry out various technical and practical tasks. These can include drawing up of plans; preparing maps and diagrams; conducting surveys and interpreting results; dealing with inquiries from the public. Much of the work is IT-based. Planning support staff also include planning administrators and enforcement officers.

Entry qualifications Minimum usually National Qualifications Framework Level 2 (GCSEs A*–C, BTEC Diplomas and Certificates) or Scottish Credit and Qualifications Framework equivalent.

Training In-house with day release for the BTEC Higher National Certificate in Land Administration (planning) or SQA Certificate in Planning, or full-time study for the BTEC/SQA Higher National Diploma award. A level 3 NVQ/SVQ in Town Planning Support is available. These qualifications, together with relevant experience, can lead to Technical Membership of the RTPI. It is possible to work towards professional membership of the RTPI by taking a town planning degree after the BTEC National Certificate.

Mature entry and career change Few opportunities although there can be opportunities for people with relevant skills and experience to become planning enforcement officers.

Work–life balance Good opportunities for flexible working in both local authorities and the Civil Service. Opportunities for part-time work are limited, but job-sharing should be possible.

Further information
The Royal Town Planning Institute, 41 Botolph Lane, London EC3R 8DL.
www.rtpi.org.uk

Related careers *architecture: Architectural Technician – cartography – economics – engineering – housing management – landscape architecture – local government – surveying*

Trading Standards Officer

Entry qualifications Professional trading standards officers require the Diploma in Trading Standards and Consumer Affairs (DCATS) award. The graduate route to the DCATS is an accredited degree in consumer protection (or a degree in a relevant subject plus an accredited postgraduate award) plus initial employment as a trainee trading standards officer combined with further study to DCATS level.

The work Trading standards officers (TSOs) are employed mainly by local authorities to ensure a fair system of trading between consumers and traders and between traders themselves. They are responsible for the enforcement of a vast array of consumer protection legislation designed to protect the consumer from, for example, unsafe electrical products or short-weight goods. At the same time they try to ensure that no other trader suffers from the effect of such unfair trading practices. TSOs are interested in subjects as wide-ranging as food safety, metrology (science of weights and measures), animal health and welfare, consumer credit, misleading advertising, counterfeit goods and sales of restricted products to under-age children.

There are two main aspects to the work. The first is routine checking and inspecting to see that, for example, the motorist gets the amount of petrol indicated on the pump, that foods are properly labelled (the actual testing of food composition is carried out by public analysts), that video films are correctly classified and labelled. Much of this is done openly, but test buying is also done. The other aspect is investigating complaints from consumers and traders. These may claim that a holiday brochure was misleading, that a 'pre-shrunk' shirt has shrunk two sizes in the wash, that a toy contained a dangerous sharp part, that the mileage on a second-hand vehicle was not what it was claimed to be, or that goods were over-priced. In each case the TSO has to gather the facts and, in the light of these, to decide whether or not the law has been broken. If it has, the TSO makes out a report and eventually decides whether to take the trader to court.

The work is diverse and mainly carried out away from the office. It also involves working some unsocial hours. TSOs meet a great variety of people and have much scope for decision-making. Most authorities offer a good career structure within the constraints of local government spending. There are now increasing opportunities for TSOs to be employed by traders to ensure that they do not inadvertently break the law.

Enforcement officers work with TSOs in the criminal enforcement aspects of the work. Consumer advisers give advice to the public and may pass queries to TSOs if they need investigation.

Training The Diploma in Consumer Affairs & Trading Standards (DCATS) is a statutory requirement for TSOs. The syllabus includes relevant civil and criminal law, metrology, statistics, trading practice, quality assurance, enforcement and advice. To study for the DCATS it is necessary to be employed by a local authority.

Trading Standards Institute (TSI) professional qualifications in consumer affairs and trading standards are at four levels: Foundation Certificate in Consumer Affairs & Trading Standards; Module Certificate in Consumer Affairs & Trading Standards; Diploma in Consumer Affairs & Trading Standards (DCATS); Higher Diploma in Consumer Affairs & Trading Standards (HDCATS).

Study can be combined with paid employment as a trainee while working up through the qualifications, or graduates of a TSI accredited degree can start professional qualifications at Diploma in Consumer Affairs & Trading Standards level.

Accredited degree courses are offered at Manchester Metropolitan University, University of Wales Institute, Cardiff, University of Teesside and Queen Margaret's University College, Edinburgh. Manchester Metropolitan University also offers a one-year graduate diploma course for students from non-accredited first degrees in other subjects.

Personal attributes Ability to grasp a great many facts and apply them in a practical way; good communication skills, written and verbal; scrupulous attention to detail; self-confidence and ability to work on one's own unsupervised; ability to explain technical points clearly to traders and consumers; diplomacy.

Mature entry and career change In theory, people with a background in business or law should have reasonable chances. In practice, when vacancies for trainees are limited, young graduates are often given preference.

Work–life balance Local authorities are introducing flexible working practices. A career break should be possible.

Further information
The Trading Standards Institute, Sylvan Court, Sylvan Way, Southfields Business Park, Basildon, Essex SS15 6TH (or contact the local Trading Standards Office).
www. tsi.org.uk and *www.tscareers.org.uk*

Related careers *consumer scientist – environmental health officer – health and safety advisers and inspectors – law*

Travel Agent/Tour Operator

Entry qualifications None specified, but typically National Qualifications Framework Level 3 (A levels, BTEC National awards) or Scottish Credit and Qualifications Framework equivalent. Also increasing graduate entry (mainly tour operators). Foreign languages especially useful for incoming tourism.

The work Travel and tourism is a major UK industry, employing 1.5 million people. It overlaps with the growing leisure industry and is essentially concerned with providing services for people who are away from home, on business or on holiday. These may be UK residents travelling within Britain or going abroad or 'incoming' tourists who make a substantial contribution to the UK economy. More people travel for necessity than for leisure but both business and leisure travellers increasingly seek a broader range of services and more sophisticated or unusual ways of spending their time and money. The business traveller may want sports facilities and saunas. The holiday-maker may want to try hang-gliding, hill-walking, wine-tasting, bird-watching or painting. Adventure tourism is a growing specialism and there are now courses for those wanting to lead expeditions.

Many jobs in tourism are concerned with providing accommodation and food – whether for farm-based holidays or international conferences. Other jobs are in transport operations – from hire-car fleets to coach companies, airline operators to Caribbean cruise ships. Others are in entertainment and visitors' attractions, tourist information services and – increasingly important – marketing and promotions. Tourist information is both general and specific, ranging from selling Britain to potential visitors all over the world to helping a family find bed-and-breakfast accommodation in Northumbria.

As the industry becomes more complex and competitive, so it needs better-trained people who are adaptable, creative and thoroughly professional.

This section deals with two distinct sectors of the industry: travel agencies and tour operators. A few large companies own agencies, operators and airlines.

Travel agents are the retailers. They sell tour operators' holidays, plan trips for people within the UK and abroad, and sell tickets for rail, air, ferry and coach travel. Some specialize in business travel, arranging travel and accommodation for company executives. Tour operators usually specialize in either incoming or outgoing operations. They put together and organize package holidays – anything from self-catering cabins in the Scottish Highlands to trekking in the Himalayas. Tour operators concentrate on planning – and selling – their holidays, with such subdivisions as British and foreign; summer and winter; business and holiday; party and individual packages. Although the bulk of the package holiday business is controlled by a few huge operators, there has been a growth in small companies catering for special interest holidays, for example cycling and art history tours.

Travel Agent/Consultant

This is essentially selling, either through a high street travel agency, telephone call centre or website. Customers may know what they want and simply buy a ticket for a train journey, or book a world tour, or want some travel literature. Others looking for a holiday have no idea of what they want. Their leisure-time tastes must be summed up and 'channelled' into the package they will most enjoy in a price range they can afford.

Travel agency staff not only need to know about the holidays they recommend but also be able to explain and/or sell the appropriate insurance or give advice on, say, vaccinations. Despite often working to strict targets, they must take trouble with each customer; their responsibility is far greater than that of most other sales assistants. Many people 'buy' only one holiday a year, and if this one is not a success, they will go to another agency next year.

Bookings are made through IT systems and by telephone. Travel agents have to make sure their customers are provided with the necessary documentation and keep them in touch if arrangements cannot be finalized immediately. Itineraries and currency conversion have to be worked out, timetables checked, car hire arranged. Minor errors can have disastrous consequences for customers' holidays and trips.

Travel agencies may be one of a large chain, a small company offering a specialized service or a small independent firm trading on its knowledge of a local area and local customers. Many of the larger firms operate call centres to handle telephone sales, and have dedicated website sales teams.

Business house clerks deal with companies making travel arrangements for their staff. Business travel agencies may offer a 24–hour service so clerks work in shifts.

Managers supervise the work of sales teams, see to the business side and, in independent agencies, select those tour operators' packages which they think will offer their clients what they want. They also need to know how to advertise and promote their services to existing and potential clients.

Tour Operator

Planning
This is done by directors or tour managers. 'Planning trips' last from one to eight weeks twice a year and are exhausting: two or three resorts and perhaps twelve hotels may be investigated in a day. Local transport, garage facilities, food, amusements, beaches will be checked and local tourist officials consulted. Planning of the tour later involves checking timetables and maps, costing, and conferring with transport and accommodation services suppliers. Costing is crucial and the success of operators depends largely on ability to negotiate discounted prices with hotels, villa companies, airlines, etc. All this has to be done

up to two years in advance, which adds to the difficulties, as the information supplied must be accurate.

Sales

Sales people visit travel agents to make sure brochures are on display. Those companies specializing in school parties (for example, to ski resorts) have a sales team which visits schools to try to win their custom.

Representative or courier

Many are freelance and are employed for the summer or winter season (occasionally both) by individual companies. The majority work with incoming tours, i.e. with overseas visitors to Britain. A minority work overseas, either travelling with groups from Britain to their holiday destination or based at a resort. Some may do secretarial work and/or planning off-season. This is not a career as such but rather a pleasant change for competent secretaries/linguists or simply good organizers. Training is mainly provided by the company (although one or two private organizations run short courses for people hoping to become couriers).

Most travel staff work long hours or may work shifts: many tour companies operate a 24-hour service.

Training Training can be full-time or part-time or by distance learning. NVQs/SVQs are well established.

- The two-year Travel Training Programme, an Apprenticeship programme run by TTC Training, is the main way into travel work for school-leavers. There are no set entry requirements, but in practice many trainees have three to four GCSEs. Most openings are in travel agencies, but there are also a few in business houses, with tour operators and with airlines. Trainees study for NVQs/SVQs level 2 or 3 in travel services, customer service, telesales or business administration.
- There are a number of other specialized courses and qualifications which can either 'stand alone' or contribute towards an NVQ/SVQ.

The ABTA Certificate in Travel (Travel Agents), can be studied at college or by distance learning. It is available at two levels and candidates sit a written examination. There is also a specialist qualification for tour operators.

- BTEC National Certificate or Diploma in Travel and Tourism (or SQA equivalent).
- BTEC/SQA Higher National award in related subjects.
- First degrees in travel and tourism, three-year full-time or four-year sandwich, plus some two-year Foundation degrees. Some other degrees, for example in tourism studies, business studies and leisure management, offer relevant options. Potential applicants should study course syllabuses carefully. Other graduate entry to the industry is possible with qualifications in, for example, marketing or accounting.
- There are some postgraduate courses and some of these may also accept HND holders. At graduate and postgraduate level tourism and hospitality management and leisure management training and work may overlap.
- The Institute of Travel and Tourism, in association with ABTA and People 1st (the Sector Skills Council for the hospitality, leisure, travel and tourism industries) is currently developing an Accredited Travel Professional Scheme (APT) for continuing professional development within the industry.
- The Guild of Travel Management Companies/City & Guilds Certificate in Business Travel is a qualification at four levels – introductory, consultant, supervisory and management. Programmes involve private study or attending courses or a combination of both, workplace assessment and written exams. There are other City & Guilds awards in travel and tourism at diploma, advanced diploma and higher professional diploma levels.

Personal attributes Aptitude for figure work; good judgement of people; a friendly manner; enthusiasm; accuracy; organizing ability; common sense; a good memory; a liking for selling.

Mature entry and career change Relatively few opportunities in travel agencies, as most posts filled by school-leavers and college-leavers, but possible for those with sales experience. Some opportunities with tour operators.

Work–life balance As in the retail industry as a whole, travel agency hours are getting longer so there may be opportunities for part-time work or job-sharing. Shift work is usual in business travel agencies. Resort workers can expect very little 'off duty' time. Opportunities for returners depend on contacts, on having kept up with changes in the industry.

Further information

TTC Training, The Quayside, Furnival Road, Sheffield S4 7YA.
www.ttctraining.co.uk

Institute of Travel and Tourism, PO Box 217, Ware, Herts SG12 8WY.
www.itt.co.uk

Guild of Travel Management Companies, Queen's House, 180–182 Tottenham Court Road, London W1T 7PD.
www.gtmc.org

People 1st Sector Skills Council, Armstrong House, 38 Market Square, Uxbridge UB8 1LH.
www.people1st.co.uk

City & Guilds, 1 Giltspur Street, London EC1A 9DD.
www.city-and-guilds.co.uk

Related careers *civil aviation: Cabin Crew; Ground Staff – hospitality and catering – languages – leisure/recreation management – secretarial, administrative and clerical work*

Working for Oneself

Creating one's own job has now established itself as an 'alternative career'. Potential entrepreneurs can get encouragement, advice, and sometimes financial help, from various sources, but their business plan has to stand up to severe scrutiny.

Entry qualifications See 'Personal attributes' and 'Training', below.

The work The variety of self-generated work is unlimited. It can be broadly divided into three overlapping types of activity: providing a service; selling; making. Most enterprises combine two activities, one of which is usually the crucial one. Deciding which type of enterprise to choose requires a great deal of research, because setting up a business is an uncharted area in conventional career terms. First impressions of what is involved tend to be misleading. They conceal any number of pitfalls – the need for compliance with health and safety regulations or for much more capital than bargained for, for example.

- *Providing a service*: This requires least capital, involves least risk, covers a vast range, e.g. dog walking, garden maintenance or domestic cleaning – activities based on using one's time, basic skills and possibly basic equipment; or repairing motorbikes, cooking directors' lunches in offices, running a word processing or Web design service, practising complementary medicine, i.e. using specific skills plus equipment and, possibly, premises – garden shed, kitchen, living room. Professionals – in law, accountancy, systems analysis, etc. – with considerable experience may set up their own computerized service and sell their expertise to companies for specific projects. This is a growing option and enables professionals to be their own boss, working from home, while retaining links with previous employers and at the same time also working for new clients. Companies like it because using people who work from home saves overheads.

- *Selling*: This usually overlaps with providing a service or with making, or it depends on 'buying-in' goods to sell (or collecting them from friends, etc.). It includes, for example, making sandwiches at home and delivering them to regular customers, or running a second-hand clothes or clutter stall. This kind of selling could be a run-up to opening a shop, restaurant, mail-order business. Selling involves more initial organization and business know-how, capital and risk than providing a service.

- *Making a product*: This usually overlaps with selling and covers anything from making chutney to highly skilled craftwork. It ranges from using talent plus basic skills to using sophisticated skills acquired through several levels of training, from craft to degree and postgraduate course, plus equipment. It requires some capital and probably premises. But if the idea is viable (see below) and the skills are there, finance and other help is available (see below).

The Law

Fewer formalities have to be complied with than would-be entrepreneurs tend to fear. Local authorities must be consulted about planning, health and safety and other regulations, but permission to go ahead is rarely 'unreasonably withheld' in the present climate of encouragement for so-called 'start-ups' – small businesses. Even HM Revenue and Customs, which has to be told, advises, informs and encourages rather than hinders. (Many people, for example, fear they will have to cope with VAT if they want to set up in business. In fact few people will reach the annual turnover limit necessary for registration in the first few years. Useful leaflets can be ordered from HM Revenue and Customs website: *www.hmrc.gov.uk*. See 'Further information' below for details of other sources of information, advice and support. Most of the listed websites offer extensive information resources.

Business Format

Again, fewer formalities have to be observed in the initial stages than generally believed. The basic formats are: (a) *Sole trader*: HM Revenue and Customs merely has to be informed that the business exists; (b) *Partnership*: if two or more people set up a business jointly, a solicitor draws up a straightforward agreement. Both sole traders and partnerships are liable for all the debts they incur should the business fail; (c) *Limited company*: requires slightly more formalities, but once set up persons involved are only liable for the money they put into the business should things go wrong; (d) *Cooperatives*: various types; to set one up solicitors' or special agencies' advice is essential (see 'Further information', below).

Another option is to buy a *franchise*, either of one outlet or agency, or to offer a particular service in a specified area. This has the advantage that the initial spadework will have been done, the trading name will already be established and training and other help may be available. However, for those wanting complete independence to develop their own ideas franchising has limitations and in any case must be as thoroughly researched and prepared for as any other enterprise.

Training No formal training structure as for conventional careers exists, but many business start-ups are based on specific skills. Welders, beauty therapists, typographers, software engineers, electronics engineers (technicians and graduates), or whatever, must first acquire the skill they intend to 'sell', i.e. which they want to use as the basis for their business. (See under individual career headings how to acquire such skills.) But to survive in the tough business world, basic business know-how is absolutely essential too. The meaning of such terms as cash-flow, balance sheets, mark-up and, say, the difference between marketing and market research must be understood. The overall failure rate of new mini-ventures is fairly high. However, the failure rate can be linked closely to the level of research done and specialist advice/training taken prior to starting up. Statistics are misleading because there are so many variables which affect success or failure, but there is general agreement among experts that successful entrepreneurship requires several indispensable ingredients:

- *A marketable idea*: No idea is good in a vacuum. It must fill a gap in a given market. A bike repair service in a seaside suburb mainly inhabited by elderly people might struggle; one in a university town stands a good chance (as long as there is no efficient competition or, if there is, the competition has more work than it can cope with and/or the local market is expanding). A mobile grocery-van on a housing estate where few shops have yet been opened sounds a good idea; a mobile grocery-van near a large shopping centre does not. A small-van removal service might flourish in bedsitter-land; it would not in a large-one-family-houses suburb. Researching the market and making a marketing plan are probably the most essential tasks when preparing to go it alone.
- *Motivation and commitment*: The self-employed have to be willing to work harder, and more irregular hours, than employees usually do (see 'Personal attributes', below).
- *Resources*: If the idea fills a gap in the market and the commitment is there, advice, possibly financial assistance and help with finding premises (if garden shed/kitchen/living room are insufficient/ unsuitable) are available.

Many locally based agencies offer help, advice and training which can help those starting a new business to avoid some of the more obvious pitfalls and to maximize their chances of success (see 'Training', below).

Points of contact for new entrepreneurs include:

- *Business Link* puts inquirers in touch with their local Business Link office, linked through their website at *www.businesslink.gov.uk*, and offers a range of services and access to personal business advisers for small firms and anyone setting up a new business. Similar services are offered through the Business Gateway (*www.bgateway.com*) and Highlands and Islands Enterprise (*www.hie.co.uk*) in Scotland, Business Eye (*www.businesseye.org.uk*) in Wales, and Invest Northern Ireland (*www.investni.com*).

- *Local Enterprise Agencies*: there are several hundreds of these privately run organizations. They help with information on the local business scene, with forming a business plan and with business counselling generally. They can give advice on tax, marketing, law, etc. The National Federation of Enterprise Agencies (NFEA) provides links to individual enterprise agencies through its website at www.nfea.com. NFEA also provides a Small Business Advisory Service, providing free advice through an online enquiry service at www.smallbusinessadvice.org.uk.
- *The Crafts Council* will advise people thinking of setting up a pottery, weaving or similar crafts workshop.
- *The Prince's Trust* and *Livewire* advise and help young people (under-30s usually) who choose the self-employment option.
- Some business studies degrees, postgraduate courses, BTEC and SQA awards (including BTEC Continuing Education units) have self-employment options.
- Some local colleges run courses which, though not necessarily planned for potential entrepreneurs, are very useful – e.g. in book-keeping, marketing, basic computer application. Some are evening classes, others are one day a week.

Personal attributes Unquenchable resilience; tenacity; decisiveness; organizing ability; being a bit bossy; exceptional stamina; business acumen; enjoying risk-taking – being a bit of a gambler; ability to put up with temporary hardship; resourcefulness; self-confidence bordering on conceit; true enjoyment of hard work; ability to get on well with other people however unreasonable their requests/criticisms/impatience; imagination; ability to work under pressure; interest in economic and social trends. (Extent of these qualities depends on extent of venturesomeness of enterprise contemplated.)

Mature entry and career change Age is a positive advantage in this 'alternative' career. Anyone who has had experience of the world of work scores over school-leavers and college-leavers when it comes to applying to banks, etc. for funds or to other agencies for premises or other help. Career changers and returners are welcome on courses.

Work–life balance In theory if you are your own boss you can arrange your own hours. In practice it is often customers or clients who dictate a working pattern so if the business is being considered in order to fit around family or other commitments, some thought needs to be given to priorities. For example, how will you respond if a vital call comes through just as you are dashing out to pick up the children from school? Working from home not only means you do not travel to work, it also means you are never away from work. Anyone who thinks self-employment is a synonym for part-time employment should think again. If the intention is to earn more than pin money, self-employed people on average probably work longer hours than employed people. However, with organization and contingency planning, it can work very well.

Further information
Business Link
   www.businesslink.gov.uk
Scotland: Small Business Gateway
   www.sbgateway.com
Business Gateway
   www.bgateway.com
Highlands and Islands Enterprise
   www.hie.co.uk
Wales: Business Eye
   www.businesseye.org.uk
Northern Ireland: Invest Northern Ireland
   www.investni.com
National Federation of Enterprise Agencies
   www.nfea.com
Small Business Advice Service

www.smallbusinessadvice.org.uk
Crafts Council
www.craftscouncil.org.uk
Livewire
www.shell-livewire.org
The Prince's Trust
www.princes-trust.org.uk
Small Business Bureau
www.smallbusinessbureau.org.uk
Several high street banks have useful booklets on running your own
business.

Related careers *management*

Youth and Community Work

Entry qualifications Depend on age and experience. See 'Training', below.

The work Youth and community workers are concerned with young people aged between 11 and 25, giving priority to those between 13 and 19. Their work has elements in common with education and social work. The social education of young people is their primary concern, helping them to explore their strengths and weaknesses, develop physical, intellectual, moral, social and emotional resources, and facilitate their growth from childhood to adulthood. Recent years have seen increased 'targeting' of disadvantaged groups, but current debate sets that against the need for more mainstream work. Many young people stay at home these days in rooms full of TVs, videos, stereos and computers – all essentially passive entertainments – and miss many opportunities for social development.

Job titles vary. People with different titles can be doing substantially the same work, while the work of people with the same title can vary greatly. Youth workers or youth and community workers may be club-based or centre-based, 'detached' or community-based. In a club or centre the youth worker plans activities to appeal to a wide range of ages and tastes. They give young people the means to mix socially and organize themselves, to develop confidence and skills, both practical (e.g. in sport or drama) and social (e.g. cooperating as part of a team), to channel their energies in a constructive way. Forming relationships with young people is a very important part of the work and may involve the youth worker in counselling or unofficial social work. For example, the youth worker may be the first person to recognize signs of drug abuse or the bottled-up effects of a family break-up.

In some centres activities are organized for other groups within the community, e.g. mother-and-toddler groups, pre-school playgroups, leisure interest classes, literacy classes or English for immigrants. Sometimes the youth and community worker is responsible for such activities; sometimes the role is one of liaison with other groups.

Many youth and community workers are 'detached', i.e. they do not work from a fixed base. Some go out into the community to make contact with young people who do not come to clubs, to identify their needs and help develop community solutions. Others do project work on, for example, drug abuse, unemployment or health education. Some youth workers are attached to schools (they usually need teaching qualifications) where their work includes contributing to PSHE (personal, social and health education), citizenship and study support programmes. A number also work in social services departments with 'at risk' young people.

Youth work is very dependent on part-time, often voluntary workers. Even in a large centre there may be only one qualified worker, and, increasingly, qualified workers are given area responsibility for a number of clubs or centres. This means that qualified youth and community workers have less face-to-face contact with young people. Their job includes lots of administration, organizing of events and activities, recruitment, training and support of part-time workers, management of budgets and premises, liaison with the management committee and other groups, and seeking grants, sponsorship and other material support.

The majority of professional youth and community workers are employed by local authorities, as members of a Youth or Youth and Community Service (this service is usually part of the education department, but sometimes comes under the leisure department) or by voluntary groups; it is estimated that 80 per cent of youth work is provided by the voluntary groups (e.g. churches and organizations like Guides and Scouts). There is, however, a great deal of cooperation between the statutory and voluntary sectors.

Training This is flexible and ensures that suitable people, whatever their age and educational qualifications, have a chance of qualifying. Though applicants for courses are normally expected to have National Qualifications Framework Level 3 (A levels, BTEC National awards) or Scottish Credit and Qualifications Framework equivalent, plus experience of voluntary or paid (for example, playleader) work with young people and/or other community work, applicants whose practical work experience has shown that they are suitable for the work may be accepted with lower educational qualifications. However, those without qualifications wishing to work with young people must commit themselves to a programme of training to achieve a qualification. Minimum entry age varies from one course to another and again depends on individuals' experience and maturity.

The National Youth Agency validates youth work training at all levels in England and a list of courses is available on their website. The professional validation of courses in Northern Ireland and in Wales is undertaken by the Youth Council for Northern Ireland and the Welsh Assembly Government respectively. (For Scotland see below.)

Qualifications in youth support work: Local authorities and many voluntary youth services offer a programme of training leading to qualifications at NVQ level 2 or 3, or vocationally related qualifications, in youth work. Some of the training may be classroom based and some supported learning in the workplace. All qualifications are based on national occupational standards for youth work.

Professional qualifications in youth work: For work at higher levels, a professional qualification is normally required. The minimum professional qualification is currently a Dip.HE in Youth Work or a Foundation degree. Honours degrees, postgraduate diplomas and higher degrees are also available. Courses can be taken by full-time or part-time study. Some institutions offer distance-learning programmes.

From 2010 all new professional qualifications in youth work will be at honours degree level, or higher.

In Scotland the minimum qualification for professionally qualified status is a degree. Programmes of study leading to professional status are validated by Community Education Validation and Endorsement or CeVe.

Personal attributes An outgoing personality; ability to communicate easily with people who may need 'drawing out'; patience; imagination to put oneself into the shoes of people who feel alienated from society; wide interests in current social and economic trends and problems; organizing ability; feeling at ease with people of all ages; creativity to think up activities.

Mature entry and career change Mature candidates are welcome on courses. This can be a suitable 'second career' for people changing direction in their 20s or 30s, if they have relevant experience.

Work–life balance Many posts require working unsociable hours. Flexible working policies are being introduced in local authorities but ample opportunities have always existed for part-time work in youth work. Job-sharing is beginning to appear. A career break should not be a problem.

Further information

The National Youth Agency, Eastgate House, 19–23 Humberstone Road, Leicester LE5 3GJ.
www.nya.org.uk and *www.youthinformation.com*
YouthLink Scotland, 9 Haymarket Terrace, Edinburgh EH12 5EZ.
www.youthlink.co.uk
Youth Scotland, Balfour House, 19 Bonnington Grove, Edinburgh EH6 4BL.
www.youthscotland.org.uk
National Assembly for Wales
www.assemblywales.org
Youth Council for Northern Ireland, Forestview, Purdy's Lane, Belfast BT8 7AR.
www.ycni.org

Related careers *leisure/recreation management – social work – sport – teaching*

Index

Index

Index

Index

Index

Index

Index

Index

Index

Index

Index

Index

Index